Lecture Notes in Computer Science   7912

Commenced Publication in 1973
Founding and Former Series Editors:
Gerhard Goos, Juris Hartmanis, and Jan van Leeuwen

T0226214

Mieczysław A. Kłopotek
Jacek Koronacki
Małgorzata Marciniak
Agnieszka Mykowiecka
Sławomir T. Wierzchoń (Eds.)

Language Processing and Intelligent Information Systems

20th International Conference, IIS 2013
Warsaw, Poland, June 17-18, 2013
Proceedings

 Springer

Volume Editors

Mieczysław A. Kłopotek
Jacek Koronacki
Małgorzata Marciniak
Agnieszka Mykowiecka
Polish Academy of Sciences
Institute of Computer Science
ul. Jana Kazimierza 5, 01-248 Warsaw, Poland
E-mail: {mieczyslaw.klopotek, jacek.koronacki,
malgorzata.marciniak, agnieszka.mykowiecka}@ipipan.waw.pl

Sławomir T. Wierzchoń
Polish Academy of Sciences
Institute of Computer Science
ul. Brzegi 55, 80-045 Gdańsk, Poland
E-mail: slawomir.wierzchon@ipipan.waw.pl

ISSN 0302-9743   e-ISSN 1611-3349
ISBN 978-3-642-38633-6   e-ISBN 978-3-642-38634-3
DOI 10.1007/978-3-642-38634-3
Springer Heidelberg Dordrecht London New York

Library of Congress Control Number: 2013939075

CR Subject Classification (1998): C.2.4, C.2.5, H.2.8, I.2.7-9, K.3.1, K.4.4, I.5

LNCS Sublibrary: SL 3 – Information Systems and Application, incl. Internet/Web
and HCI

Typesetting: Camera-ready by author, data conversion by Scientific Publishing Services, Chennai, India

Printed on acid-free paper

Springer is part of Springer Science+Business Media (www.springer.com)

Preface

The Conference on Intelligent Information Systems, organized by the Institute of Computer Science of the Polish Academy of Sciences, has been a prominent meeting place for scientists from all over the world for nearly 30 years now. This volume contains the papers presented at the 20th conference of the series Language Processing and Intelligent Information Systems Conference, which was held in Warsaw, Poland, June 17–18, 2013. This year, the main goal of the meeting was to present new ideas and tools for natural language processing and interplay between the analysis of natural language and traditional machine learning technologies.

The volume contains 28 papers selected by the Program Committee from 53 submitted papers. Each paper was anonymously reviewed by at least two independent reviewers, and the articles presented in this volume were significantly improved on the basis of the reviewers' comments. The volume consists of two types of submissions: 13 long research papers describing original research contributions to the conference topics, and 15 short papers mainly describing tools and resources. Two demonstration sessions were organized to take place during the conference. One of these sessions presented the results of the four-year Polish POIG.01.01.02 project "An adaptive system to support problem-solving on the basis of document collections on the Internet." A short description of the tools and systems to be presented are published on the conference website.

The papers presented in this volume are organized into three thematic groups: natural language processing, clustering and classification of big collections of textual documents, and classic data mining problems. The conference was opened by an invited plenary talk entitled "Syntax and Semantics in the Web-Scale Extraction of n-ary Relations" by Hans Uszkoreit—Scientific Director at the German Research Centre for Artificial Intelligence (DFKI) and Head of the DFKI Language Technology Lab, Saarbrücken, Germany. The second day started with a talk "Beyond Query Suggestions: Recommending Tasks to SE Users" given by Fabrizio Silvestri from the Institute of Information Science and Technologies at Consiglio Nazionale delle Ricerche, Pisa, Italy. In the talk, he discussed the Task Relation Graph (TRG) as a representation of users' search behaviors on a task-by-task perspective.

The problems of natural language processing are discussed in 17 articles. These papers concern the processing of a set of very diverse languages: Polish, Croatian, English, German, Dutch, Chinese, and Persian. Both machine learning and formal approaches are explored and hybrid solutions combining more than one technique are frequently proposed. A hybrid approach is used for multilingual toponyms extraction, for example. In the paper by M. Habib and M. van Keulen, an HMM module serves for the selection of potential candidates for toponyms, while the disambiguation level is done using CRF.

For many languages, the tools for performing basic syntactic analysis are not well developed. Relatively free word order and rich inflection render some of the methods used for defining English or German grammar unsatisfactory in dealing with these languages. A great number of morphological tags and the relatively small size of annotated corpora make this task more challenging. Among papers dealing with this issue is the work of K. Krasnowska, which describes a Polish LTAG grammar, while two other papers represent a partial parsing approach. A. Radziszewski and A. Pawlaczek describe recognition of CRF-based chunks, while A. Radziszewski et al. use C4.5, SVM and a memory-based classifier to classify predicate-argument relationships. A. Wróblewska and P. Sikora present an on-line service of the newly established Polish dependency parser.

Papers presenting specific NLP applications concern recognition of fake reviews (M. Rubikowski and A. Wawer), question answering (P. Przybyła), and recognition of named entities (A. L.-F. Han et al).

Another group of papers is devoted to resource building, evaluation, and sharing. These works comprise, among others, the creation of a Croatian derivational dictionary in a paper by V. Štefanec et al., the annotating of named entities by E. Hajnicz, and the detection of annotation errors in existing treebanks or corpora addressed in two papers: one by Ł. Kobyliński and another by K. Krasnowska and A. Przepiórkowski. M. Aminian et al. describe a spectral clustering algorithm used for identification of Persian semantic verb classes based on syntactic information, M. Ogrodniczuk describes a translational–based co-reference resolution for Polish, while M. Marcińczuk and A. Radziszewski present a general language for text annotation.

Two papers deal with processing older language variants. X. Zou et al. describe a method for recognizing changes in usage of a word in time on the basis of the context of its occurrences, while J. Waszczuk presents an architecture of a dictionary of old Polish.

The authors of seven articles included in the second part of the volume extend traditional tasks of machine learning, such as clustering or classification, to the domain of collections of textual documents G. Stratogiannis et al. investigate the issue of reliable search for related entities using semantic knowledge extracted from Wikipedia. With such knowledge a semantic relatedness between entities is established, and, finally, a semantic clustering is used to answer a given question. R. Szmit presents an algorithm and technological framework for the search for similar documents based on locally sensitive hashing. The proposed distributed algorithm is designed to cope with very large document collections. M. Dramiński et al. look at the clustering of user activity data from various topically related sites as a vehicle for obtaining better user profiles. Although the idea seems to be plausible, the authors demonstrate that we are far from being able to apply it in practice as the users fluctuate between the clusters. T. Kuśmierczyk and M. Sydow reiterate the old problem of focused Web crawling. They demonstrate that the usage of short lists of keywords, shallow search, and appropriately chosen starting pages may dramatically improve the Harvest Ratio. M. Łukasik and M. Sydow investigate the properties of a version of the multi-label classification algorithm based on the k-Nearest Neighbors method. They show that the modification, concentrating on choosing appropriate thresholding, performs significantly better than the standard form of the algorithm. T. Giannakopoulos et al. apply a supervised learning technique for classifying documents in a manner that allows visualization of the contents of a collection of scientific documents. M.A. Kłopotek et al. turn to the issue of balance between personalization and the required space for storing data. They propose a method for combining a personalized PageRank, computed for various categories, to obtain a PageRank for a joint category, so that a considerable number of ranking vectors need not be stored.

The last group of contributors reports on new results obtained in the domain of classic data mining. M. Lucińska and S.T. Wierzchoń propose a new spectral clustering algorithm that uses a novel way of identifying the cluster number solely on the basis of the eigenvector structure. They demonstrate that the approach yields valid clusters, even in the case of data sets that are not clearly cut. R. Kłopotek investigates a recently proposed generator of artificial social graphs with a bipartite structure. He seeks to reconstruct generator parameters from the generated graphs while posing the question of why such generators are able to provide artificial graphs that behave similarly to real ones. K. Trojanowski and M. Janiszewski investigate the issue of the influence of resource constraints on the outcome of an optimization algorithm. They introduce the concept of user impatience and demonstrate its impact on the expected value of the result of optimization. C. Sur et al. propose an algorithm for solving the traveling salesman problem that exploits new nature-based techniques of local search.

We would like to express our thanks to the invited speakers and the authors of the papers for their contribution. Likewise we thank the authors of the demonstrated systems. We extend special thanks to all the members of the Program Committee and invited reviewers for their excellent job.

March 2013

Mieczysław A. Kłopotek
Jacek Koronacki
Małgorzata Marciniak
Agnieszka Mykowiecka
Sławomir T. Wierzchoń

Conference Organization

Steering Committee

Mieczysław A. Kłopotek   Institute of Computer Science PAS, Poland
Jacek Koronacki   Institute of Computer Science PAS, Poland
Małgorzata Marciniak   Institute of Computer Science PAS, Poland
Agnieszka Mykowiecka   Institute of Computer Science PAS, Poland
    Polish Japanese Institute of Information
       Technology, Poland
Sławomir T. Wierzchoń   Institute of Computer Science PAS, Poland

Publication Chair

Leonard Bolc   Polish Japanese Institute of Information
       Technology, Poland

Program Committee

Steven Abney   University of Michigan, USA
Witold Abramowicz   Poznań University of Economics, Poland
Stanisław Ambroszkiewicz   Institute of Computer Science PAS, Poland
Pascal Bouvry   University of Luxembourg
António Horta Branco   University of Lisbon, Portugal
Luis Miguel de Campos   University of Granada, Spain
Krzysztof Cetnarowicz   AGH University of Science and Technology,
       Poland
Jan Daciuk   Gdańsk University of Technology, Poland
Piotr Dembiński   Institute of Computer Science PAS, Poland
Tomaž Erjavec   Jožef Stefan Institute, Slovenia
Dafydd Gibbon   Universität Bielefeld, Germany
Jerzy W. Grzymała-Busse   University of Kansas, USA
Mohand-Said Hacid   Université Claude Bernard Lyon 1, France
Erhard Hinrichs   University of Tübingen, Germany
Ryszard Janicki   McMasters University Ontario, Canada
Krzysztof Jassem   Adam Mickiewicz University, Poland
Janusz Kacprzyk   Polish Academy of Sciences, Poland
Waldemar W. Koczkodaj   Laurentian University, Canada
Józef Korbicz   University of Zielona Góra, Poland
Steven Krauwer   Utrecht University, The Netherlands
Vladislav Kuboň   Charles University, Prague, Czech Republic
Anna Kupść   Université Bordeaux 3, France

Halina Kwaśnicka	Wrocław University of Technology, Poland
Antoni Ligęza	AGH University of Science and Technology, Poland
Ramón López-Cózar Delgado	University of Granada, Spain
Alexander Lyaletski	Kyiv National Taras Shevchenko, Ukraine
Suresh Manandhar	University of York, UK
Krzysztof Marasek	Polish Japanese Institute of Information Technology, Poland
Stan Matwin	University of Ottawa, Canada
Archil Maysuradze	Lomonosov Moscow State University, Russia
Marie-Jean Meurs	Concordia University, Canada
Maciej Michalewicz	IBM Netezza Poland
Karel Pala	Masaryk University, Czech Republic
Maciej Piasecki	Wrocław University of Technology, Poland
Adam Przepiórkowski	Institute of Computer Science PAS, Poland
Zbigniew W. Raś	University of North Carolina at Charlotte, USA
Jan Rauch	University of Economics, Czech Republic
Henryk Rybiński	Warsaw University of Technology, Poland
Khalid Saeed	AGH University of Science and Technology, Poland
Shikhar Kr. Sarma	Guahati University, Assam, India
Franciszek Seredyński	Institute of Computer Science PAS, Poland
Kiril Simov	Bulgarian Academy of Science, Bulgaria
Roman Słowiński	Poznań University of Technology, Poland
Jerzy Stefanowski	Poznań University of Technology, Poland
Tomek Strzalkowski	University at Albany, USA
Marcin Sydow	Polish Japanese Institute of Information Technology, Poland
Stan Szpakowicz	University of Ottawa, Canada
Ryszard Tadeusiewicz	AGH University of Science and Technology, Poland
Zygmunt Vetulani	Adam Mickiewicz University, Poland
Wolfgang Wahlster	DFKI GmbH, Saarbrücken, Germany
Alicja Wakulicz-Deja	University of Silesia, Poland
Jan Węglarz	Poznań University of Technology, Poland
Peter Wittenburg	Max Planck Institute for Psycholinguistics, The Netherlands
Karsten Wolf	University of Rostock, Germany
Bożena Woźna-Szcześniak	Jan Długosz University, Poland
Janusz Zalewski	Florida Gulf Coast University, USA

Invited Reviewers

Elżbieta Hajnicz, Gregoire Danoy, Bernabe Dorronsoro, Michał Marcińczuk, Frederic Pinel, Agata Savary, Jakub Waszczuk, Marcin Woliński

Organizing Committee

Piotr Borkowski
Michał Ciesiołka
Marek Miszewski
Maciej Ogrodniczuk

Table of Contents

Natural Language Processing

Text and Web Mining

Machine Learning and Search

A Hybrid Approach for Robust Multilingual Toponym Extraction and Disambiguation

Mena B. Habib and Maurice van Keulen

Faculty of EEMCS, University of Twente, Enschede, The Netherlands
{m.b.habib,m.vankeulen}@ewi.utwente.nl

Abstract. Toponym extraction and disambiguation are key topics recently addressed by fields of Information Extraction and Geographical Information Retrieval. Toponym extraction and disambiguation are highly dependent processes. Not only toponym extraction effectiveness affects disambiguation, but also disambiguation results may help improving extraction accuracy. In this paper we propose a hybrid toponym extraction approach based on Hidden Markov Models (HMM) and Support Vector Machines (SVM). Hidden Markov Model is used for extraction with high recall and low precision. Then SVM is used to find false positives based on informativeness features and coherence features derived from the disambiguation results. Experimental results conducted with a set of descriptions of holiday homes with the aim to extract and disambiguate toponyms showed that the proposed approach outperform the state of the art methods of extraction and also proved to be robust. Robustness is proved on three aspects: language independence, high and low HMM threshold settings, and limited training data.

1 Introduction

Toponyms are names used to refer to locations without having to mention the actual geographic coordinates. The process of toponym extraction (recognition) is a subset of Named Entity Recognition (NER) that aims to identify location name boundaries in text. While toponym disambiguation (resolution) is the process of mapping between a toponym and an unambiguous spatial coordinates of the same place.

Toponyms extraction and disambiguation are highly challenging. For example, according to GeoNames[1], the toponym "Paris" refers to more than sixty different geographic places around the world besides the capital of France. Around 46% of toponyms in GeoNames have more than one reference. Duplicate geographic names comes from the fact that emigrant settlers prefer to use their original land names to denote their new homes, leading to referential ambiguity of place names [12]. Another source of ambiguity is that some common English words have references in GeoNames and might be extracted as toponyms under some conditions. For example, words like {Shop, Park, Villa, Airport} represent location names in GeoNames.

---

[1] www.geonames.org

M.A. Kłopotek et al. (Eds.): IIS 2013, LNCS 7912, pp. 1–15, 2013.

A general principle in this work is our conviction that toponym extraction and disambiguation are highly dependent [8]. Mena et al. [9] studied not only the positive and negative effect of the extraction process on the disambiguation process, but also the potential of using the result of disambiguation to improve extraction. They called this potential for mutual improvement, the *reinforcement effect*.

The extraction techniques fall into two categories: machine learning and rule-based approaches. The advantage of statistical techniques for extraction is that they provide alternatives for annotations along with confidence probabilities. Instead of discarding these, as is commonly done by selecting the top-most likely candidate, we use them to enrich the knowledge for disambiguation. It was proved that extraction probability can be used to enhance the disambiguation so that the contribution of each extracted item to the disambiguation of other extracted items is proportional to its extraction probability [9]. We believe that there is much potential in making the inherent uncertainty in information extraction explicit in this way. Certainty can also be improved using informativeness features and coherence features derived from the disambiguation results.

Most of existing extraction techniques are language-dependent as they need a POS tagger. And it is known that it takes some effort to tune the thresholds and that they are typically trained on large corpuses. In practice, one would like to have more robustness so that accuracy is not easily hampered. In this paper, we specifically address robustness against threshold settings, situations with other languages, and situations with limited training data.

In this paper we propose a hybrid extraction approach based on Hidden Markov Models (HMM) and Support Vector Machines (SVM). An initial HMM is trained and used for extraction. We used a low cutting threshold to achieve high recall resulting in low precision. A clustering based approach for disambiguation is then applied. A set of coherence features are extracted for the extracted toponyms based on the disambiguation results feedback and also on informativeness measures (like Inverse Document Frequency and Gain). A SVM is then trained with the extracted features to classify the HMM extracted toponyms into true positives and false positives resulting in improving the precision and hence the F1 measure. Our hybrid approach outperforms the Conditional Random Fields (CRF), the state of the art method of extraction and Stanford NER, the prominent Named Entity Recognition System. Furthermore, our hybrid approach is shown to be language independent as all the used methods are not based on language dependent techniques like Part Of Speech (POS) which is commonly used with the NER systems. Robustness of the proposed approach is experimentally proved by applying different HMM cutting thresholds, evaluating it across multiple languages and also with smaller training sets. More aspects of robustness like evaluating across multiple domains and using different types of named entities are left for future work.

To examine our hybrid approach, we conducted experiments on a collection of holiday home descriptions from the EuroCottage[2] portal. These descriptions contain general information about the holiday home including its location and

---

[2] http://www.eurocottage.com

its neighborhood (See figure 2 for an example). As a representative example of toponym extraction and disambiguation, we focused on the task of extracting toponyms from the description and using them to infer the country where the holiday property is located.

Contributions: We can summarize our contributions as follows: (1) We propose a hybrid toponym extraction approach based on HMM and SVM. (2) The proposed system is proved to be robust against three aspects: different languages, different cutting thresholds, and limited training data. (3) We introduce some features (informativeness and coherence-based) that can be used to enhance the process of toponym extraction.

The rest of the paper is organized as follows. Section 2 presents related work on toponym extraction and disambiguation. Our proposed approach for toponym extraction and disambiguation is described in Section 3. In Section 4, we describe the experimental setup, present its results, and discuss some observations and their consequences. Finally, conclusions and future work are presented.

2 Related Work

Toponym extraction and disambiguation are special cases of a more general problem called Named Entity Recognition (NER) and Disambiguation (NED). In this section, we briefly survey a few major approaches for NER and toponym disambiguation.

2.1 Named Entity Extraction

NER is a subtask of Information Extraction (IE) that aims to annotate phrases in text with its entity type such as names (e.g., person, organization or location name), or numeric expressions (e.g., time, date, money or percentage). The term 'named entity recognition (extraction)' was first mentioned in 1996 at the Sixth Message Understanding Conference (MUC-6) [7], however the field started much earlier. The vast majority of proposed approaches for NER fall in two categories: handmade rule-based systems and supervised learning-based systems.

One of the earliest rule-based system is FASTUS [10]. It is a nondeterministic finite state automaton text understanding system used for IE. The other category of NER systems is the machine learning based systems. Supervised learning techniques applied in NEE include Hidden Markov Models (HMM) [26], Decision Trees [21], Maximum Entropy Models [1], Support Vector Machines [11], and Conditional Random Fields (CRF) [15][4].

Multilingual NER is discussed by many researchers. Florian et al. [5] used classifier-combination experimental framework for multilingual NER in which four diverse classifiers are combined under different conditions. Szarvas et al. [24] introduced a multilingual NER system by applying AdaBoostM1 and the C4.5 decision tree learning algorithm. Richman and Schone utilized the multilingual characteristics of Wikipedia to annotate a large corpus of text with NER tags [20]. Similarly, Nothman et al. [16] automatically created multilingual training annotations for NER by exploiting the text and structure of parallel Wikipedia articles in different languages.

Using informativeness features in NER is introduced by Rennie et al. [19]. They conducted a study on identifying restaurant names from posts to a restaurant discussion board. They found the informativeness scores to be an effective restaurant word filter. Furche et al. [6] introduce a system called AMBER for extracting data from an entire domain. AMBER employs domain specific gazetteers to discern basic domain attributes on a web page, and leverages repeated occurrences of similar attributes to group related attributes into records.

Some researches focused only on toponym extraction. In [13], a method for toponym recognition is presented that is tuned for streaming news by leveraging a wide variety of recognition components, both rule-based and statistical. Another interesting toponym extraction work was done by Pouliquen et al. [17]. They present a multilingual method to recognize geographical references in free text that uses minimum of language-dependent resources, except a gazetteer. In this system, place names are identified exclusively through gazetteer lookup procedures and subsequent disambiguation or elimination.

2.2   Toponym Disambiguation

Toponym reference disambiguation or resolution is a form of Word Sense Disambiguation (WSD). According to [2], existing methods for toponym disambiguation can be classified into three categories: (i) map-based: methods that use an explicit representation of places on a map; (ii) knowledge-based: methods that use external knowledge sources such as gazetteers, ontologies, or Wikipedia; and (iii) data-driven or supervised: methods that are based on machine learning techniques.

An example of a map-based approach is [22], which aggregates all references for all toponyms in the text onto a grid with weights representing the number of times they appear. References with a distance more than two times the standard deviation away from the centroid of the name are discarded.

Knowledge-based approaches are based on the hypothesis that toponyms appearing together in text are related to each other, and that this relation can be extracted from gazetteers and knowledge bases like Wikipedia. Following this hypothesis, [18] used a toponym's local linguistic context to determine the toponym type (e.g., river, mountain, city) and then filtered out irrelevant references by this type.

Supervised learning approaches use machine learning techniques for disambiguation. [23] trained a naive Bayes classifier on toponyms with disambiguating clues and tested it on texts without these clues. Similarly, [14] used Support Vector Machines to rank possible disambiguations.

3   Proposed Hybrid Approach

The hybridness of our proposed approach can be viewed from two points of view. It can be viewed as a hybrid approach of toponym extraction and disambiguation processes. Clues derived from the disambiguation results are used to enhance

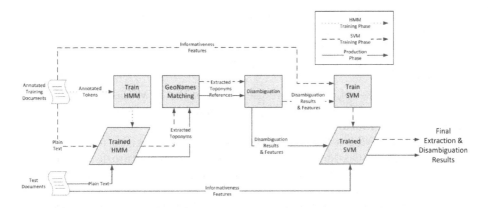

Fig. 1. Our proposed hybrid toponym extraction and disambiguation approach

extraction. Also our system can be viewed as a hybrid machine learning approach for extraction where HMM and SVM are combined to achieve better results. An initial HMM is trained and used for extraction with high recall. A SVM is then trained to classify the HMM extracted toponyms into true positives and false positives resulting in improving the precision and hence the F1 measure.

3.1 System Phases

The system illustrated in Figure 1 has the following Phases:

Phase 1: HMM training

1. Training data is prepared by manually annotating all toponyms. Tokens are tagged, following the CoNLL[3] standards, by either a LOCATION or O tag which represents words that are not part of a location phrase.
2. Training data is used to train a HMM[4,5] [3] for toponym extraction. The advantage of statistical techniques for extraction is that they provide alternatives for annotations accompanied with confidence probabilities. Instead of discarding these, as is commonly done by selecting the top-most likely candidate, we use them to enrich the knowledge for disambiguation. The probabilities proved to be useful in enhancing the disambiguation process [9].

Phase 2: SVM training

1. The trained HMM is then used to extract toponyms from the training set. A low cutting threshold is used to get high recall. The extracted toponyms are then matched against GeoNames gazeteer. For each toponym, a list of candidate references are fed to the disambiguation process.
2. The disambiguation process tries to find only one representative reference for each extracted toponym based on its coherency with other toponyms

---

[3] http://www.cnts.ua.ac.be/conll2002/ner/

[4] http://alias-i.com/lingpipe/

[5] We used an HmmCharLmEstimator which employs a maximum a posteriori transition estimator and a bounded character language model emission estimator.

mentioned in the same document. Details of the disambiguation approach used is described in section 3.2.

3. Two sets of features (informativeness and coherence-based) are computed for each extracted toponym. Details of the selected features are described in section 3.3.

4. The extracted set of features are used to train the SVM classifier[6,7] to distinguish between true positives toponyms and false positives ones.

Phase 3: Production

1. The trained HMM is applied on the test set. The extracted toponyms are matched against GeoNames and their candidate references are disambiguated. Informativeness and coherence features are computed and fed to the trained SVM to find the final results of toponyms extraction process.

2. Disambiguation process can be repeated using the final set of extracted toponyms to get the improvement reflected on the disambiguation results.

The main intuition behind our approach is to make use of more clues than those often used by traditional extraction techniques (like POS, word shape, preceding and succeeding words). We deliberately use set of language-independent features to ensure robustness across multiple languages. To make use of those features we start with high recall and then filter the extracted toponyms based on those features. Even by using a higher cutting threshold, our approach is still able to enhance the precision at the expense of some recall resulting in enhancement of the overall F1 measure. Moreover, the features are found to be highly discriminative, so that only few training samples are required to train the SVM classifier good enough to make correct decisions.

3.2   Toponym Disambiguation Approach

For the toponym disambiguation task, we only select those toponyms annotated by the extraction models that match a reference in GeoNames. We use the clustering approach of [9] with the purpose to infer the country of the holiday home from the description. The clustering approach is an unsupervised disambiguation approach based on the assumption that toponyms appearing in same document are likely to refer to locations close to each other distance-wise. For our holiday home descriptions, it appears quite safe to assume this. For each toponym t_i, we have, in general, multiple entity candidates. Let $R(t_i) = \{r_{ix} \in \text{GeoNames gazetteer}\}$ be the set of reference candidates for toponym t_i. Additionally each reference r_{ix} in GeoNames belongs to a country $Country_j$. By taking one entity candidate for each toponym, we form a cluster. A cluster, hence, is a possible combination of entity candidates, or in other words, one possible entity candidate of the toponyms in the text. In this approach, we consider all possible clusters, compute the average distance between the candidate locations in the cluster, and choose the cluster $Cluster_{min}$ with the lowest average distance. We choose the most often occurring country $Country_{winner}$ in $Cluster_{min}$ for disambiguating the country of

---

[6] http://www.csie.ntu.edu.tw/$\sim$cjlin/libsvm/
[7] We used C-support vector classification (C-SVC) type of SVM with RBF kernel.

the document. In effect the above-mentioned assumption states that the entities that belong to $Cluster_{min}$ are the true representative entities for the corresponding toponyms as they appeared in the text.

3.3 Selected Features

Coherence features derived from disambiguation results along with informativeness features are computed for all the extracted toponyms generated by the HMM. For each extracted toponym the following set of informativeness features are computed:

1. **Inverse Document Frequency (IDF)**: IDF is an informativeness score that embodies the principle that the more frequent a word is, the lower the chance it is a relevant toponym. The IDF score for an extracted toponym t is:
$$IDF = -log\frac{d_t}{D}$$
where d_t is the document frequency of the toponym t, and D is the total number of documents.

2. **Residual Inverse Document Frequency (RIDF)**: RIDF is an extension of IDF that has proven effective for NER [19]. RIDF is calculated as the difference between the IDF of a toponym and its expected IDF according to the poisson model. The RIDF score can be calculated by the formula:
$$expIDF = -log(1 - e^{-f_t/D}) \quad RIDF = IDF - expIDF$$
where f_t is the frequency of the toponym across all documents D.

3. **Gain**: Gain is a feature that can be used to identify "important" or informative terms. For a toponym t, Gain is derived as:
$$Gain(t) = \frac{d_t}{D}(\frac{d_t}{D} - 1 - log\frac{d_t}{D})$$

4. **Extraction Confidence (EC)**: Extraction confidence (probability) is the HMM conditional probability of the annotation given an input word. The goal of HMM is to find the optimal tag sequence $T = t_1, t_2, ..., t_n$ for a given word sequence $W = w_1, w_2, ..., w_n$ that maximizes:
$$P(T \mid W) = \frac{P(T)P(W|T)}{P(W)}$$
The prior probability $P(t_i|t_{i-2}, t_{i-1})$ and the likelihood probability $P(w_i|t_i)$ can be estimated from training data. The optimal sequence of tags can be efficiently found using the Viterbi dynamic programming algorithm [25]. The extraction confidence is the probability of being a part of toponym given a token $P(t|w)$.

Furthermore, the following set of coherence features are computed based on the disambiguation results:

1. **Distance (D)**: The distance feature is the kilo-metric distance between the coordinates of the selected candidate reference r_{ij} for toponym t_i and the coordinates of the inferred country $Country_{winner}$.
$$Distance = Coordinates(r_{ij}) - Coordinates(Country_{winner})$$

2. **Standard Score (SS)**: It is calculated by dividing the distance between the coordinates of the r_{ix} and $Country_{winner}$ over the standard deviation of all selected references distances to $Country_{winner}$.
$$StandardScore = \frac{Coordinates(r_{ij}) - Coordinates(Country_{winner})}{\sigma}$$

1-room apartment 80 m2, on the ground floor, simple furnishings: living/dining room 70 m2 with 4 beds and satellite-TV. Open kitchen (4 hotplates, oven, micro wave) with dining table. Shower/WC. Floor heating. Facilities: hair dryer. Internet (Dial up/ISDN). The room is separated by 4 steps in bedroom and lounge. The bedroom has no direct light.

Olšova Vrata 5 km from **Karlovy Vary**: On the edge of the **Slavkovsky** les nature reserve. Small holiday hamlet next to the hotel which has been a popular destination for **Karlsbad** inhabitants for the past 30 years new, large house with 2 apartments, 2 storeys, built in 2004, surrounded by trees, above **Karlovy Vary**, in a secluded, sunny position, 10 m from the woods edge. Private, patio (20 m2), garden furniture. In the house: table-tennis. Central heating. Breakfast and half-board on request. Motor access to the house (in winter snow chains necessary). Parking by the house. Shop 4 km, grocers 1.5 km, restaurant 150 m, bus stop 550 m, swimming pool 6 km, indoor swimming pool 6 km, thermal baths 6 km, tennis 1 km, golf course 1.5 km, skisport facilities 25 km. Please note: car essential. Airport 1.5 km (2 planes/day). On request: Spa treatments, green fee. Ski resort **Klinovec**, 20 km.

Fig. 2. An example of a EuroCottage holiday home description (toponyms in bold)

3. **Number of GeoNames candidate references (#Geo)**: It is simply the number of candidate references for the toponym ti.
$$\#\text{GeoNames Refs} = |r_{ix}|$$

4. **Belongingness to the disambiguated country (Bel)**: Indicates whether or not r_{ij} belongs to $Country_{winner}$.
$$\text{Belongingness to } Country_{winner} = \begin{cases} 1 & \text{if } Country(r_{ij}) = Country_{winner} \\ 0 & \text{otherwise} \end{cases}$$

Informativeness features tend to find those false positives that appear multiple times across the collection. Those highly repeated words are more likely to be false positives toponyms. On the other hand, some false positives appear only rarely in the collection. Those toponyms can not be caught by informativeness features. Here where we make use of coherence-based features. Coherence features tend to find those false positives that are not coherent with other toponyms. The usage of a combination of both sets of features maximizes the extraction effectiveness (F1 measure).

Unlike traditional features commonly used with NER systems like (POS), all our selected features are language independent and thus our approach can be applied to any language as the GeoNames gazetteer has representations for toponyms in different languages. Furthermore we avoid using word shape features as languages like German require the capitalization of all nouns making capitalization a useless feature to extract NE.

4   Experimental Results

In this section, we present the results of experiments with the proposed approach applied to a collection of holiday properties descriptions. The goals of the experiments are to compare our approach with the state of the art approaches and systems and to show its robustness in terms of language independence, high and low HMM threshold settings, and limited training data.

4.1   Data Set

The data set we use for our experiments is a collection of traveling agent holiday property descriptions from the EuroCottage[8] portal. The descriptions not only contain information about the property itself and its facilities, but also a description of its location, neighboring cities and opportunities for sightseeing. Descriptions are also available in German and Dutch. Some of these descriptions are direct translations and some others have independent descriptions of the same holiday cottage. The data set includes the country of each property which we use to validate our results. Figure 2 shows a representative example of a holiday property description. The manually annotated toponyms are written in bold. The data set consists of 1181 property descriptions for which we constructed a ground truth by manually annotating all toponyms for only the English version. The German and the Dutch versions of descriptions are annotated automatically by matching them against all toponyms that appear in the English version or their translations. For example "Cologne" in the English version is translated to "Köln" and matched in the German version and translated to "Keulen" and matched in the Dutch version. Although this method is not 100% reliable due to slight differences in translated versions, we believe that it is reliable enough as ground truth for showing the language independency of our approach.

We split the data set into a training set and a validation test set with ratio 2 : 1. We used the training set for training the HMM extraction model and the SVM classifier, and the test set for evaluating the extraction and disambiguation effectiveness for "new and unseen" data.

4.2   Experiment 1: Data Set Analysis

The aim of this experiment is to show some statistics about the test set in all versions through different phases of our system pipeline. Table 1 shows the number of toponyms per property description [*#Top./Doc.*], the number of toponyms per property that have references in GeoNames [*#Top./Doc. ∈ GeoNames*], and the average degree of ambiguity per toponyms [*Degree of ambiguity*] (i.e the average number of references in GeoNames for a given toponym). *Ground Truth* represents manual annotations statistics. *HMM(0.1)* represents statistics of the extracted toponyms resulting from applying HMM on the test set with cutting probability threshold 0.1, while *HMM(0.1)+SVM* represents statistics of the extracted toponyms resulting from applying SVM after HMM on the test set.

As can be observed from table 1 that HMM extracts many false positives. Examples of those false positives that have references in GeoNames are shown in figure 3[9].

It can also be noticed that the English version contains more toponyms per property description. Our method of automatically annotating the German and the Dutch texts misses a few annotations. This doesn't harm the evaluation process of the proposed method as our approach works on improving the precision

---

[8] http://www.eurocottage.com

[9] We match the extracted toponyms against names of places, their ascii representation and their alternative representations in GeoNames gazeteer.

| bath[34] shop[1]   terrace[11] shower[1] parking[3] |
| house[5] garden[24] sauna[6]   island[16] farm[5] |
| villa[49] here[7]   airport[3] table[9]   garage[1] |

(a) English

bett[1] bad[15] strand[95] meer[15] foto[11]	winkel[58] terras[3] douche[2] woon[1] bergen[59]
bergen[59] garage[1] bar[58] villa[49] wald[51]	kortom[2] verder[1] gas[9] villa[49] garage[1]
billard[3] westen[11] stadt[7] salon[12] keller[27]	tuin[2] hal[20] chalet[8] binnen[3] rond[1]

(b) German   (c) Dutch

Fig. 3. Examples of false positives (toponyms erroneously extracted by HMM(0.1)) and their number of references in GeoNames

with some loss in recall. Hence, we can claim that precision/recall/F1 measures of our proposed approach applied on German and Dutch versions shown on the section 4.4 can be regarded as a lower bound.

Table 1. Test set statistics through different phases of our system pipeline

	#Top./Doc.			#Top./Doc. ∈GeoNames			Degree of ambiguity		
	EN	DE	NL	EN	DE	NL	EN	DE	NL
Ground Truth	5.04	4.62	3.51	3.47	3.10	2.46	7.24	6.15	6.78
HMM(0.1)	12.02	11.31	11.38	6.51	5.72	5.85	8.69	9.27	10.33
HMM(0.1)+SVM	5.24	5.04	3.91	3.59	3.18	2.58	8.43	7.38	7.78

4.3   Experiment 2: SVM Features Analysis

In this experiment we evaluate the selected set of features used for SVM training on the English collection. We want to show the effect of these features on the effectivness of the SVM classifier. The aim of the SVM is to find the false positives toponyms among those extracted by the HMM. Two groups of features are used. Informativness features and coherence features (features derived from disambiguation results). Table 2 shows:

- Extraction and disambiguation results using each of the features individually to train the SVM classifier.
- Information Gain [IG] for each feature. IG measures the amount of information in bits about the class prediction (in our case true positive toponym or false positive).
- The extraction and disambiguation results using each group of features (Informativeness (Inf) and coherence (Coh)) and using both combined (All).
- Extraction and disambiguation results for only HMM with threshold 0.1 (prior to the usage of the SVM).
- Disambiguation results using manually annotated toponyms (Ground Truth).

Extraction results are evaluated in terms of precision [Pre.], recall [Rec.] and [F1] measures, while disambiguation results [Dis.] are evaluated in terms of the percentage of holiday home descriptions for which the correct country was inferred.

The coherence features can be only calculated for toponyms that belong to GeoNames. This implies that its effect only appears on false positives that belong to GeoNames. To make their effect more clear, we presented two sets of results:

- *All extracted toponyms*: where all toponyms are used to train HMM and SVM regardless of whether they exist in GeoNames or not. Evaluation is done for all extracted toponyms.
- *Only toponyms* ∈ *GeoNames*: where only toponyms existing in GeoNames are used to train and evaluate HMM and SVM.

By looking at [*IG*] of each feature we can observe that the [*Bel*], [*IDF*] and [*EC*] are highly discriminative features, while [*#Geo*] seems to be a bad feature as it has no effect at all on the SVM output.

Using manually annotated toponyms for disambiguation, the best possible input one would think, may not produce the best possible disambiguation result. For example, the disambiguation result of HMM(0.1)+SVM(Gain) is higher than that of the ground truth. This is because some holiday cottages are located on the border with other country, so that description mentions cities from other country rather than the country of the cottage. This does not mean that the correct representative candidates for toponyms are missed. Moreover, since our disambiguation result is based on voting, we attribute this effect to chance: the NER may produce a false positive toponym which happens to sway the vote to the correct country, in other words, there are cases of correct results for the wrong reasons.

It can be also observed that low recall leads to poor disambiguation results. That is because low recall may result in extracting no toponyms from the property description and hence the country of that property is misclassified.

Table 2 shows how using the SVM classifier enhances the extraction and the disambiguation results. The effect of combining both set of features is more clear in the results of [*Only toponyms* ∈ *GeoNames*]. Precision is improved significantly, and hence the F1 measure, by using the coherence features beside the informativeness ones.

Table 3 shows the extracted toponyms for the property shown in figure 2 using different methods. Informativeness features tend to find those false positives that appear multiple times across the collection like {In, Shop}. On the other hand, disambiguation features tend to find those false positives that are not coherent with other toponyms like {Airport}. The usage of a combination of both sets of features maximizes the extraction effectiveness (F1 measure).

4.4 Experiment 3: Multilinguality, Different Thresolding Robustness and Competitors

In this experiment we want to show the multiligualitiy and system robustness across different languages and against different threshold settings. Multilinguality is guaranteed by our approach as we only use language independent methods of extraction and filtering. We effectively avoided using Part-Of-Speech (POS) as feature since it is highly language-dependent and for many languages there are no good automatic POS-tagger available. Table 4 shows the effectiveness

Table 2. Extraction and disambiguation results using different features for English version

	All extracted toponyms				
	IG	Pre.	Rec.	F1	Dis.
Ground Truth		1	1	1	79.1349
HMM(0.1)		0.3631	**0.8659**	0.5116	75.0636
HMM(0.1)+SVM(IDF)	0.1459	0.5514	0.8336	0.6637	80.4071
HMM(0.1)+SVM(RIDF)	0.1426	0.5430	0.8472	0.6618	80.4071
HMM(0.1)+SVM(Gain)	0.1013	0.5449	0.8205	0.6549	**80.9160**
HMM(0.1)+SVM(EC)	0.2223	0.7341	0.7489	0.7414	78.3715
HMM(0.1)+SVM(D)	0.0706	0.6499	0.5726	0.6088	74.5547
HMM(0.1)+SVM(SS)	0.0828	0.6815	0.5166	0.5877	68.4478
HMM(0.1)+SVM(#Geo)	0.1008	0.4800	0.6099	0.5372	71.7557
HMM(0.1)+SVM(Bel)	0.3049	**0.8106**	0.4942	0.6140	73.0280
HMM(0.1)+SVM(Inf)		0.7764	0.7756	0.7760	79.8982
HMM(0.1)+SVM(Coh)		0.8106	0.4940	0.6138	73.0280
HMM(0.1)+SVM(All)		0.7726	0.8014	**0.7867**	79.8982

	Only extracted toponyms ∈ GeoNames				
	IG	Pre.	Rec.	F1	Dis.
Ground Truth		1	1	1	79.1349
HMM(0.1)		0.4874	**0.9121**	0.6353	75.0636
HMM(0.1)+SVM(IDF)	0.2652	0.7612	0.8983	0.8241	**81.1705**
HMM(0.1)+SVM(RIDF)	0.2356	0.7536	0.9107	0.8247	80.9160
HMM(0.1)+SVM(Gain)	0.1754	0.6419	0.8656	0.7372	76.3359
HMM(0.1)+SVM(EC)	0.2676	0.8148	0.8243	0.8195	78.3715
HMM(0.1)+SVM(D)	0.1375	0.6563	0.8584	0.7439	77.6081
HMM(0.1)+SVM(SS)	0.1077	0.6802	0.7444	0.7108	68.4478
HMM(0.1)+SVM(#Geo)	0.0791	0.4878	0.9121	0.6356	75.0636
HMM(0.1)+SVM(Bel)	0.3813	0.8106	0.7117	0.7579	73.0280
HMM(0.1)+SVM(Inf)		0.8181	0.8823	0.8490	80.6616
HMM(0.1)+SVM(Coh)		0.8117	0.7451	0.7770	76.3359
HMM(0.1)+SVM(All)		**0.8865**	0.8453	**0.8654**	79.8982

Table 3. Extracted toponyms for the property shown in figure 2

	HMM(0.1)	HMM(0.1)+SVM(Inf)	HMM(0.1)+SVM(Dis)	HMM(0.1)+SVM(All)
[+]Olšova Vrata	+	+	+	+
[+]Karlovy Vary	+	+	+	+
[+]Slavkovsky	+	+	+	+
[+]Karlsbad	+	+	+	+
[+]Karlovy Vary	+	+	+	+
[+]Klinovec	+	+	+	+
[-]In	+	-	+	-
[-]Shop	+	-	+	-
[-]Airport	+	+	-	-

of our proposed approach applied on English, German, and Dutch versions in terms of the F1 and the disambiguation results over the state of the art: the CRF, and the Stanford NER models[10]. CRF is considered one of the famous techniques in NER. We trained a CRF on set of features described in [9]. One

---

[10] http://nlp.stanford.edu/software/CRF-NER.shtml

Table 4. Extraction and disambiguation results for all versions

English	Pre.	Rec.	F1	Dis.
Ground Truth	1	1	1	79.1349
HMM(0.1)	0.3631	**0.8659**	0.5116	75.0636
HMM(0.1)+SVM(All)	0.7726	0.8014	0.7867	**79.8982**
HMM(0.9)	0.6638	0.7806	0.7175	78.3715
HMM(0.9)+SVM(All)	0.8275	0.7591	**0.7918**	79.3893
Stanford NER	0.8375	0.4365	0.5739	58.2697
CRF(0.9)	**0.9383**	0.6205	0.7470	69.4656

German	Pre.	Rec.	F1	Dis.
Ground Truth	1	1	1	**81.4249**
HMM(0.1)	0.3399	**0.8306**	0.4824	79.3893
HMM(0.1)+SVM(All)	0.6722	0.7321	0.7009	79.6438
HMM(0.9)	0.6169	0.7085	0.6595	77.8626
HMM(0.9)+SVM(All)	**0.7414**	0.6876	**0.7135**	77.3537
Stanford NER	0.5351	0.2723	0.3609	40.4580

Dutch	Pre.	Rec.	F1	Dis.
Ground Truth	1	1	1	**73.0280**
HMM(0.1)	0.2505	**0.8128**	0.3830	68.4478
HMM(0.1)+SVM(All)	0.6157	0.6872	**0.6495**	70.4835
HMM(0.9)	0.4923	0.6713	0.5680	67.1756
HMM(0.9)+SVM(All)	**0.6762**	0.6197	0.6467	67.6845

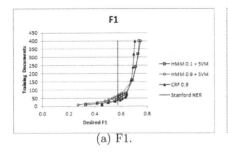
(a) F1.

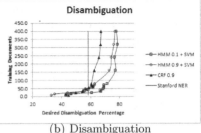
(b) Disambiguation

Fig. 4. The required training data required to achieve desired extraction and disambiguation results

of the used features is POS which we were only able to extract for the English version. Stanford is a NER system based on CRF model trained on CoNLL data collection. It incorporates long-distance information [4]. Stanford provides NER models for English and German. Unfortunately, we didn't find a suitable NER system for Dutch to compare with.

It can be observed that the CRF models achieve better precision at the expense of recall. Low recall sometimes leads to extracting no toponyms from the property description and hence the country of that property is misclassified. This results in a poor disambiguation results.

Table 4 also shows the robustness of our approach against different HMM thresholding settings. We used two different cutting thresholds (0.1, 0.9) for HMM. It is clear that our approach improves the precision and F1 measure on both cases.

4.5   Experiment 4: Low Training Data Robustness

Robustness across different languages and using different cutting probability threshold is shown in the previous sections. In this section we want to prove the third aspect of robustness of our system which is its capability to work even with limited training samples. Figures 4(a) and 4(b) shows the required size of training data to achieve a desired result for F1 and disambiguation respectively (applied on the English collection). It can be observed that our approach requires low number of training data to outperform our competitors the CRF and Stanford NER. Only 160 annotated documents are required to achieve 0.7 F1 and 75% correct disambiguation and to outperform the the CRF. Much less documents are required to outperform the CRF disambiguation results as we mentioned before that the high precision of CRF systems is accompanied by low recall leading to poor disambiguation results.

5   Conclusion and Future Work

In this paper we introduced a hybrid approach for toponym extraction and disambiguation. We used a HMM for extraction and a SVM classifier to classify the HMM output into false positive and true positive toponyms. Informativeness features beside coherence features derived from disambiguation results were used to train the SVM. Experiments were conducted with a set of holiday home descriptions with the aim to extract and disambiguate toponyms. Our system is proved to be robust on three aspects: language differences, high and low HMM threshold settings, and limited training data. It also outperforms the state of the art methods of NER.

For future research, we plan to apply and enhance our approach for other types of named entities and other domains. We claim that this approach is also robust against domain differences and can be adapted to suit any kind of named entities. To achieve this it is required to develop a mechanism to find false positives among the extracted named entities. Coherency measures can be used to find highly ambiguous named entities. We also want to estimate locations of toponyms not existing in gazetteers using other toponyms found in the textual context of the unknown toponym.

References

1. Borthwick, A., Sterling, J., Agichtein, E., Grishman, R.: NYU: Description of the MENE named entity system as used in MUC-7. In: Proc. of MUC-7 (1998)
2. Buscaldi, D., Rosso, P.: A conceptual density-based approach for the disambiguation of toponyms. Journal of Geographical Information Science 22(3), 301–313 (2008)
3. Carpenter, B.: Character language models for chinese word segmentation and named entity recognition. In: Association for Computational Linguistics, pp. 169–172 (2006)
4. Finkel, J.R., Grenager, T., Manning, C.: Incorporating non-local information into information extraction systems by gibbs sampling. In: Proc. of the 43rd ACL (2005)
5. Florian, R., Ittycheriah, A., Jing, H., Zhang, T.: Named entity recognition through classifier combination. In: Daelemans, W., Osborne, M. (eds.) Proc. of CoNLL 2003, Edmonton, Canada, pp. 168–171 (2003)
6. Furche, T., Grasso, G., Orsi, G., Schallhart, C., Wang, C.: Automatically learning gazetteers from the deep web. In: Proc. of the 21st International Conference Companion on World Wide Web, pp. 341–344 (2012)

7. Grishman, R., Sundheim, B.: Message understanding conference - 6: A brief history. In: Proc. of Int'l Conf. on Computational Linguistics, pp. 466–471 (1996)
8. Habib, M.B., van Keulen, M.: Named entity extraction and disambiguation: The reinforcement effect. In: Proc. of MUD 2011, Seattle, USA, pp. 9–16 (2011)
9. Habib, M.B., van Keulen, M.: Improving toponym disambiguation by iteratively enhancing certainty of extraction. In: Proc. of KDIR 2012, pp. 399–410 (2012)
10. Hobbs, J., Appelt, D., Bear, J., Israel, D., Kameyama, M., Stickel, M., Tyson, M.: Fastus: A system for extracting information from text. In: Proc. of Human Language Technology, pp. 133–137 (1993)
11. Isozaki, H., Kazawa, H.: Efficient support vector classifiers for named entity recognition. In: Proc. of COLING 2002, pp. 1–7 (2002)
12. Leidner, J.L.: Toponym Resolution in Text: Annotation, Evaluation and Applications of Spatial Grounding of Place Names. Universal Press, Boca Raton (2008)
13. Lieberman, M.D., Samet, H.: Multifaceted toponym recognition for streaming news. In: Proc. of SIGIR 2011, pp. 843–852 (2011)
14. Martins, B., Anastácio, I., Calado, P.: A machine learning approach for resolving place references in text. In: Proc. of AGILE 2010 (2010)
15. McCallum, A., Li, W.: Early results for named entity recognition with conditional random fields, feature induction and web-enhanced lexicons. In: Proc. of CoNLL 2003, pp. 188–191 (2003)
16. Nothman, J., Ringland, N., Radford, W., Murphy, T., Curran, J.R.: Learning multilingual named entity recognition from wikipedia. Artificial Intelligence (2012), http://www.sciencedirect.com/science/article/pii/S0004370212000276
17. Pouliquen, B., Kimler, M., Steinberger, R., Ignat, C., Oellinger, T., Fluart, F., Zaghouani, W., Widiger, A., Charlotte Forslund, A., Best, C.: Geocoding multilingual texts: Recognition, disambiguation and visualisation. In: Proc. of LREC 2006, pp. 53–58 (2006)
18. Rauch, E., Bukatin, M., Baker, K.: A confidence-based framework for disambiguating geographic terms. In: Workshop Proc. of the HLT-NAACL 2003, pp. 50–54 (2003)
19. Rennie, J.D.M.: Using term informativeness for named entity detection. In: Proc. of the 28th Annual International ACM SIGIR Conference on Research and Development in Information Retrieval, pp. 353–360 (2005)
20. Richman, A.E., Schone, P.: Mining wiki resources for multilingual named entity recognition. In: ACL 2008 (2008)
21. Sekine, S.: NYU: Description of the Japanese NE system used for MET-2. In: Proc. of MUC-7 (1998)
22. Smith, D., Crane, G.: Disambiguating geographic names in a historical digital library. In: Constantopoulos, P., Sølvberg, I.T. (eds.) ECDL 2001. LNCS, vol. 2163, pp. 127–136. Springer, Heidelberg (2001)
23. Smith, D., Mann, G.: Bootstrapping toponym classifiers. In: Workshop Proc. of HLT-NAACL 2003, pp. 45–49 (2003)
24. Szarvas, G., Farkas, R., Kocsor, A.: A multilingual named entity recognition system using boosting and c4.5 decision tree learning algorithms. In: Todorovski, L., Lavrač, N., Jantke, K.P. (eds.) DS 2006. LNCS (LNAI), vol. 4265, pp. 267–278. Springer, Heidelberg (2006)
25. Viterbi, A.: Error bounds for convolutional codes and an asymptotically optimum decoding algorithm. IEEE Transactions on Information Theory 13(2), 260–269 (1967)
26. Zhou, G., Su, J.: Named entity recognition using an hmm-based chunk tagger. In: Proc. ACL 2002, pp. 473–480 (2002)

Towards a Polish LTAG Grammar

Katarzyna Krasnowska

Institute of Computer Science, Polish Academy of Sciences
k.krasnowska@phd.ipipan.waw.pl

Abstract. This paper reports on a Lexicalised Tree Adjoining Grammar for Polish, extracted automatically from the Polish constituency treebank. The grammar consists of 23 570 elementary trees anchored by 11 515 lexemes. Running the grammar on the sentences from the treebank using a modified version of TuLiPA parser showed that it achieves a high accordance (almost 99%) with the treebank annotation – in terms of syntactic categories assigned to phrases – on the trees which were successfully parsed. For many trees, however, obtaining a TAG parse was impossible due to time or memory shortcomings of the used tool.

Keywords: Tree Adjoining Grammar, treebanks, automatic grammar extraction.

1 Introduction: LTAG Grammars

This paper describes a Lexicalised Tree Adjoining Grammar for Polish, obtained automatically from the Polish constituency treebank *Składnica* [4]. Tree Adjoining Grammars (TAGs, see [2]) are a kind of tree rewriting formalism. A TAG grammar is formally defined as a quintuple: $\langle \Sigma, NT, I, A, S \rangle$, where Σ is a finite set of terminals, NT is a finite set of nonterminals ($\Sigma \cap NT = \emptyset$), S is an initial symbol ($S \in NT$), I and A are finite sets of finite trees (*initial* and *auxiliary* trees). Initial and auxiliary trees have their internal nodes labelled with nonterminal symbols and leaves labelled with either terminals or nonterminals. A nonterminal leaf is a substitution site (usually marked "↓"). Auxiliary trees have one special nonterminal leaf called foot node (marked "∗" and labelled identically as the auxiliary tree's root). A Tree Adjoining Grammar is called *lexicalised* (LTAG) if each elementary tree has at least one terminal leaf. Such a leaf is by convention marked "◇" and called an anchor.

The trees are combined using two rewriting operations: substitution and adjunction (see Fig. 1). Derivation in a TAG grammar is a sequence of those operations, starting with an initial tree whose root is labelled with the initial symbol S. Tree substitution is fulfilled by attaching an initial tree to a nonterminal leaf. Substitution can be performed if the substitution node and the substituted tree's root have identical labels. Adjunction allows for insertion of auxiliary trees into the structure derived so far. For an adjunction to be possible, there must be an internal node (adjunction site) with a label identical as the adjoined tree's

M.A. Kłopotek et al. (Eds.): IIS 2013, LNCS 7912, pp. 16–21, 2013.

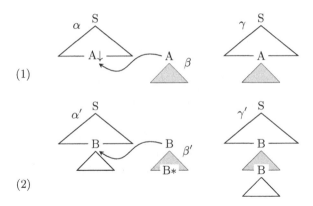

Fig. 1. Tree rewriting operations: (1) substitution of the initial tree β into α's substitution node A↓, yielding γ; (2) adjunction of the auxiliary tree β' into α''s internal node B, yielding γ'

root (and, as follows from the definition of an auxiliary tree, its foot node). The adjunction site can then be replaced with the auxiliary tree.

2   Extraction Procedure

The LTAG grammar extraction procedure is based on a technique proposed in [1], where such a grammar is obtained from the Penn Treebank. The extraction algorithm takes as its input a constituency tree and produces a set of elementary trees. It is a recursive procedure, starting in the root of the constituency tree. Extraction of an initial TAG tree α when the currently processed constituency tree node is η is performed as follows:[1]

- make η' — a copy of η — α's root;
- for each non-head child of η, decide whether it is a complement or an adjunct;
- for each child of η, if it is:
  - a non-terminal head child, run the procedure recursively on it and attach its result as η''s child;
  - a terminal head child, attach its copy as η''s child and make it α's lexical anchor;
  - a complement, attach its copy as η''s child and run the procedure recursively on it, producing a new initial tree;
  - an adjunct (to the node or its head child), run the procedure recursively on it and transform its result into an auxiliary tree as shown in Fig. 2;

The decision whether a child is a complement or an adjunct was taken according to rules such as the following:

---

[1] The described extraction procedure requires knowing which of the current node's children is a head child. [1] used a head percolation table to retrieve this information from Penn Treebank trees. In the case of *Składnica* it was not necessary since its trees have head children marked by design.

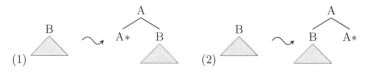

Fig. 2. Transformation of a tree extracted from A's adjunct B into an auxiliary tree
(1) if B is a left adjunct (2) if B is a right adjunct

- a node marked as mandatory phrase is a complement;
- a node marked as a loose phrase is an adjunct;
- a node bearing a category label different from its parent's is a complement;
- other nodes are adjuncts.[2]

Marking of phrases as mandatory (fw, argument, according to valence dictionary) and loose (fl, modifier) is a feature of *Składnica* which is very useful for differentiating between complement and adjunct nodes. This marking appears, however, only at the level of the ff (main finite phrase) node's siblings (see an example *Składnica* tree in Fig. 3), therefore the other rules are also necessary.

Składnica is different from Penn Treebank in that its nodes contain not only a label representing the phrase's category, but also a set of morphosyntactic features.[3] This reflects the fact that Polish is a highly inflectional language. Some of the features appearing in *Składnica* were incorporated into the extracted elementary trees. Once an elementary tree was produced, its feature values were replaced with variables. The node features which should be in agreement (e.g. the gender features of a fwe – VP – node and its subject fno – NP – are assigned the same variable. Features which are required to have a specific value (e.g. the accusative case of an fno node representing an object) have this value explicitly specified in the tree. There were also some cases where *Składnica*'s way of handling morphosyntactic features had to be slighlty modified for the TAG grammar to work. For verbs which can appear in analytical form, but are only present in *Składnica* in non-analytical form (and vice versa), appropriate elementary trees were added. An example of TAG tree extracted from a constituency tree with feature values taken from the *Składnica* tree and after replacing those values with variables is shown in Fig. 3.

3   Parsing with TuLiPA

For the purpose of testing the grammar, the TuLiPA (The Tübingen Linguistic Parsing Architecture, see [3] and https://sourcesup.cru.fr/tulipa/) parser was chosen. TuLiPA allows for including features in elementary tree nodes and assigning variables to them in order to specify which features in the resulting tree should be equal. TuLiPA uses a 3-layer architecture with the lexicon divided into 3 files:

---

[2] To the head child if they are closer to it than any node's argument, to the node otherwise.

[3] Features included in the TAG grammar are number, case, gender, person and tense.

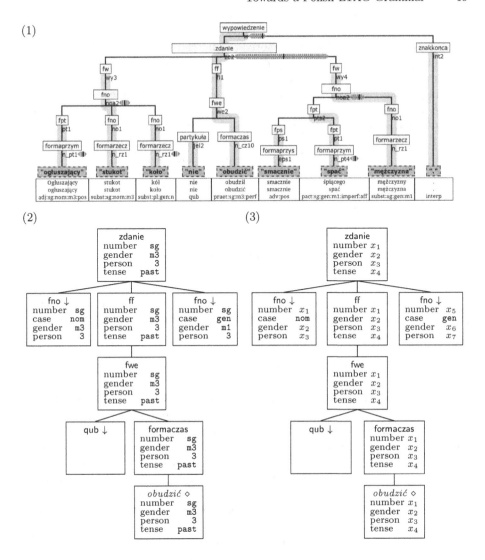

Fig. 3. (1) An example *Składnica* tree for the sentence *The deafening rattle of the train did not wake the soundly sleeping man up.* (node features hidden, highlighted branches lead to head children) and one of the TAG trees extracted from it: (2) with feature values from *Składnica*; (3) after replacing them with variables (its **wypowiedzenie** and **znakkonca↓** nodes are not shown). This is an initial tree for the verb *obudzić* (*to wake*) in negated form, taking as its arguments a nominative subject and a genitive object.

- grammar containing tree families (elementary trees with "empty" anchors, i.e. no lexical elements specified);
- lexicon, a list of lexemes and corresponding tree family identifiers (each ⟨lexeme, tree family⟩ pair specified in this file defines a lexically anchored elementary tree);
- morphology, containing all possible morphological forms for each lexeme.

In the case of Polish TAG grammar, only the first two layers (grammar and lexicon) were produced. This was motivated by the fact that the lexicon contains all lexemes appearing in *Składnica*, and given the complexity of Polish inflection the morphology file would either be incomplete (if only the forms occurring in the treebank were included) or grow unreasonably large. Instead, TuLiPA was modified to use Morfeusz, a morphological analyser for Polish (see `http://sgjp.pl/morfeusz`). This modified version of the parser was called TuLiPA-pl. When given a sentence to parse, TuLiPA-pl produces a morphology file for it on the fly, comprising all morphological interpretations of the sentence's tokens given by Morfeusz. It is also possible to run TuLiPA-pl with a morphology file provided by the user, as in original TuLiPA.

4   Evaluation

The method described in Section 2 was applied to 7 229 sentences from *Składnica*.[4] The extracted grammar contains 2 802 elementary tree families (1 825 initial and 977 auxiliary). The lexicon contains 11 515 lexemes, anchoring a total of 23 570 elementary trees (one lexeme can serve as a lexical anchor to more than one tree, e.g. in case of verbs with more than one possible valence frame). The average number of trees anchored by a lexeme is 2.05; 7 953 lexemes (69%) anchor only one tree.

Preliminary tests with parsing using the produced Polish TAG grammar and TuLiPA-pl showed serious efficiency problems: even relatively simple sentences either took a very long time to be processed or caused to parser to run out of memory. To speed up TuLiPA-pl's performance for the purpose of grammar evaluation, morphology files (one per sentence, containing morphological interpretations of token chosen in the particular tree) were extracted from the treebank. In this way, the parser did not have to deal with ambiguous word forms.

The extracted grammar was used to run TuLiPA-pl on the same sentences from *Składnica* that were used for extraction. Even with unambiguous morphology files, parsing of many sentences was unsuccessful due to time or memory shortcomings. Out of 7 229 sentences, TuLiPA-pl managed to produce a parse forest for 2 806. Table 1 summarises the outcomes of those TuLiPA-pl runs.

Table 1. Outcomes of TuLiPA runs. Time limit was 5 minutes per sentence

outcome	parse	no parse	TuLiPA error	out of memory	timed out
sentences	2678	128	640	3697	44
percentage	37%	2%	9%	51%	1%

For the sentences for which TuLiPA terminated its run (with or without a parse, a total of 2806 sentences), the trees produced by the TAG grammar were

---

[4] 998 trees were excluded due to technical problems they posed (mainly errors in head child marking).

compared to the original *Składnica* trees. For each *Składnica* tree and for each parse in the corresponding parse forest (empty in the cases when there was no parse) generated by TuLiPA-pl, the number of phrases assigned the same category (dominating node's label) was calculated. Then, the best-matching tree (i.e. the one with the most matching phrase categories) was chosen from the forest. The percentage of all phrases from *Składnica* which were assigned the same category in the best-matching TAG parse was 92%. With sentences limited to the ones with a non-empty parse forest, this score was 98.8%.

5   Conclusions

A Tree Adjoining Grammar was extracted automatically from the Polish constituency treebank. Although the grammar perform quite well on the sentences it manages to parse, achieving an almost 99% phrase category assignment match with the treebank, there are performance issues which make the grammar (at least when TuLiPA parser is used) inefficient for parsing large amounts of text. Moreover, the TAG formalism does not seem very well suited for languages with loose word order such as Polish since it requires that the elementary trees have a fixed structure. It is nevertheless worthwhile to report on this experiment since it is, as far as we know, the first attempt at creating a wide-coverage TAG grammar for Polish.

Acknowledgements. The work described in this paper is partially supported by the DG INFSO of the European Commission through the ICT Policy Support Programme, Grant agreement no.: 271022, as well as by the POIG.01.01.02-14-013/09 project co-financed by the European Union under the European Regional Development Fund.

References

1. Chen, J., Vijay-Shanker, K.: Automated extraction of Tags from the Penn Treebank. In: Proceedings of IWPT 2000 (2000)
2. Joshi, A., Schabes, Y.: Tree-adjoining grammars. In: Handbook of Formal Lanaguages and Automata. Springer, Berlin (1997)
3. Kallmeyer, L., Lichte, T., Maier, W., Parmentier, Y., Dellert, J., Evang, K.: TuLiPA: Towards a multi-formalism parsing environment for grammar engineering. In: Coling 2008: Proceedings of the Workshop on Grammar Engineering Across Frameworks, pp. 1–8. Coling 2008 Organizing Committee, Manchester (2008)
4. Woliński, M., Głowińska, K., Świdziński, M.: A preliminary version of Składnica – a treebank of Polish. In: Vetulani, Z. (ed.) Proceedings of the 5th Language & Technology Conference, Poznań, pp. 299–303 (2011)

Incorporating Head Recognition into a CRF Chunker*

Adam Radziszewski and Adam Pawlaczek

Institute of Informatics,
Wrocław University of Technology,
Wybrzeże Wyspiańskiego 27,
Wrocław, Poland

Abstract. While rule-based shallow parsers usually recognise phrases' syntactic heads, the same does not hold for statistical syntactic chunkers. The task of finding heads within already recognised chunks is not trivial for freer word order languages like German or Polish, while this information may be very useful.

We propose a simple solution that allows to incorporate head recognition into existing chunkers by extending the standard IOB2 representation with information on head location. To evaluate this approach we introduced the new representation into a CRF chunker for Polish. Although this idea is very simple, the results are surprisingly good.

1   Introduction

Syntactic chunking is a form of shallow parsing where the recognised structure is limited to phrase boundaries. Such task formulation has been proposed as a means towards full syntactic analysis [1], although chunks found other uses, e.g. in Information Extraction [3]. Later stages of processing may enrich this structure with two types of information:

1. inter-chunk syntactic dependencies,
2. intra-chunk syntactic structure, including location of chunks' syntactic heads.

In this paper we focus on the latter, namely automatic recognition of chunks' syntactic heads. In case of English the problem is next to trivial, since it is usually assumed that the syntactic head of each chunk is its last token [10, 12].

In case of other languages the situation is different. For instance, the chunk definitions proposed for German assume that post-modifiers are also allowed in NP chunks, thus syntactic heads are not necessarily chunk-final tokens [4]. Similar situation happens for Slavic languages, cf. definitions proposed for Bulgarian [6], Croatian [13, p. 124] or Polish [8]. Below we quote a sentence annotated with NP and VP chunks taken from a Polish corpus [2]:

---

* This work was financed by the National Centre for Research and Development (NCBiR) project SP/I/1/77065/10 ("SyNaT").

M.A. Kłopotek et al. (Eds.): IIS 2013, LNCS 7912, pp. 22–27, 2013.

(1)   [$_{NP}$ *Specyficzną odmianą iskry*] [$_{VP}$ *jest*] [$_{NP}$ *piorun*].

'*A specific kind of (electric) spark is a thunder*'

Most work related to chunking languages other than English is based on manually written grammars. Conceiving a rule that captures a syntactic phrase naturally involves considering the location of its syntactic head, hence many chunkers that rely on shallow grammars in fact annotate heads. The alternative approach to chunking assumes usage of Machine Learning (ML) algorithms. The standard practice is to cast the task as a sequence labelling problem by encoding chunks with so-called IOB2 tags. In this paper we propose a very simple and natural extension to this representation that allows to perform chunking and head recognition in one run. Our solution is practical, since it allows to obtain chunking and head annotation without making any changes to the underlying ML algorithms. To the best of our knowledge, no similar approach has been considered and evaluated so far. We demonstrate advantages of this simple idea by incorporating head recognition into a CRF chunker developed for Polish.

2   Encoding Chunks and Heads

The standard practice to encode text annotated with chunks of one type is to use three-tag IOB2 representation [11]:

B first token of a chunk
I non-initial token belonging to a chunk
O token outside of any chunk

When more than one chunk type is annotated in the same corpus, this IOB2 representation is naturally generalised [12]:

B-X first token of a chunk of type X
I-X non-initial token belonging to a chunk of type X
O token outside of any chunk

Our proposal is to add information on placement of syntactic heads into the IOB2 representation in the following manner:

B-X first token of a chunk of type X (non-head)
B-X-H first token of a chunk of type X (head)
I-X non-initial token belonging to a chunk of type X (non-head)
I-X-H non-initial token belonging to a chunk of type X (head)
O token outside of any chunk

We will call this representation IOB2-H from now on. Below is an example:

Specyficzną	B-NP
odmianą	I-NP-H
iskry	I-NP
jest	B-VP-H
piorun	B-NP-H
.	O

For n chunk types, the IOB2-H representation defines $4n + 1$ tags.

3   Dataset

We performed evaluation of the above idea against Polish data. Slavic languages are characterised with relatively free word order and rich inflection (therefore, large tagsets), which make them challenging for chunking and head recognition.

We use the *Polish Corpus of Wrocław University of Technology*[1] (*KPWr*) [2]. Its syntactic annotation includes the following chunk types [8]:

1. Noun phrases and prepositional phrases labelled collectively as *NP chunks*. The employed definition refers to syntactic requirements of clauses: the NP chunks closely correspond to verb arguments (sometimes also adjuncts). This assumption results in quite long chunks. Most notably, the definition requires inclusion of subordinate prepositional phrases into NP chunks (NP chunking involves PP attachment). NP heads are most often nouns, but may also be gerunds, personal pronouns, cardinal numerals, in rare cases adjectives used nominally. Prepositions are never chosen as heads for practical reasons.
2. Adjective phrases are annotated only when not part of larger NP chunks, hence they are not frequent. AdjP chunks are defined similarly to NPs, but centred around adjectival heads (adjectives or adjectival participles).
3. Verb phrase (VP) chunks are annotated around verbal predicates playing the role of their heads. The chunk definition allows for inclusion of adverbial elements that clearly modify the VPs. Verb arguments are excluded.
4. A separate 'layer' of annotation, consisting of simpler chunks defined on the grounds of morphological agreement — AgP chunks. They are noun or adjectival chunks that are limited to the extent of morphological agreement on number, gender and case. Again, chunk-initial prepositions are included. The definition includes indeclinable elements (mostly adverbs) that modify other chunk elements. AgP chunks are 'building blocks' for NPs and AdjPs. Their heads are either those typical for NPs or AdjPs. The inclusion of both AgP and NP chunks makes up an interesting comparison of head recognition performance across different task formulations.

KPWr annotation guidelines require that all heads must be one-token.

Recognition of such chunks is not an easy task. A chunker utilising Memory-Based Learning was tested against a subset of KPWr and the following F-measure values were obtained: 63% for NP, 75% for AgP, 82% for VP [5].

4   CRF Chunker for Polish

In our previous work [9] we showed that a chunker based on Conditional Random Fields (CRF) significantly outperforms three other approaches, including a hand-written grammar and Memory-Based Learning. The chunker (named *IOBBER*) is equipped with a set of features tailored for Polish, including the following items:

---

[1] The corpus is publicly available under a Creative Commons licence. We used version 1.1 downloaded from `http://www.nlp.pwr.wroc.pl/kpwr`

- the wordforms of tokens occupying a local window $(-2, \ldots, +2)$,
- grammatical class of tokens in the window,
- values for the following grammatical categories: number, gender and case in the window,
- a couple of tests for morphosyntactic agreement on the values of number, gender and case,
- two tests for orthographic form: if it starts with an upper-case letter, if it starts with a lower-case letter.

Those experiments were carried out against the data extracted from the National Corpus of Polish [7]. In this work we took the same chunker and made two modifications to its algorithm:

1. during training, chunks' syntactic heads are also read and the underlying CRF training module is fed with the IOB2-H representation (instead of standard IOB2),
2. during performance the trained CRF model is used to predict IOB2-H tags, which are decoded into chunks with heads highlighted.

In other words, we made minimal changes to the original chunker to support head recognition using the IOB2-H representation.

5   Rule-Based Alternative

We compare the results of simultaneous chunking and head recognition with performance of a simple rule set. The rules were written as a practical solution to enhance output of the chunker with chunks' syntactic heads before the work described here was started. They consist of a separate decision list for each chunk type. Each decision list consists of several rules, fired sequentially. A rule iterates over a chunk left-to-right and examines each token's grammatical class. If the class belongs to a pre-defined set, the whole search is terminated and the current token is marked as the head. For instance, the left-most noun is taken directly as NP head. If no rule fires, there is fallback rule to choose chunk-initial token.

6   Results

First, we present evaluation of the CRF chunker itself against our data set and the impact of switching from the standard CRF IOB2 representation to IOB2-H. Table 1 presents precision, recall and F-measure values[2] related to chunk boundary detection. The CRF chunker outperforms significantly the MBL chunker presented in [5]. But what we wanted to stress here is that using the new representation does not damage the quality of chunking (actually, the opposite may be observed: the figures related to IOB2-H are slightly higher).

---

[2] All the experiments described here have been carried out using the standard ten-fold cross-validation scheme. The figures reported are values averaged over ten folds.

Table 1. Impact of IOB2-H representation on chunk boundary detection

	CRF IOB2-H			CRF IOB2		
	P	R	F	P	R	F
NP	74.49	74.29	**74.38**	74.00	73.68	**73.83**
AdjP	45.53	42.67	**43.91**	46.90	39.47	**42.73**
VP	76.72	82.61	**79.55**	75.94	82.47	**79.06**
AgP	83.71	86.11	**84.89**	83.65	85.71	**84.66**

Table 2 presents the assessment of head recognition capabilities. The CRF chunker operating on the IOB2-H representation is compared to the hand-written rules (fired against output of the original CRF chunker). For each chunk type we measured the accuracy of head recognition alone (marked 'Head'), as well as the accuracy of chunk boundary detection **and** head recognition (that is, both chunk boundaries and heads had to be recognised correctly to count — 'C+H'). The immediate conslusion is that CRF chunker substantially outperforms the rules. What is more, the accuracy of head recognition alone seems impressively high: the figures related to simultaneous head recognition and chunking (C+H) are only slightly lower than chunk boundary detection alone.

Table 2. Performance of CRF chunker and hand-written rules wrt. head recognition

	CRF IOB2-H			Rules		
	P	R	F	P	R	F
NP Head	83.89	83.66	**83.77**	55.69	55.53	**55.61**
NP C+H	70.82	70.64	**70.73**	46.87	46.74	**46.80**
AdjP Head	72.42	68.02	**69.94**	58.04	54.53	**56.06**
AdjP C+H	45.11	42.25	**43.49**	34.63	32.60	**33.48**
VP Head	90.45	97.43	**93.80**	90.60	97.59	**93.96**
VP C+H	76.55	82.43	**79.38**	76.53	82.40	**79.35**
AgP Head	92.76	95.42	**94.07**	90.51	93.12	**91.79**
AgP C+H	83.05	85.43	**84.22**	81.05	83.38	**82.20**

7   Conclusion and Further Work

We proposed a solution allowing to incorporate head recognition into existing chunkers. Its practical value is confirmed by good results of head recognition against Polish data. The resulting chunker is available[3] under GNU LGPL 3.0, but also, will be used in our projects related to Question Answering and shallow semantic parsing.

It will be interesting to evaluate the presented approach against the data from the National Corpus of Polish, but also from other languages.

---

[3] http://nlp.pwr.wroc.pl/redmine/projects/iobber/wiki

References

[1] Abney, S.: Parsing by chunks. In: Principle-Based Parsing. pp. 257–278. Kluwer Academic Publishers (1991)

[2] Broda, B., Marcińczuk, M., Maziarz, M., Radziszewski, A., Wardyński, A.: KPWr: Towards a free corpus of Polish. In: Calzolari, N., Choukri, K., Declerck, T., Doğan, M.U., Maegaard, B., Mariani, J., Odijk, J., Piperidis, S. (eds.) Proceedings of LREC 2012. ELRA, Istanbul (2012)

[3] Hobbs, J.R., Riloff, E.: Information extraction. In: Indurkhya, N., Damerau, F.J. (eds.) Handbook of Natural Language Processing, 2nd edn. Chapman & Hall/CRC Press, Taylor & Francis Group (2010)

[4] Kermes, H., Evert, S.: YAC — a recursive chunker for unrestricted German text. In: Rodriguez, M.G., Araujo, C.P. (eds.) Proceedings of the Third International Conference on , vol. V, pp. 1805–1812 (2002)Language Resources and Evaluation

[5] Maziarz, M., Radziszewski, A., Wieczorek, J.: Chunking of Polish: guidelines, discussion and experiments with Machine Learning. In: Proceedings of the 5th Language & Technology Conference, LTC 2011, Poznań, Poland (2011)

[6] Osenova, P.: Bulgarian nominal chunks and mapping strategies for deeper syntactic analyses. In: Proceedings of the Workshop on Treebanks and Linguistic Theories (TLT 2002), Sozopol, Bulgaria, September 20-21 (2002)

[7] Przepiórkowski, A., Bańko, M., Górski, R.L., Lewandowska-Tomaszczyk, B. (eds.): Narodowy Korpus Języka Polskiego. Wydawnictwo Naukowe PWN, Warsaw (2012)

[8] Radziszewski, A., Maziarz, M., Wieczorek, J.: Shallow syntactic annotation in the Corpus of Wrocław University of Technology. Cognitive Studies 12 (2012)

[9] Radziszewski, A., Pawlaczek, A.: Large-scale experiments with NP chunking of polish. In: Sojka, P., Horák, A., Kopeček, I., Pala, K. (eds.) TSD 2012. LNCS, vol. 7499, pp. 143–149. Springer, Heidelberg (2012)

[10] Ramshaw, L.A., Marcus, M.P.: Text chunking using transformation-based learning. In: Proceedings of the Third ACL Workshop on Very Large Corpora, Cambridge, MA, USA, pp. 82–94 (1995)

[11] Sang, E.F.T.K., Veenstra, J.: Representing text chunks. In: Proceedings of the Ninth Conference on European Chapter of the Association for Computational Linguistics, pp. 173–179. Association for Computational Linguistics, Morristown (1999)

[12] Tjong Kim Sang, E.F., Buchholz, S.: Introduction to the CoNLL-2000 shared task: Chunking. In: Proceedings of CoNLL-2000 and LLL-2000, Lisbon, Portugal pp. 127–132 (2000)

[13] Vučković, K.: Model parsera za hrvatski jezik. Ph.D. thesis, Department of Information Sciences, Faculty of Humanities and Social Sciences, University of Zagreb, Croatia (2009)

Classification of Predicate-Argument Relations in Polish Data[*]

Adam Radziszewski, Paweł Orłowicz, and Bartosz Broda

Institute of Informatics, Wrocław University of Technology

Abstract. This paper discusses the problem of syntactic relation recognition in Polish data. We consider *subject*, *object* and *copula* relations between VP and NP or AdjP chunks. The problem has been studied for English, while it has received very little attention in the context of Slavic languages. Slavic languages, including Polish, are characterised with relatively free word order, which makes the task more challenging than in the case of English.

The task may be formulated as a classification problem and dealt with using supervised learning techniques. We propose a feature set tailored to the characteristics of Polish language and perform experiments with a number of classifiers.

1 Introduction

We present an approach to shallow parsing of Polish where the problem is decomposed into two stages: constituent chunking and recognition of selected inter-chunk relations corresponding to partial predicate-argument structure. Both stages may be expressed in terms of classification problems, which in turn allows for usage of well-known Machine Learning algorithms. This approach to shallow parsing follows the scheme proposed in [9]. Our contribution is two-fold: we adapt the feature set to the characteristics of Slavic languages and we perform experiments with recognition of syntactic relations in Polish data testing a few classifiers (the experiments presented in [9] are limited to Memory-Based Learning).

The scope of this paper is mostly limited to the second stage, that is inter-chunk relation recognition. This is because it is still an understudied problem for Slavic languages — we are aware of only one work that touches upon this issue [1] — while chunking of Slavic languages received much more attention, e.g. [11, 13, 14, 15, 18, 19, 21].

2 Syntactic Chunks and Inter-chunk Relations

Our work is based on the Polish Corpus of Wrocław University of Technology[1], abbreviated KPWr [5]. The corpus is annotated with shallow syntactic structure

---

[*] This work was financed by the National Centre for Research and Development (NCBiR) project SP/I/1/77065/10 ("SyNaT").

[1] Available at http://nlp.pwr.wroc.pl/kpwr

M.A. Kłopotek et al. (Eds.): IIS 2013, LNCS 7912, pp. 28–38, 2013.

that follows the two-stage approach. The annotation guidelines of KPWr define the following chunk types [17]:

1. Noun phrases (NP) — possibly complex noun or prepositional[2] phrases that may fill the role of arguments. The assumption that NP chunks should correspond closely to arguments entails that some NP chunks include PP modifiers. The NP chunks are limited to clause boundaries. The other situation where noun phrases are split into several chunks is coordination: if the coordination happens at the superordinate level, that is the whole NP would have several syntactic heads, the phrase is split on coordinating conjuncts. Coordinations are allowed if the whole phrase may still be assigned one noun head.
2. Adjective phrases (AdjP) are annotated only where they do not belong to any NP chunks.
3. Verb phrases (VP) — understood as verbs (simple or analytical forms) excluding arguments. VPs should also include adverbial modifiers if they clearly modify other parts of the phrase.
4. Agreement phrases (AgP) — alternative level of annotation, comprised of simple noun or adjective phrases. They are not linked to predicate-argument structure, hence we do not use this level.

The KPWr guidelines [17] define the following inter-chunk relations:

1. Subject (SUBJ) — a relation between VP and NP chunks. The definition is limited to include subjects that are manifested as NP chunks with nominative head. This leaves out null subjects, as well as some other less frequent constructs. Sometimes one VP may be attached more than one subject. This happens in the case of coordinated NPs that are split into several NP chunks — each of them is attached with a separate SUBJ link.
2. Object (OBJ) — a relation between VP and NP, sometimes also between VP and AdjP. The definition includes direct and indirect objects, as well as those adjuncts that are manifested as NP or AdjP chunks. The cases of AdjP objects are relatively infrequent, e.g. *jury uznało go [za najbardziej znaczący]* 'the jury recognised it [as most significant]'.
3. Copula (COP) — a relation between VP and AdjP or VP and NP, annotated in the case of Polish predicative constructs. The relation links the copula (*być*, 'to be', *stać się, zostać* 'to become') and an AdjP or NP. For example, *jestem głodny* 'I'm hungry' or *został dobrym policjantem* 'he became a good policeman'.

The statistics of this corpus are presented in Tab. 1.

3   Related Works

There have been a few attempts at recognising inter-chunk syntactic relations, most of them performed on the data from the Penn Treebank [3].

---

[2] Prepositional phrases and actual noun phrases are labelled collectively as NP chunks. [17] motivate this in terms of simplicity of annotation scheme as well as possibility of automatic classification with trivial rules, if needed.

Table 1. Statistics for the syntactically annotated part of KPWr

Element	Number of instances
Sentence	2004
Token	32296
VP chunk	2376
ARG chunk	6453
NP	6069
AdjP	384
SUBJ relation	1372
OBJ relation	2496
COP relation	476

In [2], the problem of verb–object and verb–subject relation recognition was cast as bracketing tasks by treating the whole stretches of text including the verb and its object as OV chunks, and similarly with verb–subject relations. This approach seems to be a bit over-simplified, since it forces to assign at most one object per verb. The work also presents a learning algorithm called Memory-Based Sequence Learning, which is based on memorising sequences of POS tags.

In [9], a shallow parser is presented. It consists of two memory-based modules: a chunker, recognising NP and VP chunks, and a module for recognition of verb–object and verb–subject relation instances. Both modules assume the respective problems are cast as sequence of classification tasks. In the case of relation recognition, both relations may hold between a VP chunk and any other word or chunk. The starting point was to generate for each sentence all possible VP–other word/chunk pairs. As this would result in a very high number of candidate instances for classification, a heuristic rule was introduced to reject all the pairs with more than one intervening VP chunk between both items. The authors make some interesting observations on the crucial role of chunking of the local context for the method to work properly. This is reflected in the proposed feature set for the relation classification tasks. The features include information concerning both items (chunks or words to be linked with a relation), the in-between material, but also some chunks outside the range, neighbouring the items in question. We will turn back to this feature set in Sec. 4.3 as a starting point for our experiments. The system achieves 84.7% precision and 81.6% recall ($F = 83.1\%$) for subject detection, while 87.3% precision and 85.8% recall ($F = 86.5\%$) for object detection. Note that those figures were obtained when including chunking errors. The observed F-measure values are higher when testing on manually annotated chunks (89.0% for subjects, 91.6% for objects).

A similar approach is presented in [7]. The chunking stage is extended to five chunk types: NP, VP, AdjP, AdvP and PP (containing only prepositions, later combined with NPs to form so-called PNP chunks). The relation recognition stage was formulated as classification of all VP–other chunk pairs. The feature set was very similar to that of [9]. The addition included a feature that obtained prepositions from PNP chunks, and some information about certain chunks occupying the in-between range. The highest reported value of F-measure was 83.1%.

An approach to classification of inter-chunk syntactic relations for Polish data is presented in [1]. This work differs from the ones previously mentioned in that the task is defined as discovering the complete dependency graph between chunks found in the sentence, not limiting the attention to subject/object relations. What is more, the set of considered chunk types include both syntactic objects corresponding to syntactic phrases, but also 'syntactic words', which are most often single tokens [12]. These two assumptions shift the task definition heavily towards full dependency parsing, hence the results obtained cannot be directly compared to ours. The proposed feature set is impressively large, including estimated collocation strength between chunks' semantic heads, but also, some items tailored for Slavic languages: grammatical case, gender and number, and also, agreement on number, gender and case (tests for agreement are useful since the task definition involves discovering dependency links between arbitrary chunks, not just subject/object). Also, some semantic information derived from a wordnet is used. The reported results are achieved using Balanced Random Forest classifier: 89% precision and 66% recall (76% F-measure). These figures include chunking (and tagging) errors only partially, for instance reference manual annotation was used to gather statistics on collocation strength between chunks' heads.

4   Proposed Solution

4.1   General Setting

To apply our shallow parsing scheme to user-provided text, the following processing stages are required:

1. morphosyntactic tagging,
2. chunking,
3. recognition of chunks' syntactic heads (the heads are used by our features),
4. the proper inter-chunk relation recognition module (next section).

4.2   Relation Recognition Algorithm

All of the syntactic relations defined in the KPWr corpus hold between either VP and NP chunks or VP and AdjP chunks. This allows for a convenient simplification: we examine all such pairs present in a sentence and classify each for one of the relations from the following set: SUBJ, OBJ, COP, *None*. We decided against filtering the pairs with respect to distance between chunks. Our motivation was that of simplicity, while as the candidate pairs in our case are limited to VP–NP/AdjP schema, the number of candidates should already be limited to reasonable ranges. The distance is embodied in two features that may be used by the classifier to exclude long-distance dependencies as unlikely.

The training procedure is simple: all the possible VP–NP and VP–AdjP pairs are generated from each sentence. For each pair a feature vector is generated. The vector is assigned a correct class label (relation name or *None*). The set of representations gathered this way is used to train a single classifier.

Performance phase, that is recognition of relation instances with a trained classifier, follows the same scheme. All the possible pairs are used for feature generation. Each feature vector is classified with relation name label (or *None*). Note that this way we do not assert some syntactic constraints that are invariant in the annotation principles. That is, our algorithm may link two different VPs with the same object, which is not permitted in KPWr. Obviously, such errors will be penalised during evaluation.

4.3 Features

Polish is a relatively free word order language and grammatical case is used to expressing syntactic roles of arguments. Nevertheless, an SVO (subject–verb–object ordering) preference is clearly visible. We tried to account for these properties:

1. we tested the original features proposed in [9] (D),
2. but also our adaptation for Polish (D+).

Both feature sets are defined in Tab. 2.

An example of manually annotated sentence is presented in Fig. 1. A couple of training instances generated from this sentence using some of the features described above are presented in Table 3. As those instances were obtained using automatic features extraction, one can see that there are errors introduced by chunker e.g. wrong head recognition of chunk VP: [może pomieścić].

Fig. 1. An example annotated sentence taken from KPWr (*'The facility was opened for public use in 2003 and it may hold 8000 spectators'*)

4.4 Classifiers

For the purpose of classification we used a few diverse classifiers:

1. Popular C4.5 decision tree induction algorithm [16] (standard Weka J48 implementation, with default parameters).
2. Support Vector Machines (SVM), using the implementation from LIBSVM package with radial basis function as a kernel [8].
3. Memory-based classifier from TiMBL package [10].

We employed standard grid search for optimisation of LIBSVM parameters. For the experiments with memory-based learning we tested several values of k (number of neighbours) and two metrics: weighted overlap as well as Modified Value Difference with inverse-linear neighbour–distance weighting scheme (the latter setting was also used for chunking of Polish; cf. [13]).

Table 2. Feature sets considered for the task. The features referring to the VP chunk are suffixed with VP, those referring to NP/AdjP — with ARG. Additional suffix designates a chunk (of any type) from local neighbourhood of the VP or ARG, e.g., base_hd_ARG-2 retrieves the head lemma of the second chunk to the left (-2) from the ARG chunk.

	D	D+	
distance	•	•	signed number of tokens between examined chunks (positive: ARG chunk is on the left of VP chunk, negative: ARG chunk is on the right)
vp_between	•	•	unsigned number of VP chunk occurrences between examined chunks
commas	•	•	number of commas between examined chunks
base_hd_VP	•	•	
base_hd_ARG-2	•	•	⎫ base form of a chunk head
base_hd_ARG-1	•	•	⎬ concerns VP or ARG chunks, as well as their neighbours
base_hd_ARG	•	•	⎭ — n chunks left/right the VP or ARG chunk
base_hd_ARG+1	•	•	
class_hd_ARG	•	•	
class_hd_ARG-2	•	•	⎫ grammatical class of a chunk head
class_hd_ARG-1	•	•	⎬ concerns VP or ARG chunks, as well as their neighbours
class_hd_ARG	•	•	⎭ — n chunks left/right the VP or ARG chunk
class_hd_ARG+1	•	•	
class_chunk_ARG		•	gram. classes of all words in ARG chunk (set)
case_chunk_ARG		•	case values of all words in ARG chunk (set)
case_hd_ARG		•	case of the head in ARG chunk

5   Evaluation

The proposed method of relation recognition has been implemented as two Python scripts: trainer and annotator. All the described features were implemented using Fextor, a feature extraction toolkit [4]. All the classifiers were accessed using the common classification API offered by the LexCSD package [6].

To evaluate the method in a setting close to real-life applications, we account for errors made at all the stages of processing:

1. Tagging error is already included as the KPWr was tagged using the WMBT tagger [20]. The impact of tagging error on chunking accuracy is substantial: the F-measure of a CRF chunker for Polish was 80% higher when evaluated against manually tagged data than when using the same corpus re-tagged with WMBT [18].

2. To account for chunking error, we incorporated chunker training into the cross-validation set-up: each training part is used to train the chunker and our relation recognition module. Each test part is processed with the trained chunker and then trained relation recogniser. The experiments use *IOB-BER*[3], a CRF chunker for Polish [18].

---

[3] We use version 1.0 from http://nlp.pwr.wroc.pl/redmine/projects/iobber/wiki

Table 3. Example training instances generated by Fextor

	Inst1	Inst2	Inst3	Inst4	...
Head VP	*został*	*może*	*został*	*został*	
Head ARG	*Obiekt*	*8000*	*otwarty*	*8000*	
distance	1	-1	-1	-9	
vp_between	0	0	0	1	
commas	0	0	0	0	
base_hd_VP	zostać	móc	zostać	zostać	
class_hd_VP	praet	fin	praet	praet	
base_hd_ARG-2	∅	∅	obiekt	∅	
class_hd_ARG-2	∅	ign	subst	ign	
base_hd_ARG-1	∅	móc	zostać	móc	
class_hd_ARG-1	∅	fin	praet	fin	
base_hd_ARG	obiekt	∅	∅	∅	
class_hd_ARG	subst	ign	adj	ign	
base_hd_ARG+1	zostać	∅	∅	∅	
class_hd_ARG+1	praet	subst	subst	subst	
class_chunk_ARG	subst	ign,subst	adj,ign,prep,subst	ign,subst	
case_chunk_ARG	nom	gen	nom,gen,loc	gen	
case_hd_ARG	nom	∅	nom	∅	
relation	SUBJ	OBJ	COP	None	

3. Relation recognition also requires information about the location of chunks' syntactic heads. IOBBER is also able to annotate chunks' syntactic heads and we exploit this capability here (the underlying CRF model recognises both chunk boundaries and heads in one run). The impact of misplaced chunk heads is also included in the overall figures.

Note that all the required information (except manual morphosyntactic tagging) is available in KPWr: chunks, chunk heads and inter-chunk relations have been manually annotated and may be used as training and testing material. To measure the impact of chunking and head recognition error on the overall relation recognition, we will also report precision and recall values for a setting where both chunking and head annotation is taken directly from the reference corpus (i.e. chunking and head annotation error is neglected).

We compare the approach based on classification with a rich baseline, namely a simple rule-based system. The rules work on the (false) assumption that every Polish sentence follows the SVO pattern:

1. If the number of VP and NP chunks (together) that appear between ARG and VP is larger than 1, classify the instance as *None*.
2. If the argument comes before the VP:
   - *SUBJ* if ARG head is in nominative case,
   - *None* otherwise.
3. If the argument comes after the VP:
   - *COP* if VP head lemma is *być*, *zostać* or *stać* and ARG is the first chunk after VP,

- *None* if VP head lemma is *być, zostać* or *stać* and ARG is *not* the first chunk after VP,
- *OBJ* otherwise.

The results for subject, object and copula recognition are presented in tables 4 and 5. The figures reported are obtained via standard ten-fold cross-validation scheme. For LIBSVM we performed additional parameter optimisation. The optimisation was carried out on a subset of the whole corpus, hence the results achieved by those classifiers might be overfit to some degree. While this should in principle be avoided, the performance of those classifiers is anyway lower than the highest achieved (TiMBL).

Although the figures presented in Table 4 seem disappointingly low, most classifiers managed to beat the baseline. Where F-measure value was significantly higher than baseline level, we marked the figure with an asterisk (paired *t*-test with 95% confidence). The comparison between two feature sets clearly shows the importance of features tailored for Polish language — in case of all three relations the best results were obtained by the proposed D+ feature set.

The other conclusion is the excellence of the memory-based classifier, TiMBL. TiMBL outperformed the other classifiers consistently in case of all the three relations, which suggests that it has been a good decision to employ it in the original study made for English [9].

Note that we count a relation instance as correct when all the following items are properly recognised: syntactic heads of both chunks (VP and ARG) as well

Table 4. Performance of relation recogniser as a function of underlying classifier and employed feature set. Chunking errors included.

			Features D			Features D+		
			P	R	F	P	R	F
SUBJ	TiMBL	mM.k20.dIL	33.6	37.2	**35.2**	49.6	43.6	**46.2**[*]
	TiMBL	mM.k5.dIL	29.5	31.4	**30.3**	45.9	42.2	**43.7**[*]
	J48		31.2	31.3	**31.2**	48.7	38.1	**42.2**[*]
	LibSVM		25.9	19.3	**22.0**	44.1	36.7	**39.6**
	Baseline		38.4	34.9	**36.5**	38.4	34.9	**36.5**
OBJ	TiMBL	mM.k20.dIL	38.9	37.2	**37.9**[*]	40.3	44.9	**42.4**[*]
	TiMBL	mM.k5.dIL	37.6	36.9	**37.1**[*]	38.9	43.9	**41.2**[*]
	J48		37.3	36.1	**36.6**[*]	38.4	44.0	**41.0**[*]
	LibSVM		30.5	39.3	**34.2**[*]	35.9	43.0	**39.1**[*]
	Baseline		28.0	31.6	**29.6**	28.0	31.6	**29.6**
COP	TiMBL	mM.k20.dIL	45.3	35.5	**39.6**	60.5	39.8	**47.5**[*]
	TiMBL	mM.k5.dIL	38.3	40.6	**38.9**	53.9	39.5	**45.1**[*]
	J48		34.4	33.1	**33.5**	45.5	35.3	**39.2**
	Baseline		33.9	36.8	**35.2**	33.9	36.8	**35.2**
	LibSVM		25.4	14.2	**17.9**	39.1	31.0	**34.1**

as the name of the relation that holds between them. If the chunker mispredicts location of a chunk's syntactic head, the whole relation instance is deemed incorrect.

The performance of the sole relation recogniser is presented in Table 5. The columns captioned *Reference* report performance values where both chunking and head recognition errors were neglected. The impact of those errors turned out to be quite substantial. To gain more insight, we also evaluated the performance of IOBBER against the very same data set (and the same division into ten folds). Table 6 reports figures for chunking (row labelled *Chunks*), recognition of heads only (*Heads*) and recognition of both (both chunk boundaries and head location must be correct to count, *Both*). Indeed, the error rates are quite substantial, which is a likely explanation for the gap between results obtained with the help of IOBBER and reference chunking.

Table 5. Impact of chunking errors on the observed performance of relation recogniser. Assuming D+ feature set.

			CRF chunker			Reference		
			P	R	F	P	R	F
SUBJ	TiMBL	mM.k20.dIL	49.6	43.6	**46.2**	77.1	68.0	**72.1**
	TiMBL	mM.k5.dIL	45.9	42.2	**43.7**	71.9	65.5	**68.1**
	J48		48.7	38.1	**42.2**	71.8	58.2	**63.8**
	LibSVM		44.1	36.7	**39.6**	63.4	50.6	**55.8**
	Baseline		38.4	34.9	**36.5**	58.5	52.6	**55.3**
OBJ	TiMBL	mM.k20.dIL	40.3	44.9	**42.4**	78.9	85.8	**82.1**
	TiMBL	mM.k5.dIL	38.9	43.9	**41.2**	76.0	83.3	**79.4**
	J48		38.4	44.0	**41.0**	75.1	83.3	**78.9**
	LibSVM		35.9	43.0	**39.1**	66.2	81.1	**72.7**
	Baseline		28.0	31.6	**29.6**	56.5	63.5	**59.7**
COP	TiMBL	mM.k20.dIL	60.5	39.8	**47.5**	84.1	65.1	**72.9**
	TiMBL	mM.k5.dIL	53.9	39.5	**45.1**	77.3	64.9	**70.0**
	J48		45.5	35.3	**39.2**	68.3	57.9	**62.0**
	Baseline		33.9	36.8	**35.2**	57.1	62.9	**59.7**
	LibSVM		39.1	31.0	**34.1**	55.9	49.5	**52.0**

Table 6. Performance of IOBBER: chunking and head recognition

	NP chunks			VP chunks			AdjP chunks		
	P	R	F	P	R	F	P	R	F
Chunks	72.4	70.6	**71.5**	81.2	84.9	**83.0**	40.2	40.0	**40.0**
Heads	82.9	80.9	**81.9**	92.7	97.0	**94.7**	69.3	69.2	**69.1**
Both	68.1	66.5	**67.3**	80.8	84.5	**82.6**	38.8	38.7	**38.7**

6 Conclusion and Further Work

We presented experiments in recognition of inter-chunk syntactic relations in Polish data. This task may be practically useful to extend the level of syntactic analysis from chunks to partial predicate-argument structure.

We should emphasize that our best results (46% F-measure for subject, 42% for object and 47% for copula) are somewhat disappointing and substantially lower than those achieved for a similarly defined task for English (83% for subject and 87% for object), [9]. This discrepancy may be attributed to the relatively free word order of Polish, but also, complex chunk definitions in KPWr corpus. The latter is confirmed by the relatively high chunking error. This leads to a conclusion that further works should focus on the improvement of chunking algorithms before any significant progress in the recognition of inter-chunk relations may be made. Nevertheless, the presented approach allowed to obtain results that are significantly better than a rich rule-based baseline, which is already of practical value.

We limited our feature set to morphosyntactic properties of chunks and their local neighbourhood. It may also be a good idea to go beyond this level, starting with re-using some of the features proposed in [1], e.g. estimated collocation strength and wordnet-induced features.

References

[1] Acedański, S., Slaski, A., Przepiórkowski, A.: Machine learning of syntactic attachment from morphosyntactic and semantic co-occurrence statistics. In: Proceedings of the ACL 2012 Joint Workshop on Statistical Parsing and Semantic Processing of Morphologically Rich Languages, pp. 42–47. Association for Computational Linguistics, Jeju (2012)

[2] Argamon, S., Dagan, I., Krymolowski, Y.: A memory-based approach to learning shallow natural language patterns. In: COLING-ACL, pp. 67–73 (1998)

[3] Bies, A., Ferguson, M., Katz, K., MacIntyre, R., Tredinnick, V., Kim, G., Marcinkiewicz, M.A., Schasberger, B.: Bracketing guidelines for treebank II style Penn Treebank project. Tech. rep., University of Pennsylvania (1995), http://nlp.korea.ac.kr/~hjchung/sprg/paper/treebank1.pdf

[4] Broda, B., Kędzia, P., Marcińczuk, M., Radziszewski, A., Ramocki, R., Wardyński, A.: Fextor: A feature extraction framework for natural language processing: A case study in word sense disambiguation, relation recognition and anaphora resolution. In: Przepiórkowski, A., Piasecki, M., Jassem, K., Fuglewicz, P. (eds.) Computational Linguistics. SCI, vol. 458, pp. 41–62. Springer, Heidelberg (2013)

[5] Broda, B., Marcińczuk, M., Maziarz, M., Radziszewski, A., Wardyński, A.: KPWr: Towards a free corpus of Polish. In: Calzolari, N., Choukri, K., Declerck, T., Doğan, M.U., Maegaard, B., Mariani, J., Odijk, J., Piperidis, S. (eds.) Proceedings of LREC 2012. ELRA, Istanbul (2012)

[6] Broda, B., Piasecki, M.: Evaluating LexCSD in a large scale experiment. Control and Cybernetics 40(2) (2011)

[7] Buchholz, S.: Memory-Based Grammatical Relation Finding. Ph.D. thesis, Tilburg University (2002)

[8] Chang, C.C., Lin, C.J.: LIBSVM: A library for support vector machines. ACM Transactions on Intelligent Systems and Technology 2, 27:1–27:27 (2011), http://www.csie.ntu.edu.tw/~cjlin/libsvm

[9] Daelemans, W., Buchholz, S., Veenstra, J.: Memory-based shallow parsing. In: Proceedings of the CoNLL 1999. Association for Computational Linguistics (1999)

[10] Daelemans, W., Zavrel, J., Ko van der Sloot, A.V.D.B.: TiMBL: Tilburg Memory Based Learner, version 6.3, reference guide. Tech. Rep. 10-01, ILK (2010)

[11] Grác, M., Jakubíček, M., Kovář, V.: Through low-cost annotation to reliable parsing evaluation. In: Proceedings of the 24th Pacific Asia Conference on Language, Information and Computation, pp. 555–562. Waseda University, Tokio (2010)

[12] Głowińska, K.: Anotacja składniowa. In: Przepiórkowski, A., Bańko, M., Grski, R.L., Lewandowska-Tomaszczyk, B. (eds.) Narodowy Korpus Języka Polskiego. Wydawnictwo Naukowe PWN, Warsaw (2012)

[13] Maziarz, M., Radziszewski, A., Wieczorek, J.: Chunking of Polish: guidelines, discussion and experiments with Machine Learning. In: Proceedings of the 5th Language & Technology Conference, LTC 2011, Poznań, Poland (2011)

[14] Osenova, P.: Bulgarian nominal chunks and mapping strategies for deeper syntactic analyses. In: Proceedings of the Workshop on Treebanks and Linguistic Theories (TLT 2002), Sozopol, Bulgaria, September 20-21 (2002)

[15] Przepiórkowski, A.: Powierzchniowe przetwarzanie języka polskiego. Akademicka Oficyna Wydawnicza EXIT, Warsaw (2008)

[16] Quinlan, J.R.: C4. 5: programs for machine learning. Morgan Kaufmann (1993)

[17] Radziszewski, A., Maziarz, M., Wieczorek, J.: Shallow syntactic annotation in the Corpus of Wrocław University of Technology. Cognitive Studies 12 (2012)

[18] Radziszewski, A., Pawlaczek, A.: Large-scale experiments with NP chunking of polish. In: Sojka, P., Horák, A., Kopeček, I., Pala, K. (eds.) TSD 2012. LNCS, vol. 7499, pp. 143–149. Springer, Heidelberg (2012)

[19] Radziszewski, A., Piasecki, M.: A preliminary noun phrase chunker for Polish. In: Proceedings of the Intelligent Information Systems (2010)

[20] Radziszewski, A., Śniatowski, T.: A memory-based tagger for Polish. In: Proceedings of the 5th Language & Technology Conference, Poznań (2011)

[21] Vučković, K.: Model parsera za hrvatski jezik. Ph.D. thesis, Department of Information Sciences, Faculty of Humanities and Social Sciences, University of Zagreb, Croatia (2009)

Online Service for Polish Dependency Parsing and Results Visualisation

Alina Wróblewska and Piotr Sikora

Institute of Computer Science, Polish Academy of Sciences, Warsaw, Poland
alina@ipipan.waw.pl, piotr.sikora@student.uw.edu.pl

Abstract. The paper presents a new online service for the dependency parsing of Polish. Given raw text as input, the service processes it and visualises output dependency trees. The service applies the parsing system – MaltParser – with a parsing model for Polish trained on the Polish Dependency Bank, and some additional publicly available tools.

Keywords: dependency parsing, Polish Dependency Bank, visualisation, BRAT, dependency parsing service.

1   Introduction

Several language processing tasks, such as machine translation, question answering or information extraction, may be successfully supported by dependency parsing. A dependency-based syntactic representation transparently encodes the predicate-argument structure of a sentence, which seems to be essential to generate a new sentence or extract relevant information. That is why dependency parsing has become increasingly important in recent years (e.g., CoNLL 2006 [2] and CoNLL 2007 [10]).

Except for grammar-based dependency parsers, the manual creation of which is very time-consuming and expensive, different data-driven approaches for dependency parsing have been proposed. The best parsing results are achieved with supervised techniques so far. Supervised dependency parsers trained on correctly annotated data may achieve high parsing performance, even for languages with relatively free word order, such as Czech [10], Russian [9] or Bulgarian [10].

This paper deals with the dependency parsing of Polish, which is another language with free word order and rich morphology. We present a new online service that processes raw text, annotates its sentences with dependency trees and visualises results. The service applies the parsing system – MaltParser [11]– with a parsing model for Polish trained on the Polish Dependency Bank [18], and some additional publicly available tools.

The paper is structured as follows. Section 2 introduces publicly available achievements in the Polish dependency parsing. Section 3 describes the dependency parsing module and the visualisation application. Section 4 concludes with some ideas for future research.

M.A. Kłopotek et al. (Eds.): IIS 2013, LNCS 7912, pp. 39–44, 2013.

2   Dependency Parsing of Polish

The first Polish dependency parser was developed by Obrębski [12].[1] This is a rule-based parser that was tested against a small artificial test set and no wide-coverage grammar seems to accompany the work. Regarding the idea of training data-driven dependency parsers for Polish, some preliminary experiments are presented in [19]. Results of these experiments show that it is possible to train dependency parsing models for Polish with publicly available parser-generation systems: *MaltParser* [11] and *MSTParser* [6]. The presented dependency parsing models have been trained on dependency trees from the Polish Dependency Bank (Pol. *Składnica Zależnościowa* [18]).

The Polish Dependency Bank consists of 8227 syntactically annotated sentences,[2] which have been semi-automatically derived from trees available in the Polish constituency treebank (Pol. *Składnica Frazowa* [17]). Dependency structures meet properties of valid dependency trees [5] and are labelled with grammatical functions defined for Polish.[3] Any dependency structure is annotated as a tree with nodes corresponding to tokens in a sentence and arcs representing dependency relations between two tokens. One of the related tokens is the governor of a dependency relation, while the other one is its dependent. An example of a Polish dependency tree is given in Figure 1.

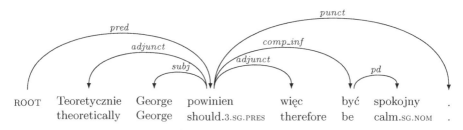

Fig. 1. Dependency tree of the Polish sentence *Teoretycznie George powinine więc być spokojny.* (Eng. 'So theoretically, George should not worry.')

A part of automatically converted dependency trees have been manually corrected by a linguist experienced in the Polish syntax. The first 1,000 trees were thoroughly checked for errors, and other trees were skimmed through focusing on potentially reoccurring errors.[4]

---

[1] This dependency parser seems to be not publicly available.

[2] In comparison to dependency treebanks for other languages, e.g., for Czech *PDT* [4], used to train dependency parsers, the size of the Polish treebank seems to be relatively small and probably not sufficient to train high-coverage parsing models. Despite this, since we do not have any larger set of training data yet, we will use the Polish Dependency Bank for the purposes of the current work.

[3] Description of Polish dependency relation types:
   `zil.ipipan.waw.pl/FunkcjeZaleznosciowe`

[4] The partially corrected Polish Dependency Bank in CoNLL format (Składnica-zależnościowa-0.5.conll.gz) is available on `http://zil.ipipan.waw.pl/Składnica`

Drawing on findings in training dependency parsing models presented in [19], we repeat one of the described experiments. A Polish dependency parser is trained on the entire partially corrected Polish Dependency Bank using *Malt-Parser* parsing system [11]. The transition-based dependency parser uses a deterministic parsing algorithm[5] that builds a dependency structure of an input sentence based on transitions (shift-reduce actions) predicted by a classifier. The classifier trained with the LIBLINEAR library [3] learns to predict the next transition given training data and the parse history. The feature model is defined in terms of token attributes, i.e., word form (FORM), part-of-speech tag (POS), morphological features (FEATS), and lemma (LEMMA) available in input data, or dependency types (DEPREL) extracted from partially built dependency graphs and updated during parsing.

Polish *MaltParser* trained on the entire Polish Dependency Bank is evaluated against a set of 50 manually annotated sentences (17.8 tokens/sentence) taken from Polish magazines. The performance of the Polish MaltParser is evaluated with two standard metrics: *labelled attachment score* (LAS)[6] and *unlabelled attachment score* (UAS).[7] Polish *MaltParser* tested against the set of 50 manually annotated sentences achieves 64.8% LAS/71.3% UAS.[8]

3 Parsing and Visualisation

Driven by the idea of making results of Polish *MaltParser* publicly available, we have prepared an online platform that allows any Internet user to input raw text that will be tagged, dependency parsed and displayed in a way convenient for perception and evaluation. To that end, a number of tools has been employed:

- *Multiservice* [13] [14],[9] a Web Service integration platform for Polish linguistic resources,
- *Pantera* [1], a morpho-syntactic rule-based Brill tagger of Polish,
- BRAT rapid annotation tool [16], an online environment for collaborative text annotation.

From the technical point of view, the dependency service is implemented as a component of *Multiservice* system, which provides a framework for different

---

[5] Since Polish dependency trees may be non-projective, the built-in `stackeager` parsing algorithm [8] is used in the experiment.

[6] Labelled attachment score (LAS) – the percentage of tokens that are assigned a correct head and a correct dependency type.

[7] Unlabelled attachment score (UAS) – the percentage of tokens that are assigned a correct head.

[8] The test sentences are much longer and more complex than sentences in the Polish Dependency Bank. [19] report that the Polish *MaltParser* results are significantly better – 84.7% LAS and 90.5% UAS, if the parser is evaluated against unseen sentences from the Polish Dependency Bank, which seem to be much simpler.

[9] *Multiservice* with an integrated dependency parsing module is publicly available on `glass.ipipan.waw.pl/multiservice`

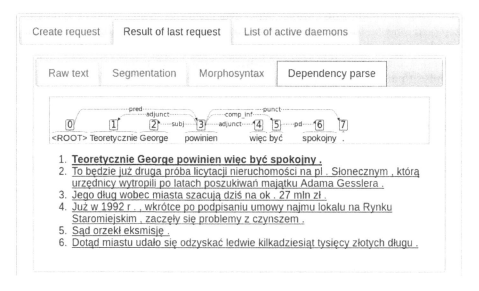

Fig. 2. Screenshot of the visualisation of the dependency tree previously presented in Figure 1

NLP-tools to work together. *Multiservice* uses Apache Thrift [15] as a basis to setup communication between various daemons[10] wrapping previously offline resources in a flexible chain of linguistic tools. As a result, the application can automatically go through all the steps from raw text to a desired output (e.g., dependency trees). Apart from providing access to linguistic resources via network, daemons have to translate the incoming Thrift data into an input format required by the wrapped tool and then do the opposite conversion for output. In order to connect dependency parsing to the *Multiservice* platform, *DependencyParserService* has been created. This service uses the *MaltParser* system with a pre-trained model to parse input sentences. Moreover, *DependencyParserService* reformats incoming and outgoing data between Thrift objects and CoNLL format [2]. The structure of Thrift object had also been modified to make it capable of containing dependency relations.

Since *MaltParser* requires sentences to be morpho-syntactically tagged before parsing, *Pantera* tagger integrated into the *Multiservice* platform fulfils this requirement. Since *Multiservice* is designed to use one communication protocol for all services, dependency parsing relies on this specific tagger only insofar as it is the only one tagger already integrated into *Multiservice*. Should another tagger become available, it can replace the current one or the user may be allowed to freely choose the source from which *DependencyParserService* would commence.

Finally, once a network based solution for the dependency parsing of Polish was ready, the only remaining task was to visualise dependency trees. At the

---

[10] Daemons are computer programs running as background processes, e.g., on a server.

beginning we intended to use *MaltEval*[11] [7] to visualise dependency trees. However, bringing the Java-based software to web environment wasn't straightforward, so we did not integrate it into the service. Meanwhile, we became aware of the recursively acronymised BRAT [16], which among other things has been used to visualise CoNLL-X Multilingual Dependency Parsing task data [2]. The BRAT tool seems to be flexible enough to be seamlessly embedded into the *Multiservice*'s Django-based web-page server. The final result is a simple web-service bringing visualised results of the dependency parsing of Polish in the form of user-friendly readable trees (see example in Figure 2).

4   Conclusions and Future Work

We have presented the online Polish dependency parsing service. The service processes raw input text, annotates sentences with dependency trees, and then visualises results. Integration of different NLP-components and the visualisation application was not a trivial task, but made it possible to present the functionality of the Polish dependency parsing to a wider audience. The dependency parsing service is freely available for research and educational purposes.

So far the online platform only enables dependency parsing of Polish sentences using *MaltParser* with one preloaded parsing model. We suppose it could be useful to be able to compare trees produced by different dependency parsing models or even different parsers. This requires expanding capabilities of the dependency parser service to allow simultaneous processing of a sentence by multiple dependency parsers. Furthermore, in order to let users see differences between multiple dependency trees at a glance, custom modificantions to BRAT visualisations need to be provided. Hence, we also plan to train Polish parsing models that will cover more linguistic facts than the current model.

Another possible path to explore is to tap BRAT's annotation capabilities and allow users to send feedback on generated results, which would lessen the workload required to train better models of Polish dependency parsing thanks to the online platform's ease of use.

Acknowledgements. This research is supported by the POIG.01.01.02-14-013/09 project which is co-financed by the European Union under the European Regional Development Fund.

References

1. Acedański, S.: A Morphosyntactic Brill Tagger for Inflectional Languages. In: Loftsson, H., Rögnvaldsson, E., Helgadóttir, S. (eds.) IceTAL 2010. LNCS, vol. 6233, pp. 3–14. Springer, Heidelberg (2010)
2. Buchholz, S., Marsi, E.: CoNLL-X shared task on Multilingual Dependency Parsing. In: Proceedings of the 10th Conference on Computational Natural Language Learning (CoNLL-X 2006), pp. 149–164 (2006)

---

[11] An evaluation tool for dependency parsers developed by the authors of *MaltParser*.

3. Fan, R.E., Chang, K.W., Hsieh, C.J., Wang, X.R., Lin, C.J.: LIBLINEAR: A Library for Large Linear Classification. Journal of Machine Learning Research 9, 1871–1874 (2008)
4. Hajič, J., Vidová-Hladká, B., Pajas, P.: The Prague Dependency Treebank: Annotation Structure and Support. In: Proceedings of the IRCS Workshop on Linguistic Databases, pp. 105–114 (2001)
5. Kübler, S., McDonald, R.T., Nivre, J.: Dependency Parsing. Synthesis Lectures on Human Language Technologies. Morgan & Claypool Publishers (2009)
6. McDonald, R., Pereira, F., Ribarov, K., Hajič, J.: Non-projective Dependency Parsing using Spanning Tree Algorithms. In: Proceedings of Human Language Technology Conferences and Conference on Empirical Methods in Natural Language Processing (HLT/EMNLP), pp. 523–530 (2005)
7. Nilsson, J., Nivre, J.: MaltEval: An Evaluation and Visualization Tool for Dependency Parsing. In: Proceedings of the 6th International Language Resources and Evaluation (LREC 2008), pp. 161–166 (2008)
8. Nivre, J.: Non-projective Dependency Parsing in Expected Linear Time. In: Proceedings of the 47th Annual Meeting of the ACL and the 4th International Joint Conference on Natural Language Processing of the AFNLP, pp. 351–359 (2009)
9. Nivre, J., Boguslavsky, I.M., Iomdin, L.L.: Parsing the SynTagRus treebank of Russian. In: Proceedings of the 22nd International Conference on Computational Linguistics (COLING 2008), vol. 1, pp. 641–648 (2008)
10. Nivre, J., Hall, J., Kübler, S., McDonald, R., Nilsson, J., Riedel, S., Yuret, D.: The CoNLL 2007 Shared Task on Dependency Parsing. In: Proceedings of the CoNLL Shared Task Session of EMNLP-CoNLL 2007, pp. 915–932 (2007)
11. Nivre, J., Hall, J., Nilsson, J., Chanev, A., Eryigit, G., Kübler, S., Marinov, S., Marsi, E.: MaltParser: A language-independent system for data-driven dependency parsing. Natural Language Engineering 13(2), 95–135 (2007)
12. Obrębski, T.: MTT-compatible computationally effective surface-syntactic parser. In: Proceedings of the 1st International Conference on Meaning-Text Theory, pp. 259–268 (2003)
13. Ogrodniczuk, M., Lenart, M.: Multipurpose Linguistic Web Service for Polish. In: Proceedings of the Language Technology for a Multilingual Europe Workshop at the German Society for Computational Linguistics and Language Technology Conference (GSCL 2011), Hamburg, Germany (2011)
14. Ogrodniczuk, M., Lenart, M.: Web Service integration platform for Polish linguistic resources. In: Proceedings of the Eighth International Conference on Language Resources and Evaluation (LREC 2012), pp. 1164–1168 (2012)
15. Slee, M., Agarwal, A., Kwiatkowski, M.: Thrift: Scalable Cross-Language Services Implementation. Tech. rep., Facebook, 156 University Ave, Palo Alto, USA (2007)
16. Stenetorp, P., Pyysalo, S., Topić, G., Ohta, T., Ananiadou, S., Tsujii, J.:BRAT: a Web-based Tool for NLP-Assisted Text Annotation. In: Proceedings of the 13th Conference of the European Chapter of the Association for Computational Linguistics, pp. 102–107 (2012)
17. Świdziński, M., Woliński, M.: Towards a Bank of Constituent Parse Trees for Polish. In: Sojka, P., Horák, A., Kopeček, I., Pala, K. (eds.) TSD 2010. LNCS (LNAI), vol. 6231, pp. 197–204. Springer, Heidelberg (2010)
18. Wróblewska, A.: Polish Dependency Bank. Linguistic Issues in Language Technology 7(1) (2012)
19. Wróblewska, A., Woliński, M.: Preliminary Experiments in Polish Dependency Parsing. In: Bouvry, P., Kłopotek, M.A., Leprévost, F., Marciniak, M., Mykowiecka, A., Rybiński, H. (eds.) SIIS 2011. LNCS, vol. 7053, pp. 279–292. Springer, Heidelberg (2012)

The Scent of Deception: Recognizing Fake Perfume Reviews in Polish

Maciej Rubikowski[1] and Aleksander Wawer[2]

[1] Institute of Computer Science
Warsaw University of Technology
ul. Nowowiejska 15/19, 00-665 Warszawa
M.Rubikowski@stud.elka.pw.edu.pl
[2] Institute of Computer Science
Polish Academy of Sciences
ul. Jana Kazimierza 5, 01-248 Warszawa
axw@ipipan.waw.pl

Abstract. Many opinion aggregation websites are injected by well-formed, fake reviews. Previous work showed that such spam is very hard to identify by a non-expert human reader and therefore, automated methods are needed to identify deceptive content. To this day, there has been no study for the Polish language and our main goal is to fill that gap. We present a corpus of fake and true reviews in Polish and describe experiments on automated opinion spam detection. Our approach turns out to be highly successful, but future systematic studies are needed to confirm the nature of our findings.

Keywords: Natural language processing, sentiment analysis, opinion spam detection.

1 Existing Work

The body of literature on automated deception detection and recognizing opinion spam is far too large to disclose here. Therefore, we only discuss two most relevant papers. [2] analyze five corpora of true and false statements (eg. views on abortion) using 72 linguistic dimensions from LIWC [4]. The method correctly classified liars and truth-tellers at a rate of 67% when the topic was constant and a rate of 61% overall. Compared to truth-tellers, liars showed lower cognitive complexity, used fewer self-references and other-references, and used more negative emotion words. In a more recent study, [3] use a corpus obtained from Amazon's Mechanical Turk and report average precision of 0.898 using an SVM classifier on LIWC categories and bigrams. The highest performing classifier significantly outperforms human judges.

2 Corpus Construction

The problem of finding a decent corpus for opinion spam detection is inevitable, especially when a research is to be conducted on a material written in a language

M.A. Kłopotek et al. (Eds.): IIS 2013, LNCS 7912, pp. 45–49, 2013.

that was not previously analyzed. This was exactly our case; lack of existing data to work on led us to the point where we were forced to define several rules that such corpus must adhere to create it accordingly.

2.1   Basic Creation Principles

We perceive the review spam detection as a two-label classification problem. Thus, we needed two disjunctive opinion sets: first one with 100%-sure authentic reviews (created by real buyers) and the second one with 100%-sure fake reviews (created by whoever). After performing such division, we decided that we should use the fake reviews written exclusively by professional opinion writers. In doing so, we would perfectly imitate real-life conditions of deceit.

The real (or, in other words, authentic) review set was much harder to obtain. As was already mentioned, it is an extraordinary hard task for a human reader to distinguish between real and fake opinions. In order to achieve this task, we developed a few binary rules which every would-be-real review has to satisfy. But before we go into details we've got to introduce the data source first.

2.2   Finding Authentic Reviews (labeled T)

The domain of our choice: *women's perfumes*. The decision was largely inspired by previous work on sentiment analysis, plus we've managed to find an extremely abundant Polish-language data source: a review site devoted solely to cosmetics (and perfumes in particular). Although this particular site has no consumer validation (i.e. there's no explicit connection between the act of buying the product and writing the review) it is possible to display users' profiles. Every account used in process of reviewing products is in fact a message board account as well, so we were able to determine users' activity.

From a wide variety of perfumes we've chosen two most popular ones:

- *Calvin Klein Euphoria*
- *Dolce & Gabbana Light Blue*

These were the most reviewed perfumes at the moment. Opinions varied, but both products were generally praised, scoring four and three-and-a-half on a five point scale.

When it came to selecting reviews, we generally adopted the following conditions:

- *The author of a review had to be an active member.* We chose only the reviews written by people who wrote at least 1 message on the message board as well. If he/she had written less than 10 such messages, we carefully analyzed all of them, searching for the link spam. This way we tried to minimize possibility of choosing messages posted from accounts created exclusively for the sake of writing opinion spam.
- Minimum length of the review: 50 characters.
- Maximum length of the review: 1100 characters.

- Reviews written in all-capitals were discarded.
- No preprocessing was performed on the data.

Apart from constraints described above, the corpus has following characteristics:

- Exactly 200 reviews were chosen, 100 for each of the two products.
- We tried to maintain normal distribution of character count across the whole set. Both longer and shorter reviews were considered, with an average text length of around 500 characters.
- No explicit constraint was put on the scores reviewers gave, but there are approximately as many positive reviews in our corpus as negative ones. This way we avoid sticking to just one language (be it praising or lessening).

2.3 Buying Fake Reviews (labeled *F*)

Obtaining fake reviews was much easier task. We simply chose to hire two free-lancers (male and female) with experience in the field and asked them to write 100 reviews each: writer *A* was to prepare 100 positive on *Light Blue* and 100 negative on *Euphoria*, while writer *B*, conversely, 50 positive opinions on *Euphoria* and 50 negative on *Light Blue*. This way we obtained the widest style range available. Other characteristics of the fake part of the corpus include:

- Writer *A* – normal distribution of text length, with minimum of around 100 characters, maximum of less than 900 characters and mean slightly higher than 500 characters.
- Writer *B* – even length distribution, with minimum of 226 characters, maximum of 298 and average of around 258 characters.
- Writer *A* – richer vocabulary, longer sentences; writer *B* – less eloquent, shorter, simpler sentences.

3 Automated Recognition of Deceptive Reviews

3.1 Features

This section describes features used in the experiment on automated recognition of deceptive reviews. The features were generated for each review as frequency vectors, reflecting following properties:

- *tags*, *POS*. In Polish, word forms are identified by morphosyntactic properties, described (in the course of text processing) by tags. Each morphosyntactic tag is a sequence of colon-separated values, e.g.: *subst:sg:nom:m1* for the segment chłopiec (boy). The first value, e.g., *subst*, determines the grammatical class, while the values that follow it, e.g., *sg*, *nom* and *m1*, are the values of grammatical categories appropriate for that grammatical class. A description of the used categories and associated tags be found in [5]. In our experiment, *tags* refer to 46 features obtained from morphosyntactic tags and *POS* (from part-of-speech) to 32 features from grammatical classes. All the text processing involved morphosyntactic disambiguation.

- *LCM.* This feature set refers to frequencies of three verb categories in the Linguistic Category Model (LCM) by [6]. The categories are as follows: Descriptive Action Verbs (IAV), Interpretative Action Verbs (IAV), State Verbs (SV). The goal of the LCM framework is to measure language abstraction and the presented verb categorization reflects verbs according to their increasing level of abstraction. Our hypothesis is that deceptive reviews may be more abstract because they are not based on experiences with reviewed products. The list of 1100 verbs used in this experiment was generated by automatically translating appropriate entries in the General Inquirer [7] into Polish and manually correcting their Polish translations and LCM category memberships.
- *sentiment.* This feature sets consists of the numbers of positive and negative words in each review. The list of such words was generated as described in [9,8] and their sentiment (as used in our experiment) computed using supervised classifiers and 3-classes (positive, neutral, negative) as in [10].
- *length.* The final feature set consists of average sentence lengths and numbers of sentences, as found in each review.

3.2 Results

Table 1 contains average precision of recognizing deceptive and real reviews as computed in 5-fold cross-validation (CV). The classification was performed using the well-known Support Vector Classification (SVC) [1]. The values presented are the highest average CV scores obtained by iterating over a range of C parameter values (from 0.0001 to 10). The experiments involved feature selection using recursive feature elimination (RFE) method resulting in the identification of 25 relevant features.

Table 1. Average precision in 5-fold cross-validation using an SVC classifier

Features	Nr	Selection	C	Precision
tags, POS, sentiment, LCM, length	82	RFE->25	1.0	0.835
tags, POS	78	-	0.01	0.809
sentiment, LCM, length	8	-	0.01	0.711
adjectives, LCM	4	-	1.0	0.639

4 Conclusions

Overall, the results are surprisingly good. Although the presented results are preliminary and should be interpreted with caution, it seems possible to automatically distinguish true and false reviews with high precision. Notably, the problem can be nearly solved using non-lexical, very likely less domain dependent than lexical features consisting of unigrams or n-grams.

The LCM feature set combined with adjective frequency corresponds to the measure of language abstraction [6]. The results are initially promising, but perhaps could be improved when applied to other types of products than perfumes (a very special product described using poetic language, full of highly abstract descriptions and figurative expressions).

Our findings generally confirm the results reported by [2] and [3], discussed in Section 1. One especially interesting finding is the difference in the performance of part-of-speech features. [3] report that this type of features, using an SVM classifier, reaches the average accuracy of 0.73. The likely explanation of this difference is the fact that rich morphology of the Polish language carries more information relevant to distinguishing true and false reviews than part-of-speech in English. However, the difference could be also caused by different corpus structures. Here, the most desirable extension of our work would be to enlarge the dataset with texts written by many more fake reviewers. Unfortunately, this does not seem realistic and one can not directly replicate the corpus such as [3] in Polish, because there are not enough Polish native speakers on the Mechanical Turk.

References

1. Fan, R.E., Chang, K.W., Hsieh, C.J., Wang, X.R., Lin, C.J.: LIBLINEAR: A library for large linear classification. Journal of Machine Learning Research 9, 1871–1874 (2008)
2. Newman, M.L., Pennebaker, J.W., Berry, D.S., Richards, J.M.: Lying words: Predicting deception from linguistic styles. Personality and Social Psychology Bulletin 29(5), 665–675 (2003)
3. Ott, M., Choi, Y., Cardie, C., Hancock, J.: Finding deceptive opinion spam by any stretch of the imagination. In: Proceedings of the 49th Annual Meeting of the Association for Computational Linguistics: Human Language Technologies, ACL HLT (2011)
4. Pennebaker, J.W., Francis, M.E., Booth, R.J.: Linguistic Inquiry and Word Count: LIWC 2001. Erlbaum Publishers (2001)
5. Przepiórkowski, A.: A comparison of two morphosyntactic tagsets of Polish, pp. 138–144 (2009)
6. Semin, G.R., Fiedler, K.: The cognitive functions of linguistic categories in describing persons: Social cognition and language. Journal of Personality and Social Psychology 54, 558–568 (1988)
7. Stone, P.J., Dunphy, D.C., Ogilvie, D.M., Smith, M.S.: The General Inquirer: A Computer Approach to Content Analysis. MIT Press (1966)
8. Wawer, A.: Extracting Emotive Patterns for Languages with Rich Morphology. International Journal of Computational Linguistics and Applications 3(1) (January-June 2012)
9. Wawer, A.: Mining Co-Occurrence Matrices for SO-PMI Paradigm Word Candidates. In: Proceedings of the Student Research Workshop at the 13th Conference of the European Chapter of the Association for Computational Linguistics, EACL 2012 SRW, pp. 74–80. Association for Computational Linguistics, Avignon (2012)
10. Wawer, A., Rogozińska, D.: How Much Supervision? Corpus-based Lexeme Sentiment Estimation. In: 2012 IEEE 12th International Conference on Data Mining Workshops, ICDMW, SENTIRE 2012, pp. 724–730. IEEE Computer Society, Los Alamitos (2012)

Question Classification
for Polish Question Answering

Piotr Przybyła

Institute of Computer Science, Polish Academy of Sciences,
ul. Jana Kazimierza 5, 01-248 Warszawa, Poland
P.Przybyla@phd.ipipan.waw.pl

Abstract. This paper deals with a problem of question type classification for Polish Question Answering (QA). The goal of this task is to determine both a general type and a class of an entity which is expected as an answer. Three types of approaches: pattern matching, WordNet-aided focus analysis and machine learning are presented and evaluated using a test set of 1137 manually classified questions from a Polish quiz TV show. Quantitative results supported with an analysis of error sources help to find possible improvements.

1 Introduction

Question Answering (QA) is an area of Natural Language Processing (NLP) focused on answering questions asked by a user in his natural language. This term refers to a huge variety of systems; for example they could be divided by a type of knowledge base (database or text corpus) or broadness of domain (closed- or open-domain systems). Although different, they usually base on similar architectural schemes, of which a question type determination is an indispensable part. The goal of this module is to analyse a question and determine its type, necessary for finding an answer.

In this paper results of applying several approaches to the case of Polish questions are reported. Polish belongs to Slavonic languages, whose structure differs substantially from that of English, for which a majority of QA-related studies were done. Therefore, their performance needs to be carefully evaluated before implementing analogous solutions in a Polish QA system. For reader's convenience most of examples were put in English.

In fact, the term "question type" refers to two types of categorial information. First, henceforth called **general question type**, describes its general structure. In this paper, the following general types are distinguished:

- **Verification** questions (herein abbreviated as TRUEORFALSE), containing a hypothesis, which is to be verified by an answerer, e.g. *Did Lee Oswald kill John F. Kennedy?*,
- **Option** questions (abbreviation: WHICH), containing a number of options, from which the answerer chooses one, e.g. *Which one killed John F. Kennedy: Lance Oswald or Lee Oswald?*,

M.A. Kłopotek et al. (Eds.): IIS 2013, LNCS 7912, pp. 50–56, 2013.

- **Named entity** questions (abbreviation: NAMED_ENTITY), which could be answered by providing a single named entity,
- **Unnamed entity** questions (abbreviation: UNNAMED_ENTITY), similar to above - answer is still a single entity, but not necessarily a named one (from categories like: professions, sciences, species, things, body parts, ...), e.g. *What did Lee Oswald use to kill John F. Kennedy?*,
- **Other name** questions (abbreviation: OTHER_NAME), which seeks for another, non-standard, name for an entity mentioned in the question, e.g. *What nickname did John F. Kennedy use during his military service?*,
- **Multiple named entities** questions (abbreviation: MULTIPLE), which could be answered by providing a set of named entities, satisfying conditions imposed by the question, e.g. *Which U.S. presidents were assassinated in office?*.

Above list does not exhaust the variety of possible question constructions, leaving cases like *What is the global warming?*, *Why did the World War II begin?* or *What is the product of 6 and 32?* out. Those types of questions, demanding elaborate answers or complex reasoning, require different techniques for answer formulation, which puts them out of the scope of this work.

The second question type, henceforth referred to as **named entity type**, describes the subtype of NAMED_ENTITY general question type. The list of possible labels is shown in Table 2. The list was manually created in order to cover the most frequent types of questions from general knowledge and could easily be expanded to suit any specific domain. One could notice that these categories are not independent, some are more general than others (e.g. continents, islands and countries are places), some include others (e.g. date notation includes year). We aim to be as specific as possible, i.e. select place only if it does not belong to any narrower category, e.g. in case of a city district.

2   Related Work

Although question classification plays a vital role in QA systems, it has not grabbed a lot of attention so far. In the most popular QA task at *Text REtrieval Conference (TREC)* [2], a general question type was given: FACTOID (referring to both named and unnamed entities), LIST (corresponding to MULTIPLE above) or OTHER (interesting information about a subject not mentioned so far). At the NTCIR-6 Cross-Lingual Question Answering Task [12] all questions were to be answered by named entities.

However, a named entity type is usually not given, so a correct decision at this level gets crucial for finding a correct answer. Some interrogative pronouns uniquely define an answer type (e.g. *When*), which can be easily employed by a set of hand-written pattern; in [7] it is the only tool for question classification, but as much as 1273 rules are necessary.

In case of ambiguous questions, beginning with *what* or *which* (e.g. *Which famous Dutch painter lost his ear?*, in Polish *Który sławny holenderski malarz stracił ucho?*), a more sophisticated approach becomes necessary. Namely, a question focus, following those interrogative pronouns (in this case *famous Dutch painter*), needs to be analysed, as its type corresponds to a type of an expected answer (here: a person). For that purpose, ontological resources, such as word classes [13], WordNet [3] or other [4], are used.

Finally, a machine learning (ML) approach is possible, in which we extract a set of features from question formulation (even 200,000 for each, see [8]) and use a classifier to learn types from a training set.

Each of these solutions has been designed for English, so applying them to Polish QA requires special attention and taking into account its features, mainly rich nominal inflection [10]. In case of pattern matching a number of necessary rules is much bigger, for example one English pattern *Whose ... ?* corresponds to 11 Polish (*Czyj ... ?, Czyjego ... ?, Czyjemu ... ?, Czyim ... ?, Czyja ... ?, Czyjej ... ?, Czyją ... ?, Czyje ... ?, Czyi ... ?, Czyich ... ?, Czyimi ... ?*). To use the ontological resources in the disambiguation process we also need to take it into account; in the question *Which American cyclist was disqualified for life in 2012?* the focus is *cyclist*, which exists in the WordNet. However, in Polish equivalent *Którego amerykańskiego kolarza zdyskwalifikowano dożywotnio w 2012 roku?*, the focus *kolarza* appears in genitive and needs morphological analysis before becoming a WordNet search query. Such analysis also needs to precede the ML approach. For example let us consider the features corresponding to the existence of a specified word in two formulations of the same problem: active *Which composer created the Jupiter Symphony?* and passive *By which composer was the Jupiter Symphony created?*. They have 6 common words and 2 differences (*by* and *was* in passive). Their Polish equivalents *Który kompozytor stworzył Symfonię "Jowiszową"?* and *Przez którego kompozytora została stworzona symfonia "Jowiszowa"?* have no common features unless preceded by the morphological analysis.

3   Question Classifiers

In this study all three approaches are compared in case of classification of Polish questions. An input of a classifier is a question string; it responds with a set of the types described previously: general question type or named entity type if named entity question is recognized or no answer if it fails to find one. A set may be returned because of a possible ambiguity in question (e.g. *Who started World War II?* could be answered by PERSON, COUNTRY, NATIONALITY or ORGANISATION).

3.1   Pattern Classifier

The simplest approach bases on a list of 104 regular expressions and sets of question types associated with them. The classifier scans the list and if any of the expressions matches, returns a corresponding type set. If it reaches the end of the table, no answer is returned. Such a large number of rules is necessary because of the properties of Slavonic languages: rich nominal inflection and free word order. A few examples are shown in Table 1.

Table 1. Exemplary rules of the pattern classifier: regular expressions and their corresponding results. English constructions close in meaning are also shown.

Regular expression	Set of types	English construction
^Czy[,](.*)\?$	TRUEORFALSE	*Did ... ?* or other
^(.*[,])?[Ii]le[,](.*)\?$	COUNT,PERIOD, QUANTITY	*How many ... ?*
^(.*[,])?[Kk]omu[,](.*)\?$	PERSON,COUNTRY, COMPANY,BAND,...	*To whom ... ?*
^W którym wieku[,](.*)\?$	CENTURY	*In which century ... ?*

The patterns were created manually using general linguistic knowledge about the interrogative pronouns available in Polish and their meanings. Because of the properties of Polish, i.e. rich nominal inflection and relatively free word order, numerous regular expressions are necessary.

3.2 WordNet-Aided Classifier

This classifier uses the pattern classifier as a preliminary step, but its pattern list is expanded by the ambiguous question structures (e.g. *What ... ?*). If a question matches any of the unambiguous expressions, the corresponding type set is returned as previously, but for the ambiguous patterns a focus analysis becomes necessary. Morphological analyser Morfeusz [14], tagger PANTERA [1] and shallow parser Spejd [11] annotate the sentence. A nominal group directly following (or including) the interrogative pronoun is assumed to be a question focus. For example, in *Który sławny holenderski malarz stracił ucho?*, the nominal group *sławny holenderski malarz* plays a role of a focus. It is then used to find a lexem in Polish WordNet [9]. As long as no lexem corresponds to the focus string, the focus group is replaced by its semantic head (e.g. *sławny holenderski malarz* by *holenderski malarz* and then *malarz*). The we look for a path leading from it, by hypernymy relations, to any of specified synsets, corresponding to named entity types (in this case *malarz* belongs to subtypes of synset connected with PERSON). The classifier returns corresponding type if successful, UNNAMED_ENTITY otherwise.

3.3 Machine Learning Classifiers

The last approach employs general-purpose classifiers to questions. First, each question is annotated by the same tools and converted into a list of root forms appearing in it. Feature set is very simple compared to [8] - it consists of boolean values, indicating existence of a particular root form in the question and morphological interpretations of the first five segments. Two classifiers, implemented in R statistical environment, were chosen for the task: decision trees with pruning (for human-readable results) and random forests (for high performance).

4 Evaluation

To evaluate question classifiers, a set of 1137 questions from Polish quiz TV show *"Jeden z dziesięciu"*, published in [5], was manually reviewed and classified to one of the types. Distribution of question types is shown in Table 2. One may easily notice the unevenness of the distribution; rare classes will most likely cause troubles for machine learning classifiers. To estimate precision of ML classifiers, 100-fold cross-validation[1] was used.

Table 2. The 6 general question types and the 31 named entity types and numbers of their occurrences in test set

Question type	N. o.	Question type	N. o.	Question type	N. o.
NAMED_ENTITY	657	ISLAND	5	DYNASTY	6
WHICH	28	ARCHIPELAGO	2	ORGANISATION	20
TRUEORFALSE	25	SEA	2	COMPANY	2
MULTIPLE	28	CELESTIAL_BODY	8	EVENT	7
UNNAMED_ENTITY	377	COUNTRY	52	TIME	2
OTHER_NAME	22	STATE	7	CENTURY	9
PLACE	33	CITY	52	YEAR	34
CONTINENT	4	NATIONALITY	12	PERIOD	1
RIVER	11	PERSON	260	COUNT	31
LAKE	9	NAME	11	QUANTITY	6
MOUNTAIN	4	SURNAME	10	VEHICLE	10
RANGE	2	BAND	6		
TITLE	38	ANIMAL	1		

For each of the classifiers three measures have been calculated: percentage of classified cases, precision of classification and the product of these two fractions, corresponding to the number of the questions from the whole test set, classified correctly.

5 Results

Results of the evaluation are shown in Table 3. Only a small part of questions turned out to be simple enough to match prepared patterns. On the other hand, the precision of that stage seems satisfactory. WordNet-aided classifier handles almost all cases, but its precision still leaves room for improvement. Unfortunately, the ML classifiers yielded worse results. The structure of decision tree was examined - its leaves correspond either to unambiguous interrogative pronouns or question foci. Unfortunately, they cover only a few most popular types, which clearly suggests that it would benefit from a larger training set.

For better understanding of difficulties, all wrong answers of WordNet-aided classifier and its justifications were carefully analysed. Table 4 enumerates the

Table 3. Results of evaluation of the four question type classifiers: percentages of questions classified, precisions of results and products of these two fractions, corresponding to the number of questions from the whole test set classified correctly

Classifier	Classified	Precision	Overall
pattern matching	32.54%	95.14%	30.96%
WordNet-aided	98.32%	79.61%	78.27%
decision tree	100%	67.02%	67.02%
random forest	100%	72.91%	72.91%

Table 4. Results of an analysis of error causes for the WordNet-aided classifier, ordered by a number of failures of the classification caused by each of them

Error cause	Number of errors
Ambiguous question focus, wrong meaning chosen	99
Particular named entity instead of a general class	55
No rules for OTHER_NAME	14
Poor multiple entities detection	12
Too complex question syntax	12
Insufficient pattern matching	11
Not enough WordNet parents specified	10
Semantic relations not present in WordNet	8
Tagging error	6
Shallow parsing error	1

error causes. The two most important weaknesses of this approach are ambiguous question foci (the lexem is connected to several synsets in WordNet with different hypernyms), reported also in [6], and difficulties in deciding whether a goal of the question is a particular named entity or a general class (e.g. consider *Which dog has the strongest bite?* and *Which dog was the first to travel to space?*).

6   Conclusion

In this paper, the three different approaches to question type determination were reported and evaluated basing on the set of Polish questions. Pattern matching for easy questions and WordNet matching for questions with ambiguous interrogative pronouns turned out to be the most promising methods. There still remains a couple of possible improvements, but the methods designed for English proved to work also in the Polish question classification. This study is part of an effort of building an open-domain text-based question answering system for Polish, which was supported by research fellowship within "Information technologies: research and their interdisciplinary applications" agreement number POKL.04.01.01-00-051/10-00.

---

[1] The test set was divided into 100 subsets and each of them was classified using a classifier trained on the remaining 99 subsets.

References

1. Acedański, S.: A morphosyntactic Brill Tagger for inflectional languages. In: Proceedings of the 7th International Conference on Advances in Natural Language Processing (IceTAL 2010), pp. 3–14 (August 2010),
   `http://dl.acm.org/citation.cfm?id=1884371.1884376`
2. Dang, H.T., Kelly, D., Lin, J.: Overview of the TREC 2007 Question Answering track. In: Proceedings of The Sixteenth Text REtrieval Conference, TREC 2007 (2007),
   `http://trec.nist.gov/pubs/trec16/papers/QA.OVERVIEW16.pdf`
3. Harabagiu, S., Moldovan, D., Pasca, M., Mihalcea, R., Surdeanu, M., Bunescu, R., Gîrju, R., Rus, V., Morarescu, P.: The role of lexico-semantic feedback in open-domain textual question-answering. In: Proceedings of the 39th Annual Meeting on Association for Computational Linguistics, ACL 2001, pp. 282–289 (July 2001),
   `http://dl.acm.org/citation.cfm?id=1073012.1073049`
4. Hermjakob, U.: Parsing and question classification for question answering. In: Proceedings of the Workshop on Open-domain Question Answering (ODQA 2001), vol. 12 (July 2001), `http://dl.acm.org/citation.cfm?id=1117856.1117859`
5. Karzewski, M.: Jeden z dziesięciu - pytania i odpowiedzi. Muza SA (1997)
6. Katz, B., Lin, J., Loreto, D., Hildebrandt, W., Bilotti, M., Felshin, S., Fernandes, A., Marton, G., Mora, F.: Integrating Web-based and corpus-based techniques for question answering. In: Proceedings of the Twelfth Text REtrieval Conference, TREC 2003 (2003),
   `http://citeseerx.ist.psu.edu/viewdoc/summary?doi=10.1.1.111.4868`
7. Lee, C., Wang, J.H., Kim, H.J., Jang, M.G.: Extracting Template for Knowledge-based Question-Answering Using Conditional Random Fields. In: Proceedings of the 28th Annual International ACM SIGIR Workshop on MFIR, pp. 428–434 (2005),
   `http://citeseerx.ist.psu.edu/viewdoc/summary?doi=10.1.1.112.7960`
8. Li, X., Roth, D.: Learning Question Classifiers. In: Proceedings of the 19th International Conference on Computational Linguistics, COLING 2002, vol. 1 (2002),
   `http://portal.acm.org/citation.cfm?id=1072228.1072378`
9. Maziarz, M., Piasecki, M., Szpakowicz, S.: Approaching plWordNet 2.0. In: Proceedings of the 6th Global Wordnet Conference (2012)
10. Przepiórkowski, A.: Slavonic information extraction and partial parsing. In: Proceedings of the Workshop on Balto-Slavonic Natural Language Processing Information Extraction and Enabling Technologies, ACL 2007 (2007),
    `http://portal.acm.org/citation.cfm?doid=1567545.1567547`
11. Przepiórkowski, A.: Powierzchniowe przetwarzanie języka polskiego. Akademicka Oficyna Wydawnicza EXIT, Warszawa (2008)
12. Sasaki, Y., Lin, C.J., Chen, K.H., Chen, H.H.: Overview of the NTCIR-6 Cross-Lingual Question Answering (CLQA) Task. In: Proceedings of NTCIR-6 Workshop Meeting (2007)
13. Srihari, R., Li, W.: Information Extraction Supported Question Answering. In: Proceedings of The Eighth Text REtrieval Conference (TREC-8), pp. 185–196 (1999), `http://citeseerx.ist.psu.edu/viewdoc/summary?doi=10.1.1.29.5096`
14. Woliński, M.: Morfeusz—a Practical Tool for the Morphological Analysis of Polish. In: Kłopotek, M., Wierzchoń, S., Trojanowski, K. (eds.) Intelligent Information Processing and Web Mining, pp. 511–520 (2006)

Chinese Named Entity Recognition with Conditional Random Fields in the Light of Chinese Characteristics

Aaron L.-F. Han, Derek F. Wong, and Lidia S. Chao

University of Macau, Department of Computer and Information Science
Av. Padre Toms Pereira Taipa, Macau, China
hanlifengaaron@gmail.com, {derekfw,lidiasc}@umac.mo

Abstract. This paper introduces the research works of Chinese named entity recognition (CNER) including person name, organization name and location name. To differ from the conventional approaches that usually introduce more about the used algorithms with less discussion about the CNER problem itself, this paper firstly conducts a study of the Chinese characteristics and makes a discussion of the different feature sets; then a promising comparison result is shown with the optimized features and concise model. Furthermore, different performances are analyzed of various features and algorithms employed by other researchers. To facilitate the further researches, this paper provides some formal definitions about the issues in the CNER with potential solutions. Following the SIGHAN bakeoffs, the experiments are performed in the closed track but the problems of the open track tasks are also discussed.

Keywords: Natural language processing, Chinese named entity recognition, Chinese characteristics, Features, Conditional random fields.

1 Introduction

With the rapid development of information extraction, text mining, machine translation and natural language processing (NLP), named entity recognition (NER) and detection become more and more important for its critical influence on the information and knowledge management. Lev and Dan [1] talk about the difficulties in the English NER task testing on three data sets with the use of some external knowledge including Unlabeled Text and Wikipedia gazetteers. Sang and Meulder [2] conduct the NER research on German language. Furthermore, many people have applied NER in special areas, e.g. geological text processing [3] and biomedical named entity detection [4]. On the other hand, Chinese named entity recognition (CNER) are more difficult due to the lack of word boundary and the complex characteristics of Chinese.

There were several CNER shared tasks under the Chinese language processing (CLP) conference supported by SIGHAN (a special interest group for Chinese in ACL) [5] [6] before 2008. However, CNER task was latterly replaced by Chinese personal name disambiguation [7] and Chinese word sense induction

M.A. Kłopotek et al. (Eds.): IIS 2013, LNCS 7912, pp. 57–68, 2013.

[8]. The applied methods on CNER include Maximum Entropy (ME) [9] [10], Hidden Markov Model (HMM) [11], Support Vector Machine (SVM) [12] and Conditional Random Field (CRF) algorithms (e.g. [13], extraction for product attribute). Some people combine the CNER with word segmentation, sentence chunking, and word detection [14] while others deal with the CNER alone [15] [16]. All of the employed methods have both advantages and weaknesses. Markov Model assumes a strong independence assumption between text putting an obstacle to consider the context information, and Maximum Entropy employs a locally optimal solution which leads to label bias problems. CRF has overcome these two kinds of disadvantages using global optimal solution; however, it also brings new challenges e.g. the selection of best features etc.

The conventional research papers about CNER tend to speak more about the applied methods or algorithms while the analysis of CNER issues is usually less mentioned [17] [18]. In this paper we pay attention to this point. In addition, we analyze the characteristics of Chinese with three kinds of named entities including the different attributes of prefix, suffix and the number of combined characters in n-gram factor. Then we discuss the effects of different feature sets employed by other researchers and propose optimized features with promising performances. In the discussion section, to facilitate the further researches, we provide the formal definitions of the problems that underlie the CNER framework.

2   Chinese Characteristics

Three kinds of Chinese named entities are introduced in this section including personal name (PER), location name (LOC) and organization name (ORG). First, most Chinese personal names have clear format using a family name in front of the given name. In this paper, we use "Surname Given-name" as Chinese name expression and "$x + y$" as the corresponding character number of surname x and given-name y. According to the survey and statistical results of Chinese academy of science [19] [20], there have been developed to 11,939 Chinese surnames, 5313 of which consist of one character, 4311 of two characters, 1615 of three characters and 571 of four characters, etc. On the other hand, the Chinese given name usually contains one or two characters as shown in Table 1.

Secondly, for the Chinese location names, there are some commonly used suffixes including "路" (road), "區" (district), "縣" (county), "市" (city), "省" (province), "洲" (continent), etc. In their generation, most of them also have several standard formats, for instance, using the building name as representation (e.g. "故宮博物館" (the Imperial Palace Museum), "天安門" ($TianAnMen$), etc.), which is also shown in Table 1 ("Pl.", "Org", "Bud.", "Suf." and "Abbr." mean characterized by Place, organization, building, suffix and abbreviation respectively).

Lastly, some of the organization names also possess suffixes, but the organization suffixes have various expressions and a much larger amount than the one of locations. What is more, many of the organization names do not have apparent suffixes and contain various characters due to the fact that they are sometimes generated by only one or several persons i.e. the owner of the organization, e.g. "笑開花" (*XiaoKaiHua*, a small art association). In Table 2, we list some kinds of organizations and the corresponding examples with the areas of administrative unit, company, arts, public service, association, education and cultural. Even in the same class, the organization names have abundant expressions of suffixes. This phenomenon is potentially implying that the organization name may be the most difficult category to recognize among the three kinds of named entities.

Table 1. The PER and LOC categories with examples

PER		LOC	
Class	Samples	Class	Samples
1+1	王明 (*Wang Ming*)	Bud.	天安門 (*TianAnMen*)
1+2	李自成 (*Li ZiCheng*)	Pl.Bud.	北京圖書館 (*BeiJing* Library)
2+2	歐陽蘭蘭 (*OuYang LanLan*)	Pl.Org	北京市公安局 (*BeiJing* Police Station)
4+2	愛新覺羅恒山 (*AiXinJueLuo HengShan*)	Mix.Suf	南沙群島 (*NanSha* Islands)
4+4	愛新覺羅努爾哈赤 (*AiXinJueLuo NuErHaChi*)	Abbr.	港 (Hong Kong), 澳 (Macau)

Table 2. The ORG categories with examples

ORG	
Class	Samples
Administrative	香港社會福利署 (The Hong Kong Social Welfare Department)
Company	獨山子化石總廠 (*DuShanZi* Fossil Main Workshop)
Arts	越秀藝苑 (*YueXiu* Art)
Public service	中國青少年科技俱樂部 (Science and Technology Club of Chinese Youth)
Association	天津市婦女聯合會 (*TianJin* Women's Federation)
Education	香港教育學院 (The Hong Kong Institute of Education)
Cultural	中國國家文物局 (China's State Bureau of Cultural Relics)

3   Optimized Features

In the NER task of English text, employing a regularized averaged perceptron algorithm, Ratinov and Roth [1] use the tokens in the window of size two around each token instance as features and get the highest test score 0.8653 on CoNLL03 and lowest score 0.7121 on the Web pages data in the closed task. On the other hand, in the CLP and CNER literature, when dealing with the strings, there have been various window sizes of features employed by researchers, some of which are less than two surrounding characters and others may consider more than five as surrounding radius.

With the features of two surrounding characters, Huang et al. [21] utilize the SVM and ME model to deal with the boundaries of organization names and use CRF method for the personal and location names. The test F-score on MSRA (Microsoft Research of Asia) corpus is 0.855 for closed test and 0.8619 in open test with the external lexicon and name list. Feng et al. [18] propose a CNER system NER@ISCAS under the CRF framework with the use of an external part-of-speech (POS) tagging tool and some collected character lists as open knowledge. The main features include text feature (two window sizes), POS (four window size), derived vocabulary lists (even considering the 7th following token), word boundary (four window size) etc. with some heuristic post process steps applied to complement the limitations of local features. Sun et al. [22] utilize Maximum entropy model (ME) for open track NER task, with the external knowledge including Chinese name dictionary, foreign name dictionary, Chinese place dictionary and organization dictionary. The applied features are both unigram and bigram for word tokens, named entity (NE) tags, POS tags etc. Other related works include [17] and [23] etc.

Table 3. Designed feature sets

Features	Meaning
$U_n, n \in (-4, 2)$	Unigram, from previous 4th to following 2nd character
$B_{n,n+1}, n \in (-2, 1)$	Bigram, four pairs of characters from the previous 2th to the following 2th

According to the analysis about the characteristics of Chinese named entities in previous sections, we held some different opinions. To begin with, the surrounding two characters of window size are not enough for CNER. There are several reasons: 1). The longest chunk it considered is five characters for the surrounding two characters of window size. 2). Many Chinese named entities have long spans, especially the location name (e.g. "那然色布斯臺音布拉格" *Na Ran Se Bu Si Tai Yin Bu La Ge*, a border port containing ten characters) and organization names (e.g. "香港特別行政區民政總署" The Hong Kong Special Administrative Region Civil Affairs Administration, eleven characters). Secondly, we think that the previous characters of the cased token play more important roles. Most location names and organization names have commonly used suffixes and the lengths of the suffixes have few number of characters. Last, the window size for the following characters should be smaller than the previous characters and it will generate noises if the considered length is longer than reasonable. According to the analysis above, the optimized feature set for Chinese NER is listed in Table 3 (for each token case, we consider the information from the previous fourth to following second in unigram, and surrounding two characters for bigram window size).

4   CRF Model

The CRFs are first introduced by Lafferty et al. [24] in the NLPP literature to conduct the segmenting and labeling of sequence data. After that, many researchers have tried to employ CRFs in their own areas. To define CRFs, assume X is the variable representing sequence we want to label, and Y is the corresponding label sequence to be attached to X, the conditional model in mathematics is $P(Y|X)$. Then the definition of CRFs: assume a graph $G = (V, E)$ comprising a set V of vertices or nodes together with a set E of edges or lines and $Y = \{Y_v | v \in V\}$ so Y is indexed by the vertices of G; thus (X, Y) is a Conditional Random Field model [24]. The distribution over X and Y is presented as:

$$P_\theta(y|x) \propto \exp\left(\sum_{e \in E, k} \lambda_k f_k(e, y|_e, x) + \sum_{v \in V, k} \mu_k g_k(v, y|_v, x)\right) \tag{1}$$

The variable y and x are described as above Y and X respectively, f_k and g_k are the feature functions, and λ_k and μ_k are the parameters that are trained from the specific dataset. The bar "|" is the mathematical symbol to express that the right part is the precondition of the left. The training methods which can be used for the CRFs include Iterative Scaling Algorithms [24], Non-Preconditioned Conjugate-gradient [25], Voted Perceptron Training [26], etc. and we use a quasi-newton algorithm in the experiments [27] and some implementation tools[1].

5 Experiments

5.1 Data

There were some SIGHAN bakeoffs about CLP including CNER task before 2008 [6], and latterly the tasks of Chinese word segmentation [28] and Chinese parsing [29] remained while the CNER was replaced by Chinese personal name disambiguation [7], which focused on a single category of named entity. To deal with a extensive kinds of named entities, we select the Bakeoff-4 corpus in our experiments. There are seven corpora in total offered in the Bakeoff-4, however only two of them were applied in the CNER task including CityU (Traditional character corpora) and MSRA (Simplified character). Traditionally, there are two kinds of tracks including open track (without the limit of using external knowledge) and closed track (where the use of external data sets is not allowed including vocabulary, corpus etc.). In this paper, we undertake the closed track to perform our experiments. The detailed information about the volume of the data is shown in Table 4 and Table 5. NE means the total of three kinds of named entities, OOV means the entities of the test data that do not exist in the training data, and Roov means the OOV rate. The samples of training corpus are shown as Table 6. In the test data, there is only one column of Chinese characters.

---

[1] http://crfpp.googlecode.com/svn/trunk/doc/index.html

Table 4. Statistics of used CNER data

Source	Training					Truth				
	Character	NE	PER	LOC	ORG	Character	NE	PER	LOC	ORG
CityU	1772202	66255	16552	36213	13490	382448	13014	4940	4847	3227
MSRA	1089050	37811	9028	18522	10261	219197	7707	1864	3658	2185

Table 5. OOV statistics of CNER truth data

Source	NE		PER		LOC		ORG	
	OOV	Roov	OOV	Roov	OOV	Roov	OOV	Roov
CityU	6354	0.4882	3878	0.7850	900	0.1857	1576	0.4884
MSRA	1651	0.2142	564	0.3026	315	0.0861	772	0.3533

Table 6. Samples of training data

Character List	Label
本 (Local)	N
港 (Hong Kong)	B-LOC
梅 (*Mei*)	B-PER
豔 (*Yan*)	I-PER
芳 (*Fang*)	I-PER

5.2   Results

The experiment results of entity recognition for PER, LOC and ORG respectively are shown in Table 7, which are evaluated in Table 8. The evaluation is performed on NE level (not token-per-token). For example, if a token is supposed to be B-LOC but it is labeled I-LOC instead, then this will not be considered as a correct labeling. In Table 8, there are three criteria commonly used in the literature of natural language processing for the evaluation (precision, recall and F-score). The performances of precision scores are especially inspiring (around 90% of the accuracy) for all the three kinds of named entities.

There are several main conclusions derived from the experiment results. First, the Roov rate (in Table 5) of LOC is the lowest (0.1857 and 0.0861 respectively for CityU and MSRA) and the recognition of LOC also performed very well (0.8599 and 0.8988 respectively in F-score). Second, in the MSRA corpus, the Roov of ORG (0.3533) is larger than PER (0.3026) and the F-scores of ORG also are lower; however, in CityU corpus, the Roov of ORG (0.4884) is much lower than PER (0.7850) while the recognition result of ORG also perform worse (0.6646 and 0.8036 respectively of F-scores for them). These experiments results corroborate our analysis of the Chinese characteristics in different named entities in previous sections (most of the PER and LOC have simpler structures and expressions that make the recognition easier than the ORG). Last, the total OOV entity number in CityU (0.4882) is larger than MSRA (0.2142), and the

Table 7. Summary of test results

Type	CityU			MSRA		
	Truth	Output	Correct	Truth	Output	Correct
PER	4940	3716	3478	1864	1666	1599
LOC	4847	4580	4053	3658	3418	3180
ORG	3227	1937	1716	2185	1954	1733

Table 8. Evaluation scores

Type	CityU				MSRA			
	PER	LOC	ORG	ALL	PER	LOC	ORG	ALL
Recall	0.7040	0.8362	0.5318	0.7105	0.8578	0.8693	0.7931	0.8449
Precision	0.9360	0.8849	0.8859	0.9036	0.9598	0.9304	0.8869	0.9253
F-score	0.8036	0.8599	0.6646	0.7955	0.9059	0.8988	0.8374	0.8833

corresponding final F-score of CityU (0.7955) is also lower than MSRA (0.8833), which shows that the recognition of the OOV entities is the principal challenge for the automatic systems.

Table 9. Comparisons of test scores with baselines

Type	F-score							
	CityU				MSRA			
	PER	LOC	ORG	ALL	PER	LOC	ORG	ALL
Ours	0.8036	0.8599	0.6646	0.7955	0.9059	0.8988	0.8374	0.8833
Baseline	0.3272	0.8042	0.5598	0.5955	0.7591	0.5731	0.5575	0.6105

5.3   Comparisons with Related Works

The experiments have yielded much higher F-scores than the baselines in SIGHAN Bakeoff-4 [6] as compared in Table 9 (we list the F-scores on PER, LOC, ORG and total named entities). The baselines are produced by a left-to-right maximum match algorithm applied on the testing data with the named entity lists generated from the training data. The baseline scores are unstable on different entities resulting synthetically in the total F-scores of 0.5955 and 0.6105 respectively for CityU and MSRA corpus. On the other hand, our results show that the three kinds of entity recognitions get high scores generally without big twists and turns. This proves that the approaches employed in this research are reasonable and augmented. The improvements on ORG and PER are especially larger on both two corpora, leading to the total increases of F-scores 33.6% and 44.7% respectively. To compare with other related works that use different features (various window sizes), algorithms (CRF, ME, SVM, etc.) and external resources (external vocabularies, POS tools, name lists, etc.), we list some works briefly in Table 10. Furthermore, to show the performances of different sub features in our experiments, we also list the corresponding results respectively in

Table 11. In Table 10, we use number n to represent the previous nth character when n is less than zero, the following nth character when n is larger than zero, and the current token case when n equal to zero. For instance, B(-10,01,12) means the three bigram features (former one and current, current and next one, next two characters). Due to the fact that most researchers undertake the test only on MSRA corpus, we list the comparison test on MSRA.

Table 10. Comparisons with related works

	Features and methods	Results(F-score)
[30]	Features: Surname{0}, personal name {T(012),B(01)}, person title {B(-2-1)}, location name {B(01),T(012),F(0123)}, location suffix{0} and organization suffix {0} External: No Algorithm: CRF and Maximum Probability	Closed:85.26%
[18]	Features: Character text {U(-2,...,2), B(-10,01,12)}, POS{U(-4,...,4)}, Vocabulary-list {U(-2,...,7), B(01,12)}, word-boundary {U(-1,0,1)}, named-entity {U(-4,...,4), B(-2-1,...,12)} External: POS tagging and collected character-lists Algorithm: CRF	Open:88.36%
[17]	Features: {Unigram(-2,...,2)} External: entity dictionary, a few linguistic rules Algorithm: ME, CRF	Open: Sys_1:85.84% Open: Sys_2:89.12%
Ours	Features: {Unigram(-4,...,2), B(-2-1,...,12)} External: No Algorithm: CRF	**Closed: 88.33%**

From Table 10, we first see that when the window size of the features is smaller, the performance shows worse. Second, too large window size cannot ensure good results while it will bring in noises and cost more running time simultaneously. Third, the combination of segmentation and POS will offer more information about the test set; however, these external materials do not necessarily ensure better performances, which may be due to the fact that the segmentation and POS accuracy also influence the system quality. Finally, the experiment of this paper has yielded promising results by employing optimized feature set and a concise model. Table 11 shows that, generally speaking, more features lead to more training time, and when the feature set is small this conclusion also fit the case of iteration number; however, this conclusion does not stand when the feature set gets larger e.g. testing on the MSRA corpus, the feature set (FS) FS4 needs 314 iteration number which is less than 318 by FS2 although the former feature set is larger. This may be due to the fact that the feature set FS2 needs more iterations to converge to a fixed point. Employing the CRF algorithm, the optimized feature set is chosen as FS4, and if we continue to expand the features the recognition accuracy will decrease as in Table 11.

Table 11. Performances of sub features in experiments

NO.	Sub features	Training info(MSRA,CityU)	Result(F-score)
FS1	{U(-2,...,2)}	Iterations=(77,82) Time=(145.66s,248.70s)	MSRA:0.5553 CityU:0.5392
FS2	{U(-2,...,2),B(-10),(01)}	Iterations=(318,290) Time=(746.25s,1071.2s)	MSRA:0.8721 CityU:0.7851
FS4	{U(-4,...,2),B(-2-1),...,(12)}	Iterations=(314,261) Time=(862.71s,1084.01s)	MSRA:**0.8833** CityU:**0.7955**
FS5	{U(-4,...,3),B(-2-1),...,(12)}	Iterations=(278,NA) Time=(760.93s,NA)	MSRA:0.8803 CityU:NA

6 Discussion

Due to the changeful and complicated characteristics of Chinese, there are some special combinations of characters, and sometimes we can label them with different performances with all results reasonable in practice. These make some confusion for the researchers. So how do we deal with these problems?

First, we define the Function-overload (also called as metonymy in some place) problem: one word bears two or more meanings in the same text. For instance, the word "大山" (*DaShan*) means an organization name in the chunk "大山國際銀行" (*DaShan* International Bank) and the whole chunk means a company, while " 大山" (*DaShan*) also represents a person name in the sequence "大山悄悄地走了" (*DaShan* quietly went away) with the whole sequence meaning a person's action. So it is difficult for the computer to differ their meaning and assign corresponding different labels (ORG or PER), and they must be recognized through the analysis of context and semantics.

Furthermore, we define the Multi-segmentation problem in CNER: one sequence can be segmented into a whole or more fragments according to different meanings, and the labeling will correspondingly end in different results. For example, the sequence "中興實業" (*ZhongXing* Corporation) can be labeled as a whole chunk as "B-ORG I-ORG I-ORG I-ORG" which means it is an organization name, however, it also can be divided as "中興 / 實業" (*ZhongXing* / Corporation) and labeled as "B-ORG I-ORG / N N" meaning that the word "中興" (*ZhongXing*) can represent the organization entity and "實業" (Corporation) specifies common Chinese word whose usage is widespread in Chinese documents. For another example of this kind of problem, the sequence "杭州西湖" (*Hang Zhou Xi Hu*) can be labeled as "B-LOC I-LOC I-LOC I-LOC" as a place name, but it can also be labeled as "B-LOC I-LOC B-LOC I-LOC" due to the fact that "西湖" (*XiHu*) is indeed a place that belongs to the city "杭州" (*HangZhou*). Which label sequences shall we select for them? Both of them are reasonable. This is a difficult problem for manual work, let alone for computer. Above discussed problems are only some of the existing ones in CNER. If we can deal with them well, the performances will be better in the future.

7   Conclusion and Future Works

This paper undertakes the researches of CNER which is a difficult issue in NLP literature. The characteristics of Chinese named entities are introduced respectively on personal names, location names and organization names. Employing the CRF algorithm, optimized features have shown promising performances compared with related works that use different feature sets and algorithms. Furthermore, to facilitate further researches, this paper discusses the problems existing in the CNER and puts forward some formal definitions combined with instructive solutions. The performance results can be further improved in the open test through employing other resources and tools such as Part-of-speech information, externally generated word-frequency counts, common Chinese surnames and internet dictionaries.

Acknowledgments. This work is partially supported by the Research Committee of University of Macau, and Science and Technology Development Fund of Macau under the grants UL019B/09-Y3/EEE/LYP01/FST, and 057/2009/A2.

References

1. Ratinov, L., Roth, D.: Design Challenges and Misconceptions in Named Entity Recognition. In: Proceedings of the Thirteenth Conference on Computational Natural Language Learning (CoNLL 2009), pp. 147–155. Association for Computational Linguistics Press, Stroudsburg (2009)
2. Sang, E.F.T.K., Meulder, F.D.: Introduciton to the CoNLL-2003 Shared Task: Language-Independent Named Entity Recognition. In: HLT-NAACL, pp. 142–147. ACL Press, USA (2003)
3. Sobhana, N., Mitra, P., Ghosh, S.: Conditional Random Field Based Named Entity Recognition in Geological text. J. IJCA 1(3), 143–147 (2010)
4. Settles, B.: Biomedical named entity recognition using conditional random fields and rich feature sets. In: Collier, N., Ruch, P., Nazarenko, A. (eds.) International Joint Workshop on Natural Language Processing in Biomedicine and its Applications, pp. 104–107. ACL Press, Stroudsburg (2004)
5. Levow, G.A.: The third international CLP bakeoff: Word segmentation and named entity recognition. In: Proceedings of the Fifth SIGHAN Workshop on CLP, pp. 122–131. ACL Press, Sydney (2006)
6. Jin, G., Chen, X.: The fourth international CLP bakeoff: Chinese word segmentation, named entity recognition and Chinese pos tagging. In: Sixth SIGHAN Workshop on CLP, pp. 83–95. ACL Press, Hyderabad (2008)
7. Chen, Y., Jin, P., Li, W., Huang, C.-R.: The Chinese Persons Name Disambiguation Evaluation: Exploration of Personal Name Disambiguation in Chinese News. In: CIPS-SIGHAN Joint Conference on Chinese Language Processing, pp. 346–352. ACL Press, BeiJing (2010)
8. Sun, L., Zhang, Z., Dong, Q.: Overview of the Chinese Word Sense Induction Task at CLP2010. In: CIPS-SIGHAN Joint Conference on CLP (CLP2010), pp. 403–409. ACL Press, BeiJing (2010)
9. Jaynes, E.: The relation of Bayesian and maximum entropy methods. J. Maximum-entropy and Bayesian Methods in Science and Engineering 1, 25–29 (1988)

10. Wong, F., Chao, S., Hao, C.C., Leong, K.S.: A Maximum Entropy (ME) Based Translation Model for Chinese Characters Conversion. J. Advances in Computational Linguistics, Research in Computer Science. 41, 267–276 (2009)
11. Ekbal, A., Bandyopadhyay, S.: A hidden Markov model based named entity recognition system: Bengali and Hindi as case studies. In: Ghosh, A., De, R.K., Pal, S.K. (eds.) PReMI 2007. LNCS, vol. 4815, pp. 545–552. Springer, Heidelberg (2007)
12. Mansouri, A., Affendey, L., Mamat, A.: Named entity recognition using a new fuzzy support vector machine. J. IJCSNS 8(2), 320 (2008)
13. Putthividhya, D.P., Hu, J.: Bootstrapped named entity recognition for product attribute extraction. In: EMNLP 2011, pp. 1557–1567. ACL Press, Stroudsburg (2011)
14. Peng, F., Feng, F., McCallum, A.: Chinese segmentation and new word detection using conditional random fields. In: Proceedings of the 20th international conference on Computational Linguistics (COLING 2004), Article 562. Computational Linguistics Press, Stroudsburg (2004)
15. Chen, W., Zhang, Y., Isahara, H.: Chinese named entity recognition with conditional random fields. In: Fifth SIGHAN Workshop on Chinese Language Processing, pp. 118–121. ACL Press, Sydney (2006)
16. Zhu, F., Liu, Z., Yang, J., Zhu, P.: Chinese event place phrase recognition of emergency event using Maximum Entropy. In: Cloud Computing and Intelligence Systems (CCIS), pp. 614–618. IEEE, ShangHai (2011)
17. Qin, Y., Yuan, C., Sun, J., Wang, X.: BUPT Systems in the SIGHAN Bakeoff 2007. In: Sixth SIGHAN Workshop on CLP, pp. 94–97. ACL Press, Hyderabad (2008)
18. Feng, Y., Huang, R., Sun, L.: Two Step Chinese Named Entity Recognition Based on Conditional Random Fields Models. In: Sixth SIGHAN Workshop on CLP, pp. 120–123. ACL Press, Hyderabad (2008)
19. Yuan, Y., Zhong, W.: Contemporary Surnames. Jiangxi people's publishing house, China (2006)
20. Yuan, Y., Qiu, J., Zhang, R.: 300 most common surname in Chinese surnames-population genetic and population distribution. East China Normal University Publishing House, China (2007)
21. Huang, D., Sun, X., Jiao, S., Li, L., Ding, Z., Wan, R.: HMM and CRF based hybrid model for chinese lexical analysis. In: Sixth SIGHAN Workshop on CLP, pp. 133–137. ACL Press, Hyderabad (2008)
22. Sun, G.-L., Sun, C.-J., Sun, K., Wang, X.-L.: A Study of Chinese Lexical Analysis Based on Discriminative Models. In: Sixth SIGHAN Workshop on CLP, pp. 147–150. ACL Press, Hyderabad (2008)
23. Yang, F., Zhao, J., Zou, B.: CRFs-Based Named Entity Recognition Incorporated with Heuristic Entity List Searching. In: Sixth SIGHAN Workshop on CLP, pp. 171–174. ACL Press, Hyderabad (2008)
24. Lafferty, J., McCallum, A., Pereira, F.C.N.: Conditional random fields: Probabilistic models for segmenting and labeling sequence data. In: Proceeding of 18th International Conference on Machine Learning, pp. 282–289. DBLP, Massachusetts (2001)
25. Shewchuk, J.R.: An introduction to the conjugate gradient method without the agonizing pain. Technical Report CMUCS-TR-94-125, Carnegie Mellon University (1994)
26. Collins, M., Duffy, N.: New ranking algorithms for parsing and tagging: kernels over discrete structures, and the voted perceptron. In: Proceedings of the 40th Annual Meeting on Association for Computational Linguistics (ACL 2002), pp. 263–270. Association for Computational Linguistics Press, Stroudsburg (2002)

27. The Numerical Algorithms Group. E04 - Minimizing or Maximizing a Function, NAG Library Manual, Mark 23 (retrieved 2012)
28. Zhao, H., Liu, Q.: The CIPS-SIGHAN CLP2010 Chinese Word Segmentation Back-off. In: CIPS-SIGHAN Joint Conference on CLP, pp. 199–209. ACL Press, BeiJing (2010)
29. Zhou, Q., Zhu, J.: Chinese Syntactic Parsing Evaluation. In: CIPS-SIGHAN Joint Conference on CLP (CLP 2010), pp. 286–295. ACL Press, BeiJing (2010)
30. Xu, Z., Qian, X., Zhang, Y., Zhou, Y.: CRF-based Hybrid Model for Word Segmentation, NER and even POS Tagging. In: Sixth SIGHAN Workshop on CLP, pp. 167–170. ACL Press, India (2008)

Detecting Syntactic Errors
in Dependency Treebanks
for Morphosyntactically Rich Languages

Katarzyna Krasnowska and Adam Przepiórkowski

Institute of Computer Science, Polish Academy of Sciences
k.krasnowska@phd.ipipan.waw.pl, adamp@ipipan.waw.pl

Abstract. The paper introduces a new method for detecting and correcting errors in large dependency treebanks with rich morphosyntactic annotation. The technique uses error correction rules automatically extracted from the treebank. The procedure of rule extraction is based on a comparison of similar – but not identical – subgraphs of dependency structures. The outcome of applying the method to a 3-million-sentence dependency treebank of Polish is presented and evaluated. The method achieves satisfactory precision in the task of automatic error correction and relatively high precision in the task of error detection.

Keywords: dependency treebank, error mining, automatic error detection, automatic error correction.

1 Introduction

Treebanks are an important type of linguistic resource and are currently maintained or developed for numerous languages. They play a crucial role in the task of training probabilistic parsers and, hence, in many natural language processing applications. This is why it is necessary to ensure their high quality. One of the ways of eradicating erroneous structures in a treebank is to develop a method of automated detection of wrongly annotated structures once the resource is created.

The aim of this paper is to present one such method for detecting errors in a dependency treebank. There were previous reports on application of some methods for pointing out wrongly annotated structures in this type of resource [2,3]. This paper presents an alternative method, inspired by a technique designed for finding errors in constituency treebanks [5] which was successfully adapted for use with the Polish constituency treebank [6].

The treebank used for the evaluation of the proposed method is an automatically created corpus comprising of a little more than 3 million trees.[1] The method used for creating the treebank (described in detail in [10]) involved the use of a large English-Polish word-aligned parallel corpus. The English part of

---

[1] The exact number is 3 162 800.

M.A. Kłopotek et al. (Eds.): IIS 2013, LNCS 7912, pp. 69–79, 2013.

the corpus was parsed automatically using a comprehensive LFG parser for English.[2] Dependency structures for the Polish part were then induced on the basis of the English parse and the word alignment between parallel sentences.

The paper is organised as follows. Section 2 introduces the proposed method of error detection, section 3 describes relevant experiments, and section 4 contains evaluation of the obtained results.

2   Method

The proposed method relies on the assumption that constructions which appear in the treebank relatively rarely are likely to be erroneous. Moreover, similar constructions encountered more frequently can be expected to be correct counterparts of the erroneous constructions (the notion of similarity will be explained later on). Although this may not hold in all cases, we are hoping to be able to detect dependency annotation errors with sufficient precision. The idea behind the technique proposed in this paper is thus to define sub-structures of dependency trees that the method will compare, as well as what it means for them to be similar. After extracting relevant structures from the treebank and determining their frequencies, pairings of similar structures are found, possibly representing erroneous constructions and their correct counterparts.

The method is based on connected subgraphs of the dependency trees. As a first step, all such subgraphs of a given size[3] are extracted from each tree. For convenience, we assume that the dependency relations are marked in the child node, not attached to the edge between parent and child, and that the (artificial) root note of the tree is not taken into account for the purpose of subgraph extraction. The subgraphs retain information about parent-child relations and are in fact themselves dependency trees, it is therefore relevant to refer to a subgraph's *root*.

Our approach differs from the one proposed by Kato and Matsubara [5], who extracted subtrees from constituency structures and then truncated them by cutting off all children of specific nodes. In other words, each node in the tree substructures they considered had either all its original children removed, or all its original children retained. In the method proposed here, it is possible for a subgraph's node to retain only a subset of its children from the original dependency tree. In this way the technique presented here achieves greater flexibility, especially given the fact that arguments of verbs can be (and frequently are) omitted or freely ordered in Polish.

Experiments on error detection in small, syntactically annotated corpora of highly inflectional languages, reported in [6], suggest that abstraction from exact word forms (i.e., taking into consideration only their part of speech and

---

[2] See [1] and `http://www2.parc.com/isl/groups/nltt/xle/doc/xle_toc.html`

[3] In this work, we only considered subgraphs of sizes 4 and 5 (i.e., based on 4 or 5 words). Smaller subtrees seemed to carry too little information to prove substantially useful. What is more, allowing more possible subtree sizes would increase the already long – because of the treebank's size – time required to run the procedure.

morphological tags) can help in obtaining sufficient amount of data for drawing statistical generalisations. In the case of the study described in this paper, this coarse granularity of information does not seem essential, given the very high number of sentences in the treebank. Moreover, some preliminary experiments conducted with a small (about 8000 trees) dependency treebank described in [9] showed that ignoring word forms may lead to unacceptable loss of lexical information.

For instance, when it abstracted away from lexical information, the method failed in case of sentences containing the common verb *mieć* (*to have*), which has an accusative nominal argument that is not passivisable and is therefore labelled as a complement (COMP), not an object (OBJ), in the dependency schema adopted here. On the other hand, for the vast majority of Polish verbs, the accusative argument is actually a passivisable object. As a result, subgraphs with an OBJ dependency relation between a verb and a noun in accusative case were much more frequent in the treebank than similar subgraphs with a COMP relation, and the method wrongly reported many trees with the verb *mieć* and its accusative complement as errors.

To strike a reasonable balance between the need for generalisation and the necessity to retain some lexical information, graph nodes are represented by base forms of words, together with their CPOS tags[4] and morphological case. This way, the current method is capable of drawing a parallel between, e.g., two sentences containing the same verb with the same arguments, but differing in the verb's person and gender.

To illustrate the above considerations, Figure 1 shows an example dependency tree and all its connected subgraphs of size 4. CPOS tags combined with morphological cases will be referred to as CPOS-case tags. For instance, a noun in dative will be assigned the noun-DAT CPOS-case tag.

Once the subgraphs are extracted, all subgraph pairs are found such that:

- their roots are identical in terms of dependency relation, word base form and CPOS-case tag;
- the sequences base forms and CPOS-case tags of all nodes (ordered the same way as corresponding words in the sentence) are identical;
- their internal structures (i.e., subgraph shapes and/or dependency relations) diverge.

An example of a rule extracted in this way from the treebank is presented in Figure 2.

For each rule, all trees containing the source of the rule (the first substructure) are marked as possibly incorrect. Trees created by transforming the subgraph matching the source into one matching the target are suggested as correct.

---

[4] CPOS tags are coarse-grained POS tags, where fine-grained grammatical classes (e.g., various types of adjectives) are grouped into more traditional parts of speech.

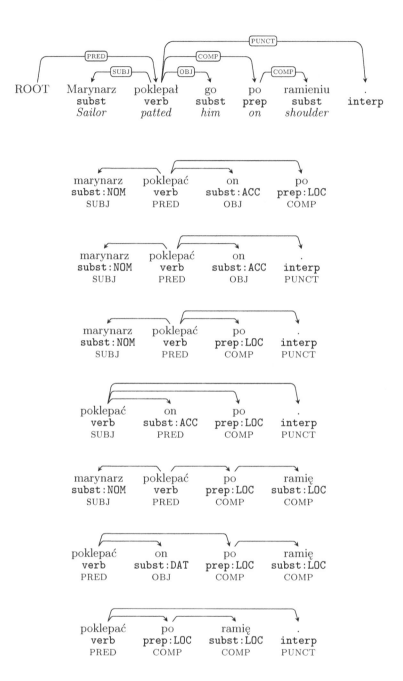

Fig. 1. An example dependency tree for the sentence *Marynarz poklepał go po ramieniu.* '*The sailor patted him on the shoulder.*' (taken from the 3-million-sentence dependency treebank) with all its subgraphs of size 4. Orthographic word forms have been replaced in the subgraphs by base forms combined with CPOS-case tags.

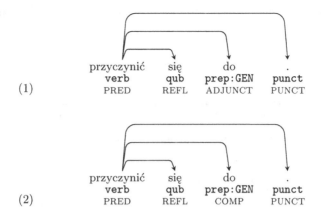

(1)

(2)

Fig. 2. An example rule: (1) is the source of the rule, (2) is the target. The rule changes the dependency relation between the (inherently reflexive) verb *przyczynić się* '*to contribute*' and a preposisional phrase headed by the preposition *do* '*to*' from the incorrect ADJUNCT to the correct COMP.

3   Experiments

2 variants of the method described above were run on the 3-million-sentence dependency treebank:

variant I: exactly as presented in the previous section;
variant II: for some parts of speech, their base forms were ignored, i.e., only CPOS-case tags were taken into account; additionally the dependency relations in the subtrees' roots were ignored.

The modifications to the method were introduced in variant II so as to increase the generality of extracted rules and, as a result, be able to identify more trees as possibly erroneous (see Section 4).

The first modification is motivated by the intuition that for some parts of speech the base form is less important from the point of view of the method. For instance, it is relevant to make a distintion between different verbs because of their different argument structure. On the other hand, it seems that as far as nouns, pronouns, adjectives, numerals and adverbs are concerned, their base form can be omitted without much loss of information, especially, as they typically do not have idiosyncratic combinatorial (or argument structure) properties.

The second introduced modification consists in ignoring dependency relations in the roots of subtrees. Those dependency relations tie the subgraph's root node to its parent from the complete dependency tree. As this parent is not present in the subgraph, this particular dependency relation is much less relevant than the "internal" ones (i.e., those between the subgraph's nodes). What is more, abstracting from the root's dependency relations enables rule extraction in the case where, for example, two similar noun phrases appear as the subject of a sentence and a conjunct in a coordinated structure, respectively.

Table 1 gives the numbers of trees pointed out as wrongly annotated by each variant.

Table 1. The number of trees reported as erroneous by the two methods (some trees were reported more than once)

method variant	I	II
number of error reports	18 885	852 323
number of distinct trees	10 237	265 460
distinct trees percentage	54.2%	31.1%

4   Evaluation

It is difficult to estimate the recall of the implemented method, as the number of erroneous parses in the treebank is not known. It is probably for this reason that some works on error detection do not report recall at all (e.g., [4], [5]). Nevertheless, it is perhaps worthwhile to mention two issues concerning recall of error detection. Previous experiments with automatic error detection in a Polish constituency treebank reported in [6] suggest that high recall might be more difficult to achieve than high precision. What is more, the procedure of obtaining the 3-million-sentence dependency treebank used in the experiments involves several steps (sentence alignment, dependency parsing of English sentences, tree projection), all of which are likely to contribute for errors. It is therefore unrealistic to assume that only a small fraction of dependency structures are wrongly annotated (for instance, the percentage of erroneous trees in a Polish constituency treebank, annotated semi-automatically, is estimated to be around 18%, see [8]).

What can be directly estimated is the precision of the method. After applying the method to the treebank, we carefully examined two samples of 100 error reports for each method variant (i.e., four samples were taken into account). Not all error reports could have been included in the samples since preliminary attempts at examining them using the *MaltEval* tool for visualisation[5] showed that some of the structures in the treebank were discontinuous. Since *MaltEval* does not handle discontinuous trees, they were excluded from further examination.

The error reports to include in the samples were chosen as follows. First, an ordered list of rules was created (the orderings were different for each sample type, as explained further on). Second, for each rule, the first tree it indicated as wrong was taken to form a list consisting of one error report per rule. The samples were formed by truncating (i.e., taking only its n first elements for some n) the lists so that they contained 100 *distinct* trees. Table 2 gives the size of sample for each method (sample sizes are greater than 100 since some trees appeared more than once on the list).

---

[5] With the trees after rule application as gold standard, see [7] and
http://w3.msi.vxu.se/~nivre/research/MaltEval.html

Table 2. Sample sizes for both variants of the method and both rule ordering strategies. For each sample, the number of trees appearing more than once is also given.

sample	sample size	trees reported more than once
I_O	107	7
I_R	103	2
II_O	118	14
II_R	101	1

Two types of sample were created, depending on the rule ordering strategy, as mentioned before. The following ordering strategies were applied:

O — the rules were sorted in the decreasing order of the sum of occurrences of their source and target in the treebank.

R — the rules were sorted randomly.

The first ordering, O, is a heuristic for promoting rules which were expected to be more efficient: if there is more material in the treebank to serve as "evidence" for the rule, it might be that not only the rule is more probable to be sound, but also that it detects a common error. The second ordering is expected to allow for better approximation of the method's overall precision. One can think of more possible orderings, e.g., the proportion of rule's source and target occurrences in the treebank (similarly to the approach adopted in [5]).

As a result, four samples were created. The samples will be referred to as I_O (i.e., method variant I, rule ordering O), I_R, II_O, II_R

Each error report from a sample was examined and assigned one of the following categories:

correct for genuine errors with an appropriate correction suggestion,
partial for genuine errors with a wrong correction suggestion,
wrong for correct structures pointed out as erroneous.

In the case of trees which were included in the sample more than once, only one error report, assigned the best category,[6] was taken into account. This is because for each tree, we are interested in whether the method succeeded in detecting an annotation error. In Table 3, the numbers of error reports assigned each category are given.

The precision of each method variant was estimated as the number of reports which pointed out genuine errors divided by the total number of reports considered, i.e., 100. Two measures of precision were used. The first one, P_0, is the number of reports classified as *correct* divided by 100. The second one, P_1, was less strict in that it also admitted *partial* error reports. In other words, P_0 is the fraction of correctly identified errors with a good correction suggestion, while P_1

---

[6] In the sense that *correct* is better than *partial*, and *partial* is better than *wrong*.

Table 3. The number of trees for which the error report was assigned each category, given for each evaluated sample

sample	correct	partial	wrong
I_O	53	30	17
I_R	42	30	28
II_O	57	19	24
II_R	52	21	27

Table 4. Precision estimates for each sample

sample	P_0	P_1
I_O	53%	83%
I_R	42%	72%
II_O	57%	76%
II_R	52%	73%

is the fraction of correctly identified errors regardless of whether their correction suggestion was appropriate. Estimations for P_0 and for P_1, depending on method variant and rule sorting strategy, are given in Table 4.

It is clear that the method is much more efficient when it comes to the simple detection of errors, but the precision of error correction is also satisfactory. This makes the proposed method a good candidate for use in semi-automatic error correction, where the correction suggestions are presented to a human annotator who can accept, modify or reject the correction suggested by the system. Variant II of the method outperforms variant I in terms of P_0. As far as P_1 is concerned, variant II also achieved higher results with exception of the case where O strategy was adopted. Higher precision estimates obtained using the O rule ordering than when the R ordering was applied show that it can be worthwile to somehow arrange the error reports (perhaps using a more sophisticated strategy) in the case where for some reason not all of them can be examined (e.g., due to the large treebank size).

Given the estimation for precision, it is possible to calculate the estimated number of annotation errors that the method managed to find – it can be approximated by the estimated precision multiplied by the total number of distinct trees pointed out as possibly erroneous. As in the case of precision, two estimations can be given depending on whether P_0 or P_1 is taken into account. As stated before, we are not able to compare them to the actual number of erroneous structures in the treebank, but suspect that many errors are still left undetected given the estimates ranging from 2.1% to 6.4%. Table 5 presents the estimated numbers of correctly identified errors for both method variants.

Table 5. The approximate number of all errors found by the method based on precision estimations P_0 and P_1. The percentages below numbers are the proportions of the approximate number of found errors to the whole treebank size.

sample	approx. number of errors	
	using P_0	using P_1
I_O	82975	129943
	2.6%	4.1%
I_R	65754	112721
	2.1%	3.6%
II_O	151312	201749
	4.8%	6.4%
II_R	138039	193785
	4.4%	6.1%

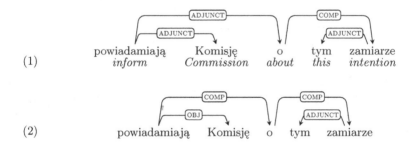

(1)

(2)

Fig. 3. An example of error detected by the method: (1) wrong dependency structure from the treebank (2) proposed correction

Figures 3 and 4 present two examples of detected errors together with the correct version of the tree suggested by the method as a replacement. For clarity, only the fragment of the tree affected by the rule is shown. In the case of the sentence in Figure 3, the phrases *Commission* and *about this intention* were wrongly annotated as two adjuncts, whereas the correct dependency relations between them and their head *inform* are OBJ (object) and COMP (complement), respectively, as in the structure proposed by the method. In the second case, presented in Figure 4, the phrase *applying sanctions* was assigned a wrong dependency relation and the phrase *from institutions* had a wrong head (*applying* instead of *request*) and a wrong dependency relation. Both errors are corrected in the alternative structure proposed by the method.

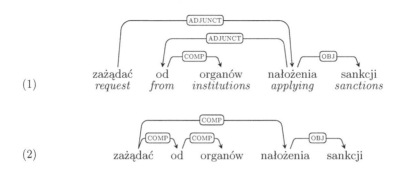

(1)

(2)

Fig. 4. Another example of error detected by the method: (1) wrong dependency structure from the treebank (2) proposed correction

5   Conclusions

A method for detecting and correcting annotation errors in a dependency treebank for a highly inflectional language was proposed, implemented and evaluated. The evaluation showed that the method achieves reasonable estimated precision for error correction (52%) and good estimated precision when the task is limited to error detection (73%).

Acknowledgements. The work described in this paper is partially supported by the DG INFSO of the European Commission through the ICT Policy Support Programme, Grant agreement no.: 271022, as well as by the POIG.01.01.02-14-013/09 project co-financed by the European Union under the European Regional Development Fund.

References

1. Butt, M., Dyvik, H., King, T.H., Masuichi, H., Rohrer, C.: The parallel grammar project. In: Proceedings of the COLING 2002 Workshop on Grammar Engineering and Evaluation, Taipei, pp. 1–7 (2002)
2. Dickinson, M.: Correcting dependency annotation errors. In: Proceedings of the 12th Conference of the European Chapter of the Association for Computational Linguistics (EACL 2009), Athens, Greece (2009)
3. Dickinson, M.: Detecting errors in automatically-parsed dependency relations. In: The 48th Annual Meeting of the Association for Computational Linguistics (ACL 2010), Uppsala, Sweden (2010)
4. Dickinson, M., Meurers, D.W.: Detecting inconsistencies in treebanks. In: Nivre, J., Hinrichs, E. (eds.) Proceedings of the Second Workshop on Treebanks and Linguistic Theories (TLT 2003), Växjö, Sweden, pp. 45–56 (2003)

5. Kato, Y., Matsubara, S.: Correcting errors in a treebank based on synchronous tree substitution grammar. In: Proceedings of the ACL 2010 Conference Short Papers, ACLShort 2010, pp. 74–79. Association for Computational Linguistics, Stroudsburg (2010)

6. Krasnowska, K., Kieraś, W., Woliński, M., Przepiórkowski, A.: Using tree transducers for detecting errors in a treebank of Polish. In: Sojka, P., Horák, A., Kopeček, I., Pala, K. (eds.) TSD 2012. LNCS, vol. 7499, pp. 119–126. Springer, Heidelberg (2012)

7. Nilsson, J., Nivre, J.: MaltEval: An evaluation and visualization tool for dependency parsing. In: Proceedings of the Sixth International Language Resources and Evaluation, LREC (2008)

8. Woliński, M., Głowińska, K., Świdziński, M.: A preliminary version of Składnica – a treebank of Polish. In: Vetulani, Z. (ed.) Proceedings of the 5th Language & Technology Conference, Poznań, pp. 299–303 (2011)

9. Wróblewska, A.: Polish dependency bank. Linguistic Issues in Language Technology 7(1) (2012)

10. Wróblewska, A., Przepiórkowski, A.: Induction of dependency structures based on weighted projection. In: Nguyen, N.-T., Hoang, K., Jędrzejowicz, P. (eds.) ICCCI 2012, Part I. LNCS, vol. 7653, pp. 364–374. Springer, Heidelberg (2012)

A Method for the Computational Representation of Croatian Morphology

Vanja Štefanec[1], Matea Srebačić[1], and Krešimir Šojat[2]

[1] University of Zagreb
[2] Faculty of Humanities and Social Sciences, University of Zagreb

Abstract. In this paper we present the development of the Croatian Derivational Database (CroDeriV), a unique language resource for the Croatian language. We describe the initial stage of its development as well as its redesign according to insight gained from data analyzed thus far. We believe that the data model we have presented will enable us to encode all derivational processes in Croatian. We also believe that our model is sufficiently flexible and abstract that it could be used for other morphologically "rich" languages.

Keywords: CroDeriV, morphological resources, derivation, Croatian.

1 Introduction

In this paper we present the development of the Croatian Derivational Database (CroDeriV). The computational processing of Croatian morphology so far has focused primarily on inflectional phenomena ([10]; [12]; [3]) and the enlargement procedures of the Croatian Morphological Lexicon ([11]). During the process of building Croatian Wordnet ([6]), especially when dealing with derivationally connected members of different synsets ([9]), it became obvious that large-scale data indicating which affixes are used or can be used with particular lexical morphemes do not exist for Croatian. In other words, the data about the derivational spans of particular lexical morphemes have not yet been systematically and extensively presented in the Croatian morphological literature.

A derivational span refers to all attested combinations of derivational affixes and one or more lexical morpheme. Large-scale data on such combinations are necessary not only for the further development of Croatian WordNet, but also for the development of various NLP tools for Croatian, such as stemmers, lemmatizers, Q&A systems, etc.

The CroDeriV database is designed to comprise four major POS, i.e. nouns, verbs, adjectives, and adverbs, and to represent their morphological structure in terms of roots (lexical morphemes) and derivational affixes attached to the roots. The aim of the database is to serve as the basis for future research on Croatian derivational morphology by enabling the recognition of words with the same root of the same or a different POS as well as word-formation processes between words sharing the same root.

M.A. Kłopotek et al. (Eds.): IIS 2013, LNCS 7912, pp. 80–91, 2013.

Lexical entries in CroDeriV contain lemmas analyzed for lexical and derivational morphemes, i.e. each lemma is divided into one or more roots and derivational affixes attached to those roots. In the first phase of the database development, 14,000 verbal lemmas, i.e. verbs in infinitive form, were collected from freely available digital dictionaries of Croatian and semi-automatically analyzed for morphemes.[1] So far, no language resource containing morphologically analyzed lemmas has been developed for Croatian.

In Sects. 2 and 3 we shall briefly discuss related work and word-formation processes in Croatian. In Section 4 we present the present shape of CroDeriV, and in Section 5 we present the reasons for our complete redesign of CroDeriV, as well as the new data model on which it is based. Section 6 comprises future work and conclusions.

2   Related Work

As mentioned, the computational processing of Croatian has been primarily focused on inflection. The Croatian Morphological Lexicon [10] comprises 120,000 lemmas and their inflectional forms. Ćavar et al. [3];[2] describe the development of *CroMo*, a finite state lexical transducer used for morphological analysis and lemmatization. The transducer is based on a database of ca. 250,000 lexical, derivational, and inflectional morphemes. This database is unfortunately not publicly available. Šnajder [8] deals with the procedures of automatic processing and the acquisition of inflectional lexicon for Croatian. Derivational processing is limited to nouns, verbs and adjectives formed by suffixation. The data obtained through lemmatization and stemming are used for further information extraction from raw corpora. Stemmers for Croatian presented in [4] and [5] are developed for the recognition of derivational suffixes and inflectional endings. Although all stemmers are based on linguistic rules, none of them recognizes base forms and derivatives obtained through prefixation. Morphological analyzers for other Slavic languages, e.g. *ajka* for Czech [7] or *Morfeusz* for Polish [13] are also restricted to inflection.

3   Word-Formation Processes in Croatian

As in other Slavic languages, word-formation processes in Croatian comprise derivation and compounding. Derivation is a significantly more productive process than compounding, which does not play an important role in Croatian morphology if compared with languages such as German. In some cases it is hard to draw a sharp line between derivation and inflection in Croatian, since, for instance, the formation of gerunds, participles, and comparatives/superlatives are considered to be inflectional processes, whereas the formation of verbal aspectual pairs is treated as derivation.

---

[1] A similar resource exists for Russian (http://courses.washington.edu/unimorph/).

Derivation in Croatian is basically affixation. Affixation can comprise prefixation (*pisati* - **po**pisati, **is**pisati, **na**pisati, **pre**pisati), suffixation (*popisati* - *popisivati*, *pisati* - *pisač*, *pisar*) and simultaneous prefixation and suffixation (*pisati* - **s**pis**atelj**).

Compounding is the word-formation process of putting two lexical morphemes together. In Croatian there are three kinds of compounding: bare compounding (stem1 + (interfix) + stem2; stem2 can stand as a separate lexeme; *kuć-e-pazitelj* 'housekeeper'), simultaneous compounding and suffixation (stem1 + interfix + stem2 + suffix, where stems cannot stand as separate lexemes; e.g. *rukopis* 'manuscript' = *ruk-o-pis-Ø*), and finally semi-compounding (two lexemes preserve their meaning, marked with a hyphen between them, e.g. *književno-povijesni* 'litero-historical').

The recognition and description of complex word-formation processes in Croatian is a non-trivial task due to their non-predictability and numerous phonological changes at morpheme boundaries. We tend to overcome these obstacles by recognizing all allomorphs[2] of the same morpheme and linking them to it. Moreover, we do not only want to recognize the specific word-formation rule in question, but also the complete morphological structure of each lemma in CroDeriV. In other words, we want to be able to recognize its root in order to gain insight into complete derivational spans, as has been already pointed out in the preceding sections.

Word-formation processes in Croatian are very similar to word-formation processes in other Slavic languages, particularly to South Slavic languages as e.g. Slovene or Serbian. Therefore, a resource built along the principles as described here could be useful for the development of NLP tools for these languages, as well.

4   The Initial Stage of CroDeriV Development

The main impulse for the building of CroDeriV was the incorporation of derivationally related verbs into Croatian WordNet. This is the reason we decided to start from the verbal part of the lexicon. We have collected approximately 14,000 verbal lemmas (verbs in the infinitive form).

For the purpose of speeding up the morphological analysis, we devised a simple naïve brute-force algorithm based on a small set of linguistic rules. In the first step, we removed 19 productive prefixes. Since prefixation is a recursive process in Croatian (one base can have from zero to four prefixes), this enabled the recognition of the attested prefixal combinations used in verb formation. In the second step, the rules for the removal of suffixes were applied. All Croatian verbs have at least two suffixes denoting aspect and conjugational class before the infinitive ending *-ti* or *-ći*. Optionally, verbs can have another derivational suffix, attached to the root and bearing specific, diminutive or pejorative meanings. Finally, a manual check of the automatic analysis was performed due to the phonological overlapping of affixes and roots, which often resulted in incorrect segmentation.

---

[2] An allomorph is a variant form of a morpheme.

In this step we also connected all allomorphs to one mutual morph in the underlying representation and added some additional linguistic information about verbal aspect and reflexivity. Moreover, the stems were attached to the roots they are related to. Stems can be either productive (i.e. used in the derivation of at least two verbs) or unproductive (used in a single verb formation).

Therefore, the next step was to devise a data model which would enable us to store this data in a structured way and thus facilitate various types of research. Since the verbal morphological structure is rather rigid, the generalization of this structure for all verbs seemed the most logical. Our decision was to present every lemma as a series of slots which can be either filled or empty. These slots were arranged as follows (P = prefix, St = stem, I = interfix, Su = suffix, E = inflectional ending; square brackets = slot can be empty): [P4] + [P3] + [P2] + [P1] + [St2] + [I] + St1 + [Su3] + Su2 + Su1 + E. In this model, every slot is assigned its own semantics. For instance, Su1 will always contain suffixes which define the verb's inflectional class. However, when we started to explore the possibility of expansion of CroDeriV to the nominal part of the lexicon, a rigid structure with a predefined number and order of slots turned out to be inappropriate. When it comes to nouns, the meanings of either prefixes or suffixes in a particular "slot" are not predetermined (e.g. *šal-ic-|a* 'a cup' vs. *šal-ic-|a* 'a little joke', where *šal-* in the first word is not the same root as *šal-* in the second word, and the suffix *-ic-* in the first one has the meaning of a container, whereas in the second one it has a diminutive meaning), and suffixes of the same form with some shared meaning components can come in different relative distances from the root (*prija-telj-ic-|a* 'a female friend' vs. *lav-ic-|a* 'a female lion'). Since the morphological structure of nouns differs significantly from the morphological structure of verbs, we decided to introduce a completely different data-model which would be able to comprise lemmas of different POS.

5   Redesigning CroDeriV

In the inital phase of CroDeriV development, the morphological structure of the entries was predefined, the derivation was described in the form of a final state, and a derivational process could be computed as a change between two states. In the redesigned database, derivation is represented as a sequence of derivational steps (or phases) which consist of simply adding one combining element (a morpheme or a derivative) to some previous phase. The process starts with a single morpheme, which gets combined (prepended or appended) by only one combining element in each step.

The product of each step is one type of derivative, which inherits the morphological structure from its predecessor and is built upon it. For example, the noun *učiteljica* 'female teacher' is derived form *uč-i-telj-* (*uč-i-telj-|Ø* 'male teacher') by adding the suffix *-ic-* and the inflectional ending *-a*. However, it inherits the complete morphological structure of *uč-i-telj-*, and its underlying representation is *uč-i-telj-ic-|a*. With this design, we automatically solved the problem of alloting a definite number of slots for morphemes and determining their order (see the *prijateljica* - *lavica* example). The semantics of a morpheme is not defined by its slot in the morphological structure, but is rather provided by a set of assigned features, which will be further explained later.

It is important to stress that we did not change the way we understand derivation; we simply chose a more flexible model of description. Derivation is comprehended as a sequential process, but in the previous design, it was implicitly coded as the difference between two states. In the redesigned database, the products of each step in the derivational process are stored regardless of whether they:

a) can form words by adding inflectional endings (these will be referred to as *full derivatives*, e.g. *pis-ač-* → *pis-ač-|Ø* 'printer'),

b) can productively form other derivatives serving as stems, (e.g., *pis-Ø-iva-* (**pis-Ø-iva-|ti*) will serve as a stem for *na-pis-Ø-iva-|ti*, *ras-pis-Ø-iva-|ti*, etc.),

c) can simply be an intermediate phase in becoming one or the other.

The types of derivatives are described in more detail in the following section.

Since the new model of the database is not based upon a predefined morphological structure, the exact order of the derivational processes had to be established. By establishing the exact order of derivational processes we ensured that sequential building of the morphological structure will always branch in a predictable way and that there will be no derivational phases stored in the database that cannot be considered plausible nor can be defended by any formal morphological theory (e.g. **do-√pis-Ø-* in *na-do-√pis-Ø-a-|ti*). In our model we chose the following order: 1) suffixation, 2) prefixation, and 3) compounding. Complex derivational processes described in Croatian grammars, such as prefixal-suffixal derivation, are decomposed into simple phases and executed in the default order.

This will minimize the number of derivational phases necessary for the morphological description of all words in the database. Also, the phases stored in the database do not always reflect the actual derivational stages words undergo. For example, *uč-i-telj-|Ø* 'teacher' is derived from *uč-Ø-i-|ti* 'to teach', but in this model we cannot produce *uč-i-telj-* from *uč-Ø-i-* since the elision of one suffix, which is not supported as an operation, would be required. So, in the database *uč-i-telj-* will be represented as being derived from *uč-*. Therefore, the derivational phases are simply an economical way of storing morphological data. Although in our derivational model *učitelj* is not represented as directly derived from *učiti*, the direct derivational relation between them is established separately. These "real" derivational relations are established only between lemmata, i.e. full-fledged words.

Besides the process-like description of derivation, the other significant difference between the previous and the present model is that we separated derivation from inflection. These two morphological processes are described in separate tables in the database. The database comprises four main tables:

1. a derivational table,

2. an inflectional table,

3. a morpheme table (including all morphemes, lexical and grammatical),

4. a relations table (modeling the relations between lemmata).

5.1 Derivation

Each entry in a derivational table represents one step in a derivational process in which only one combining element is added. Each entry consists of:

1. a **derivative text** - the surface form of an entry;

2. a **starting derivative** - the derivative from which the formation of the present phase starts. When this field is empty, derivation starts from this point;

3. a **combining element** - a derivational morpheme or morpheme cluster which takes part in a derivational step. This element is appended or prepended to a starting derivative with respect to the derivation type, e.g. the starting derivative *uč-i-telj-* (*uč-i-telj-|Ø* 'teacher') and the combining element *ic-* form the full derivative *uč-i-telj-ic-* (*uč-i-telj-ic-|a* 'a female teacher') via suffixation;

4. a **derivative type** – thus produced derivatives can be classified as follows[3]:
   (a) *Full derivatives* can produce words by adding inflectional endings but also can continue their derivational process serving as a stem. For example, *uč-i-telj-* can undergo inflection and become *uč-i-telj-|Ø* 'teacher', but also can derive *uč-i-telj-ic-* (*uč-i-telj-ic-|a* 'female teacher'). Only derivatives classified as *full derivatives* will serve as inflectional stems and therefore are referenced in the inflectional table. If they participate in further derivational processes, they serve as derivational stems (here the word *stem* is used in its strict sense as a linguistic term). In other words, they can serve at the same time as an inflectional and derivational base.

   (b) *Intermediate derivatives* are those that have not finished some non-optional process. They can not form words, nor can they serve as a combining element for derivation - they must continue their derivational process and the choice of combining elements which can be combined with them is very limited. For example, the derivative *-Ø-*, consisted

---

[3] The purpose of these categories is merely for filtering and they have no deeper linguistic meaning.

only of the verbal aspectual suffix, will be referred to as *intermediate*, because it has to be first appended by the verbal class suffix to participate in any other derivational process;

(c) *Stems* cannot form words but are productive and serve as the basis for further derivation (e.g., *uč-Ø-ava-* → *na-uč-Ø-ava-|ti, pod-uč-Ø-ava-|ti*, etc.). Stems normally serve as derivational stems and continue the derivation process which can branch in more than one direction;

(d) *Prefix clusters* and *suffix clusters* are derivatives composed of one or more affixes of the same type. In the process of affixation (prefixation or suffixation) these derivatives will function as a combining element.

5. a **derivational type** - there are seven derivational types recognized in CroDeriV:

(a) *cloning* (in which a morpheme starts the derivation process),

(b) *suffixation* (in which a derivative is appended by a suffix cluster),

(c) *prefixation* (in which a derivative is prepended by a prefix cluster),

(d) *suffix composition* (in which a suffixal derivative is appended by another suffix),

(e) *prefix composition* (in which a prefixal derivative is prepended by another prefix),

(f) *compounding_interfix* (in which a derivative is prepended by an interfix),

(g) *compounding* (in which a derivative gets prepended by a derivative);

6. a **derivative slug** – a textual representation of the morphological analysis of the derivative's surface form in which morphemes are segmented with hyphens. The purpose of this field is twofold: first is to present the morphological analysis in a human-readable manner, and second is to facilitate faster and more efficient search of database entries according to morphemes they consist of.[4]

7. the corresponding **underlying representation** is a complex structure to which a derivative is linked. It consists of all the morphemes contained within it with their respective order in the structure.

---

[4] This type of "slug" field will be also used in a table in which underlying representations of the entries are stored (see 7.), with a difference that it will contain underlying, instead of a surface form segmented with hyphens. Every "slug" field in the database will be indexed and easily searchable using regular expressions.

A partial representation of the derivational processes including the root *pis-* in a derivational table is shown in Figure 1.

5.2 Inflection

The derivational table represented above is connected to the inflectional table. When a full derivative from the derivational table receives its inflectional ending, the actual word is formed. For example, the full derivative *uč-i-telj-* becomes a masculine noun in the nominative singular only by acquiring the nominative ending -Ø. Every entry from this table is a lemma tagged with the following attributes: surface form, reference to the corresponding full derivative in the derivation table, inflectional ending, underlying representation and grammatical categories (POS and MSD). The final set of features or feature values is assigned to a word by particular morphemes.

Feature values are listed in a separate table which is referenced both in the morpheme table and inflectional table. Values are grouped by feature types (morphological, syntactic, semantic, morphosemantic, etc...) and feature names. Values pertaining to the same name are logically mutually exclusive. For example, one of the morphological features is the aspect, which can be perfective, imperfective, or biaspectual. Aspect is encoded by the particular verbal suffix, and the same verb cannot be at the same time perfective and imperfective. This constraint is ignored when features are attached to single morphemes and not to words, because a single morpheme often carries mutually incompatible or exclusive features (e.g., the morpheme -Ø- can have either imperfective or perfective meaning, but in a particular word, only one of them is realized). The set of features attached to an inflected form is usually a subset of the union of features attached to the morphemes from which a particular full derivative is combined. Not all of these features are already included in CroDeriV, but they can easily be incorporated at later stages of development, due to its flexible design.

The lemmas, or the entries in the inflectional table, are connected by a set of relations. The new model supports various, but always symmetrical relations. One of the most important relations in the database is, of course, the relation *derives↔is_derived_from*. As we said earlier, the direct derivational relation between two lemmas in some cases cannot be straightforwardly established. In other words, the direct derivational relations have to be explicitly established. By connecting words using derivational relations, we are actually building a network-like structure which illustrates the complete derivational span of a particular lexical morpheme across different POS.

The other types of relations have yet to be included in the CroDeriV.

A graphical representation of the CroDeriV structure is shown in Figure 2.

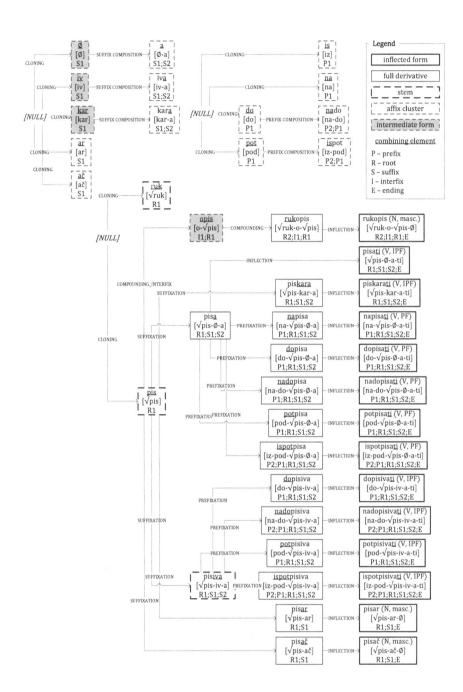

Fig. 1. Schematic representation of the database entries and their mutual relations

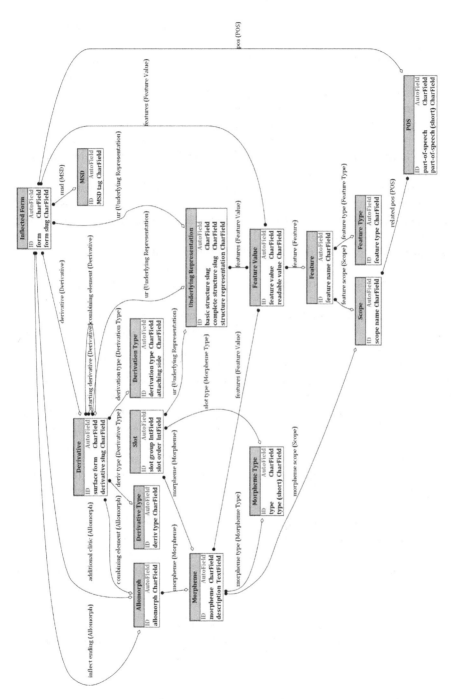

Fig. 2. CroDeriV Data Model

6 Future Work and Conclusion

As we have already stated, CroDeriV is a unique language resource for the Croatian language. Even in the earliest stage of its development, it has been shown to be an extremely valuable source of data for different kinds of linguistic research. For now, we have carried out only a preliminary analysis on the frequency of particular derivational affixes and their attested combinations. These results have already provided new insight into derivational processes in Croatian, since this kind of information cannot be found in Croatian grammars, nor have studies of this type, to the best of our knowledge, ever been done on a representative language data sample. Our plan is to go further: we would like to explore how certain affixes (or their combinations) are good predictors of grammatical (morphological, syntactic, semantic, etc...) features and how they are correlated. One of the features that especially interests us is the alteration of verbal aspect which can occur under different derivational processes. Another interest of ours is to see how syntactic features, such as verbal syntactic frames, are influenced by prefixation. Furthermore, we would like to explore the possibilities of (semi-)automatic expansion of Croatian WordNet by making use of morphosemantic features of derivational affixes. Also, our plans go towards building language tools on the basis of this data, such as a morphological analyzer which would be able to perform both deep and shallow analysis. A good morphological (derivational) analyzer would be useful not only as a part of other language tools, but also for the further expansion of the database.

In this paper we have presented the redesign of CroDeriV, the Croatian Derivational Database. Despite the fact that it is merely a technical solution, we tried to build it in accordance with morphological theories. We believe that the data model we have presented will enable us to encode all derivational processes in the Croatian language. We also believe that our model is flexible and abstract enough to be used for other morphologically "rich" languages.

Derivational morphology is an important part of lexicalization processes in Slavic languages. In predominantly analitical languages, as e.g. English, derivational morphology does not have such a prominent role when compared to Slavic. We believe that derivational databases as the one described in this paper could facilitate the development of NLP tools for Slavic languages or improve the quality of existing ones. We are convinced that the theoretical model that CroDeriV is based upon can be applied to other Slavic languages with only minor modifications. This especially pertains to South Slavic languages as e.g. Slovene and Serbian. [5]

Acknowledgments. This work has been supported by XLike (Cross-lingual Knowledge Extraction), a project in the area of Language Technologies (ICT-2011.4.2) funded by the European Community's Seventh Framework Programme FP7/2007-2013.

---

[5] This resource will be freely available as soon as possible, probably under CC BY-NC-SA 3.0 licence.

References

1. Bernhard, D., Cartoni, B., Tribout, D.: Evaluating Morphological Resources: a Task-Based Study for French Question Answering. In: Proceedings of the International Workshop on Lexical Resources at ESSLII, Slovenia (2011)
2. Ćavar, D., Jazbec, I., Runjaić, S.: Interoperability and Rapid Bootstrapping of Morphological Parsing and Annotation Automata. In: Erjavec, T., Žganec, G., Jerneja (eds.) Proceedings of the Sixth Language Technologies Conference, Proceedings of the 11th International Multiconference Information Society, IS 2008, October 16-17, vol. C, pp. 80–85 (2008)
3. Ćavar, D., Jazbec, I., Stojanov, T.: CroMo Morphological Analysis for Standard Croatian and its Synchronic and Diachronic Dialects and Variants. In: Finite-State Methods and Natural Language Processing - Post-proceedings of the 7th International Workshop FSMNLP, pp. 183–190. IOS Press, Italy (2009)
4. Ljubešić, N., Boras, D., Kubelka, O.: Retrieving information in Croatian: Building a simple and efficient rule-based stemmer. In: Seljan, S., Stančić, H. (eds.) INFuture2007: Digital Information and Heritage, pp. 313–320. Odsjek za informacijske znanosti Filozofskoga fakulteta, Zagreb (2007)
5. Pandžić, I.: Oblikovanje korjenovatelja za hrvatski jezik u svrhu pretrazivanja informacija. MA thesis. University of Zagreb, Faculty of Humanities and Social Sciences, Department of Linguistics
6. Raffaelli, I., Tadić, M., Bekavac, B., Agić, Z.: Building Croatian WordNet. In: Proceedings of the 4th Global WordNet Conference, pp. 349–359. Global WordNet Association, Szeged (2008)
7. Sedláček, R., Smrž, P.: Automatic Processing of Czech Inflectional and Derivative Morphology. In: FI MU Report Series. Masaryk Univesity: Faculty of Informatics (2001)
8. Šnajder, J.: Morfološka normalizacija tekstova na hrvatskome jeziku za dubinsku analizu i pretraživanje informacija. PhD thesis. University of Zagreb, Faculty of Electrical Engineering and Computing (2008)
9. Šojat, K., Srebačić, M., Tadić, M.: Derivational and Semantic Relations of Croatian Verbs. Journal of Language Modelling. O.1, 111–142 (2012)
10. Tadić, M., Fulgosi, S.: Building the Croatian Morphology Lexicon. In: Proceedings of the EACL 2003 Workshop on Morphological Processing of Slavic Languages, pp. 41–46. ACL, Budapest (2003)
11. Tadić, M., Oliver, A.: Enlarging the Croatian Morphological Lexicon by Automatic Lexical Acquisition from Raw Corpora. In: LREC 2004 Proceedings, pp. 1259–1262. ELRA, Paris-Lisabon (2004)
12. Tadić, M., Bekavac, B.: Inflectionally Sensitive Web Search in Croatian using Croatian Lemmatization Server. In: Proceedings of ITI 2006 Conference, SRCE, Zagreb (2004)
13. Woliński, M.: Morfeusz a practical tool for the morphological analysis of Polish. In: Kłopotek, M.A., Wierzchoń, S.T., Trojanowski, K. (eds.) Proceedings of the International Intelligent Information Systems: Intelligent Information Processing and Web Mining 2006 Conference, pp. 511–520. Wisła, Poland (2006)

Mapping Named Entities from NKJP Corpus to *Składnica* Treebank and Polish Wordnet

Elżbieta Hajnicz

Institute of Computer Science, Polish Academy of Sciences

Abstract. In this paper a method of mapping named entities from NKJP corpus, where their annotation is rather coarse, to *Składnica* treebank, where their annotation is wordnet-based, is discussed. The method is based on the fact that *Składnica* is a subcorpus of the one-million-word manually annotated balanced subcorpus of NKJP. The method to find a corresponding node in a parse tree is presented. Next, several heuristics to match the lemma of an NE in Polish Wordnet and to choose the most probable semantic interpretation of ambiguous ones are suggested. The results of the mapping are evaluated.

1 Introduction

The ultimate goal of our research is to create a semantic valence dictionary and to establish automatic methods supporting achievement of this goal. Such a dictionary combines syntactic (by means of syntactic frames and slots) and semantic (by means of semantic roles and selectional preferences) information. Therefore, an important resource for our research is a semantically annotated treebank.

Named entities (NEs) play an important role in natural language texts and they occur quite frequently in them. Therefore, the methods of identifying NEs in texts is a vital part of NLP. However, named entities do not have meanings: one cannot say that *Warsaw, Berlin* or *London* means a city, they are cities. Nevertheless, named entities can be in a way semantically interpreted: even though they do not have senses, they do have their *semantic types*.

During semantic annotation of a text, named entities are often ignored. However, as a consequence many sentences are not completely semantically interpreted, which causes a drastic reduction of the language material. This has negative consequences in automatic semantic preferences detection [1, 2, 3], diathesis alternation detection [4, 5] and semantic valence frame extraction [6].

Therefore, we decided to annotate named entities as a preprocessing phase of a complete semantic annotation of treebank *Składnica*.

Our task is quite untypical for the community of named entities, mainly devoted to named entities classification [7, 8] and recognition [9, 10, 11], whereas we deal with already identified and classified NEs.

M.A. Kłopotek et al. (Eds.): IIS 2013, LNCS 7912, pp. 92–105, 2013.

2   Data Resources

The presented work was based on three resources: National Corpus of Polish
(pl. *Narodowy Korpus Języka Polskiego*, NKJP), Polish Treebank *Składnica* and
Polish Wordnet *Słowosieć* (PLWN).

2.1   NKJP

The National Corpus of Polish (http://nkjp.pl) [12] is the largest text corpus of Polish annotated on several levels. In our work we use the one-million-
word manually annotated balanced subcorpus of NKJP. Its texts are annotated
linguistically at the following levels:

- segmentation into sentences and word-level tokens (called segments),
- morphosyntactic,
- syntactic [13],
- named entities,
- word senses (a little over 100 frequent and clearly ambiguous lexemes were
  annotated).

Technically, all kinds of annotation are encoded in XML, using mark-up
schemata based on TEI guidelines [14]. On morphosyntactic level, each token
has its unique identifier of the form morph_<p>.<s>-seg, where <p> is the number of a paragraph and <s> is the number of a token. This identifier is referred
to in the other levels of annotation.

On the named entities level, the following types and subtypes of NEs are
distinguished [15]:

- personal names
  - forename (e.g., *Lech*),
  - surname (e.g., *Wałęsa*),
  - nickname;
- names of organisations and institutions (e.g., *Uniwersytet Warszawski* 'Warsaw University');,
- geographical names (e.g., *Warta* river);,
- place names (referring to geopolitical entities)
  - bloc (e.g., *Unia Europejska* 'European Union'),
  - country (e.g., *Polska* 'Poland'),
  - region (e.g., *Wielkopolska*),
  - settlement (e.g., *Poznań*),
  - district (e.g., *Jeżyce*, a district of *Poznań*);
- basic temporal expressions;
- words related to (most often derived from) the above categories: relational
  adjectives (e.g., *poznański*), names of inhabitants (e.g., *Poznaniak*), both
  derived from *Poznań*, and organisation members (e.g., *gestapowiec* derived
  from *gestapo*—secret police of Nazi Germany).

```
<seg xml:id="named_1.28-s_n3">
  <fs type="named">
    <f name="type">
      <symbol value="geogName"/>
    </f>
    <f name="base">
      <string>ulica Piaskowa</string>
    </f>
  </fs>
  <ptr target="ann_morphosyntax.xml#morph_1.22-seg"/>
  <ptr target="ann_morphosyntax.xml#morph_1.25-seg"/>
</seg>
```

Fig. 1. Representation of a single named entity in NKJP

The XML representation of a name contains its lemma, semantic type and (optionally) subtype. For our goals it is important that the boundaries of an NE are marked as `ptr` links (recursively) targeted at subnames of compound named entities or at tokens of morphosyntactic level. For example, the representation of the NE *ulica Gdyńska w Koziegłowach* from sentence (1) targets at its subnames *ulica Gdyńska* and *Koziegłowy*, which in turn target at their elements on morphosyntactic level. The representation of the NE *ulica Gdyńska* (*Gdyńska street*) is presented in Fig. 1.

(1) *Pierwsza z wymienionych sygnalizacji pojawi   się u zbiegu*
     First   of listed   signaling   appear$_{FUT}$ self at junction
     ulic   Gdyńskiej   i   Piaskowej   w Koziegłowach.
     street$_{PL}$ STREET NAME *and* STREET NAME *in* VILLAGE NAME
     (*First of the mentioned traffic lights will appear at the crossroad of Gdyńska and Piaskowa streets at Koziegłowy.*)

(2) *Kolejna sygnalizacja pojawi   się u zbiegu*
     Next   signaling   appear$_{FUT}$ self at junction
     ulic   Okrężnej   i   Gdyńskiej.
     street$_{PL}$ STREET NAME *and* STREET NAME
     (*Next traffic lights will appear at the crossroad of Okrężna and Gdyńska streets.*)

2.2 Składnica

Składnica is a bank of constituency parse trees for Polish sentences taken from the balanced hand-annotated subcorpus of NKJP. To attain consistency of the treebank, a semi-automatic method was applied: trees were generated by an automatic parser[1] and then selected and validated by humans. The resulting version 0.5 of *Składnica* contains 7841 manually validated trees.

---

[1] *Świgra* parser [16] based on the revised version [17, 18] of metamorphosis grammar GFJP [19].

```
<node nid="59" from="9" to="10" subtrees="2" chosen="true">
    <nonterminal>
        <category>fpt</category>
    </nonterminal>
    <children rule="pt1" chosen="true">
        <child nid="60" from="9" to="10" head="true"/>
    </children>
</node>
<node nid="60" from="9" to="10" subtrees="2" chosen="true">
    <nonterminal>
        <category>formaprzym</category>
    </nonterminal>
    <children rule="n_pt1" chosen="true">
        <child nid="61" from="9" to="10" head="true"/>
    </children>
    <children rule="n_pt1">
        <child nid="62" from="9" to="10" head="true"/>
    </children>
</node>
<node nid="61" from="9" to="10" subtrees="1" chosen="true">
    <terminal token_id="morph_1.23-seg"
        interp_id="morph_1.23.2.1-msd" disamb="true" nps="false">
        <orth>Gdyńskiej</orth>
        <base>Gdyński</base>
        <f type="tag">adj:sg:gen:f:pos</f>
    </terminal>
</node>
<node nid="77" from="9" to="12" subtrees="4" chosen="true">
    <nonterminal>
        <category>fpt</category>
    </nonterminal>
    <children rule="ptsz3" chosen="true">
        <child nid="59" from="9" to="10" head="false"/>
        <child nid="63" from="10" to="11" head="true"/>
        <child nid="78" from="11" to="12" head="false"/>
    </children>
</node>
```

Fig. 2. A fragment of the representation of a sentence in *Składnica*

Parse trees are encoded in XML, each parse being stored in a separate file. Each tree node, terminal or nonterminal, is represented by means of an XML **node** element, having two attributes **from** and **to** determining the boundaries of the corresponding phrase. Terminals additionally contain a **token_id** attribute linking them with corresponding NKJP tokens. As a result, the first and last NKJP tokens of a phrase represented by a particular node can be determined. Nonterminal nodes contain sub-elements **children** pointing at child nodes of the node in the parse tree. The **head** attribute shows whether a child is a head of a phrase.

A fragment of the representation of sentence (1) in *Składnica* is shown in Fig. 2.

Fig. 3 (a) contains a subtree of the phrase *ulic Gdyńskiej i Piaskowej w Koziegłowach* (*Gdyńska and Piaskowa streets in Koziegłowy*) from sentence (1), whereas Fig. 3 (b) contains a subtree of the phrase *ulic Okrężnej i Gdyńskiej* from sentence (2). Thick gray shadows emphasising some branches in the tree show heads of phrases.

(a)   (b)

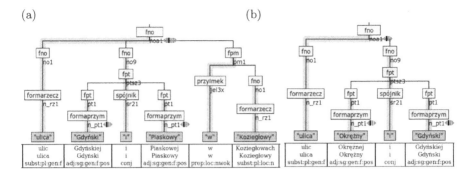

Fig. 3. Exemplary parse subtrees from *Składnica*

124	aparycja	1
136	apteka	1
139	arbiter	2
198	atrybut	3
199	atrybut	1
18382	atrybut	2
19474	arbiter	1

Fig. 4. The fragment of the table of triples ⟨identifier, lemma, meaning⟩ of PLWN 1.6

2.3   Polish Wordnet—*Słowosieć*

In contrast to NKJP, we decided to annotate named entities with very fine-grained semantic types represented by wordnet synsets. For this sake we used the Polish WordNet [20], called *Słowosieć* (English acronym PLWN).

PLWN is a network of lexical-semantic relations, an electronic thesaurus with a structure modelled on that of the Princeton WordNet and those constructed in the EuroWordNet project. Polish WordNet describes the meaning of a lexical unit comprising one or more words by placing this unit in a network representing relations such as synonymy, hypernymy, meronymy, etc.

A lexical unit [LU] is a string which has its morphosyntactic characteristics and a meaning as a whole. Therefore, it may be an idiom or even a collocation, but not a productive syntactic structure [21]. An LU is represented as a pair ⟨lemma, meaning⟩, the last being a natural number. Technically, any LU has also its unique numeric identifier. Each lexical unit belongs to a synset, which is a set of synonyms. Synsets have their unique numeric identifiers as well. A fragment of the table of triples ⟨identifier, lemma, meaning⟩ is presented in Fig. 4.

Named Entities in PlWN. Polish WordNet contains some number of named entities, selected rather randomly. They are represented by means of analogous lexical units as common words. LUs representing NEs are grouped in synsets as well, since the same object can be identified by means of several NEs (e.g., a full name and its acronym). The only difference is that they are connected by 'type' and 'instance' relations instead of 'hypernym' and 'hyponym'.

The representation of NEs in PLWN is far unsatisfactory. Therefore, a table of names was created, in which a list of semantic types represented by PLWN synset identifiers is assigned to every NE lemma. The order of synsets in a list reflects their preference.

3   A Method of Mapping

Differences in the representation of named entities in NKJP and *Składnica* influence the method and scope of their conversion. The main difference lies in the way of representing information itself. In *Składnica*, each sentence is stored in separate XML file; in NKJP a single XML file contains a whole document divided into paragraphs and sentences. NKJP representation is linear, i.e., a sentence is a sequence of tokens; *Składnica* contains parse trees. On the other hand, NKJP has mechanisms for representing discontinuous phenomena which are ignored in *Składnica*.

Since the named entities are identified and interpreted in NKJP and *Składnica* contains complete parses of sentences, the method is strongly resource-dependent but completely language independent.

In order to map named entities from NKJP to *Składnica*, we have to perform two subtasks:

1. Identify a node representing a particular NE in the parse tree of a sentence,
2. Find a fine-grained PLWN-based semantic type of the NE.

These two subtasks are completely independent.

3.1   Identifying a Phrase in a Parse

Named entities are often multi-word units, and their semantic interpretation is often not compositional. Because of that we decided to ascribe the semantic type of an NE to the lowest corresponding nonterminal in a parse tree. In the case of single-word named entities, they are nodes having category formarzecz (nounform) for noun names and category formaprzym (adjform) for adjective names.

The method uses the fact that each terminal in *Składnica* contains information which NKJP token it represents, hence we can assign corresponding from and to attributes to each token.

NKJP NEs are sets of tokens which have identifiers that can be numerically ordered. Thus, we can find the first and last token of any NE. The from attribute of the first token and the to attribute of the last token determine from and to attributes of the whole NE. This enables us to link every NE with a corresponding node in a parse tree, on condition that the NE is represented in *Składnica* as a separate phrase.

This is however not always the case. Observe that neither *ulica Gdyńska* (*Gdyńska street*) nor *ulica Piaskowa* (*Piaskowa street*) from sentence (1) have a corresponding subtree in the parse (see Fig. 3 (a)). On the other hand, *ulica Gdyńska* from sentence (2) was mapped to the whole phrase *ulic Okrężnej i Gdyńskiej* (*Okrężna and Gdyńska streets*), whereas *ulica Okrężna* (*Okrężna street*) obtained no mapping. The reason is that *ulic* is the first token, whereas *Gdyńskiej* is the last token of both NE *ulica Gdyńska* and phrase *ulic Okrężnej i Gdyńskiej*. The above is the consequence of differences in the representation of various units in both solutions and cannot be overcome in any way.

3.2 Finding a PlWN Semantic Interpretation

Finding the semantic type for a named entity seems to be an easy task. Named entities are lemmatised in NKJP. Therefore, the only thing to do should be finding it in PLWN itself or in table of names and copying the corresponding unit or type. Unfortunately, many NEs are absent in both resources on one hand, and on the other hand some names are ambiguous. Therefore, we should first find a corresponding lemma, and then disambiguate it.

Finding the Lemma of an NE. In order to find the most likely lemma for an NE absent in our resources, the following heuristics were implemented:

1. change of the case:
    - first letter to upper case (*lis* to *Lis*)[2],
    - all letters to upper case (*bmw* to *BMW*),
    - all letters to lower case (*BANK* to *bank*),
    - all letters but the first to lower case (*JAWORSKI* to *Jaworski*);
2. changing a female form of a surname to the male form[3];
3. choosing the head of a phrase;
4. heuristics 1 and 2 applied together;
5. heuristics 1 and 3 applied together.

The heuristics are applied in the above order; finding a match terminates the procedure. The need for using the changing case heuristics is caused by the fact that lemmatising in NKJP is not consistent w.r.t. case.

Surnames are the largest group in the table of names, they constitute above 50% of all names. They are the largest set of names in NKJP as well. The characteristic feature of Polish, similarly as other Slavic languages, is the existence of female forms of surnames. The first group of such surnames are forms ending with *-cka, -dzka, -ska* (*Lipnicka, Gilowska*), derived from male forms ending with *-cki, -dzki, -ski* (*Lipnicki, Gilowski*). Such forms are completely regular. The second group are forms ending with *-owa, -ówna* (*Boryczkowa, Florczakowa, Gawlikowa, Skowronówna*) derived from male forms ending with a consonant (*Florczak, Gawlik, Skowron*) or with *-o* preceded by a consonant (*Boryczko*). Such derivatives are not as regular as the previous ones, but they are rather

---

[2] Lis is an example of surname being also a common word meaning *fox*.
[3] Only male forms of surnames are represented in the table of names.

rare in contemporary Polish. The third group are surnames having adjectival inflection (*Cicha, Dymna, Konieczna*).

The most important heuristics in the process of matching a lemma in PLWN to a named entity is the head heuristics. The important feature of named entities is that they are often multi-word units. Some of them are represented directly in PLWN or in the table of names. Usually, they are semantically non-compositional. Most of them are geographic names (cities *Los Angeles, Rio de Janeiro, Góra Kalwaria*, countries *New Zealand*, rivers *Rio Grande*), but also surnames (*ben Laden, di Palma*), companies (*Canal Plus*) or even political parties (*Platforma Obywatelska*, literally *Citizen Platform*). Nevertheless, many named entities, especially names of firms and institutions, are semantically compositional. For such names, the interpretation of the head (usually a common word) of a corresponding phrase already interprets the name as a whole. This concerns factories (*Warszawska Fabryka Dźwigów—Warsaw Lift Factory*), schools, universities (*Uniwersytet Warszawski—Warsaw University*), banks (*Wielkopolski Bank Kredytowy— Credit Bank of Wielkopolska*), ministries (*Ministerstwo Rolnictwa—Ministry of Agriculture*) etc., etc. This also concerns some geographic names, e.g., names of streets often contain the word *ulica* or its abbreviation *ul.*

In order to implement the head heuristic for mapping named entities from NKJP to *Składnica* we use the fact that each phrase in *Składnica* has its head marked. Actually, it only shows which child of a node is its head child. Nevertheless, it is easy to link the head terminal descendant to each nonterminal node by a simple recursive procedure. The lemma of that head terminal descendant is then identified in PLWN or the table of names.

Disambiguation. Quite a lot of named entities are ambiguous. For instance, *Mars* denotes a planet, a Roman god of war and a chocolate bar, *Alberta* is a female name, a lake and a Canadian province. On the other hand, the common word *szkoła* (*school*) being a lemma of head terminal descendant of many particular school names has 10 lexical units in PLWN. Such names need to be disambiguated.

We do not apply any elaborated WSD algorithm [22]. Instead, we used information about NKJP type and subtype of each NE (cf. section 2.1). We assigned a list of PLWN-based semantic types (synset's identifiers used in the table of names) to each NKJP type and subtype. The length of these lists varies a lot, see Table 1 (columns denoted 'Syns').

The set of senses (corresponding synset identifiers) of each named entity was intersected with the list of synsets assigned to its NKJP type and subtype. In the case of NEs present in PLWN itself, all the hypernyms were considered as well. If the resulting set was empty, the whole set of senses was taken into consideration.

For the resulting set of senses (lexical units for NEs present in PLWN itself or synsets for NEs considered in the table of names), the variation of *the most*

Table 1. The number of PLWN synsets assigned to particular NKJP types and subtypes and the number of mapped NEs of that types

geogName	orgName	persName		placeName		time
Syns Freq	Syns Freq		Syns Freq		Syns Freq	Syns Freq
23 268	55 683		89 1915		1 1233	8 29
		addName	1 81	bloc	1 9	
		forename	2 759	country	3 553	
		surname	1 721	district	2 19	
				region	11 38	
				settlement	5 587	

frequent sense heuristic [23, 22] was applied. This means the lowest sense number for NEs present in PLWN and the first synset identifier for NEs considered in the table of names.

4   Evaluation of Automatic Mapping of Named Entities

The method of automatic mapping of named entities from NKJP to *Składnica* presented above was applied to *Składnica 0.5* and PLWN 1.6. From among 4473 NEs present in NKJP sentences having a correct parse tree in *Składnica*, 4294 NEs (96%) were mapped to *Składnica*, i.e., the corresponding tree nodes were assigned to them. Fiasco of mapping of the remaining NEs was caused by differences between the range of the NE in NKJP and the boundaries of the corresponding phrase in *Składnica*. The resulting annotation was manually corrected and evaluated w.r.t. this correction. Among them, there were 473 adjective named entities that are not discussed in the present paper.

4.1   Manual Correction of Named Entities Annotation

The goal of the manual correction of NEs annotation in *Składnica* automatically mapped from NKJP was four-fold:

1. correcting heuristically chosen lemmas and PLWN-based semantic types of NEs,
2. establishing semantic types of NEs absent both in PLWN and in the table of names,
3. finding corresponding nodes for NEs ignored during the automatic procedure,
4. adding NEs ignored in NKJP.

The last two tasks were performed only if omitting given NE resulted in leaving uninterpreted words that cannot be correctly interpreted as common words.

The main task 1 was performed in the case when NEs were incorrectly annotated. If the correct unit or type existed, the choice was modified. Otherwise the corresponding semantic type was added. Differentiating these situations is important for two reasons. First, it influences evaluation. Second, it shows the

```
<named name_id="named_4.62-s_n2">
    <nambase>Wik</nambase>
    <nkjp_type type="geogName"/>
    <plwn_types part="whole" case_agreement="Full" polysemy="false">
        <type typid="n2-tv1" status="auto" chosen="false">
            <nbase>Wik</nbase>
            <plwntype>200001</plwntype>
        </type>
        <type typid="n2-tv2" status="added" chosen="true">
            <nbase>Wik</nbase>
            <plwntype>4267</plwntype>
        </type>
    </plwn_types>
</named>
```

Fig. 5. NE with added correct interpretation

lack of the corresponding NE in the table of names. An example of an NE with added interpretation is presented in Fig. 5. Task 2 is similar.

Realisation of task 3 led to assigning 15 subphrases and 28 superphrases of corresponding NEs, realisation of task 4 led to adding 122 NEs, 7 foreign expressions, 5 lexicalisations, 4 neologisms, 3 cases of metonymy and 1 dialectal expression.

4.2   Actual Evaluation

Evaluation concerns only NEs that were automatically mapped. Table 1 contains the number of mapped NEs w.r.t. their NKJP types and subtypes (columns denoted 'Freq'). The largest group of names are personal names (45%), geographical and place names constitute 35% of all names. For 493 of 3821 (13%) NEs the lemma matching procedure failed. For 56 of the remaining 3319 NEs there was not a correct interpretation among the suggested ones, hence the corresponding heuristics had no chance to work properly. On the other hand, 151 NEs were interpreted both in PLWN itself and in the table of names.

The number of detected female forms of surnames is 28.

The task 1 of manual correction consists in changing the automatic choice, which results in one false positive (the automatically chosen wrong interpretation) and one false negative (the different, manually chosen, proper interpretation). Therefore, the number of false positives and false negatives is equal, hence precision, recall and F-measure are equal as well. Actually, they equal correctness, since the number of true positives denotes the number of NEs annotated properly, whereas the number of false positives denotes the number of NEs annotated improperly.

Table 2. Evaluation of all named entities w.r.t. lemma matching heuristics

info	Full			AllLow			FirstUp			TOTAL		
	H	W	T	H	W	T	H	W	T	H	W	T
PLWN freq	429	940	1369	20	118	138	0	0	0	449	1058	1507
acc	93.9	98.0	95.9	90.7	95.8	95.3	—	—	—	93.8	97.5	95.8
corr	92.3	98.9	96.9	90.0	94.1	93.5	—	—	—	92.2	98.4	96.5
added	6	1	7	0	2	2	0	0	0	7	3	10
table freq	43	1762	1805	0	0	0	0	1	1	43	1764	1807
acc	100	99.6	99.6	—	—	—	—	100	100	100	99.6	99.6
corr	100	99.8	99.8	—	—	—	—	100	100	100	99.8	99.8
added	14	29	43	0	2	2	0	0	0	16	31	47
both freq	472	2702	3174	20	118	138	0	1	1	492	2822	3314
acc	94.2	99.0	97.7	90.7	95.8	95.2	—	100	100	94.1	98.7	97.5
corr	93.0	99.5	98.5	90.0	94.1	93.5	—	100	100	92.9	99.2	98.3
added	20	30	50	0	4	4	0	0	0	0	0	0

Table 2 shows the evaluation of all named entities w.r.t. lemma matching heuristics: case heuristics (Full means that the case of the NE lemma was not changed). Each corresponding column is divided into tree subcolumns w.r.t. head heuristics: H meaning that the head of NE was found in the resources, W meaning that an NE was interpreted as a whole and T for total figures. The 'freq' row shows how often a particular heuristic was applied. The 'acc' row contains the accuracy, whereas the 'corr' row includes the correctness calculated for NEs with a particular heuristics applied to find its lemma. Finally, the 'added' row sums up situations in which the lemma found in PLWN or in the table of names was not the actual lemma of an NE or it was not interpreted in the resource.

It is easy to notice that the case change heuristics was applied occasionally; whereas head heuristics is quite often. On the other hand, both lemma heuristics are much more often used to much lemma in PLWN than in the table of names. Obviously, the reason is that the table of names contains actual NEs' lemmas. The head heuristics could be applied if there exists a multi-word NE having its head being a single-word NE (e.g., villages *Bartodzieje, Bartodzieje Podleśne*, rivers *Nida, Czarna Nida*). In the case of PLWN, head heuristics is much more appropriate, as it was explained in section 3.2.

The evaluation shows that the proposed heuristics work properly: the total accuracy for all NEs is 97.5 whereas the total correctness is 98.3. The results are better for the table of names than for PLWN, the reason is that attempts to interpret named entities as common nouns often fail. It is not surprising that applying the heuristics lowers the figures. The results for ambiguous NEs presented in Fig. 3 are still really good. Note that accuracy better than correctness suggests that the task was hard (the level of ambiguity was high).

Table 3. Evaluation of ambiguous named entities w.r.t. lemma matching heuristics

	info	Full			AllLow			FirstUp			TOTAL		
		H	W	T	H	W	T	H	W	T	H	W	T
PLWN	freq	285	54	339	14	92	106	0	0	0	299	146	445
	acc	92.9	82.8	91.8	89.2	95.5	94.8	—	—	—	92.8	92.0	92.6
	corr	88.4	81.5	87.3	85.7	92.4	91.5	—	—	—	88.3	88.4	88.3
table	freq	11	115	126	0	0	0	0	1	1	11	116	127
	acc	100	96.9	97.2	—	—	—	—	100	100	100	96.9	97.2
	corr	100	96.5	96.8	—	—	—	—	100	100	100	96.6	96.9
both	freq	296	169	465	14	92	106	0	1	1	310	262	572
	acc	93.1	92.6	93.0	89.2	95.5	94.8	—	100	100	92.9	93.9	93.3
	corr	88.9	91.7	89.9	85.7	92.4	91.5	—	100	100	88.7	92.0	90.2

5 Conclusions and Future Work

The present paper reports on the task of mapping named entities annotation from NKJP corpus to *Składnica* treebank. Even though the method was elaborated for particular resources, the heuristics used to accomplish it can be applied for mapping semantic or named entities annotation between other corpora, especially when the target annotation schema is more fine-grained than the source one.

The result of the actual mapping performed on *Składnica* 0.5 are good, but there is still room for improvement. For instance, PLWN contains many single-letter LUs, such as vitamins (A, B, C, D, E, K) or chemical element symbols (H for hydrogen, O for oxygen, etc.). This led to misinterpreting initials represented by a letter in upper case followed by a dot. Their PLWN type shows clearly that this is a misinterpretation to be corrected. Second, when an attempt at matching lemma of an NE fails, the more coarse heuristics based on its NKJP type and subtype may be used, for instance person identified by their surname/forename for personal names, town as most often settlement etc.

Acknowledgements. This research is supported by the POIG.01.01.02-14-013/09 project which is co-financed by the European Union under the European Regional Development Fund.

References

[1] Agirre, E., Martinez, D.: Learning class-to-class selectional preferences. In: Proceedings of the Conference on Natural Language Learning, Toulouse, France, pp. 15–22 (2001)

[2] Brockmann, C., Lapata, M.: Evaluating and combining approaches to selectional preference acquisition. In: Proceedings of the 10th Conference of the European Chapter of the Association for Computational Linguistics (EACL 2003), Budapest, Hungary, pp. 27–34 (2003)

[3] Ribas, F.: An experiment on learning appropriate selectional restrictions from parsed corpus. In: Proceedings of the 15th International Conference on Computational Linguistics (COLING 1994), Kyoto, Japan, pp. 769–774 (1994)

[4] Lapata, M.: Acquiring lexical generalizations from corpora: a case study for diathesis alternations. In: Proceedings of the 37th Annual Meeting of the Association for Computational Linguistics (ACL 1999), College Park, MA, pp. 397–404 (1999)

[5] McCarthy, D.: Lexical Acquisition at the Syntax-Semantics Interface: Diathesis Alternations, Subcategorization Frames and Selectional Preferences. PhD thesis, University of Sussex (2001)

[6] Hajnicz, E.: Automatyczne tworzenie semantycznego słownika walencyjnego. Problemy Współczesnej Nauki. Teoria i Zastosowania: Inżynieria Lingwistyczna. Academic Publishing House Exit, Warsaw, Poland (2011)

[7] Cimiano, P., Völker, J.: Towards large-scale, open-domain and ontology-based named entity classification. In: Proceedings of the Recent Advances in Natural Language Processing (RANLP 2005), Borovets, Bulgaria, INCOMA Ltd., pp. 166–172 (2005)

[8] Fleischman, M., Hovy, E.: Fine grained classification of named entities. In: Proceedings of the 19th International Conference on Computational Linguistics (COLING 2002), Taipei, Taiwan, pp. 1–7 (2002)

[9] Cucchiarelli, A., Velardi, P.: Unsupervised named entity recognition using syntactic and semantic contextual evidence. Computational Linguistics 27(1), 123–131 (2001)

[10] Etzioni, O., Cafarella, M., Downey, D., Popescu, A.M., Shaked, T., Soderland, S., Weld, D.S., Yates, A.: Unsupervised named-entity extraction from the web: An experimental study. Artificial Intelligence 165(1), 91–134 (2005)

[11] Nadeau, D., Sekine, S.: A survey of named entity recognition and classification. Lingvisticae Investigationes 30(1), 3–26 (2007)

[12] Przepiórkowski, A., Górski, R.L., Łaziński, M., Pęzik, P.: Recent developments in the National Corpus of Polish. In: [24]

[13] Głowińska, K., Przepiórkowski, A.: The design of syntactic annotation levels in the National Corpus of Polish. In: [24]

[14] Przepiórkowski, A., Bański, P.: XML text interchange format in the National Corpus of Polish. In: Goźdź-Roszkowski, S. (ed.) Practical Applications in Language Corpora (PALC 2009), Frankfurt am Main, Peter Lang, pp. 55–65 (2009)

[15] Savary, A., Waszczuk, J., Przepiórkowski, A.: Towards the annotation of named entities in the National Corpus of Polish. In: [24]

[16] Woliński, M.: An efficient implementation of a large grammar of Polish. In: Vetulani, Z. (ed.) Proceedings of the 2nd Language & Technology Conference, Poznań, Poland, pp. 343–347 (2005)

[17] Świdziński, M., Woliński, M.: A new formal definition of Polish nominal phrases. In: Marciniak, M., Mykowiecka, A. (eds.) Aspects of Natural Language Processing. LNCS, vol. 5070, pp. 143–162. Springer, Heidelberg (2009)

[18] Świdziński, M., Woliński, M.: Towards a bank of constituent parse trees for polish. In: Sojka, P., Horák, A., Kopeček, I., Pala, K. (eds.) TSD 2010. LNCS, vol. 6231, pp. 197–204. Springer, Heidelberg (2010)

[19] Świdziński, M.: Gramatyka formalna języka polskiego. Rozprawy Uniwersytetu Warszawskiego. Wydawnictwa Uniwersytetu Warszawskiego, Warsaw, Poland (1992)

[20] Piasecki, M., Szpakowicz, S., Broda, B.: A Wordnet from the Ground Up. Oficyna Wydawnicza Politechniki Wrocławskiej, Wrocław, Poland (2009)

[21] Derwojedowa, M., Piasecki, M., Szpakowicz, S., Zawisławska, M., Broda, B.: Words, concepts and relations in the construction of Polish WordNet. In: Tanacs, A., Csendes, D., Vincze, V., Fellbaum, C., Vossen, P. (eds.) Proceedings of the Global WordNet Conference, Seged, Hungary, pp. 162–177 (2008)

[22] Agirre, E., Edmonds, P. (eds.): Word Sense Disambiguation. Algorithms and Applications. Text, Speech and Language Technology, vol. 33. Springer, Dordrecht (2006)

[23] Gale, W., Church, K., Yarowsky, D.: Estimating upper and lower bounds on the performance of word-sense disambiguation programs. In: Proceedings of the 30th Annual Meeting of the Association for Computational Linguistics (ACL 1992), Newark, DL, pp. 249–256 (1992)

[24] Proceedings of the 7th International Conference on Language Resources and Evaluation (LREC 2010), Valetta, Malta, ELRA (2010)

Automatic Detection of Annotation Errors in Polish-Language Corpora

Łukasz Kobyliński

Institute of Computer Science, Polish Academy of Sciences,
ul. Jana Kazimierza 5, 01-248 Warszawa, Poland
lkobylinski@ipipan.waw.pl

Abstract. In this article we propose an extension to the variation n-gram based method of detecting annotation errors. We also show an approach to finding anomalies in the morphosyntactic annotation layer by using association rule discovery. As no research has previously been done in the field of morphosyntactic annotation error correction for Polish, we provide novel results based on experiments on the largest available Polish language corpus, the National Corpus of Polish (NCP). We also discuss the differences in the approaches used earlier for English language data and the method proposed in this article, taking into account the characteristics of Polish language.

1 Introduction

Annotated text corpora are one of the most important resources used in linguistics. Particularly, in computational linguistics, they serve as a basis for training automated taggers, as well as may be used as a source of information for speech recognition and machine translation systems. These corpora are either annotated manually by qualified linguists, or automatically, using taggers. Unfortunately even the most recent automated taggers are far from being 100% accurate. For example, in the case of part-of-speech tagging of Polish texts, the best-performing automated taggers achieve "weak correctness" (measured as the percent of words for which the sets of interpretations determined by the tagger and the gold standard are not disjoint) of between 91.06% (TaKIPI, [1]) to 92.44% (PANTERA, [2]). The reliability of annotation has a direct impact on the results of most other language-related research, as the methods used there usually rely on corpora and their annotation to perform their tasks. There is thus a burning need to improve the tagging accuracy, as each incorrectly annotated word potentially lowers the results of other, higher-level text processing techniques.

As manual correction of errors in the entire corpus is impractical, it is therefore necessary to employ an automated method of tagging error detection in the corpus to filter only potential mistakes and present them to human annotators.

2 Previous Work

Below we discuss some of the prominent representatives of the approaches previously proposed to the problem of annotation error detection.

M.A. Kłopotek et al. (Eds.): IIS 2013, LNCS 7912, pp. 106–111, 2013.

Dickinson and Meurers [3] show an effective approach to annotation error detection, which is based on the idea of finding "variation n-grams" in a corpus. Variation n-grams are sequences of tokens, which appear multiple times in the text and contain at least one word that has been assigned different annotation tags throughout the corpus. The word with ambiguous annotation is called the "variation nucleus" and is a potential place, where an annotation error might have occurred. The n-grams are discovered in the corpus using an incremental approach: at first unigrams are found and their position stored; next, each unigram is extended left or right by one word (if possible) and the resulting n-gram stored; the second step is repeated until no n-gram can be further extended. It is thus a method of finding the largest contexts of words, for which a tagging error might have been introduced during the annotation process.

A method of using association rules directly mined from the corpus data to find frequent relationships between the annotations of segments appearing in similar contexts has been proposed by [4]. Rules with high confidence and support have then been used to detect word occurrences, which violate these strong rules. The authors have concluded that the method achieved ca. 20% precision and that the limiting factor was the sparse annotation of the Czech PDT corpus.

There are no published works dealing with automated detection of morphosyntactic annotation errors in Polish language corpora. Having in mind the fact that very large corpus of Polish has just been released (the National Corpus of Polish [5] is a reference corpus of Polish language containing over fifteen hundred millions of words) and that they are used regularly in most other projects related to language processing, it is an important research problem to provide such a method, which would provide accurate results for Polish and to improve the approaches already described in the literature for other languages.

3   Variation N-grams in Annotation Error Detection

A variation n-gram ([3]) is an n-gram of words from a collection of texts, which contains one or more words annotated differently in another occurrence of the n-gram in the corpus. For example, the following is a variation 9-gram taken from the manually annotated 1 million word subcorpus of the NCP:

- Zamykam dyskusję. Do **głosowania** [głosować:ger:sg:n:imperf:n] nad uchwałą Senatu przystąpimy *jutro rano.*
  I close the discussion. We will proceed to **a vote** on the resolution of the Senate *tomorrow morning.*
- Zamykam dyskusję. Do **głosowania** [głosowanie:subst:sg:gen:n] nad uchwałą Senatu przystąpimy *w bloku głosowań.*
  I close the discussion. We will proceed to **a vote** on the resolution of the Senate *in a series of votings.*

The word "głosowania" in above example is annotated as a gerund in one occurrence, while in another occurrence it is tagged as a noun. Dickinson and Meurers call such a word a "variation nucleus", as it constitutes a variation n-gram, which indicates an existence of inconsistency in corpus annotation.

In the original formulation of the algorithm, a variation n-gram is created by first finding words in a corpus, which have exactly the same orthographic form, but different annotation. Such unigrams are then extended to neighboring words, if their orthographic form appears in more than one fragment. Application of this method to the manually annotated 1 million subcorpus of the NCP resulted in finding variation n-grams of length up to 67. Intuitively, longer variation n-grams, representing more similar contexts with annotation anomaly, are the most promising candidates for annotation errors. Unfortunately, the vast majority of unique n-grams found was not longer than 6 words. Unique n-grams are understood as n-grams, which are not contained by any longer n-gram discovered.

To evaluate the actual accuracy of the method, we have firstly prepared a list of annotation errors spotted and corrected manually in the corpus by a trained linguist. In course of his work the linguist corrected 2 692 mistakes in the corpus, of which 1 332 corrections considered the morphosyntactic annotation layer. We have used this information to estimate the recall of the approach, understood as the fraction of previously found annotation mistakes in the corpus, which were also detected by the automatic method. Table 1 presents the number of manually corrected segments, which have also been detected by the variation n-gram approach.

Table 1. Errors detected automatically vs errors corrected manually in the corpus; minN – minimum length of variation n-grams that were inspected, TP – true positives (among the 1 332 manual corrections), FP – false positives, F – value of the F measure

minN	suspicious segments	TP	FP	precision	recall	F
3	54970	398	38	0.72%	29.88%	1.41%
4	10448	97	3	0.93%	7.28%	1.65%
5	2513	24	0	0.96%	1.80%	1.25%
6	873	12	0	1.37%	0.90%	1.09%

We have also performed a direct evaluation of the precision of the method, by inspecting manually the list of possible annotation mistakes produced by the algorithm. The results of such an experiment are presented in Table 2.

The previously stated intuition that longer n-grams have a much greater probability of indicating an actual annotation error is clearly backed by the experimental data, as precision of variation n-grams longer than 10 surpasses 70%, while global average was 52.55%. Another intuition, suggested by the authors of [3], is that variation nuclei appearing on a verge of a variation n-gram are usually not an annotation error, as the context is different on that side of the n-gram. We have repeated such an experiment, including only non-verge variation n-grams and the results show an increase in precision of the method, but at a cost of lower recall (see Table 3).

Table 2. Manual verification of the list of errors detected automatically; N - length of variation n-grams, verified – number of manually verified contexts, errors – number of actual annotation errors

N	suspicious contexts	verified	errors	precision
4	1192	19	10	52.63%
5	373	9	5	55.56%
6	104	21	9	42.86%
7	32	16	11	68.75%
8	24	15	5	33.33%
9	23	20	6	30.00%
>=10	37	37	26	70.27%
	1785	137	72	52.55%

Table 3. Errors detected automatically using the non-fringe heuristic vs errors corrected manually in the corpus

minN	segments	TP	FP	precision	recall	F
3	18855	203	10	1.08%	15.24%	2.01%
4	4870	73	2	1.50%	5.48%	2.35%
5	1605	23	0	1.43%	1.73%	1.57%
6	678	11	0	1.62%	0.83%	1.09%

4   Increasing Recall of the N-gram Detector

Experiments with the original annotation error detection method proposed by [3] have shown a difficulty in the direct application of the approach to Polish language texts. The number of discovered variation n-grams in corpora of similar sizes is much lower for Polish than it is for English. As Polish is inflectional, the number of n-grams that can be built on the basis of orthographic word forms is far more limited than for English. It thus possible to achieve similar precision ratio as for English, but the number of detected suspicious contexts and consequently the (estimated) recall is much lower. Based on the original variation n-gram method, here we propose modifications to increase the recall of the approach and make the algorithm more suitable for inflectional languages.

Firstly, we have experimented with generalization of certain word types, by eliminating the need of two words to have exactly the same orthographic form to be included in an n-gram. For example, in case of punctuation, abbreviations and numbers the exact word form used should not differentiate two similar contexts. Table 4 shows the results of experiments, in which n-grams have been extended to neighboring words of such types, regardless of their orthographic form (e.g. an n-gram has been extended to include a comma, even if in another context a period was used in that place).

Secondly, we have experimented with building variation n-grams based solely on the part-of-speech tags of words, ignoring their orthographic form. In such a scenario we assume that similar sequences of POS tags represent contexts, having similar grammatical structure. Table 5 presents the results of error detection

Table 4. Errors detected automatically vs errors corrected manually in the corpus; orthographic form of *interp, brev, num, numcol* types ignored

minN	segments	TP	FP	precision	recall	F
4	8939	90	2	1.01%	6.76%	1.75%
5	2878	32	0	1.11%	2.40%	1.52%
6	1107	16	0	1.45%	1.20%	1.31%

using that approach. Clearly, the recall of the method has successfully been increased, at a cost of lower precision.

Table 5. Errors detected automatically vs errors corrected manually in the corpus; n-grams extended based on their POS tags

minN	segments	TP	FP	precision	recall	F
4	28499	257	30	0.90%	19.29%	1.72%
5	9547	98	9	1.03%	7.36%	1.80%
6	2762	36	0	1.30%	2.70%	1.76%

5 Detecting Anomalies in Annotation Using Association Rules

Association rule mining has been proposed in [6], originally as a method for market basket analysis. This knowledge representation method focuses on showing frequent co-occurrences of attribute values in data. Based on the original idea of [4], we have used association rule mining to identify relationships in corpus morphosyntactic annotation, which were of very high confidence, but still not equal to 100%. This allowed us to detect word-annotation pairs, which were suspiciously rare and therefore could constitute an error. We have mined rules having support greater or equal to 0.1% and confidence above 99% in a random sample of corpus contexts. We have then transformed the discovered rules into search queries, allowing us to identify instances, which did not support the 99% confident rules. Given a rule of the form:

$$attr_1, \ldots, attr_n \longrightarrow attr_{n+1}, \ldots, attr_m,$$

we have formed a search query as follows:

$$attr_1 \ \& \ \ldots \ \& \ attr_n \ \& \ !attr_{n+1} \ \& \ \ldots \ \& \ !attr_m.$$

Below we give an example of several rules mined from the corpus and associated search queries, along with the number of actual errors identified by the query. Numbers in parenthesis indicate the number of segments that supported the rule antecedent / rule consequent.

- base=my $\longrightarrow$ ctag=ppron12 (276/274)
  - query [base=my&pos!=ppron12] returns 1 error in 7 results,
- ctag=aglt $\longrightarrow$ base=być (290/288)
  - query [pos=aglt&base!=być] returns 10 errors in 24 results,
- base=no msd=[null] $\longrightarrow$ ctag=qub (446/442)
  - query [base=no&pos!=qub] returns 2 errors in 13 results,
- base=tak ctag=adv $\longrightarrow$ msd=pos (118/117)
  - query [base=tak&pos=adv&degree!=pos] returns 27 errors in 27 results.

6 Conclusions and Future Work

We have presented experimental results of two approaches to automatic detection of annotation errors applied to the National Corpus of Polish, a reference linguistic resource for Polish. We have successfully adapted methods proposed earlier for English language corpora to inflectional Polish language and proposed extensions, which may be used to increase recall of the detector, regardless of the target language. Described approaches to automatic detection of annotation errors proved to reduce the amount of time needed to identify mistakes and facilitated correction of a large corpus, namely the National Corpus of Polish.

In the future, we plan to combine various detection methods to further improve both the precision and recall of the system. As each of the approaches may identify different contexts as potentially erroneous, aggregating their results is a promising direction of further work.

Acknowledgements. The author would like to thank Łukasz Szałkiewicz for his linguistic work and Michał Lenart for sharing algorithm implementations. The work has been funded by the National Science Centre project number DEC-2011/01/N/ST6/01107.

References

1. Piasecki, M.: Polish tagger TaKIPI: Rule based construction and optimisation. Task Quarterly 11(1-2), 151–167 (2007)
2. Acedański, S.: A morphosyntactic brill tagger for inflectional languages. In: Loftsson, H., Rögnvaldsson, E., Helgadóttir, S. (eds.) IceTAL 2010. LNCS, vol. 6233, pp. 3–14. Springer, Heidelberg (2010)
3. Dickinson, M., Meurers, D.: Detecting errors in part-of-speech annotation. In: Proceedings of the 10th Conference of the European Chapter of the Association for Computational Linguistics (EACL 2003), Budapest, Hungary (2003)
4. Novák, V., Razímová, M.: Unsupervised detection of annotation inconsistencies using apriori algorithm. In: Proceedings of the Third Linguistic Annotation Workshop, Suntec, Singapore, pp. 138–141. Association for Computational Linguistics (August 2009)
5. Przepiórkowski, A., Bańko, M., Górski, R.L., Lewandowska-Tomaszczyk, B. (eds.): Narodowy Korpus Języka Polskiego. Wydawnictwo Naukowe PWN, Warsaw (2012)
6. Agrawal, R., Imielinski, T., Swami, A.N.: Mining association rules between sets of items in large databases. In: Proceedings of the ACM SIGMOD International Conference on Management of Data, Washington, D.C., USA, pp. 207–216 (May 1993)

Unsupervised Induction of Persian Semantic Verb Classes Based on Syntactic Information

Maryam Aminian[1], Mohammad Sadegh Rasooli[2], and Hossein Sameti[1]

[1] Department of Computer Engineering,
Sharif University of Technology, Tehran, Iran
`maminian@ce.sharif.edu, sameti@sharif.edu`
[2] Department of Computer Science, Columbia University, New York, NY, USA
`rasooli@cs.columbia.edu`

Abstract. Automatic induction of semantic verb classes is one of the most challenging tasks in computational lexical semantics with a wide variety of applications in natural language processing. The large number of Persian speakers and the lack of such semantic classes for Persian verbs have motivated us to use unsupervised algorithms for Persian verb clustering. In this paper, we have done experiments on inducing the semantic classes of Persian verbs based on Levin's theory for verb classes. Syntactic information extracted from dependency trees is used as base features for clustering the verbs. Since there has been no manual classification of Persian verbs prior to this paper, we have prepared a manual classification of 265 verbs into 43 semantic classes. We show that spectral clustering algorithm outperforms KMeans and improves on the baseline algorithm with about 17% in Fmeasure and 0.13 in Rand index.

1 Introduction

Persian is an Indo-European language as the first language by more than 100 million speakers in Iran, Afghanistan, Tajikestan, and a few other countries. Several challenges such as free order of words, colloquial texts, pro-drop and complex inflections [1] in addition to the lack of efficient annotated linguistic data have made processing of Persian texts very hard. As an instance, there are more than 100 verb conjugates and 2800 noun declensions for some word forms in Persian [2], some words in the Persian language do not have a clear word category (i.e. lexical category mismatching) [3] and so many compound verbs (complex predicates) can be separable (i.e. the non-verbal element can have a distance from the position of the light verb) [4]. Despite the high importance of computational lexical semantics, there have not been much considerable researches on this area for the Persian language.

Many verbs have similar semantic components, e.g. *walk* and *run* are two verbs that have similar meanings. In both, an actor moves from a source to a location. In addition to the semantic redundancy, knowing the similar frequent words of a rare word (i.e. having a prior knowledge of lexical classes) may help overcome data sparsness. This seems an interesting issue for researchers as a

M.A. Kłopotek et al. (Eds.): IIS 2013, LNCS 7912, pp. 112–124, 2013.

means to improve common natural language processing tasks such as parsing [5], word sense disambiguation [6], subcategorization acquisition [7] and semantic role labeling [8].

The large amount of the applications of lexical classification has lead to the popularity of the task in natural language processing. In addition to the expenses of manually classifying words, the existing available lexical resources which are manually constructed lack useful statistical information. While the existing manually constructed lexicons are hard to be extended, automatic classification is cost-effective and provides statistical information as a consequence of the classification process. Unsupervised clustering methods are more popular than other machine learning techniques for lexical classification. These algorithms do not require any annotated corpora. Moreover, unsupervised methods can be used as a starting point for manual annotation in order to speed up the annotation process.

Among all word categories, verbs usually act as the main part of the sentence and provide useful information about the meaning and structure of the whole sentence. The centrality of verbs in linguistic approaches such as dependency grammar makes the task of semantic classification of verbs very important. Manual classifications of semantic verb classes exist for several languages. Levin verb taxonomy [9] is one of these lexical semantics resources that is mostly used by researchers. It is based on the hypothesis that there is a tight relation between the verb meaning and its alternation behavior which is captured by diathesis alternation. Diathesis alternation is an alternation in the expression of the arguments of a verb, such as different mappings between transitive and intransitive aspects. Based on Levin's idea, verbs that are in the same semantic classes are expected to have similar syntactic behaviors. Since recognizing the syntactic behavior of verbs is a challenging task and has many ambiguities, the syntactic behavior of verbs is captured by just finding the subcategorization frames in so many studies just for the sake of simplicity. As an example, consider two Persian verbs "صحبت کردن" (to speak) and "فرار کردن" (to escape) which govern prepositions "با" (with) and "از، به" (from, to) respectively. While these verbs have similar syntactic behavior, they do not belong to the same semantic clusters. However, considering the lexical features (such as prepositions), the ambiguity may decrease.

To the best of our knowledge, no comparable Persian verb classification study has been reported so far. Therefore, such a research can fill gaps in lexical knowledge for Persian. In this paper, we use diathesis alternation as an approach to characterize verb behavior. Subcategorization frames for each verb is extracted from the Persian Dependency Treebank [10]. Two clustering algorithms (KMeans [11] and Spectral Clustering [12]) are used for the clustering task. Evaluation is done based on the manual conversion of German verb classes in [13] to Persian by considering Persian verbs in the Persian verb valency lexicon [14]. This type of conversion is done for the first time in the Persian language by the authors of this paper[1]. The evaluation results show an improvement on the baseline methods.

The remainder of the paper is as follows. In Sect. 2, previous studies on verb classification is reviewed. In Sect. 3, we present a brief introduction to the clustering algorithms used in the paper. Sect. 4 describes the procedure of evaluation data preparation and experimental results. In Sect. 5, mathematical analysis and evaluation are presented. In the last Section, conclusions are made.

2   Related Work

One of the first considerable studies on verb clustering is proposed by Schulte im Walde [15] for German verbs. In that work, subcategorization frame acquisition is done by a robust statistical head-lexicalized parser. Lexical heads for each syntactic complement is included in the extracted frames, e.g. each prepositional phrase is accompanied by the lexical prepositional head plus the head noun of the subordinated noun phrase. Lexical heads are used to extract selectional preferences for each verb argument. Selectional preferences are the amount of information that a verb provides about its semantic arguments [16]. In [15], selectional preferences extraction is done using the co-occurrence of verbs with their WordNet synsets for calculating the probability of WordNet conceptual classes for each verb-frame type. Clustering is done in two ways: I) a pairwise clustering algorithm is initialized by assuming each data point as a singleton cluster and clusters are merged by measuring the distance between clusters; and II) unsupervised latent class analysis where a verb cluster is assumed as a latent variable that is to be optimized during E and M steps of the EM algorithm.

Since subcategorization frames are the main features used for verb clustering, the clustering accuracy is directly affected by the subcatgorization frame acquisition process [13]. In [17], spectral clustering is used in order to transform high dimensional original data points to a set of orthogonal eigen vectors. This transformation reduces the risk of being trapped in local optima which may happen in certain classic algorithms such as KMeans. In [17], 38 subcategorization frames are extracted from a subcategorization lexicon and information about prepositional phrases for each verb are used as the feature vectors. In [18], attempts are made to cluster 57 German verbs into 14 classes utilized by subcategorization frame acquisition using the lexicalized form of a probabilistic grammar for German which is trained on a large corpus with KMeans algorithm. In [19,20], the effect of prepositional information is studied. In those studies, results show that prepositional information may improve verb clustering. Furthermore, the number of prepositions that are used are not significantly effective.

As mentioned earlier in this paper, in Levin's idea, verbs in the same semantic clusters are expected to have similar syntactic behavior while verbs with similar syntactic features may not be categorized similarly. Therefore, with subcategorizaion frames, the semantic classes of verbs can not be distinguished completely.

---

[1] The dataset is available from
http://www.cs.columbia.edu/~rasooli/index_files/pvc.tar.gz

Sun and Korhonen [21] showed that selectional preferences for different arguments such as *subject* and *object* in addition to the prepositional information improve the verb clustering accuracy. This improvement is not significantly better than using prepositional information alone.

Polysemous verbs (i.e., verbs that have multiple meanings) are one of the challenging problems in verb clustering. Several works consider the most frequent sense of verbs as the dominant sense and ignore polysemy. A number of other researches have tried to overcome this connivance [22,23]. In [22], a generative model and in [23], the information bottleneck as an iterative soft clustering method based on information theoretic grounds, are used to overcome the verb polysemy.

Sun et al. [24] employed hierarchical graph factorization clustering (HGFC) as a graph-based probabilistic clustering algorithm. The method had been applied to the identification of social network communities prior to this study and Vlachos et al. used it for natural language processing tasks for the first time. Results show that this algorithm outperforms other hierarchal clustering algorithms such as AGG for verb clustering. Bayesian nonparametric models based on Dirichlet process mixture models (DPMM) are also used for lexical semantic classification of verbs [25]. In DPMM, unlike other clustering methods, there is no need to specify the number of target clusters.

The only study about computational semantics for Persian verbs that we are aware is done by Saeedi and Faili [26] which is about argument classification of Persian verbs using syntactic frames (valency structures) and chunks.

3   Semantic Clustering of Persian Verbs

3.1   Persian Lexical-Semantic Verb Classes

Since no semantic verb classification exists for Persian verbs, we have constructed an evaluation data in a manual process. We used Levin style verb classes used in [13] where 168 German verbs were manually classified into 43 semantic verb classes based on their common semantic properties. We translated the equivalent English verbs of those verbs using Google translate API to Persian. There were a number of polysemous verbs among the translations prepared by Google. To overcome the problem of polysemy, we assigned each verb to the class that has the dominant sense of that verb. We ignored the translations that do not act as verbs in Persian and tried to substitute them manually with their equivalent Persian verbs. Therefore, some clusters were removed in this process because their members did not have proper equivalent Persian verbs. Semantic classes were given in two levels including coarse and fine labels; however we combined fine labels and formed them as a coarse class to increase classification generality.

We only consider verbs in the Valency Lexicon for Persian verbs [14] to construct the gold verb classes and ignore irrelevant verbs. In the conversion process, the main question is whether transferring verb classes to Persian preserves the verb syntactic-semantic relations or not. Our linguistic investigation confirms the

hypothesis that semantic relations are not transferred completely after translation, therefore some clusters are modified manually in order to integrate verb
classes. This modification is done based on semantic intuitions completely and is
not affected by the facts about the syntactic behavior of verbs. The final Persian
verb classes consist of 265 verbs that are classified into 30 coarse grained (43 fine
grained) classes. We use the coarse grained classes in our experiments. Details
about the classes are shown in Table 1.

3.2   Empirical Distribution for Persian Verbs

Verbs are represented by distributional vectors with values acquired from the
Persian Dependency Treebank [10]. The value of each feature in the feature vector represents the probability of each syntactic frame that is obtained from the
syntactic relations in the Persian Dependency Treebank. Base structures show all
possible combinations of syntactic complements that can generate all sentences
of the language. Table 2 represents these structures in Persian. Possible complements in these frames include nine kinds of syntactic complements for verbs in
Persian which Rasooli et al. [14] enumerate: *subject* (SBJ), *object* (OBJ), *prepositional complement* (VPP), *Ezafe complement* (EZC), *complement clause* (VCL),
Mosnad (MOS), *Tamiz* (TAM), *adverbial complement* (ADVC), and *second object* (OBJ2). Among the 28 Persian base structures as syntactic frame types in
Persian, we consider only 25 structures and ignore the structure with the null
subject (obligatory absence of subject). Null subjects are rare in Persian and it
is hard to distinguish between pro-drops and null subjects. We extract features
in two levels:

1. *Frequency Distributions of Persian Verbs over 25 Subcategorization Frames.*
   For each verb (v_i), the empirical distribution of each frame (f) is obtained
   by $\frac{C(v_i, f)}{C(v_i)}$ where $C(v_i, f)$ is the joint frequency of a verb-frame couple and
   $C(v_i)$ is the total number of the specified verb in the corpus. We constrain
   our verb clustering task to the verbs that exist in the Persian verb valency
   lexicon [14] and among all verbs in the lexicon, we only consider verbs with
   a frequency higher than 100, leaving a final list of 653 verbs. Among the list,
   only 129 verbs exist in the semantic verb classes in Table 1. Therefore, we
   only consider 129 verbs for the clustering task.
2. *Information about Prepositions in Each Frame.* Since subcategorization frames
   can only capture pure syntactic information about the verb behavior, we attach information about the prepositions accompanied by each verb in special
   frame types to the verb feature vector. We capture all possible preposition
   combinations for Persian verbs using the Persian dependency trees and add
   them to the feature vector. The values of these new features are calculated
   by $\frac{C(v_i, pps)}{C(v_i)}$ in which $C(v_i, pps)$ is the joint frequency of each verb with the
   special preposition groups.

Table 1. Persian verb classes based on [13]. Some class labels include finer levels shown in sub-columns. *Eng. Trans.* refers to the English translation of the sample verbs. Only coarse grained classes are used in the experiment and evaluation. There are no verbs in some of the clusters; however we keep such clusters in the table in order to provide a comparative view with [13].

Class label			No.Mem.	Sample verb(s)	Eng. trans.
Aspect			12	آغاز کردن	start
Propositional Attitude			13	حدس زدن	guess
Desire	wish		3	امید بستن	hope
	need		0	-	-
Transfer of Possession	Obtaining		4	حاصل کردن	obtain
	Giving	Gift	10	اهدا کردن	present
		Supply	10	فرستادن	send
Manner of Motion	Locomotion		8	رفتن	go
	Rotation		4	چرخاندن	rotate
	Rush		3	شتافتن	hurry
	Vehicle		5	پریدن	fly
	Flotation		3	سریدن	glide
Emotion	Origin		2	رنجیدن	be annoyed
	Expression		8	ناله کردن	cry
	Objection		2	ترساندن	frighten
Facial Expression			4	لبخند زدن	smile
Perception			14	حس کردن	feel
Manner of Articulation			8	جیغ زدن	scream
Moaning			5	شکایت کردن	complain
Communication			11	حرف زدن	talk
Statement	Announcement		5	خبر کردن	announce
	Constitution		10	آراستن	arrange
	Promise		2	تضمین کردن	ensure
Observation			7	مشاهده کردن	observe
Description			7	ترجمه کردن	interpret
Presentation			6	نشان دادن	demonstrate
Speculation			4	اندیشیدن	think
Insistence			4	اصرار کردن	insist
Teaching			6	درس دادن	teach
Position	Be in Position		7	قرار دادن	set
	Bring into Position		8	دراز کشیدن	lie
Production			6	ساختن	produce
Renovation			9	پیراستن	decorate
Support			13	حمایت کردن	support
Quantum Change			9	کاهش دادن	diminish
Opening			5	گشادن	open
Existence			5	زیستن	live
Consumption			5	آشامیدن	drink
Elimination			8	حذف کردن	delete
Basis			0	-	-
Inference			4	نتیجه گرفتن	conclude
Result			0	-	-
Weather			6	باریدن	rain

Since the version of the Persian Dependency Treebank that is used in this paper has 25497 sentences[2] which seems insufficient for robust statistics, we have extended the treebank by automatically converting Bijankhan corpus [27] into a dependency treebank. After finding the sentence boundaries based on punctuation clues and refining unicode characters with Virastyar open source library [28][3], we have used a Persian verb analyzer [29][4] to preprocess the corpus. Finally, a trained MST parser [30] is run on Bijankhan corpus with sentences of the length less than or equal to 200. After attaching the automatically created dependency corpus with 354879 sentences to the original dependency treebank, a treebank with 381983 sentences is created.

Table 2. Possible sentence base structures in Persian [14]

Persian Sentence Base Structures	
||SBJ||	||SBJ,VPP,VPP||
||NULL-SBJ,VCL||	||SBJ,VPP,EZC||
||SBJ,OBJ||	||SBJ,VPP,ADVC||
||SBJ,VPP||	||SBJ,VPP,VCL||
||SBJ,EZC||	||SBJ,VPP,TAM||
||SBJ,VCL||	||SBJ,EZC,VCL||
||SBJ,MOS||	||NULL-SBJ,VCL,VPP||
||SBJ,ADVC||	||NULL-SBJ,OBJ,VPP,VPP||
||SBJ,OBJ,VPP||	||SBJ,VPP,VPP,ADVC||
||SBJ,OBJ,EZC||	||SBJ,EZC,ADVC||
||SBJ,OBJ,VCL||	||SBJ,OBJ,VPP,TAM||
||SBJ,OBJ,TAM||	||SBJ,OBJ,VPP,ADVC||
||SBJ,OBJ,MOS||	||SBJ,OBJ,VPP,OBJ2||
||SBJ,OBJ,ADVC||	||SBJ,VPP,VPP||

3.3 Clustering Algorithm and Evaluation Techniques

We employ two clustering algorithms in this paper: *KMeans* [11] and *spectral clustering* [12].

KMeans for Verb Clustering. Since KMeans is one of the best performed algorithms that has been used for the lexical-semantic verb clustering task, we use it for Persian verb clustering. KMeans is an unsupervised hard clustering method assigning n data objects to k clusters. In this algorithm, k verbs are

---

[2] The treebank is just a middle version of the main dependency treebank that was available during our experiments. The official version of the treebank is available at http://dadegan.ir/en

[3] The open source code is available at http://sourceforge.net/projects/virastyar/

[4] The source code is available at https://github.com/rasoolims/PersianVerbAnalyzer

selected as initial centroid of clusters randomly. Clusters are reorganized by assigning each verb to the closest centroids and by recalculating cluster centroids iteratively until meeting certain criteria. In our experiments, the algorithm iterates until certain number of iterations occurs. The number of semantic classes for verbs is chosen as the number of clusters in the KMeans algorithm.

Spectral Clustering Algorithm for Verb Clustering. Spectral clustering is the second clustering method used in this paper. Other multivariate clustering algorithms such as KMeans do not guarantee to reach the global optimum, specially in high dimensional spaces. Spectral methods, first reduce data dimension and then cluster data points by using a multivariate algorithm. The key steps of spectral clustering algorithm for a set of points $S = \{s_1, ..., s_n\}$ are:

1. Constructing the distance matrix $D \in \mathbb{R}^2$: We use Euclidean distance and Skew divergence as two different distance measures to construct D and investigate the effect of the distance measure in spectral clustering results. Since Lee [31] has shown that *Skew divergence* measure (cf. (1)) is the most effective measure for distributional similarity, we use this measure as a distance measure to construct distance matrix. In (1), α is a parameter close to 1 for controlling the smoothing rate. We set it to 0.9 following [31]. In (1), v and $\acute{v}$ are two feature vectors which v is smoothed with $\acute{v}$ and D is the *KL-divergence* measure.

$$D_{skew}(v, \acute{v}) = D(\acute{v} \parallel \alpha \cdot v + (1 - \alpha).\acute{v}) \tag{1}$$

2. Calculating affinity matrix A from D following (2) where σ^2 is a scaling parameter that controls the rate at which affinity drops with distance.

$$A_{ij} = \begin{cases} \exp(\frac{D_{ij}^2}{\sigma^2}) & \text{for } i \neq j, \\ 0 & \text{otherwise,} \end{cases} \tag{2}$$

3. Creating the matrix $L = D^{-\frac{1}{2}} A D^{-\frac{1}{2}}$ where D is the diagonal form of the distance matrix in which the (i, i)th element is the sum of elements in the $A's$ ith row.
4. Taking the eigen values and eigen vectors of L.
5. Finding the $\{x_1, ..., x_k\}$ k largest eigen vectors of L and making the matrix $X = [x_1, ..., x_n] \in \mathbb{R}^{n \times k}$. Ng et al. [32] show that usually k well separated clusters exist in a reduced dimension space. Hence, k is the number of classes in the gold standard and the number of selected eigen vectors is equal to the number of Persian verb classes in our task. We also use this approach to find the number of clusters. After normalizing each row in X to have a unit length which forms the matrix Y following (3), each row of Y is treated as a data point in the reduced dimension space $\mathbb{R}^k$.

$$Y_{ij} = \frac{X_{ij}}{(\sum_j X_{ij}^2)^{\frac{1}{2}}} \tag{3}$$

6. Clustering data points in the new dimension space using KMeans or other clustering algorithms. Eventually, the original data point s_i is assigned to cluster j if and only if the row i in the matrix X is assigned to the cluster j.

We test the clustering task for different values of σ between 0.01 to 0.09 in steps of 0.005 to choose the best solution since our experiments show that the results are degraded out of this range of σ. After transforming the data points to the reduced dimension space, Kmeans clustering is used to cluster data points.

4   Evaluation Metrics

Evaluation is done using four measures:

(I) *Modified purity (mPUR)*, which evaluates the mean precision of the clusters as shown in (4). Each cluster is associated with its prevalent class. The number of verbs in a cluster K that take this class is denoted by $n_{prevalent(K)}$. Singleton clusters are ignored by conditioning on $n_{prevalent(k_i)} > 2$.

$$mPUR = \frac{\sum_{n_{prevalent(k_i)}>2} n_{prevalent(k_i)}}{number\ of\ verbs} \tag{4}$$

(II) *weighted class accuracy (ACC)* which is shown in (5) and denotes the proportion of members of dominant clusters $DOM\text{-}CLUST_i$ within all of possible verb classes c_i.

$$ACC = \frac{\sum_{i=1}^{C} verbs\ in\ DOM\text{-}CLUST_i}{number\ of\ verbs} \tag{5}$$

The two measures, $mPUR$ and ACC, can be explained as precision and recall respectively [24] .

(III) *Fscore* that can be rewritten as the harmonic mean of precision and recall as in (6).

$$F = \frac{2 \cdot mPUR \cdot ACC}{mPUR + ACC} \tag{6}$$

(IV) *Adjusted Rand index* is another measure that is used to evaluate agreement vs. disagreement between clusters, cf. (7). The agreement between clustering results (C) and manual classification (M) is represented in a contingency matrix $C \times M : t_{ij}$ denotes the number of common verbs in clustering result C_i and manual class M_j. In (7), $t_{.i}$ and $t_{j.}$ represent the number of verbs in cluster C_i and manual class M_j respectively.

$$Rand_{adj}(C, M) = \frac{\sum_{ij} \binom{t_{ij}}{2} - \frac{\sum_i \binom{t_{i.}}{2} \sum_j \binom{t_{j.}}{2}}{\binom{n}{2}}}{\frac{1}{2}\left(\sum_i \binom{t_{i.}}{2} + \sum_j \binom{t_{j.}}{2}\right) - \frac{\sum_i \binom{t_{i.}}{2} \sum_j \binom{t_{j.}}{2}}{\binom{n}{2}}} \tag{7}$$

Table 3. Experimental results for semantic clustering of Persian verbs. *mPUR*, *ACC*, and *Rand_{adj}* represent *modified purity*, *accuracy*, and *adjusted Rand index* respectively.

		$mPUR$	ACC	$FScore$	$Rand_{adj}$
Random Basline		32.55	41.96	34.76	0.015
KMeans	SCFs	37.20	**58.14**	45.37	0.043
	SCFs+PPs	43.20	55.20	48.47	0.078
Spectral Clustering	SCFs (Euc.)	40.62	55.47	46.90	0.067
	SCFs (Skew)	41.40	57.03	47.98	0.067
	SCFs+PPs (Euc.)	41.93	57.26	48.41	**0.142**
	SCFs+PPs (Skew)	**45.97**	58.06	**51.31**	0.099

5 Experimental Results

We employ KMeans and spectral clustering algorithms for our verb clustering task. Verbs are represented by two levels of information. The first includes un-lexicalized syntactic information, captured by subcategorization frames and for the second level, the syntactic information in the first level is enriched by adding information about prepositions accompanied by verbs. We only consider verbs with a frequency higher than 100 in the Persian Dependency Treebank. This constraint results to 129 verbs.

We have initialized KMeans cluster centers with k randomly chosen data points. Euclidean distance is used as distance measure in the KMeans algorithm. Choosing the number of clusters as an input parameter for KMeans is done using a prior information about number of semantic classes in the gold data which is 28 classes. Table 3 shows experimental results. Evaluation is done using four evaluation measures mentioned in Sect. 4. Results of evaluation by each measure is reported for each clustering algorithm and feature set separately in Table 3 where *SCFs* and *PPs* show subcategorization frames and prepositional lexical head which are used as features to represent verbs respectively. In this paper, distance matrix construction in the first step of spectral clustering algorithm is done using two distance measures, *Euclidean distance (Euc.)* and *Skew divergence (Skew)* which is separated in the parenthesis. The first row of Table 3 refers to the experiment baseline which is obtained by assigning the verbs randomly to a cluster with the number between 1 and the number of gold classes.

6 Analysis and Conclusion

As a comparison, we can make the following observations according to the experimental results in Table 3. The first observation is the effect of using syntactic features to represent verb behavior. The comparison between the results and the baseline demonstrates that using purely syntactic features gives rise to the verb clustering task above the baseline. Although syntactic information seems to be the most informative features in the verb classification task, it is not sufficient to use them in isolation and selectional restrictions must be added to the syntactic information at both syntactic and semantic levels [33].

The second observation is the effect of lexical information. As shown in Table 3, both *Fscore* and *adjusted rand index* are improved by adding information about prepositions accompanied by verbs regardless of the clustering algorithm and distance measures used in it. This improvement indicates that prepositions have distinctive information for distinguishing semantic clusters of Persian verbs. In cases such as the example in Sect. 1, when lexical information about the prepositions are added to the features, the algorithm will be able to distinguish their semantic clusters correctly. The third observation is the effect of the clustering algorithm. Our experiments show that spectral clustering generally outperforms KMeans having similar feature sets.

The final observation is the effect of the distance measures. Results of spectral clustering with different distance measures indicate that distance matrix construction with Skew divergence achieve better results than Euclidean distance in the terms of *Fscore*. These results confirm arguments in [31] which stated that Skew divergence is the most effective measure for distributional vectors. On the other hand, with Euclidean measure, we can gain better *adjusted Rand index* in comparison to the Skew divergence. We can conclude that with Skew divergence more pure clusters can be achieved, while with the Euclidean measure we may have so many verb couples which are in the same real semantic clusters but are not in the dominant class of their assigned clusters. It seems that our choice of the distance measure for building the distance matrix is strongly dependent on what our aim is. If one aims to have more pure and accurate clusters, Skew divergence may be a good choice. On the other hand, if the goal is to have a clustering in which the dominant clusters are not very important, Euclidean measure seems to be better.

In this paper, we assume that each verb belongs to one cluster which involves the most dominant sense of that verb. This assumption allows us to use (I) hard clustering algorithms such as KMeans and spectral clustering; and (II) constructing the Persian semantic verb classes in which each polysemous verb is assigned to its most dominant sense. Therefore, considering polysemy and employing soft clustering algorithms is an important direction in the future research in order to improve the task. Other approaches for future works include: extending manual definition of Persian verb classes to cover a greater number and larger variety of Persian verbs, employing other initialization methods for KMeans algorithm such as hierarchal clustering and enriching the feature vectors by adding selectional preferences extracted from resources such as FarsNet [34] or information about named entities.

Acknowledgments. We would like to thank Behrang Mohit, Nizar Habash, Morteza Rezaei and anonymous reviewers for their helpful comments on the draft.

References

1. Shamsfard, M.: Challenges and open problems in Persian text processing. In: 5th Language & Technology Conference (LTC): Human Language Technologies as a Challenge for Computer Science and Linguistics, Poznań, Poland, pp. 65–69 (2011)

2. Rasooli, M.S., Kashefi, O., Minaei-Bidgoli, B.: Effect of adaptive spell checking in Persian. In: 7th International Conference on Natural Language Processing and Knowledge Engineering (NLP-KE), pp. 161–164 (2011)
3. Karimi-Doostan, G.: Lexical categories in Persian. Lingua 121(2), 207–220 (2011)
4. Karimi-Doostan, G.: Separability of light verb constructions in Persian. Studia Linguistica 65(1), 70–95 (2011)
5. Agirre, E., Bengoetxea, K., Gojenola, K., Nivre, J.: Improving dependency parsing with semantic classes. In: Proceedings of the 49th Annual Meeting of the Association for Computational Linguistics: Human Language Technologies (ACL:HLT), Portland, Oregon, USA, pp. 699–703 (June 2011)
6. Chen, J., Palmer, M.: Improving english verb sense disambiguation performance with linguistically motivated features and clear sense distinction boundaries. Language Resources and Evaluation 43(2), 181–208 (2009)
7. Korhonen, A.: Semantically motivated subcategorization acquisition. In: Proceedings of the ACL 2002 Workshop on Unsupervised Lexical Acquisition, Philadelphia, USA, pp. 51–58 (2002)
8. Titov, I., Klementiev, A.: A Bayesian approach to unsupervised semantic role induction. In: Proceedings of the 13th Conference of the European Chapter of the Association for Computational Linguistics (EACL), Avignon, France, pp. 12–22 (April 2012)
9. Levin, B.: English verb classes and alternations: A preliminary investigation, vol. 348. University of Chicago press (1993)
10. Rasooli, M.S., Kouhestani, M., Moloodi, A.: Development of a persian syntactic dependency treebank. In: The 2013 Conference of the North American Chapter of the Association for Computational Linguistics: Human Language Technologies (NAACL HLT), Atlanta, USA (2013)
11. Forgy, E.: Cluster analysis of multivariate data: efficiency versus interpretability of classifications. Biometrics 21, 768–769 (1965)
12. Alpert, C., Kahng, A., Yao, S.: Spectral partitioning with multiple eigenvectors. Discrete Applied Mathematics 90(1), 3–26 (1999)
13. Schulte im Walde, S.: Experiments on the automatic induction of German semantic verb classes. Computational Linguistics 32(2), 159–194 (2006)
14. Rasooli, M.S., Moloodi, A., Kouhestani, M., Minaei-Bidgoli, B.: A syntactic valency lexicon for Persian verbs: The first steps towards Persian dependency treebank. In: 5th Language & Technology Conference (LTC): Human Language Technologies as a Challenge for Computer Science and Linguistics, Poznań, Poland, pp. 227–231 (2011)
15. Schulte Im Walde, S.: Clustering verbs semantically according to their alternation behaviour. In: Proceedings of the 18th Conference on Computational Linguistics (COLING), Saarbrücken, Germany, vol. 2, pp.747–753 (2000)
16. Resnik, P.: Selectional preference and sense disambiguation. In: Proceedings of the ACL SIGLEX Workshop on Tagging Text with Lexical Semantics: Why, What, and How, Washington DC., USA, pp. 52–57 (1997)
17. Brew, C.,Schulte im Walde, S.: Spectral clustering for German verbs. In: Proceedings of the ACL 2002 Conference on Empirical Methods in Natural Language Processing (EMNLP), Philadelphia, USA, pp. 117–124 (2002)
18. Schulte im Walde, S., Brew, C.: Inducing German Semantic Verb Classes from Purely Syntactic Subcategorisation Information. In: Proceedings of 40th Annual Meeting of the Association for Computational Linguistics, Philadelphia, Pennsylvania, USA, pp. 223–230 (July 2002)

19. Sun, L., Korhonen, A., Krymolowski, Y.: Verb class discovery from rich syntactic data. In: Gelbukh, A. (ed.) CICLing 2008. LNCS, vol. 4919, pp. 16–27. Springer, Heidelberg (2008)
20. Sun, L., Korhonen, A., Krymolowski, Y.: Automatic classification of English verbs using rich syntactic features. In: Third International Joint Conference on Natural Language Processing (IJCNLP), Hyderabad, India, pp. 769–774 (2008)
21. Sun, L., Korhonen, A.: Improving verb clustering with automatically acquired selectional preferences. In: Proceedings of the 2009 Conference on Empirical Methods in Natural Language Processing (EMNLP), Suntec, Singapore, vol. 2, pp. 638–647 (2009)
22. Lapata, M., Brew, C.: Verb class disambiguation using informative priors. Computational Linguistics 30(1), 45–73 (2004)
23. Korhonen, A., Krymolowski, Y., Marx, Z.: Clustering polysemic subcategorization frame distributions semantically. In: Proceedings of the 41st Annual Meeting on Association for Computational Linguistics (ACL), Sapporo, Japan, vol. 1, pp. 64–71 (2003)
24. Sun, L., Korhonen, A.: Hierarchical verb clustering using graph factorization. In: Proceedings of the Conference on Empirical Methods in Natural Language Processing, pp. 1023–1033. Association for Computational Linguistics (2011)
25. Vlachos, A., Korhonen, A., Ghahramani, Z.: Unsupervised and constrained Dirichlet process mixture models for verb clustering. In: Proceedings of the Workshop on Geometrical Models of Natural Language Semantics (GEMS), Athens, Greece, pp. 74–82 (2009)
26. Saeedi, P., Faili, H.: Feature engineering using shallow parsing in argument classification of Persian verbs. In: Proceedings of the 16th CSI International Symposiums on Artificial Intelligence and Signal Processing (AISP 2012), Shiraz, Iran (2012)
27. Bijankhan, M.: The role of the corpus in writing a grammar: An introduction to a software. Iranian Journal of Linguistics 19(2) (2004)
28. Kashefi, O., Nasri, M., Kanani, K.: Automatic Spell Checking in Persian Language. Supreme Council of Information and Communication Technology (SCICT), Tehran, Iran (2010)
29. Rasooli, M.S., Faili, H., Minaei-Bidgoli, B.: Unsupervised identification of persian compound verbs. In: Batyrshin, I., Sidorov, G. (eds.) MICAI 2011, Part I. LNCS (LNAI), vol. 7094, pp. 394–406. Springer, Heidelberg (2011)
30. McDonald, R., Crammer, K., Pereira, F.: Online large-margin training of dependency parsers. In: Proceedings of the 43rd Annual Meeting on Association for Computational Linguistics (ACL), Sydney, Australia, pp. 91–98 (2005)
31. Lee, L.: On the effectiveness of the skew divergence for statistical language analysis. In: Artificial Intelligence and Statistics, vol. 2001, pp. 65–72 (2001)
32. Ng, A., Jordan, M., Weiss, Y.: On spectral clustering: Analysis and an algorithm. In: Advances in Neural Information Processing Systems, vol. 2, pp. 849–856 (2002)
33. Croce, D., Moschitti, A., Basili, R., Palmer, M.: Verb classification using distributional similarity in syntactic and semantic structures. In: Proceedings of the 50th Annual Meeting of the Association for Computational Linguistics (ACL), Jeju Island, Korea (2012)
34. Shamsfard, M., Hesabi, A., Fadaei, H., Mansoory, N., Famian, A., Bagherbeigi, S., Fekri, E., Monshizadeh, M., Assi, S.: Semi Automatic Development of FarsNet; the Persian WordNet. In: Proceedings of 5th Global WordNet Conference, Mumbai, India (2010)

Translation- and Projection-Based Unsupervised Coreference Resolution for Polish*

Maciej Ogrodniczuk

Institute of Computer Science, Polish Academy of Sciences

Abstract. Creating a coreference resolution tool for a new language is a challenging task due to substantial effort required by development of associated linguistic data, regardless of rule-based or statistical nature of the approach. In this paper, we test the translation- and projection-based method for an inflectional language, evaluate the result on a corpus of general coreference and compare the results with state-of-the-art solutions of this type for other languages.

1 Introduction

A widely known problem of coreference resolution — the process of "determining which NPs in a text or dialogue refer to the same real-world entity" [1], crucial for higher-level NLP applications such as text summarisation, text categorisation and textual entailment — has so far been tackled from many perspectives. However, there still exist languages which do not have state-of-the-art solutions available, which is most likely caused by the substantial effort required by development of language resources and tools, some of them knowledge-intensive, either leading to development of language-specific rules or preparation of training data for statistical approaches.

One of the solutions to this problem is following the translation-projection path, i.e., (1) translating the text (in the *source* language) to be coreferentially annotated into the *target* language, for which coreference resolution tools are available, (2) running the target language coreference resolver, (3) transferring the produced annotations (mentions — discourse world entities and clusters — sets of mentions referring to the same entity) from the target to the source language. Such a solution has so far been proposed e.g. by Rahman and Ng [2] and evaluated for Spanish and Italian with projection from English (see Section 2). Although the source and target languages in this setting come from two different language families, they differ markedly from inflectional languages such as Polish, which makes the approach interesting to test with different language pairs.

---

* The work reported here was carried out within the *Computer-based methods for coreference resolution in Polish texts (CORE)* project financed by the Polish National Science Centre (contract number 6505/B/T02/2011/40) and *University Research Program for Google Translate*.

M.A. Kłopotek et al. (Eds.): IIS 2013, LNCS 7912, pp. 125–130, 2013.

For Polish, there currently exist two resolvers of general coreference, a rule-based [3] and a statistical one [4], yet they were evaluated with a dataset of limited size — unavailable at the time of their preparation. Presently, a new corpus is being built to improve development and evaluation of coreference resolution tools — a Polish Coreference Corpus [5], parts of which have been used to evaluate our experimental results.

2   Related Work

Rahman and Ng's paper refers to many previous projection attempts in NLP tasks, mostly in the context of projecting annotations from a resource-rich to a resource-scarce language, starting from parallel corpus-based solutions to newer, machine translation-based ones. In the context of coreference resolution, two Romanian-English works are mentioned: [6] and [7] and a Portuguese-English one [8], all involving projection of hand-annotated data. Unlike others, Rahman and Ng's approach concentrated on "a technology for projecting annotations that can potentially be deployed across a large number of languages without coreference-annotated data"[1].

The article presents three settings differing in terms of application of linguistic tools, potentially caused by their (un)availability for the source language. Setting 1 assumes no linguistic tools available, which results in projecting not only coreference clusters, but also complete mentions. Setting 2 employs existing mention extractors (as in our case), while setting 3 makes use of all available linguistic processing tools used to generate features and train coreference resolvers on the projected coreference annotation.

As expected, the results of Setting 1 are highly unsatisfactory, with CONLL[2] F1 = 37.6% for Spanish and 21.4% for Italian. Results of setting 2 and 3 show considerable improvement, amounting to 50-60% F-measure.

3   The Experiment

Our experiment concentrated on a configuration combining Rahman and Ng's settings 1 and 2. A Polish text has been translated into English and mentions have been identified in the Polish part (as with setting 2), but an English coreference resolver was running on plain English text — and not on pre-identified Polish mentions transferred to English (as with setting 1). Only then English coreference clusters were used to form Polish clusters using original Polish mentions aligned with English mentions. We believe that this configuration can generally improve translation-based coreference resolution since predetermining mentions might propagate errors resulting e.g. from incorrect classification of nominal constituents of idiomatic expressions as referential. With no mentions

---

[1] See [2], bottom of p. 721.
[2] Calculated as (MUC + B^3+ CEAFE) / 3.

predefined, the resolver can exclude non-referential expressions in the very first step of the process.

Google Translate service has been used for producing translations, end-to-end coreference baseline system presented in [3] was used for Polish mention detection (see Table 1 for results of mention detection) and Stanford CoreNLP [9], one of the best coreference resolution systems up to date, has been used for English mention detection and coreference resolution. Instead of using external aligners such as GIZA++ [10] employed by Rahman and Ng, we decided to make use of the internal alignment algorithm of Google[3], concentrating the two steps of the process into one, potentially offering better coherence of the result due to internal dependence of both steps — translation and alignment.

Table 1. Polish mention detection

Mention statistics		Mention detection results	
Gold mentions	23069	Precision	68.89%
Sys mentions	21861	Recall	65.28%
Common mentions	15060	F1	67.04%

Texts for the experiment were acquired from the Polish Coreference Corpus to facilitate evaluation. They constituted 260 gold samples (all currently available), each between 250 and 350 segments, manually annotated with information on mentions and coreference clusters[4].

The following algorithm was used:

Algorithm 1. Translation and projection-based coreference resolution

---

annotate *pl-text* to detect *pl-mentions*
translate *pl-text* into *en-text* with word-to-word alignment
run *en-coreference resolution tool* on *en-text* to detect *en-mentions* and *en-clusters*
for all *en-clusters* (including singletons) **do**
    for all *en-mentions* in *en-cluster* **do**
        if exists alignment between *en-mention* head with any *pl-mention* head **then**
            put *pl-mention* in *pl-cluster* corresponding to *en-chain*
        end if
    end for
end for
for all *pl-mentions* not in any *pl-cluster* **do**
    create singleton *pl-clusters*
end for

---

[3] Made available by the University Research Program for Google Translate, see
http://research.google.com/university/translate/
[4] See [5], Section 5, for detailed information on organization of the annotation procedure.

4   Evaluation

All usual evaluation metrics have been calculated by comparing projection results with the golden data:

Table 2. Experimental results

Evaluation metrics	P	R	F
MUC	50.30%	29.62%	37.28%
B^3	93.34%	84.20%	88.53%
CEAFM	81.51%	81.51%	81.51%
CEAFE	81.06%	89.62%	85.12%
BLANC	71.43%	60.51%	64.01%
CONLL	74.90%	67.81%	70.31%

The final results show a promising direction and surpass figures given by Rahman and Ng for Spanish and Italian (as compared with best results — except for MUC — in all settings). They even withstand comparison with the official scores of CoNLL-2011 for the top ranked system[5] (below 60% average F1).

The figures could be further improved by investigating how target language-specific properties are being used by the translation-projection process, since inability to fully capture such features is usually considered to be the major weakness of projection-based approaches. However, the commonly cited problematic example of zero pronouns does not hold in the case of languages such as Polish, since their features can easily be propagated onto verbs based on inflectional endings, as in:

(1)   *Maria od zawsze kochała Jana. Gdy Øpoprosił ją o rękę, Øbyła szczęśliwa.*[6]
      'Maria has always loved John. When he asked her to marry him, she was happy.'

This fact, along with the integration of alignment into translation, might explain the better results for Polish than for Italian or Spanish.

It has also been noticed that the translation-based approach benefited from pragmatic information integrated in the source coreference resolver and propagated without integrating any similar resources into the resolution process for the target language. For example, *atrakcja* 'attraction' mention has been correctly linked by the process with *parada* 'parade' and *miano* 'appellation' with *tytuł* 'title'. This seems to be a very interesting feature since it introduces the idea of exploiting the knowledge used by various coreference resolution tools, also from

---

[5] See e.g. http://nlp.stanford.edu/software/dcoref.shtml
[6] Actual translation from Polish to English produced by Google Translate, as of March 2013.

different languages. Similarly, a voting mechanism between several target language coreference resolvers could be used in the process to improve the final result.

5   Conclusions and Further Work

We believe that the presented approach can facilitate construction of computational coreference resolvers in two respects: firstly, by creating a useful baseline for languages still lacking coreference resolution tools, and secondly, by applying external knowledge resources to current systems.

A new branch of research could concentrate on the application of different algorithms of alignment of coreference clusters; for languages which have coreference resolvers available, their efficiency could be improved e.g. by testing how corresponding clusters align in the source vs. target language. This could attach singleton mentions in the source language to existing clusters, pointed out by a respective cluster in the target language (i.e. containing a "target" mention aligned with the singleton "source" mention). Investigating how translation quality influences projection results seems another interesting issue.

Last, but not least, the combined translation-alignment procedure could be applied to the data sets used by Rahman and Ng to further improve their results.

References

1. Ng, V.: Supervised Noun Phrase Coreference Research: The First Fifteen Years. In: Proceedings of the 48th Annual Meeting of the Association for Computational Linguistics, Uppsala, Sweden, pp. 1396–1411 (2010)
2. Rahman, A., Ng, V.: Translation-Based Projection for Multilingual Coreference Resolution. In: Proceedings of the Conference of the North American Chapter of the Association for Computational Linguistics: Human Language Technologies (HLT-NAACL 2012), Montréal, Canada, pp. 720–730. Association for Computational Linguistics (2012)
3. Ogrodniczuk, M., Kopeć, M.: End-to-end coreference resolution baseline system for Polish. In: Vetulani, Z. (ed.) Proceedings of the Fifth Language and Technology Conference: Human Language Technologies as a Challenge for Computer Science and Linguistics, Poznań, Poland, Wydawnictwo Poznańskie, pp. 167–171 (2011)
4. Kopeć, M., Ogrodniczuk, M.: Creating a Coreference Resolution System for Polish. In: Proceedings of the Eighth International Conference on Language Resources and Evaluation, LREC 2012, Istanbul, Turkey, pp. 192–195. ELRA, European Language Resources Association (2012)
5. Ogrodniczuk, M., Zawisławska, M., Głowińska, K., Savary, A.: Coreference annotation schema for an inflectional language. In: Gelbukh, A. (ed.) CICLing 2013, Part I. LNCS, vol. 7816, pp. 394–407. Springer, Heidelberg (2013)
6. Harabagiu, S.M., Maiorano, S.J.: Multilingual coreference resolution. In: Proceedings of Sixth Applied Natural Language Processing Conference, North American Chapter of the Association for Computational Linguistics (ANLP-NAACL 2000), Seattle, Washington, USA, pp. 142–149 (2000)

7. Postolache, O., Cristea, D., Orasan, C.: Transferring Coreference Chains through Word Alignment. In: Proceedings of the Fifth International Conference on Language Resources and Evaluation (LREC 2006), Genoa, Italy, pp. 889–892. ELRA, European Language Resources Association (2006)

8. de Souza, J.G.C., Orăsan, C.: Can projected chains in parallel corpora help coreference resolution? In: Hendrickx, I., Lalitha Devi, S., Branco, A., Mitkov, R. (eds.) DAARC 2011. LNCS, vol. 7099, pp. 59–69. Springer, Heidelberg (2011)

9. Lee, H., Chang, A., Peirsman, Y., Chambers, N., Surdeanu, M., Jurafsky, D.: Deterministic coreference resolution based on entity-centric, precision-ranked rules. Computational Linguistics 39(4) (forth., 2013)

10. Och, F.J., Ney, H.: Improved statistical alignment models. In: Proceedings of the 38th Annual Meeting on Association for Computational Linguistics. ACL 2000, Stroudsburg, PA, USA, pp. 440–447. Association for Computational Linguistics (2000)

WCCL Match – A Language
for Text Annotation

Michał Marcińczuk and Adam Radziszewski

Institute of Informatics
Wrocław University of Technology
Wybrzeże Wyspiańskiego 27,
Wrocław, Poland
{michal.marcinczuk,adam.radziszewski}@pwr.wroc.pl

Abstract. In this paper we present a formalism for text annotation called *WCCL Match*. The need for a new formalism originates from our works related to Question Answering for Polish. We examined several existing formalisms to conclude that none of them fulfills our requirements. The new formalism was designed on top of an existing language for writing morphosyntactic functional expressions, namely *WCCL*. The major features of *WCCL Match* are: creation of new annotations, modification of existing ones, support for overlapping annotations, explicit access to tagset attributes and referring to context outside of captured annotation. We discuss three applications of the formalism: recognition of proper names, question analysis and question-to-query transformation. The implementation of *WCCL Match* is language-independent and can be used for almost any natural language.

1   Background

The work presented here originates from our efforts at development of a Question Answering system for Polish. We faced the necessity to annotate texts with several types of linguistic entities using hand-written rules. One of the project assumptions was to be able to enrich morphosyntactically tagged text with several layers of annotation, including: (1) proper names, (2) semantic relations between proper names and (3) annotations related to question analysis, such as question stems and answer type term [4].

It was also important to be able to process texts already annotated with some structural information. The rules should be able to add new annotations, but also, modify or remove existing ones (e.g. post-processing of a statistical named entity recogniser). Also, support for overlapping annotations was crucial as we planned to include several annotation layers corresponding to independent or partially dependent task definitions. For instance, to peek at syntactic chunks while attempting at recognition of named entities, while still being able to capture those named entities that cross chunks boundaries (the chunking guidelines are different to the principles of named entity annotation).

Another requirement stemmed from the characteristics of Polish language. It is an inflectional language and substantial amount of inflectional and syntactic

M.A. Kłopotek et al. (Eds.): IIS 2013, LNCS 7912, pp. 131–144, 2013.

information is typically stored in morphosyntactic tags. We use the positional tagset of the National Corpus of Polish [5], where tags encode not only part of speech, but also values of grammatical case, number, gender, aspect and many other important grammatical categories. Thus, the requirement was to be able to refer to the values of these categories instead of treating the tags as atomic symbols.

There was also a couple of important technical requirements. We sought a solution that would be able to process large amounts of text in reasonable time. The rules were to be fired against questions, but also against large corpora containing possible answers. As the rule-based component was to be integrated into a whole system, it should support pipeline processing or at least ability to process smaller portions of input without considerable start-up time (e.g., user's questions should be processed real-time).

We reviewed a couple of existing solutions (next section) and decided to develop our own formalism, which we built on top of an existing language for writing morphosyntactic functional expressions, namely *WCCL* [8]. In the next sections we motivate our decisions, present the resulting formalism and its applications.

2   Why Another Formalism?

We reviewed a few formalisms and their implementations with respect to the requirements stated in the previous section.

Spejd [6] is a formalism devised for rule-based partial parsing and morphosyntactic disambiguation of Polish (and possibly other languages). The formalism seems very attractive, since it was tailored for Polish and features full support for positional tagsets. Spejd allows for writing rules that group together tokens or already captured sequences of tokens. There is, however, a limitation that excludes its usage in our scenario: new groups may be added only on top of existing groups without the possibility of having separate layers of annotation. This means that it is impossible to have two annotations of different type partially overlapping. What is more, Spejd is not well suited to enhance partially annotated text with new annotations, e.g. it is impossible to write a rule that adds a smaller group that would be 'covered' by one already existing. This means that if we were to adapt it to our requirements, we would have not only to extend the language with new constructs, but also to redefine the behaviour of the existing matching expressions.

JAPE [2] is a popular formalism for writing annotation rules whose implementation is a part of the GATE platform. Each annotation rule consists of a matching part and an action part. The matching mechanism corresponds to a regular language over tokens and annotations. Those latter may be referred to by their name or attribute value assertions. The rules may also reference external dictionaries (*gazetteers*) and it is possible to embed arbitrary Java code in rule actions. The main disadvantage of JAPE from our point of view is the lack of any direct support for positional tagsets. In JAPE and other GATE components [1], tags are normally encoded as strings attached to tokens, which is quite a crude and cumbersome solution for a structured tagset and a language with about 1000 different tags appearing in real corpora. A possible work-around would be to use additional processing stage to decompose each tag and encode it as multiple key–value pairs assigned to each token. Note that if rule application is to be followed by another processing stage that operates on the level of tags, this GATE key–value decomposition would have to be converted back into standard tag representation.

We also considered using the NooJ platform [9]. The very first problem we faced is a technical one: at least until recently, NooJ was strictly bound to Microsoft .NET platform and as such it worked only under Microsoft Windows operating systems. One of the requirement of our project was to integrate the tool being developed with existing tools and architectures for processing of Polish, most of which are developed for UNIX platforms. Also, the computational servers and clusters (at least academic) are UNIX-based.

XTDL is a grammar formalism utilized by a multi-purpose engine for text processing called SProUT [3]. The formalism combines regular and unification-based grammars. XTDL grammars consist of pattern–action rules. Patterns are regular expressions over Typed Feature Structures (TFS), actions create new TFS. Although SProUT has already been applied successfully in several projects, not all of our requirements are met. Most notably, XTDL does not support the following: contextual constraints, modification of existing annotations, as well as testing if tokens overlap with annotations.

The immediate conclusion was that we couldn't take any of the above solutions and use it 'as-is' in our processing pipeline. If we had to put considerable effort into integration, we preferred to use some of the tools already available for Polish and build our own formalism and its implementation on top of them.

3   WCCL

A significant part of a desired formalism would have to deal with matching tokens that satisfy given constraints, including morphosyntactic information inferred from positional tags. Such constraints are part of the Spejd formalism, but also, of another formalism developed for Polish called WCCL [8]. WCCL is a language of functional expressions that are evaluated against morphosyntactically annotated sentences. These functional expressions may return values belonging to one of four data types:

1. Boolean: such functions are predicates, either simple (e.g. if the wordform is '*Berlin*') or complex (e.g. arbitrary number of conjunctions and alternatives of other predicates, constraint satisfaction search, tests for set intersection).
2. Set of strings, e.g., functions gathering wordforms or lemmas from tokens.
3. Set of symbolic values taken from the tagset, e.g. possible values of grammatical case.
4. *Position*, that is, an index designating a particular token in a sentence (useful for further processing).

A functional expression may be built from other expressions of various types. For instance, the following WCCL expresion checks if there exists a token of the noun class (assuming that nouns bear **subst** mnemonic in the tagset definition file used) and returns a set of grammatical case values assigned to it (assuming **cas** mnemonic for this category) or an empty set otherwise. The token is sought in the range starting from the token currently being processed (position 0) and the end of the sentence (**end**).

```
if (
  rlook (
    0, end, $S,
    equal(class[$S], {subst})
  ),
  cas[$S],
  {}
)
```

The above example shows that simple expressions may be combined to form more complex ones. For instance, `class[$S]` obtains the grammatical class of a token at the position pointed to by the variable $S, while `equal(class[$S],` `{subst})` turns it into a predicate — if the returned value equals a set containing noun class only (if corpus annotation is unambiguous, there should always be exactly one class per token).

We found it very convenient to use this flexible formalism as a means of expressing rule constraints. The main advantage is that WCCL was designed with the intention that the functional expressions, simple or complex, may be used as standalone functors for various purposes. The language is strongly typed and the syntax and semantics of each singular expression is well defined in the language specification. This allowed us to reuse all the existing language expressions without introducing any changes to their semantics. Instead, we built our rule formalism, which we called *WCCL Match*, on top of this functional language. As WCCL defines uniform syntax for 'whole WCCL file' where functional expressions of given types may be grouped under given names, we also extended this syntax to optionally contain a special section for *WCCL Match* rules. What is more, the assumptions underlying the formalism are consistent with our requirements regarding the annotation structure: it is assumed that annotations are organised in independent 'channels', each containing chunk-style annotations with the possibility to mark chunk heads. This allows referring to arbitrary number of annotation layers, whose elements may mutually overlap. WCCL provides a couple of predicates checking annotations in a given 'channel', e.g. if there is any noun phrase that crosses the given token position (assuming the input data contains a 'channel' with the results of NP chunking).

WCCL also comes with an open-source implementation. We extended this implementation with the *WCCL Match* language, thanks to which we could benefit from the existing parser, support for positional tagsets, corpus I/O routines and implementations of the functional expressions.

4 WCCL Match

Each rule consists of three sections:

1. match specification (match),
2. additional condition that may be used to reject a match (cond, optional),
3. actions (actions).

Below is an example rule that annotates highlands' names assuming that adjectives (possibly multiword) that belong to a dictionary have already been annotated as dict_adj.

```
apply(
  match(
    in( ["wyżyna"], base[0] ),          // eng. highland
    is( "dict_adj" )
  ),
  cond(
    agrpp(first(:1), first(:2), {nmb,gnd,cas})
  ),
  actions(
    mark(M, "HIGHLAND_NAM")
  )
)
```

The rule first matches a token whose base form is *wyżyna* (*highlands*), or, strictly speaking, the set of possible base forms that are left after disambiguation contains this one. Then an annotation of type dict_adj is expected. If matched, the additional condition is checked, which in this case tests for agreement on number, gender and case between the two elements of this match. If succeeded, an annotation of HIGHLAND_NAM is added around the whole matched sequence, which is accessible via M keyword[1]. :1 and :2 are notational shorthands for M:1, M:2. vec:index is a simple subscripting operator for *match vectors* (explained in the following subsection).

4.1 Match Specification

A match specification may consist of the following expression types:

1. Single-token match, which is essentially any valid WCCL predicate, e.g. in(["wyżyna"], base[0]) in the above example. The WCCL functional expresions are evaluated against a sentence with one of the tokens set as the *current position* (position 0). In *WCCL Match* the current position is shifted automatically by the match operator and position 0 always refers to the token being matched at the moment, while any other integer designates a token relatively to this token.

---

[1] M is syntactic sugar for $m:_M, that is a variable named _M of *match* data type (we added fifth data type to the core functional language to represent match vector elements).

2. Annotation match. It is required that a whole annotation bearing the given name starts at the current position.
3. Nested match: `repeat` (one or more repetitions of the matching expressions given), `optional` (zero or one repetition), `text` (a sequence of tokens whose forms make up the given text), `longest` (each of the given match specifications is examined and the longest one is selected).

While attempting at a match, a *match vector* is being built. If succeeded, the vector may be referred to in the additional condition and in rule actions. A nested match expression also produces a nested match vector. This way it is possible to refer to arbitrary fragments of the matched sequence.

4.2   Additional Conditions

The additional conditions are convenient means of performing more sophisticated post-checking of a match. There are two kinds of expressions allowed here:

1. Any valid WCCL predicate. Hence WCCL functional expressions did not operate on matches, we added two auxiliary functions to the functional language — `first` and `last`. The functions allow to convert match vectors to the *position* data type, which is already supported by a number of WCCL functions.
2. Two convenience tests: `ann` and `annsub`, allowing to check if a given match has the same boundaries or is a subsequence of an existing annotation.

4.3   Actions

There are two kinds of actions:

1. Related to annotations, that is adding, modification or removal of annotations (`mark`, `remark`, `unmark`).
2. Adding of key–value properties (`setprop`).

5   Applications

To present the usefulness of the formalism we present a couple of use cases in which its features were utilised.

5.1   Named Entity Recognition

We used *WCCL Match* to construct a set of rules to disambiguate category of proper names on the basis of their context. The candidate proper name is being recognised using gazetteers or general rules based only on orthographical features (for example, a sequence of upper case letters). Listing 1.1 presents a simple rule which disambiguates city and country name appearing in a phrase "the capital of COUNRTY is CITY".

```
apply(
  match(
    in("stolica", base[0]), // eng. capital
    is("dict_country_nam"),
    in("być", base[0]),     // eng. is
    is("dict_city_nam")
  ),
  actions(
    mark(:2, "COUNTRY_NAM"),
    mark(:4, "CITY_NAM")
  )
)
```

Listing 1.1. Sample WCCL Match rule disambiguating city and country name

Listing 1.2 presents another rule which disambiguates two first names one after another. One interpretation can be one person name containing two first names if both names agree in case (one PERSON_NAM annotation). The other interpretation is two person names when they do not agree in case (two PERSON_NAM annotations). The cond section is used to test the case agreement.

```
apply(
  match(
    is("dict_first_nam"),
    is("dict_first_nam")
  ),
  cond(
    not(agrpp(first(:1), first(:2), {cas}))
  ),
  actions(
    mark(:1, 'PERSON_NAM'),
    mark(:2, 'PERSON_NAM')
  )
)
```

Listing 1.2. Sample WCCL Match rule disambiguating two first names in a row

5.2   Question Analysis

During question analysis we perform a couple of subtasks. These include heuristic identification of questions among sentences (non-question sentences are assigned to *question context*, which is processed with a different pipeline) as well as identification of *question phrases*. By question phrases we understand noun or prepositional phrases that contain question word stems. Question phrases are sometimes limited to question stems as in *[Gdzie] urodził się Chopin?* ('*[Where] was Chopin born?*'). In other cases they may contain multiple elements, e.g., *[Na ilu kandydatów] można głosować? ([For how many candidates] one may vote?)*.

Below is one example rule that tries to recognises question phrases containing the question word stem *ile* (*how many* or *how much*). Recognised phrases are marked as `qphrase` annotations with phrase head set to *ile*. Besides, this word is assigned a property that it is a good indicator that the whole sentence is a question. The match specification tests for an optional preposition followed by any wordform having the base form of *ile*, followed by an optional noun in genitive. In the additional condition a safety check is performed to avoid capturing relative pronouns as question stems (e.g. *Nie wiem, ile . . .* — 'I don't how many. . . '). Left context of the match is examined and first token to the left is sought such that it is not a punctuation mark nor particle, adverb or interjection. If such token is found, the token must not belog to any verbal class. The match is also accepted if the token is not found (i.e., sentence begin was reached).

```
apply(
  match( // prep? ile genitive?
    optional(in({prep}, class[0])),
    in(["ile"], base[0]),
    optional(and(in({subst}, class[0]), in({gen}, cas[0])))
  ),
  cond(
    if(
      // go left from the match, set $L there
      skip(first(M), $L, // skip punctuation and indeclinable
        inter(class[$L], {interp,qub,adv,interj}),
        -1), // one token left not counting the above
      // if still within sentence, assert this is not a verb
      not(inter(class[$L], {praet,fin,bedzie,imps,impt,inf,
                            pant,pcon,aglt,winien})),
      True // if out of bounds, it is ok
    )
  ),
  actions(
    mark(M, M, M:2, "qphrase"),
    setprop(M:2, "question", "yes")
  )
)
```

5.3 Question Transformation

WCCL Match was also used as a means of writing rules performing transformation of natural language questions into SQL queries. Such queries were posed to a database containing semantic relations between named entities. First, we defined a set of question patterns reflecting different ways of asking about proper names being in a given semantic relation. For each question pattern we constructed a pair of elements — a *WCCL Match* rule and a SQL query pattern. The task of each rule is to match for relevant questions and capture all their arguments. When a rule matches, the associated query pattern is instantiated with captured arguments. The generated query is used to extract an answer from the database. Also, a set of question attributes (question type, subtype, object category, argument category) is defined for each rule. Listing 1.3 contains a sample rule matching a question about facilities located by a given street in a given city. The rule matches two arguments — a street name and a city name.

```
apply(
  match(
    inter(base[0], ["jaki"]),         // eng. what
    inter(base[0], ["budowla"]),      // eng. facility
    inter(base[0], ["znajdować"]),    // eng. located
    inter(base[0], ["się"]),
    inter(base[0], ["przy"]),         // eng. by
    inter(base[0], ["ulica"]),        // eng. street
    is("road_nam"),
    inter(base[0], ["w"]),            // eng. in
    is("city_nam"),
    inter(base[0], ["?"])
  ),
  actions(
    mark(:8, "arg_road_nam"),         // argument: road name
    mark(:10, "arg_city_nam")         // argument: city name
  )
)
```

Listing 1.3. Sample WCCL Match rule matching a question about facilities located at given street in given city

6   WCCL Match Is Language-Independent

WCCL Match is not bound to any particular language. It may be used to process any language as long as the tagset used conforms to the following requirements:

- the tagset defines a non-empty set of grammatical classes (parts of speech),
- the tagset defines a possibly empty set of attributes (grammatical categories),
- each grammatical class is assigned a set of attributes that are required for the class and a set of optional attributes,
- each attribute is assigned a set of its possible values,
- mnemonics used for grammatical classes and attribute values are unique,
- the tags are represented as a string of comma-separated mnemonics.

Note that in case of simple tagsets, such as those for English, the whole tagset definition is limited to a set of grammatical classes and their mnemonics.

The WCCL implementation uses simple configuration files to define tagsets (this is handled by the Corpus2 library, [7]). Tagset definitions consist of three sections: declaration of attributes and their values (ATTR), declaration of grammatical classes and applicable attributes (POS) and a tag selected to represent

```
┌──────── nkjp.tagset ─────────┐      ┌─ ptb.tagset ──┐
│ [ATTR]                       │      │ [ATTR]        │
│ nmb     sg pl                │      │               │
│ cas     nom gen dat acc inst loc voc│ [POS]        │
│ gnd     m1 m2 m3 f n         │      │ CC            │
│ ...                          │      │ CD            │
│ [POS]                        │      │ DT            │
│ adja                         │      │ ...           │
│ ...                          │      │ UNK           │
│ subst   nmb cas gnd          │      │               │
│ depr    nmb cas gnd          │      │ [IGN]         │
│ ...                          │      │ UNK           │
└──────────────────────────────┘      └───────────────┘
```

Fig. 1. Sample tagset definitions for Polish (nkjp.tagset) and English (ptb.tagset)

unknown words (IGN). Figure 1 presents fragments of tagset definitions for Polish (nkjp.tagset) and English (ptb.tagset).

The implementation handles data in several formats including two based on XML (XCES, CCL) and some simple plain-text formats that are convenient for storage of large corpora and script processing. The complete list of input/output formats can be found at . http://www.nlp.pwr.wroc.pl/redmine/projects/corpus2/wiki/Inputoutput_formats.

7 Conclusion

WCCL Match is a language-independent formalism for text annotation which may be used in many natural language processing tasks that involve text matching and annotation. The language has already been used for several applications including question analysis and proper name recognition.

The presented formalism has several unique features which make it an attractive alternative for other related tools. *WCCL Match* is now part of the *WCCL* toolkit. The toolkit provides core C++ implementation, which compiles into a shared library and a set of command-line utilities, but also, simple Python wrappers that facilitate rapid application development. The whole package is available under GNU LGPL 3.0[2].

The current implementation assumes sequential firing of rules, while the possibility of using finite-state techniques should be considered. On the other hand, the current processing speed seems quite satisfactory for the applications tested.

Acknowledgements. The work was funded by the NCBiR NrU.: SP/I/1/ 77065/10.

---

[2] Project site: http://www.nlp.pwr.wroc.pl/redmine/projects/joskipi/wiki

References

1. Cunningham, H., Maynard, D., Bontcheva, K., Tablan, V., Aswani, N., Roberts, I., Gorrell, G., Funk, A., Roberts, A., Damljanovic, D., Heitz, T., Greenwood, M.A., Saggion, H., Petrak, J., Li, Y., Peters, W.: Text Processing with GATE (Version 6) (2011), `http://tinyurl.com/gatebook`
2. Cunningham, H., Maynard, D., Tablan, V.: JAPE: a Java Annotation Patterns Engine. Tech. Rep. CS–00–10, University of Sheffield, Department of Computer Science (2000)
3. Drozdzynski, W., Krieger, H.U., Piskorski, J., Schäfer, U., Xu, F.: Shallow processing with unification and typed feature structures — foundations and applications. Künstliche Intelligenz 1, 17–23 (2004), `http://www.kuenstliche-intelligenz.de/archiv/2004_1/sprout-web.pdf`
4. Paşca, M.: Open-Domain Question Answering from Large Text Collections. University of Chicago Press (2003)
5. Przepiórkowski, A.: A comparison of two morphosyntactic tagsets of Polish. In: Koseska-Toszewa, V., Dimitrova, L., Roszko, R. (eds.) Representing Semantics in Digital Lexicography: Proceedings of MONDILEX Fourth Open Workshop, pp. 138–144. Warszawa (2009)
6. Przepiórkowski, A.: A preliminary formalism for simultaneous rule-based tagging and partial parsing. In: Data Structures for Linguistic Resources and Applications: Proceedings of the Biennial GLDV Conference 2007, pp. 81–90. Gunter Narr Verlag, Tuebingen (2007)
7. Radziszewski, A., Śniatowski, T.: Maca — a configurable tool to integrate Polish morphological data. In: Proceedings of FreeRBM 2011 (2011)
8. Radziszewski, A., Wardyński, A., Śniatowski, T.: WCCL: A morpho-syntactic feature toolkit. In: Habernal, I., Matoušek, V. (eds.) TSD 2011. LNCS, vol. 6836, pp. 434–441. Springer, Heidelberg (2011)
9. Silberztein, M.: NooJ manual (2003), user's manual available on-line at `http://www.nooj4nlp.net`

A   WCCL Match Grammar

This appendix contains a brief definition of WCCL Match grammar. A comprehensive documentation can be found at `http://www.nlp.pwr.wroc.pl/wccl`.

A.1   Set of Rules and Rule Structure

```
wccl_file  := match_rules(
                  rule(; rule)*
              )

rule       := apply(
                  sec_match,
                  (sec_cond,)?
                  sec_actions
              )
```

A.2   Match Section (*sec_match*)

It contains a list of operators matching a sequence of tokens and annotations.

```
sec_match       := match(
                       op_match(, op_match)*
                   )

op_match        := op_match_token | op_match_seq |
                   op_match_ann

op_match_token  := op_equal | op_inter | op_regex |
                   op_isannpart | op_isannhead |
                   op_isannbeg | op_isannend |
                   ... (any WCCL predicate)

op_match_seq    := op_text | op_optional | op_repeat |
                   op_longest | op_oneof

op_match_ann    := op_is

op_match_token_list := op_match_token
                       (, op_match_token)*
```

Operators matching a single token (op_match_token)
Any WCCL predicate may be used to match the current token, including the following.

- equal(arg1, arg2) — arg1 is equal to arg2 (defined for all data types),
- inter(arg1, arg2) — $arg1 \cap arg1 \neq \emptyset$ (set of strings or set of symbols),
- regex(arg1, arg2) — string arg1 matches regular expression arg2,
- isannpart(arg1) — current token is a part of annotation of type arg1,
- isannhead(arg1) — current token is a head of annotation of type arg1,
- isannbeg(arg1), isannend(arg1) — current token starts (ends) an annotation of type arg1,
- not(...), or(...), and(...) — usual Boolean connectives

Operators matching a sequence of tokens (op_match_seq):
Matches sequence of tokens if given condition is satisfied.

- text(arg1) — concatenation of orthographic forms is equal to arg1,
- optional(match) — zero or one match of the parenthesized expression,
- repeat(match) — one or more repetitions of the parenthesized match,
- longest(variants) — choose the longest match,
- oneof(variants) — choose the first matched.

Matching a single annotation (`op_match_ann`):

– `is(arg1)` — matches an annotation of type `arg1`.

A.3   Additional Condition Section (*sec_cond*)

It contains a list of additional conditions to be satisfied to accept a completed match.

```
sec_cond       := cond(
                       op_cond
                       (, op_cond)*
                   )

op_cond        := op_cond_token | op_ann | op_annsub

op_cond_token  := op_match_token
```

Token-level conditions (`op_cond_token`) are used to test token attributes. Any WCCL predicate may be used here. The token index may be obtained from matched groups using **first** or **last** (returns first/last token from a match vector element).

There are two condition operators to examine annotations, possibly occupying different 'channels':

– `ann(arg1, arg2)` — test if a sequence of tokens spanning over group with index `arg1` is annotated with `arg2`,
– `ann(arg1, arg2, arg3)` — test if a sequence of tokens spanning from group `arg1` to `arg2` (inclusive) is annotated with `arg3`,
– `annsub(arg1, arg2)` — test if a sequence of tokens spanning over group with index `arg1` is a part of annotation of type `arg2`,
– `annsub(arg1, arg2, arg3)` — test if a sequence of tokens spanning from group `arg1` to `arg2` (inclusive) is part of annotation of type `arg3`.

A.4   Action Sect ion (*sec_actions*)

It contains a set of actions performed on the matched elements.

```
sec_actions := actions(
                   op_action
                   (, op_action)*
               )

op_action   := op_mark | op_remark | op_unmark | op_setprop
```

Operators:

- `mark(vec, chan)` — creates an annotation of type `chan` spanning over tokens belonging to the given vector,
- `mark(vec_from, vec_to, chan)` — as above, but the annotation will span from the first token of `vec_from` to the last vector of `vec_to`,
- `mark(vec_from, vec_to, vec_hd, chan)` — as above, but the annotation head will be set to the first token of `vec_hd`.
- `remark(...)` — as `mark` but removes any annotations in the given channel that would intersect with the one being added.
- `unmark(vec, chan)` — removes the annotation matched.
- `setprop(vec, key, val)` — adds a key–value property to the first token of `vec`.

Diachronic Corpus Based Word Semantic Variation and Change Mining

Xiaojun Zou[1], Ni Sun[1], Hua Zhang[2], and Junfeng Hu[1,*]

[1] Key Laboratory of Computational Linguistics, Ministry of Education,
School of Electronics Engineering & Computer Science, Peking University,
Beijing, 100871, P.R. China
[2] School of Foreign Languages, Peking University
{xiaojunzou,sn96,zhang.hua,hujf}@pku.edu.cn

Abstract. The study of language variation has achieved a significant growth in the past half-century, but there is seldom research conducted from the aspect of computational lexical semantics. This paper applies a typical computational based algorithm to a diachronic corpus and attempts to track word semantic variation and change. The preliminary experiments show that our approach achieves a helpful result in semantic variation and change analysis in both overall trends and word level characteristics.

Keywords: Language Variation and Change, Computational Lexical Semantics, Distributional Semantic Model.

1 Introduction

The study of language variation and change has achieved a significant growth in the past half-century, and it has now become a highly productive subfield of research in sociolinguistics [1–3]. However, the methods of language study adopted by sociolinguists are generally empirical investigation (which may contain qualitative or quantitative analysis) based on fieldwork [3], which are usually laborious and time consuming, and there is seldom such research conducted from the aspect of computational lexical semantics.

The key difference between the two methodologies is that the former aims to give accurate description of the language variation by meticulous data collection and analysis [3], while the latter is a typical corpus based statistical method which relies on the context (lexical or syntactic) of the target words and gives their statistical trends in semantic or usage [4–6]. The former attempts to tracking the style of speaking which most closely approximates "everyday speech" [7], while the latter analyzes and reflects the statistical characteristics of any given text corpus computationally.

As an important method of language research, corpus based approach has gained extensive attentions for centuries. Initially, it was widely adopted by linguists in dictionary construction and grammar research. With the birth and

---

* To whom all correspondence should be addressed.

M.A. Kłopotek et al. (Eds.): IIS 2013, LNCS 7912, pp. 145–150, 2013.
© Springer-Verlag Berlin Heidelberg 2013

development of sociolinguistics in the last half-century, it was attached importance to by the sociolinguists and utilized as a helpful tool in the research of language variation and change.

This paper proposes to conduct word semantic variation and change mining on a diachronic corpus from the aspect of computational lexical semantics. Intuitively, it reveals the lexical semantic variation and change laws on the diachronic text corpus. The written text at each period can in some way reflects the real language usage at that time, thus this result can also supply important clues for sociolinguists and save their efforts in seeking for such potential cases for variation study. Moreover, since many words and phrases bear a distinctive characteristic of a particular time, by collecting and analyzing these words, the trajectory of times change and social development can be discerned.

The rest of this paper is organized as follows. In the second section, the computational approach to mining word semantic variation and change is elaborated. The preliminary experimental results are presented in Section 3. The last section concludes this paper and discusses the future work.

2   Computational Based Approach

Although language varies across both time and space [8], in this paper, we take a nationwide publication, *People's Daily*, as the corpus, ignore the geographical factors and just consider word semantic variation and change over time. We also take the collection of the most semantically similar words to represent the senses (or meanings) of a word in each particular period. The advantage is that polysemies can be easily represented by all the similar words of each sense. As all the similar words are scored and ranked, even the distribution of the senses can be reflected by the proportion of their corresponding similar words—the main or more commonly used senses may have more corresponding words selected to this collection.

Further, we adopt the typical distributional method [6], which is also referenced as distributional semantic model (DSM), to compute the similarity between two words on the corpus of each period. DSM is known to be based on distributional hypothesis [9], of which the essence is that a word is characterized by the company it keeps [10]. In other words, it assumes words appearing in analogous contexts tend to be similar. The contexts considered fall roughly into two categories, one is *syntactic context*, the other is *lexical context*.

The construction of syntactic contexts relies on the syntactic trees of sentences, which are typically the output of a syntactic parser [4, 5, 11] and are extremely time-consuming to obtain on a large corpus. As an alternative, lexical context has been studied. One commonly used lexical context is *text window*, where a context c for a word w_0 in a sentence S is defined as a substring of sentence containing but removing w_0. For instance, given sentence "$\ldots w_{-3}w_{-2}w_{-1}w_0w_1w_2w_3 \ldots$", a text window context for w_0 with size 4 can be "$w_{-2}w_{-1}w_1w_2$" [12]. For the sake of simplicity, we adopt lexical context in this preliminary research.

By tracking the semantic similarity collection of a word in each period, we can obtain its semantic variation and usage preference evolution over time. We call the word whose senses change remarkably with time *diachronic sensitive word*, whereas the one whose senses change little with time *diachronic insensitive word*. The diachronic sensitive words witness the times change and social development.

3   Experimental Results

The preliminary experiments were based on a diachronic corpus of *People's Daily* in half-century (from 1947 to 1996). For simplicity, we ignored the influence of linguistic variation in word segment and the Chinese Lexical Analysis System (ICTCLAS) [13] was applied to segment the raw text and tag the words with a part of speech. In lexical context construction, we defined the co-occurrence as, if and only if the two words are within the same clause, or exactly a sub-sentence separated by any punctuation. In other words, we used a *variable text window*, the boundaries of which are determined by the most nearest punctuations on each side of the target word. Frequent words (e.g., stop words) that tend not to be very discriminative were ignored to keep these contexts efficient. The *pointwise mutual information* (PMI) [14] was adopted as the weight in building the co-occurrence vectors and the cosine or normalized dot product was applied to compute the distributional similarity for each word pair.

Based on the experimental setup above, the similarity of each word pair was calculated throughout the corpus from 1947 to 1996 respectively. In this section, we study word semantic variation and change from the following two aspects: one is the overall data analysis, and the other is word level analysis.

3.1   Word Semantic Variation and Change Trends Analysis

In order to measure the intensity of word semantic variation, we define the K level *Semantic Stability Index* (SSI) of word w from time y_1 to y_2 as

$$SSI_{y_1,y_2}^K(w) = \frac{Similar_{y_1}^K(w) \cap Similar_{y_2}^K(w)}{K} \times 100\% , \qquad (1)$$

where $Similar_{y_1}^K(w)$ and $Similar_{y_2}^K(w)$ denote the top K similar words collection for word w at time y_1 (in the year y_1, for example) and time y_2 respectively. (Note that we also refer *similar words collection* as *semantic similarity collection*.) The numerator on the right side denotes the intersection of semantic similarity collections (ISSC). Intuitively, SSI describes the semantic stability degree of a word by evaluating the ratio of items in semantic similarity collection that remain unchanged. Meanwhile, the K level *Semantic Variation Index* (SVI) of word w from time y_1 to y_2 can be defined as

$$SVI_{y_1,y_2}^K(w) = 1 - SSI_{y_1,y_2}^K(w) . \qquad (2)$$

In Table 1, we take the word "变色" (change color) in 1976 (here we mean y_2 is 1976) as an example, where K is set as 100. It can be seen that the SSI declines from 27% to 2% (Column 3) as the year gap (namely the $y_2 - y_1$) increasing from

1 to 20 (Column 1). This result accords with people's intuition: the semantic or usage of a word tends to keep stable within a shorter time gap. Limited by the computational burden, we randomly selected a thousand words to do the overall analysis. We calculated yearly the SSI of each selected word taking the year gap of 1, 2, 3, 5, 10, and 20 respectively. Table 2 shows the average SSI on the thousand words on each year gap. It can be seen that the average SSI also declines as the increasing of year gap.

This preliminary experiment reveals that the semantic or usage of a word tends to keep stable within a shorter time gap and semantic variation and change exhibits a characteristic of gradualness.

Table 1. The ISSC and SSI of the word "变色" (change color) when $y_2 = 1976$ with the year gap of 1, 2, 3, 5, 10, and 20 respectively ($K = 100$)

Year Gap	ISSC Size	SSI	ISSC
1	27	27%	松动/loosen, 停步/halt, 生锈/rust, 打下/overcome, 枯竭/drain, 休战/truce, 颜色/color, 人道/humanity, 改变颜色/change color, 江山/landscape, 千秋万代/throughout the ages, 永不/forever, 娘子军/detachment of women, 欧格利姆/Φgrim, 凋谢/perish, 击破/destroy, 造福/benefit, 红色/red, 褪色/fade, 螺丝钉/screw, 磨灭/obliterate, 电波/radio wave, 锦绣/splendid, 老前辈/doyen, 迷航/lose one's course, 指点/give directions, 浙江省/Zhejiang Province
2	17	17%	塘边/pool side, 红色/red, 锦绣/splendid, 江山/landscape, 螺丝钉/screw, 老花/presbyopia, 千秋万代/throughout the ages, 来之不易/hard-won, 停步/halt, 永不/forever, 娘子军/detachment of women, 迷航/lose one's course, 凋谢/perish, 休战/truce, 磨灭/obliterate, 颜色/color, 生锈/rust
3	14	14%	停步/halt, 褪色/fade, 打下/overcome, 江山/landscape, 螺丝钉/screw, 千秋万代/throughout the ages, 永不/forever, 迷航/lose one's course, 枯竭/drain, 休战/truce, 磨灭/obliterate, 凋谢/perish, 颜色/color, 生锈/rust
5	14	14%	松动/loosen, 红色/red, 锦绣/splendid, 褪色/fade, 枯竭/drain, 紧急/urgency, 江山/landscape, 螺丝钉/screw, 千秋万代/throughout the ages, 停步/halt, 永不/forever, 磨灭/obliterate, 迷航/lose one's course, 生锈/rust
10	10	10%	创下/perform, 褪色/fade, 壮美/magnificent, 枯竭/drain, 江山/landscape, 螺丝钉/screw, 千秋万代/throughout the ages, 永不/forever, 颜色/color, 生锈/rust
20	2	2%	磨灭/obliterate, 永不/forever

Table 2. The average SSI on each year gap

Year Gap	1	2	3	5	10	20
SSI(%)	1.65	1.38	1.26	1.13	0.98	0.73

3.2 Diachronic Sensitive and Insensitive Words Mining

The average SSI of each word on all the year gaps can also be calculated. This value reflects the diachronic sensitivity of a word to semantic variation and change. By ranking the words in SSI, we can obtain the diachronic sensitive and insensitive words. Table 3(a) and 3(b) display the top 10 diachronic sensitive and insensitive words respectively over the half-century by ranking the thousand randomly sampled words mentioned above. Taking "中下层" (middle and poorer classes) as an example, it generally has two senses in the corpus, one is middle- and lower-level of something (usually thick or deep), the other is middle and poorer social groups. The emphasis of each sense in the corpus varies with time going by. We take the former sense as an example. At first, it describes things such as haystacks (agricultural industry), with the economic development, it describes rivers or seas (fishery industry), and then the mines (mining industry). Thus its similar words collections vary notably and have few intersections, in other words, "中下层" is a diachronic sensitive word in the corpus. On the contrary, the similar words collections of "友谊" (friendship) keep relatively stable with time and the intersections between different years always include "永久"(forever), "深厚" (deep), "维护"(maintain) and so on. Thus, "友谊" is a diachronic insensitive word in the corpus.

Table 3. The ranked diachronic sensitive and insensitive words

(a) The top 10 diachronic sensitive words.

Rank	Word	SSI(%)	Rank	Word	SSI(%)
1	中下层/middle and poorer classes	0.10	6	折子/bankbook	0.14
2	远涉重洋/across vast oceans	0.10	7	朝思暮想/yearn day and night	0.14
3	闹别扭/be at odds with sb.	0.12	8	走运/be lucky	0.15
4	黄毛丫头/a silly little girl	0.13	9	粗陋/coarse	0.15
5	产品制造/product manufacture	0.14	10	聚餐/dine together	0.15

(b) The top 10 diachronic insensitive words.

Rank	Word	SSI(%)	Rank	Word	SSI(%)
1	总司令/commander in chief	8.65	6	混凝土/concrete	7.37
2	友谊/friendship	8.36	7	革命/revolution	7.09
3	印度/India	8.15	8	物理/physics	7.02
4	松劲/slacken	7.85	9	美元/dollar	6.82
5	毛里塔尼亚/Mauritania	7.47	10	政治部/political department	6.28

4   Conclusions and Future Work

This paper studies word semantic variation and change mining on a diachronic corpus from the aspect of computational lexical semantics. The preliminary experiments show that our approach achieves a helpful result in words diachronic semantic variation and change analysis in both overall trends and word level characteristics (eg., diachronic sensitivity). Our future work will focus on the following aspects. Firstly, using more refined algorithm to process the diachronic corpus and designing more elaborate model in word semantic mining. Secondly, many other social historical changes mining can be conducted based on the diachronic corpus of *People's Daily*.

Acknowledgments. We thank Ma Yongfang for her initial work on synonymous relationship extraction [15] and Shi Weijia for his web based demo system based on Ma's work [16]. Thanks to Dou Xiaotian for his further improvement on this demo system. This work is supported by the Chiang Ching-kuo Foundation for International Scholarly Exchange under the project "Building a Diachronic Language Knowledge-base" (RG013-D-09) and the Open Project Program of the National Laboratory of Pattern Recognition (NLPR).

References

1. Labov, W.: The Social Stratification of English in New York City. Center for Applied Linguistics, Washington, D.C (1966)
2. Chambers, J.K., Trudgill, P., Schilling-Estes, N. (eds.): The Handbook of Language Variation and Change. Blackwell, Oxford (2002)
3. Bayley, R., Lucas, C.: Sociolinguistic Variation: Theories, Methods, and Applications. Cambridge University Press, Cambridge (2007)
4. Hindle, D.: Noun Classification from Predicate-Argument Structures. In: ACL 1990, pp. 268–275. Association for Computational Linguistics, Stroudsburg (1990)
5. Lin, D.: Automatic Retrieval and Clustering of Similar Words. In: COLING/ACL 1998, pp. 768–774. Association for Computational Linguistics (1998)
6. Jurafsky, D., Martin, J.H.: Speech and Language Processing: An Introduction to Natural Language Processing, Computational Linguistics, and Speech Recognition. Prentice-Hall, Englewood Cliffs (2000)
7. Cedergren, H.J., Sankoff, D.: Variable Rules: Performance as a Statistical Reflection of Competence. Language 50, 333–355 (1974)
8. Radford, A., Atkinson, M., Britain, D., Clahsen, H., Spencer, A.: Linguistics: An introduction. Cambridge University Press, Cambridge (1999)
9. Harris, Z.S.: Distributional Structure. Word, pp. 146–162 (1954)
10. Firth, J.R.: A Synopsis of Linguistic Theory, 1930-1955. Studies in linguistic analysis. Philological Society Blackwell, Oxford (1957)
11. Pantel, P., Lin, D.: Discovering Word Senses from Text. In: SIGKDD 2002, pp. 613–619. ACM Press (2002)
12. Shi, S., Zhang, H., Yuan, X., Wen, J.R.: Corpus-based Semantic Class Mining: Distributional vs. Pattern-Based Approaches. In: COLING 2010, pp. 993–1001. Association for Computational Linguistics (2010)
13. Zhang, H.P.: ICTCLAS. Institute of Computing Technology, Chinese Academy of Sciences (2002), http://ictclas.org/index.html
14. Fano, R.M.: Transmission of Information: A Statistical Theory of Communications. American Journal of Physics 29, 793–794 (1961)
15. Ma, Y.: Synonymous Relationship Extraction and Evaluation Based on Large-scale Corpus. Bachelor Degree Thesis. Peking University (2012) (in Chinese)
16. Shi, W.: A Web Application of Semantics Visualization Based on Synonyms Networks. Bachelor Degree Thesis. Peking University (2012) (in Chinese), http://162.105.80.205:8080/keywords/key.swf

A Representation of an Old Polish Dictionary Designed for Practical Applications

Jakub Waszczuk

Institute of Computer Science, Polish Academy of Sciences
Jakub.Waszczuk@ipipan.waw.pl

Abstract. We describe an efficient representation of an old Polish dictionary designed for practical applications. This representation consists of two components: a memory-efficient automaton and a binary version of the dictionary. We have developed a separate automata library and we show some practical applications of the library within the context of the old Polish dictionary.

1 Introduction

Machine-readable dictionaries can be represented in many different ways. A dictionary resource in its primary form should be stored using a standard format which makes the dictionary more interoperable. Another advantage of the standard representation is that it suggests a verified structure of the dictionary which should be easily extensible with additional information characteristic for resources of the particular type. Nevertheless, when it comes to a particular application of the dictionary, other factors often become more important: lookup speed and memory performance, for example.

A preliminary version of the old Polish dictionary has been constructed on the basis of the paper dictionary ([1,2]). An XML structure compatible with an LMF (Lexical Markup Framework, http://www.lexicalmarkupframework.org, [3]) meta-format has been chosen as the primary representation of the dictionary. The dictionary has been also complemented with new word forms on the basis of a collection of historical documents and part of speech tags has been assigned to individual lexical entries on the basis of their contemporary equivalents (unlike part of speech tags, equivalents were included in the paper dictionary). The process of part of speech inferring has been described in [4].

Here we describe a structure of the old Polish dictionary developed with analysis of old Polish texts in mind. This dictionary version allows fast and memory-efficient lookup and it can be used in practice to label words with dictionary data such as contemporary equivalents or definitions. The dictionary structure consists of two complementary elements:

- A minimal, acyclic finite-state automaton in which a morphology-related part of the dictionary is stored. See section 2 for a description of an automata library. Details about a method of storing the old Polish dictionary in the automaton can be found in section 3.
- A binary version of the old Polish dictionary. See section 4 for more details.

M.A. Kłopotek et al. (Eds.): IIS 2013, LNCS 7912, pp. 151–156, 2013.

Using the dictionary to analyze old Polish texts can be problematic because descriptions of many lexical entries in the historical dictionary are incomplete. Fortunately, there are language resources (morphological dictionary PoliMorf, http://zil.ipipan.waw.pl/PoliMorf, in particular) developed for contemporary Polish which can be used to supplement the historical dictionary with missing word forms. This process is described in section 3.4.

2   Automata Library

Acyclic, deterministic finite-state automata (also called directed acyclic word graphs, DAWGs) provide a memory-efficient way to store language dictionaries. They can be used to represent a map from words to domain-specific annotations and, as long as the set of distinct annotations is small, a minimized DAWG is usually much more compact than a corresponding trie built with respect to the same dictionary.

We have developed a generic DAWG implementation in a Haskell language in order to store the old Polish dictionary in the automaton. The implementation is available in a form of a library at http://hackage.haskell.org/package/dawg under the 2-clause BSD license.

2.1   Interface

The library provides a high-level interface and from a user perspective a DAWG can be treated as a map from words[1] to totally ordered values. All elements equal with respect to an ordering relation are represented with one distinct value in the automaton. Here is a list of basic functions provided by the library interface:

```
empty        :: DAWG a
lookup       :: String -> DAWG a -> Maybe a
insert       :: Ord a => String -> a -> DAWG a -> DAWG a
insertWith   :: Ord a => (a -> a -> a)
                        -> String -> a -> DAWG a -> DAWG a
delete       :: Ord a => String -> DAWG a -> DAWG a
```

DAWG a is a polymorphic type which represents a DAWG with elements (values kept in automaton states) of type a. Ord a is a type class which states that elements of type a are totally ordered. A lookup function can be used to search for an element assigned to a particular word. Functions insert, insertWith and delete can be used to modify the DAWG. The insertWith function takes an additional argument which tells what action should be performed when a word is already a member of the DAWG. All three functions preserve minimality of the automaton.

---

[1] The actual interface is parametrized over a type of alphabet symbols, but for simplicity we assume that words are built over the set of Unicode characters.

2.2 Incremental Construction

There are two main methods of building a DAWG from a finite collection of (word, value) pairs. The first one involves an additional, prior stage during which a trie of the input collection is constructed. Only afterwards the DAWG is built on the basis of the trie. Disadvantage of such a solution is that the trie can be very inefficient in terms of memory usage, which sometimes makes the method impossible to use in practice.

Another solution is to build the automaton incrementally. It doesn't require any intermediate stage of trie construction and it works directly on the finite set of (word, value) pairs. The DAWG construction method implemented in the DAWG library is a functional version of the incremental algorithm described in [5].

3 Automaton Representation of a Dictionary

The old Polish dictionary can be viewed as a version of a morphological dictionary extended with additional data: contemporary equivalents, definitions etc. Only the morphology-related part is kept in the automaton while the rest of information is stored in a binary part of the dictionary (see section 4). We start by showing how a morphological dictionary PoliMorf can be stored in a DAWG.

3.1 PoliMorf

A lexical entry in PoliMorf consists of three components: a base form (Base), a part of speech (POS) and a set of word forms (WordForms, each form accompanied with a set of potential morphosyntactic descriptions, MSDs). Therefore, an entry can be represented with a (Base, POS, Map WordForm (Set MSD)) triple, where Set a corresponds to a set with elements of type a and Map a b corresponds to a map from keys of type a to values of type b.[2] In order to reduce the number of distinct values stored in automaton states and, consequently, to make the automaton minimization process more efficient, a rule (Rule) which translates a base form into a particular word form can be used in place of the word form itself. This modification yields the following representation of an entry: (Base, POS, Map Rule (Set MSD)). Since a (Base, POS) pair uniquely identifies a lexicon entry, the entire dictionary can be represented with a DAWG of type

```
type PoliMorf = DAWG (Map POS (Map Rule (Set MSD))),
```

where keys of the DAWG correspond to base forms of individual entries.

Assuming that POS, Rule and MSD types are already instances of the Ord class,[3] an appropriate Ord instance will be automatically generated for the entire Map POS (Map Rule (Set MSD))) type, which makes it possible to use functions defined in the library interface (see section 2.1) on the DAWG specific to the

---

[2] A http://hackage.haskell.org/package/containers package provides standard, functional implementations of Set and Map.

[3] In Haskell, instances of the *Ord* class can be usually derived automatically.

PoliMorf dictionary. The DAWG can be constructed by folding the `insertWith` function over the collection of dictionary entries starting with the `empty` DAWG. This shows that adapting the polymorphic DAWG type to a particular dictionary is a straightforward task.

3.2   Old Polish Dictionary

Since only the morphology-related part of the old Polish dictionary is stored in the DAWG, structure of this specific DAWG is very similar to the structure described in the previous section. However, there is one important difference regarding the assumptions under which the two DAWG structures are designed. The assumption that lexical entry can be uniquely identified by its base form and its part of speech is too strong within the context of the constantly evolving old Polish dictionary, which contains a lot of automatically generated data (in particular, some `POS` tags may be assigned incorrectly).

Therefore, we assume a weaker condition which states that every lexical entry contains at least one word form. Based on this basic assumption an object which uniquely identifies a particular entry can be defined as a pair of:

- `KEY`: A first textual representation of a first word form described within the entry (base form is preferred, when available).
- `UID`: An identifier unique among all entries with the same `KEY`.

This definition can be used to specify a DAWG adapted to the old Polish dictionary as

```
type OldPolish = DAWG (Map UID (Map Rule (Set MSD))),
```

where keys of the DAWG correspond to `KEY` values assigned to individual dictionary entries.

3.3   Inverse Automaton

Both automata described in the two previous sections can be used to map a textual representative of a lexical entry (base form in case of PoliMorf, `KEY` in case of the old Polish dictionary) into a morphological description of the entry using the `lookup` function provided by the DAWG library. However, a DAWG can be used to represent an inverse dictionary as well, in which keys correspond to word forms and rules kept in automaton states are used to translate word forms into corresponding base forms (or `KEY`s, in case of the old Polish dictionary). In fact, this representation is used in a morphological analysis tool Morfeusz (`http://sgjp.pl/morfeusz`, [6]). It is important to note that this modification doesn't change the type of the DAWG and both specific DAWG types described earlier (`PoliMorf` and `OldPolish`) are still adequate. Moreover, in case of PoliMorf and the old Polish dictionary, both automata – direct and the inverse one – yield the same compression level.

3.4   Updating the Old Polish Dictionary with Contemporary Forms

Since the old Polish dictionary is still under development, its coverage of the old Polish language is not perfect at this point. It doesn't contain entries corresponding to many old Polish lexemes and descriptions of lexemes which are included in the dictionary are often incomplete. Based on the similarity between the contemporary Polish language and its older version, we can alleviate this problem by using PoliMorf as an alternative source of morphological knowledge. The problem is that, if we look up a word in both dictionaries and find only the contemporary interpretation, there is no guarantee that there is no lexical entry in the old Polish dictionary which also corresponds to this word form. It may be just that this particular word form is not yet included in the lexical entry of the old Polish dictionary.

A solution to this problem is to supplement the old Polish automaton with contemporary word forms which can be directly linked with forms already present in the old Polish dictionary. A process which utilize two PoliMorf automata (the standard and the inverse one, see sections 3.1 and 3.3) can be used to identify PoliMorf entries which correspond to a particular old Polish dictionary entry:

1. For each word form of the entry a set of contemporary entries which contain the same word form is identified,
2. Contemporary entries which do not agree on the part of speech tag with the historical entry are rejected. This step can be used to reduce the number of false-positive links between entries at the expense of the number of false-negatives which, due to possible errors in automatic POS assignment, can be increased.

4   Binary Representation of the Old Polish Dictionary

The first step in designing a binary representation of the old Polish dictionary was to develop a Haskell data structure which mirrors the original, LMF structure of the lexical entry. This structure is used in Haskell programs which operate on the dictionary and, additionally, constitutes an intermediate structure between the XML and the binary form of the lexical entry. Lexical entry serialization method has been developed using the Haskell **binary** library (http://hackage.haskell.org/package/binary) which provides methods for encoding Haskell values as streams of bytes. An interface has been developed which provides functions for reading and writing individual lexical entries from and to a disk, respectively. Path at which a particular entry is located is uniquely identified with a (KEY, UID) pair (as well as the entry itself, as described in section 3.2).

5   Summary and Future Works

An efficient representation of the old Polish dictionary can be obtained by combining the automaton, which includes morphological data and provides a fast lookup method, with the binary version of the dictionary, which consists of a collection of serialized lexical entries from the original, LMF dictionary. In order to look up a word in the old Polish dictionary:

1. A morphological description and a (KEY, UID) identifier has to be found by looking up the word in the automaton,
2. Additional data which may be relevant for a particular application has to be extracted from the binary representation of the entry. The location at which the entry is stored can be determined on the basis of the (KEY, UID) pair.
3. When the word is not found in the automaton, PoliMorf (or Morfeusz) can be consulted to obtain morphological information about the input word.

The binary version of the old Polish dictionary doesn't hold information about multiword lexical entries and syntactic relations. Support for these structures is planned to be added in the next release of the binary dictionary implementation.

Acknowledgments. This work was financed by the National Centre for Research and Development (NCBiR) project SP/I/1/77065/10 (SYNAT).

References

1. Mykowiecka, A., Głowińska, K., Rychlik, P., Waszczuk, J.: Construction of an electronic dictionary on the base of a paper source. In: Vetulani, Z. (ed.) Proceedings of the 5th Language & Technology Conference: Human Language Technologies as a Challenge for Computer Science and Linguistics, Poznań, Poland, pp. 506–510 (2011)
2. Reczek, S.: Podręczny słownik dawnej polszczyzny. Ossolineum (1968)
3. Francopoulo, G., Bel, N., George, M., Calzolari, N., Monachini, M., Pet, M., Soria, C.: Multilingual resources for nlp in the lexical markup framework (lmf). Language Resources and Evaluation 43, 57–70 (2009)
4. Mykowiecka, A., Rychlik, P., Waszczuk, J.: Building an electronic dictionary of an old polish basing on the paper resource. In: Calzolari, N (Conference Chair), Choukri, K., Declerck, T., Doğan, M.U., Maegaard, B., Mariani, J., Odijk, J., Piperidis, S. (eds.) Proceedings of the Adaptation of Language Resources and Tools for Processing Cultural Heritage Objects Workshop Associated with the 8th International Conference on Language Resources and Evaluation (LREC 2012), Turkey, Istanbul. European Language Resources Association (ELRA) (2012)
5. Daciuk, J., Watson, B.W., Mihov, S., Watson, R.E.: Incremental construction of minimal acyclic finite-state automata. Comput. Linguist. 26, 3–16 (2000)
6. Woliński, M.: Morfeusz a practical tool for the morphological analysis of Polish. In: Kłopotek, M.A., Wierzchoń, S.T., Trojanowski, K. (eds.) Intelligent Information Processing and Web Mining. Advances in Soft Computing, pp. 503–512. Springer, Berlin (2006)

Related Entity Finding Using Semantic Clustering Based on Wikipedia Categories

Georgios Stratogiannis, Georgios Siolas, and Andreas Stafylopatis

National Technical University of Athens,
Department of Electrical and Computer Engineering Intelligent Systems Laboratory
Zografou Campus Iroon Polytexneiou 9, 15780 Zografou
{stratogian,gsiolas}@islab.ntua.gr, andreas@cs.ntua.gr

Abstract. We present a system that performs Related Entity Finding, that is, Question Answering that exploits Semantic Information from the WWW and returns URIs as answers. Our system uses a search engine to gather all candidate answer entities and then a linear combination of Information Retrieval measures to choose the most relevant. For each one we look up its Wikipedia page and construct a novel vector representation based on the tokenization of the Wikipedia category names. This novel representation gives our system the ability to compute a measure of semantic relatedness between entities, even if the entities do not share any common category. We use this property to perform a semantic clustering of the candidate entities and show that the biggest cluster contains entities that are closely related semantically and can be considered as answers to the query. Performance measured on 20 topics from the 2009 TREC Related Entity Finding task shows competitive results.

Keywords: Related Entity Finding, Wikipedia category vector representation, Semantic clustering.

1 Introduction

Question Answering (QA), offline or online, is a complex task. In most cases, the question is transformed into keywords which enter to a search engine and retrieve all web pages containing these keywords. These pages possibly contain the answers we are looking for. The drawback of this search method is that we are not taking into account any Semantic Information in the form of already acquired knowledge. Initial QA approaches were restricted asking very simple questions that could be answered by factoid answers (e.g. "What is the name of the managing director of Apricot Computer?" or "How far is Yaroslavl from Moscow?"). To answer these queries they used classic textual question answering approaches that rely on statistical keyword relevance scoring [6]. These approaches did not make use of any kind of semantic knowledge, so the answers to the questions consisted of a small text excerpt returned from a database search that was meant to include the correct information.

With the maturation of structured knowledge sources like Wikipedia and the more recent projects of ontologies like DBpedia and Freebase, a number of richer

M.A. Kłopotek et al. (Eds.): IIS 2013, LNCS 7912, pp. 157–170, 2013.

knowledge bases became available for use by QA systems. In ontologies the knowledge about entities and the relations between them are semantically organized and information can be extracted easily. Unfortunately, this approach also has limitations; most ontologies cover a specific domain of knowledge and this means that one has to search in more than one ontology. This adds complexity to the task because usually ontologies are different in their construction and need different methods to be accessed. An additional problem is that ontologies are manually constructed, so an important human effort is needed for their construction.

Recently, QA has made progress in handling queries that require more than one answer. A direction of QA systems of this kind is the Related Entity Finding (REF) track of the Text Retrieval Conference (TREC) [2], which actually searches both the entities that answer to a question and their representative URIs that might be their homepages or other pages that contain information for some entities.

In this paper we present a system that makes use of the TREC dataset in order to achieve automated Related Entity Finding. Our system makes use of both Information Retrieval (IR) and structured knowledge extraction methods. First, it uses IR methods to obtain a large number of potential answers, called candidate entities. At this step, the system aims to achieve high recall and inevitably has low precision. For this reason it is followed by a second step which makes use of Semantic Information in the online ontology of Wikipedia that helps to discriminate the subset of right answers.

In more detail, in the IR part, starting with the initial question, its searches in the World Wide Web (WWW) using a search engine and the narrative of the question. Then, it uses a Part-Of-Speech Tagger on the top ranked web pages and detects all the candidate entities from the search results, extracting the *noun phrases*. After the collection of all different entities it uses IR measures to get the ranking of the potential importance of the candidate entities. Next, in the Semantic part, for a number of the top ranked entities, it gets the Wikipedia pages whenever this is possible. Our contribution is that our system tries to get the Semantic Information of the category names of the Wikipedia pages using a new vector representation for each entity. It constructs each vector by leveraging the category names of the Wikipedia pages and splitting them to words. Every vector's attributes contain the number of appearances of each word in the category names, excluding its stopwords. Afterwards, it clusters these vectors by using an intelligent method of clustering and automatically decides the total number of the clusters. The cluster which contains the maximum number of entities is considered to be the winning cluster, as it contains entities that share the same Wikipedia categories vocabulary and hence are more related to each other. Then it exploits the category information of the winning cluster to decide for the rest of the candidate entities if they are related to the question. Subsequently it searches for the homepages (or relevant pages) retrieving three URLs for each entity. Finally, we test our experimental results using the ClueWeb09 Dataset[1]

---

[1] `http://lemurproject.org/clueweb09.php/`

and the track files released from TREC 2009 Entity. Obviously it is required to find the corresponding IDs in ClueWeb09 Dataset of the entity's homepages and Wikipedia pages, so a batch query service[2] is used.

The paper is structured as follows. Section 2 discusses related work in the fields of QA and REF. Section 3 analyzes the first part of our system, that is, using IR methods to get a set of ranked candidate entities. Section 4 describes the Semantic part of the method which returns the final set of answers. Section 5 describes how the system finds the homepages of the entities returned from the previous section. Section 6 reports the experimental results. Finally, in Section 7 we draw our conclusions.

2   Related Work

With the rapid development of WWW, web data offers a huge amount of information to many fields. Before that, users would have to collect a lot of different documents in order to find information related to their query. In our days all the information is widely available online but problems persist; a lot of work is needed by users if they want to pinpoint the exact information they are looking for, which can be not only plain text answers but also homepages or URIs. QA tasks have evolved over time to reflect this differentiation in user needs.

2.1   Question Answering from Texts

QA is a task requiring a good expertise in several natural language processing fields to properly understand information needs in the questions, to obtain a list of candidate answers from documents and to filter them based on solid evidence that justifies each answer's correctness. Historically, in the first years of the development of this task, due to the weak spread of the WWW, QA systems were grown on offline text collections. Most state-of-the-art QA approaches are textual QA systems built around a passage retrieval core, where questions or affirmative re-phrasings of a question are treated only as bag-of-words or n-grams, ignoring all their semantic content. These question representations, which are very simplified, are given into an information retrieval engine to obtain the paragraphs or the article that is most likely to contain answers. The candidates are then extracted based on their type and ranked based on their frequency in the article or the union of the articles returned from the information retrieval engine. Passage-retrieval QA systems have their share of success in QA evaluation tracks such as QA@CLEF [17], which include a considerable amount of concrete questions (such as factoid or definition questions). Answers to these questions can usually be found in the collection within a paragraph containing a sentence similar to the question, for example for question "Where is X located ?" something like "X is located in Y", or by exploiting redundant information in large collections such as the WWW. As textual QA systems focus on selecting

---

[2] http://boston.lti.cs.cmu.edu/Services/batchquery/

text excerpts from the collection, it is true that they cannot address structurally complex questions that require advanced reasoning over key entities, nor questions whose answers are not explicitly represented in a text excerpt, but must be inferred from knowledge that may be automatically derived from those text excerpts.

2.2 Semantic QA

With the recent rapid growth of the Semantic Web (SW) and projects like DBpedia [1], YAGO [20] and the recent interest in Linked Open Data[3], the processes of searching and querying content that is both massive in scale and heterogeneous have become increasingly challenging. The main difference between textual and semantic QA is that in systems of the second kind, external sources of knowledge are used empowering the system with semantic capabilities. Also, in contrast to textual QA, semantic QA employs processes that go beyond matching questions and documents: external knowledge in a formal representation (such as RDF) can be used to reason over disambiguated concepts and entities, derive relations between them and infer answers from the question representation. While textual QA approaches can be successful in finding explicitly stated answers from documents, semantic QA aims at complex questions where several information sources must be merged. The main differences between textual and semantic QA are presented in Table 1 [3].

Table 1. Key differences between textual QA and semantic QA approaches

Textual QA	Semantic QA
[web of] documents	[web of] data
document retrieval (IR core)	search for and derive facts (IE core)
query expansion on word level	question expansion on entity level
keywords & co-occurrence	concepts & relations
ambiguous words (or even word forms)	disambiguated concepts
textual snippets	graph patterns
gazetteers	RDF data
lexical semantics (thesaurus oriented)	formal semantics
Text with entities	Linked entities with text

2.3 Related Entity Finding (REF)

An evolution of semantic QA is Related Entity Finding. REF is defined as follows: Given an input entity, by its name and homepage, the type of the target entity, as well as the nature of their relation, described by a narrative, we seek to find related entities that are of target type, standing in the required relation to the input entity. The main differences between REF and the two previous

---
[3] http://linkeddata.org/

types of question answering (textual and semantic) are i) the answer in general consists of many entities so the system must return a list and ii) instead of returning only plain text containing the answer, the system must return the entities with their URIs, homepages and optionally related web pages. Systems that perform REF share a common multiple-stage framework which consists of the following five stages: document retrieval, entity extraction, entity filtering, entity ranking and homepage detection. REF has been investigated by the Text REtrieval Conference (TREC) in 2009 [2]. Table 2 shows an example of a topic of this track.

Table 2. Topic 4 of TREC 2009

```
<query>
<num>4</num>
<entity_name>Philadelphia</entity_name>
<entity_URL>clueweb09-en0011-13-07330</entity_URL>
<target_entity>organization</target_entity>
<narrative>Professional sports teams in Philadelphia.</narrative>
</query>
```

3 Implementation: Information Retrieval Part

3.1 Candidate Entity Extraction

In this part, we investigate how to gather candidate entities that might be answers to the question. In our implementation we shall consider as questions the narratives of the TREC REF topics[4]. The motivation for using this dataset is that the topics are simplified questions and extra information about the category of the target entities is given. Some of the narratives of the topics are "Professional sports teams in Philadelphia", "Airlines that currently use Boeing 747 planes" and "CDs released by the King's Singers". An example of a full topic is defined in XML form in Table 2.

At first, for each narrative-question we search the WWW by using the Bing Search API[5] and the narrative as the query, after the removal of stopwords. The first 40 HTML page results are retrieved. After this, all the pages retrieved are parsed and plain text is extracted from HTML. It is well known that the entities which answer to the queries are *noun phrases*. For this acceptance we use the Stanford Log-linear Part-Of-Speech Tagger (POS Tagger)[6] for each word (and other token) contained in the text. A part of speech tag, such as noun, verb, adjective, etc is assigned to every word. Next, we extract all the noun phrases in every plain text using a pattern for the tagged words. The pattern used is `<JJ>?<NN.*|FW>+<IN>?<DT|CC>?<JJ>?<JJ>?<NNP.*>+`, where JJ, NN.*, FW, IN, DT, CC and NNP.* are for adjectives, nouns, foreign words, prepositions or

---

[4] http://trec.nist.gov/data/entity/09/09.entity-topics
[5] https://datamarket.azure.com/dataset/5BA839F1-12CE-4CCE-BF57-
    A49D98D29A44
[6] http://nlp.stanford.edu/software/tagger.shtml

subordinating conjunctions, determiners, coordinating conjunctions and proper nouns, respectively, used in the Penn Treebank Project [16]. For creating the pattern we started from [7] which we further developed to make it more efficient.

Usually, the related entities that are possible answers to a query are located near the entity name (see Table 2, third line) or the remaining words of the narrative of the query. For this reason we retain only the entities that are in the same sentence with the target entity or at least one of the words contained in the narrative, after stopwords removal. Additionally, we remove all the common nouns that might be retrieved, since answers to the REF task cannot contain common nouns. These entities constitute the set of our candidate entities. Our next task is to rank these entities so that the candidate entities that are ranked at the top of the list are more likely to be in the set of the correct answers.

3.2   Entity Ranking

We have a set of all the extracted candidate entities and we need to find the most relative ones. We rank them using a *linear combination* of five measures. These are: *a*) the Term Frequency (TF); *b*) the Inverse Document Frequency (IDF); *c*) the average number of the appearances of the candidate entity in the pages in which appeared in at least at once; *d*) the average number of the entities between the candidate entity the entity name of the topic; and *e*) the sum of the inversed rank of the web pages the candidate entity appeared in (SumRank). All of them are normalized in [0,1]. To find the optimal weights of the above measures for the linear combination we used a small dataset, taking as answers for the topics the examples of the topics for the ELC task [2], a task similar to the REF task, sharing the same topics and narratives. The optimal weights are the ones that used in a linear combination rank higher the entities that we know beforehand are correct answers to the queries. Only two of the measures we used ended up with non-zero weights, IDF and SumRank:

IDF [15]. IDF is a measure of whether the term is common or rare across all documents. It is obtained by dividing the total number of web pages returned by the Bing Search API by the number of web pages containing the candidate entity and then taking the logarithm of the quotient (1)

$$idf(t, D) = \log \frac{|D|}{|\{d \in D : t \in d\}|}, \qquad (1)$$

where $|D|$ is the total number of web pages returned by the Bing Search API and $|\{d \in D : t \in d\}|$ is the number of web pages where the candidate entity t appears in the sentences we have kept. The base of the log function does not matter and constitutes a constant multiplicative factor towards the overall result.

Sum Rank. Sum Rank is the sum of the inversed rank of the web pages, returned by the Bing Search API, in which the candidate entity appeared at least once. For example, if a candidate entity appears in the sentences of the first, the fourth and the fifteenth web page, returned by Bing Search API, and the total number of the pages we keep is 40, the sum is $(40-1)+(40-4)+(40-15) = 100$. *Sum Rank* is a measure of the quality of the pages an entity appears in, since the first returned by a search engine are usually the most relevant.

So the final linear combination is:

$$rank = a \times IDF + b \times SumRank. \tag{2}$$

The weights a and b found to give the best results for the values *0.9* and *0.1* respectively. In the end, we keep the top 75 entities for every query topic and we assign a ranking ID from 1 (the top ranked) to 75 (the least ranked).

4 Implementation: Semantic Part

4.1 Entity Vector Representation Based on Wikipedia Categories

In this part, we start by using the ranked candidate entities from the previous part. We choose only the top 25 best ranked entities and search for their corresponding Wikipedia page if one exists. For every candidate entity we find its corresponding article using the MediaWiki API[7]. Mediawiki is a free server-based software written in PHP, which helps access the Wikipedia articles, searching for the respective articles of an entity, their categories and their links. In many cases, more than one Wikipedia article may correspond to an entity, so a link to a disambiguation page also exists. A disambiguation page may be used to disambiguate a number of homonym terms that are written in the same way but have different meanings. For example, the term "Eagle" may refer to the bird, to the Philadelphia Eagles team or to a film named "Eagle". The title of a disambiguation page contains the ambiguous term itself, concatenated with the word "disambiguation" for example "Eagle (disambiguation)". If only one Wikipedia article corresponds to a candidate entity, then there is no disambiguation page. We first collect this single-meaning entities in a set called the *disambiguated set*. The rest of the entities, having more than one meaning, which could correspond to different Wikipedia pages, form another set that we call *set for disambiguation*. We will propose a Word Sence Disambiguation (WSD) method in Section 4.3. After the WSD process we gather all category names of each entity in the disambiguated set. The category names in Wikipedia consist, in general, of more than one word. For example, for the Wikipedia page "Philadelphia Eagles" three of its categories are "Steagles", "National Football League teams" and "Sports in Philadelphia, Pennsylvania". Although the first category consists of only one word (Steagles) the next two consist of four words. As the Wikipedia category names for every page are manually added, it is very common to be inconsistent. For example, noticing the category names "Sports in Philadelphia, Pennsylvania" and "National Football League teams" for the entity "Philadelphia Eagles" and the category names "Soccer clubs in Philadelphia, Pennsylvania" and "Pennsylvania soccer teams" for the entity "Philadelphia KiXX", we presume that both

---

[7] http://en.wikipedia.org/w/api.php

entities are "teams in Philadelphia, Pennsylvania" although they don't belong to any common category. We then proceed to splitting all these categories into the individual words they are made of. Furthermore, all stopwords like "and", "or" etc are removed. The remaining words are stemmed with the Porter2 stemming algorithm [14]. Finally, a vector is constructed with its dimension equal to the cardinality of all the different stemmed words that are found in all the categories of every candidate entity included in the disambiguated set. The attributes of this vector are the stemmed category words. The value of each attribute for each candidate entity is the *term frequency* of every stemmed word found in its Wikipedia page categories. For example, if we have the candidate entities "Philadelphia Eagles" and "Philadelphia Flyers" and the Wikipedia page of the first one belongs to the categories "National Football League teams", "Philadelphia Eagles", "Sports in Philadelphia, Pennsylvania" and the Wikipedia page of the second to "Philadelphia Flyers" and "Professional ice hockey teams in Pennsylvania", the resulting vectors are shown in Table 3. Zero values mean that the corresponding attributes do not exist in any category of this candidate entity. Representing the information given by the category names of the entities in vectors, such as the example above, helps use unsupervised methods, such as clustering, to get the relevance between the candidate entities.

Table 3. Vectors of the entities "Philadelphia Eagles" and "Philadelphia Flyers"

entity name	ice	hocke	philadelphi	sport	pennsylvani	nation	football	leagu	team	professional	flyer	eagl
Philadelphia Eagles	0	0	2	1	1	1	1	1	1	0	0	1
Philadelphia Flyers	1	1	1	0	1	0	0	0	1	1	1	0

4.2   Data Pre-processing

Before proceeding to clustering we need to pre-process the data to eliminate any differences between two vectors, such as differences of scale. We use the *Standard score* or *Z-value* [5], which indicates by how many standard deviations an observation or datum is above or below the mean. It is a dimensionless quantity derived by subtracting the population mean from an individual raw score and then dividing the difference by the population standard deviation. Our processed values of the vectors are estimated by Equation (3)

$$y_{iu} = \frac{x_{iu} - \bar{x}_u}{Range(x_u)},$$
(3)

where x is the dataset, i a given vector of an entity and u are the attributes of the vector. The result y_{iu} is the standardized form of x_{iu}.

4.3   Semantic Clustering

We will describe our entity clustering method and illustrate how clustering the entities in this new vector space provides semantic properties to the resulting clusters, in the sense that entities belonging to the same cluster are more closely related semantically.

Defining the Number of Clusters. We now have a set of vectors pre-processed by Standard score that we wish to cluster. In this step, we must decide for the number of clusters. We set the number of clusters between two and six using the *silhouette width* [12], a well-balanced coefficient, which has shown good performance in experiments [13]. The concept of silhouette width involves the difference between within-cluster tightness and separation from the remaining clusters. Specifically, the silhouette width $s(i)$ for entity $i \in I$ is defined by Equation (4)

$$s(i) = \frac{b(i) - a(i)}{\max{(a(i), b(i))}},\tag{4}$$

where $a(i)$ is the average distance between i and all other entities of the cluster to which i belongs and $b(i)$ is the minimum of the average distances between i and all entities in each other cluster. The silhouette width values lie in the range from -1 to 1.

Clustering Using k-Means. We use the simple k-means clustering algorithm [18]. Its input is the set of vectors returned from the previous step. The number of clusters is defined as the minimum number between two and six, such that the mean silhouette width value of the clusters is more than 0.5. If the mean silhouette width is not more than 0.5 for any number of clusters between two and six, then we arbitrarily set the number of clusters equal to six.

Fig. 1 shows the clusters resulting for the query of topic 4 ("Professional sports teams in Philadelphia") after *Principal Component Analysis* (PCA) [11] [9] is applied for two-dimensional visualization of the clustered vectors. We observe that 3 clusters were created for the candidate entities. Cluster 1 contains the entity "NASCAR" which is a motor racing championship. Cluster 2, which is the biggest, contains entities that are sport teams which is the right type of category for the answers. Finally, cluster 3 contains entities that are stadiums. As we can see the system already has the capacity to discriminate groups of entities belonging to different semantic categories.

Choosing the Winning Cluster and Obtaining the Rest of the Seed Entities. To choose the cluster that corresponds to the right categories we simply select the cluster with the most data points in it and, if there is a tie between two clusters, the cluster that contains entities that have the lesser sum of the ranking IDs. For example, for the clusters in Fig. 1, cluster 2 is chosen, because it contains the most entities. We call these entities, included in the winning cluster, *seed entities*. These entities enter the answer set.

WSD for the Rest of the Entities. We first get the stemmed words from the category names of the seed set in the same way we did before. We also keep the frequency of every unique stemmed word from all the category names of all the *seed entities*, which were in the winning cluster. These values are normalized to (0,1). After this procedure, for each entity for disambiguation, we get all the different Wikipedia articles that this entity could be assigned to. Obviously, every different meaning and corresponding different Wikipedia page of each entity

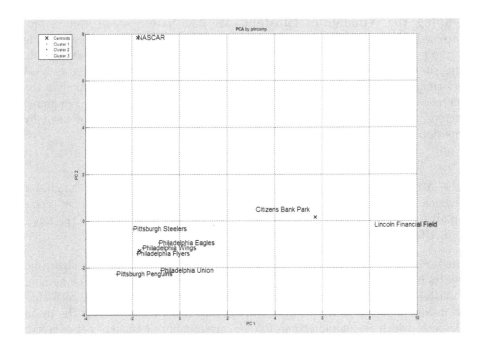

Fig. 1. Clusters for the candidate entities of disambiguated set of topic 4 after Principal Component Analysis is applied for visualization in a two-dimensional graph

belongs to different categories. For every Wikipedia article corresponding to a different meaning, all its categories are again collected, split into words, have their stopwords removed and finally stemmed. Then, for each meaning we produce the inner product of the term frequency vector of the words in the categories in common with the categories of the winning cluster and the normalized vector of the previous procedure. For each of these entities we keep only the meaning with the highest score. This meaning is much more probable than the others to answer the query, because it shares similar Semantic Information with the entities in the answer set. We must then decide whether this chosen meaning of the entity shares enough category words with the winning cluster to be relevant and enter the answer set. To achieve this goal, we first define a quantity, called *minimumb*,

$$minimumb = \min_{e \in E} \frac{score_e}{|W_e|}, \tag{5}$$

where E is the *seed entities set*, e is every entity in *seed entities set* and $|W_e|$ is the cardinality of the words found in the categories of the seed's entity e Wikipedia article, excluding stopwords. $Score_e$ is computed by the Equation (6)

$$score_e = \sum_{w \in c:C_e} \frac{w}{w_E},\qquad(6)$$

where C_e is the set of categories of seed entity e, w is every word in the categories, excluding stopwords and w_E is the maximum number of appearances of the most frequent word of the categories. We have empirically found that if the inner product is more than three quarters of the *minimumb*, then the entity is very likely to share very common Semantic Information with the entities in the remaining answer set and therefore be one of the query answers.

If the entities that have been appended to the answer set are more than 60% of the initial 25 candidate entities, that is more than 15, there is a high probability that there exist more entities that could be added to the answer set from the remaining 50 candidate entities. For this reason, we check whether some of the next 25 ranked entities, with rank IDs from 26 to 50, could be added to the answer set. This is done in the same way we did for the candidate entities of the set for disambiguation before. Again, if the total number of entities entering the answer set continues to be more than 40% of the candidate entities that have been checked, we proceed to check the remaining last 25.

5   Finding Primary and Relevant Homepages

In order to be able to compare our system with other algorithms on the TREC 2009 REF data, we need to retrieve three candidate homepages for every entity in the answer set in addition to its Wikipedia page. Starting from the already known Wikipedia page, it is possible in some cases to find the official homepage of the entity by parsing the Infobox, if one exists. If there is no Infobox, we simply collect the top links returned by Bing so as to have three candidate homepages for each entity, outside its Wikipedia page. Table 4 shows an example of three URLs the system retrieved for the entity "British Airways". The first one is evaluated in the track as the primary homepage of the entity, the second one as a relevant homepage and the last one as an irrelevant page. Furthermore, all evaluations of this track are performed by using ClueWeb09 dataset, so it is also required to find the corresponding ClueWeb09 IDs of the homepages. This is easily done by using a batch query service[8].

6   Results

In this section we present our experiments. We evaluated our method in the TREC 2009 Entity Track Dataset which contains 20 topics. These topics give additional information about the type of the target entity and the entity name.

The evaluation of the REF task is complicated since it is not always possible to gather all possible answers with certainty. For topics such as "carriers that BlackBerry makes phones for" finding all the answers is feasible. On the other

---

[8] http://boston.lti.cs.cmu.edu/Services/batchquery/

Table 4. Pages retrieved for the entity "British Airways"

ID 'URI
1 'http://ba.com
2 'http://www.guardian.co.uk/business/britishairways
3 'http://www.justtheflight.co.uk/news/18339089-aer-lingus-announces-british-airways-codeshare.html

hand, for topics such as "airlines that currently use Boeing 747 planes" this is more difficult, since the set of correct answers changes rapidly over time and, even if an airline has ceased to use Boeing 747 planes, a number of web pages in the WWW may still list it as an answer, a problem known as *Concept Drift* [19]. Because of these difficulties, in order to evaluate our results, we use the "Category B" subset of ClueWeb09 dataset, manually annotated pages considered pertinent to the topics. First, we have to pass our resulting URLs to their respective ClueWeb09 IDs. For this task we use the ClueWeb09 batch query service. If a URL exists in ClueWeb09, then its ClueWeb09 ID is returned, otherwise -1. To evaluate our results we used the qrel file[9], released by the TREC 2009 Entity Track. For every topic in this file, there exist a number of records that have a ClueWeb09 ID or a name of an entity, and help us check whether the homepages (or entities) retrieved are primary or relevant. It must be noted that a name was judged correct if it matched up in the record, even if the record was neither primary nor relevant to the topic. This means that the qrel file may include false entries. Evaluation results are computed using a script[10] developed specifically for the 2009 edition of the Entity track.

The main evaluation measures we use are the number of primaries and relevant homepages for all topics, P@10 (the fraction of records in the first ten ranks with a primary homepage) and the normalized discounted cumulative gain (NDCG) [10] at rank R (NDCG@R). A record with a primary homepage (or an entity name) scores 2 points, and a record with a relevant page scores 1 point. For example for the URIs retrieved for the entity "British Airlines" (see Table 4), the first URI scores 2 points, the second scores 1 and the last scores 0. Table 5 shows our evaluation results compared with the results obtained by other groups presented within the Related Entity Finding task of TREC 2009 Entity Track, ordered by the number of primary homepages found.

Comparative results show that our system yields the best performance for the primary retrieved homepages and the fraction of records in the first 10 ranks with a primary homepage. It also scores comparable results for the relevant retrieved homepages and the NDCG at rank R measure.

---

[9] http://trec.nist.gov/data/entity/09/09.entity.qrels
[10] http://trec.nist.gov/data/entity/09/eval-entity.pl

Table 5. Number of primary retrieved, number of relevant retrieved, P@10 and NDCG@R measures for each group as reported in [2]

Group	#pri	#rel	P@10	NDCG@R
Our system	**93**	56	**0.25000**	0.1020
uogTr	79	**347**	0.1200	0.2662
CAS	70	80	0.2350	0.2103
NiCT	64	99	0.1550	0.1907
Purdue	61	126	0.2350	**0.3061**
TUDelft	42	108	0.0950	0.1351
UAms (Amsterdam)	19	198	0.0450	0.1773
EceUdel	10	102	0.0000	0.0488
BIT	9	81	0.0200	0.0416
Waterloo	5	55	0.0100	0.0531
UALR CB	4	15	0.0200	0.0666
BUPTPRIS	3	48	0.0150	0.0892
UIUC	3	64	0.0100	0.0575
UAms (ISLA)	1	30	0.0000	0.0161

7   Conclusion and Future Work

We presented a system that performs Related Entity Finding. It collects candidate answers from the WWW and ranks them using IR measures, thus overcoming usual content shortcomings of QA systems based on specialized ontologies. We propose a novel vector representation for the entities by splitting into words the Wikipedia categories they belong to. This representation gives our system the ability to calculate a measure of the semantic relatedness between entities, even if they don't share common categories or are not related in an hierarchical way like in most ontologies. We exploit this property by proposing a Semantic Clustering which groups semantically related entities and show that the most important (winning) cluster corresponds to the right category for answers. Finally, we show how to effectively enlarge the winning cluster so as to include more candidate answers. Results on the TREC 2009 REF Track show very competitive performance, outperforming all other algorithms on the two criteria related to finding primary homepages and performing comparably on the other two criteria, taking also into account related homepages.

In the future we will try to further enhance the performance of our system by using LingPipe [4] as a noun phrase extractor or the Stanford NER [8] for Named Entity Recognition. We would also try to leverage the semantics of additional ontologies, exploiting the properties of Linked Data. Finally, it would be useful to explore better methods for extracting the relevant pages.

References

1. Auer, S., Bizer, C., Kobilarov, G., Lehmann, J., Cyganiak, R., Ives, Z.G.: DBpedia: A nucleus for a web of open data. In: Aberer, K., et al. (eds.) ASWC 2007 and ISWC 2007. LNCS, vol. 4825, pp. 722–735. Springer, Heidelberg (2007)
2. Balog, K., de Vries, A.P., Serdyukov, P., Thomas, P., Westerveld, T.: Overview of the trec 2009 entity track. In: TREC (2009)
3. Cardoso, N., Dornescu, I., Hartrumpf, S., Leveling, J.: Revamping question answering with a semantic approach over world knowledge. In: Braschler, M., Harman, D., Pianta, E. (eds.) CLEF (Notebook Papers/LABs/Workshops) (2010), http://dblp.uni-trier.de/db/conf/clef/clef2010w.html#CardosoDHL10
4. Carpenter, B., Baldwin, B.: Natural Language Processing with LingPipe 4. LingPipe Publishing, New York, draft edn. (June 2011), http://alias-i.com/lingpipe-book/lingpipe-book-0.5.pdf
5. Cheadle, C., Vawter, M.P., Freed, W.J., Becker, K.G.: Analysis of microarray data using z score transformation. The Journal of Molecular Diagnostics 5(2), 73–81 (2003), http://www.sciencedirect.com/science/article/pii/S1525157810604552
6. Demner-fushman, D., Lin, J.: Answering clinical questions with knowledge-based and statistical techniques. In: Computational Linguistics 2006, pp. 63–103 (2007)
7. Figueroa, A., Neumann, G.: Mining web snippets to answer list questions. In: Proceedings of the 2nd International Workshop on Integrating Artificial Intelligence and Data Mining, vol. 84, pp. 61–71. Australian Computer Society, Inc. (2007)
8. Finkel, J.: Named entity recognition and the stanford ner software (2007)
9. Jackson, J.: A User's Guide to Principal Components. Wiley series in probability and mathematical statistics: Applied probability and statistics. Wiley (1991), http://books.google.com.sg/books?id=f9s6g6cmUTUC
10. Järvelin, K., Kekäläinen, J.: Cumulated gain-based evaluation of ir techniques. ACM Transactions on Information Systems (TOIS) 20(4), 422–446 (2002)
11. Jolliffe, I.T.: Principal Component Analysis, 2nd edn., Springer (October 2002), http://www.amazon.com/exec/obidos/redirect?tag=citeulike07-20&path=ASIN/0387954422
12. Leonard, K., Peter, R.: Finding groups in data: an introduction to cluster analysis (1990)
13. Pollard, K., Van Der Laan, M.: A method to identify significant clusters in gene expression data. U.C. Berkeley Division of Biostatistics Working Paper Series, p. 107 (2002)
14. Porter, M.F.: The Porter2 stemming algorithm (2002)
15. Robertson, S.: Understanding inverse document frequency: On theoretical arguments for idf. Journal of Documentation 60, 2004 (2004)
16. Santorini, B.: Part-of-speech tagging guidelines for the penn treebank project (3rd revision) (1990)
17. Santos, D., Cabral, L.M.: Gikiclef: Crosscultural issues in an international setting: asking non-english-centered questions to wikipedia. In: Cross Language Evaluation Forum: Working Notes of CLEF 2009, Corfu (2009)
18. Seber, G.A.F.: Frontmatter, in Multivariate Observations. John Wiley & Sons, Inc., Hoboken (2008), doi:10.1002/9780470316641.fmatter
19. Šilić, A., Dalbelo Bašić, B.: Exploring classification concept drift on a large news text corpus. In: Computational Linguistics and Intelligent Text Processing, pp. 428–437 (2012)
20. Suchanek, F.M., Kasneci, G., Weikum, G.: Yago: a core of semantic knowledge. In: Proceedings of the 16th International Conference on World Wide Web, WWW 2007, pp. 697–706. ACM, New York (2007), http://doi.acm.org/10.1145/1242572.1242667

Locality Sensitive Hashing for Similarity Search Using MapReduce on Large Scale Data

Radosław Szmit

Warsaw University of Technology - Electrical Engineering
Institute of Control and Industrial Electronics

Abstract. The paper describes a very popular approach to the problem of similarity search, namely methods based on Locality Sensitive Hashing (LSH). To make coping with large scale data possible, these techniques have been used on the distributed and parallel computing framework for efficient processing using MapReduce paradigm from its open source implementation Apache Hadoop.

1 Introduction

Similarity search is an important problem present in many branches of science like databases, data mining, machine learning, information retrieval, clustering and near-duplicate detection [1]. In the XXI century the amount of data increases tenfold every five years. For this reason we are forced to take advantage of new approaches in computing such large data sets. We can do it thanks to MapReduce paradigm implemented in Apache Hadoop project.

2 Problem Definition

The aim of similarity search is in general to retrieve the top-k most similar objects to searched object q from a given collection D [1,2]. It is also possible to search for all objects such that their similarity is stronger then given threshold t.

This article presents a more specific version of similarity search problem, *All Pairs similarity search problem*, where we do not have any query object and we are searching for all pairs of objects with similarity greater than some threshold [1].

3 Jaccard Similarity

The Jaccard similarity coefficient, also known as the Jaccard index or Tanimoto coefficient, is a simple and effective coefficient which measures similarity of two sets [2].

It is defined as:

$$J(A, B) = \frac{|A \cap B|}{|A \cup B|},$$

(1)

M.A. Kłopotek et al. (Eds.): IIS 2013, LNCS 7912, pp. 171–178, 2013.

where A and B are two sets to be compared. As we see, the more the two sets overlap, the stronger similarity they display; it is a number between 0 and 1 - when sets are more similar then their Jaccard index is closer to 1, when more dissimilar then Jaccard index is closer to 0.

In this paper, Jaccard similarity index is used to measure similarity between documents.

4   Locality Sensitive Hashing

Locality Sensitive Hashing (LSH) is an algorithm used for solving probabilistic dimension reduction of high dimensional spaces. It is widely used in nearest neighbour search on large scale data. It was introduced in [3].

The main idea is to hash the input data and put it into some buckets. The more similar the objects are, the higher probability they are in the same bucket.

5   MinHash

MinHash or the min-wise independent permutations locality sensitive hashing scheme was introduced in [4] and used to detect duplication in [5]. MinHash was used initially to detect duplicated web pages and eliminate them from search result in AltaVista search engine [6]. Currently used for example in the recommendations of Google News [7].

Let h be a random hash function that transforms members of set into distinct integers (or some other bigger space). The Min-Hashing function is defined as:

$$m_h(S) = m_h(v) = argmin\{h(v[i])\}, \tag{2}$$

where v is a vector of set S and v[i] is the i-th component of v. As we see, MinHashing function returns the smallest hash value from given collection of hashes calculated by function h.

For two different sets A and B, the results of Min-Hash function are equal $m_h(A) = m_h(B)$ when the minimum hash value of the union $A \cup B$ lies in the common part of $A \cap B$ [2], therefore:

$$Pr[m_h(A) = m_h(B)] = J(A, B), \tag{3}$$

where:

- Pr - probability
- $m_h(S)$ - Min-Hash value for set S
- $J(A, B)$ - The Jaccard similarity coefficient (see section 3)

Defining random variable such that it has the value of one when $m_h(A) = m_h(B)$ and zero in the opposite case, we can assume that is an unbiased estimator of $J(A, B)$. This estimator has too high variance to be useful, therefore in the MinHash scheme the idea is to reduce variance by averaging together several variables constructed in a similar way (see section 5.2).

5.1   MinHash with Many Hash Functions

One of the simplest ways to implement MinHash scheme is to use k different hash functions. In this approach we get k values of $m_h(S)$ for these k functions.

In this scheme to estimate $J(A, B)$ we use y/k as the estimate, where y is the number of hash function for which $m_h(A) = m_h(B)$. As we see, this estimate is the average of k different 0-1 random variables, each of which is an unbiased estimator of $J(A, B)$, therefore their average is also an unbiased estimator with the expected error $O(1/\sqrt{k})$.

Number of hashes depends on an expected error and similarity threshold. For example, with an expected error lower than or equal to 0.05, we need 350 hashes for similarity equal to 0.5 and only 16 hashes for similarity of 0.95 [1].

5.2   MinHash with a Single Hash Functions

Calculating multiple hash function very often is expensive computationally, therefore in this variant of MinHash scheme to avoid this hindrance we can use only one hash function and use it to select multiple values from given set S rather than selecting the smallest value per one hash function.

In this approach we define $m_k(S)$ to be function returning the subset of the k smallest values of h function. This subset $m_k(S)$ is used as a signature of set S, and the similarity is evaluated by comparing two signatures of any two sets.

To estimate $J(A, B)$ for two given sets A and B let define

$$X = m_k(m_k(A) \cup m_k(B)) = m_k(A \cup B). \tag{4}$$

X is a set of k smallest elements of $A \cup B$. The subset:

$$Y = X \cap m_k(A) \cap m_k(B), \tag{5}$$

is the set of members belonging to the intersection $A \cap B$. The unbiased estimator for this variant is $|Y|/k$ with expected error $O(1/\sqrt{k})$. As we see, this version gives the same result with the same expected error, but is computationally cheaper. The second difference is between estimators, where for multi hash variant we can get k or less values because two different hash functions may return the same value, but in the second approach of single hash function, subset Y always has exactly k members. However, when k is small compared to the size of sets, this difference is irrelevant.

6   Apache Hadoop

Hadoop is an open source, free, Java-based software framework that supports the distributed processing of large data sets. It was developed for reliable, scalable and distributed computing across clusters of computers using simple programming models. It is core of the Apache Hadoop project sponsored by the Apache Software Foundation [8,9].

It is constructed to scale up from single machine to thousands of nodes and more without any limits. The preferred operating systems is Linux but Hadoop can also work with BSD, OS X and Windows on any kind of computer without special hardware requirements. This library is designed to detect and handle failures on runtime, so allows the system to continue operating uninterrupted in case of a node failure.

The whole project includes modules like Hadoop MapReduce, Hadoop Distributed File System (HDFS) and related sub projects eg. HBase, ZooKeeper, Mahout etc.

Hadoop is used by companies and organizations such as Google, Yahoo, Facebook, Amazon, Allegro, eBay, IBM, ICM [8].

6.1   MapReduce

Hadoop implements a computational paradigm named MapReduce introduced by Google inc. in [10]. MapReduce is a programming model for processing and generating large data sets.

Input data is divided into many small fragments of work and passed into user specified function called *map* and *reduce*. *Map* function processes a key/value pair of input data to generate a set of intermediate key/value pairs and a *reduce* function merges all intermediate values associated with the same intermediate key together generating key/value output pairs of proceeded data.

MapReduce programs are automatically parallelized and executed on a cluster. Hadoop takes care of the details of partitioning the input data, scheduling the job's execution across a set of nodes, handling node failures, and managing the required communication between nodes and *map-reduce* functions. Every job may be executed or re-executed on any node in the cluster, but Hadoop tries to maximize local computation storaged data effectively. This allows for writing parallel and distributed jobs using large scale data without any specialist knowledge.

Hadoop implementation of MapReduce can run on a large cluster of commodity machines and is highly scalable; Yahoo cluster has 11000 nodes and it is used to manage 40 petabytes of enterprise data [11].

6.2   HDFS

Hadoop Distributed File System (HDFS) is a second core project of Apache Hadoop platform. It is a distributed file system invented to run on standard, various and low-cost hardware. HDFS is optimized for storing large data sets and providing high throughput access to this data. A typical file is the size of gigabytes to terabytes and it supports tens of millions of files in a single instance. It can be used like standard standalone file systems, but it implements write-once-read-many access model for files with the ability to append them.

HDFS is secured and designed to automatically detect and handle failures. Each node stores a part of the file system's data. It achieves reliability by replicating the data across multiple nodes with the default replication value equal to

3 and that means that data is stored on three nodes: two on the same rack, and one on a different rack. It also rebalances data, moves copies around and keeps the replication of data high.

7 System Architecture

The architecture of tested system is a standard Hadoop architecture (master/slave) with one master node called *NameNode* and 18 slave nodes called *DataNodes*. The *NameNode* has the ability to execute file system operations like opening, closing, and renaming files and directories and also to determine the mapping of blocks to DataNodes. The *DataNodes* are responsible for serving read and write requests from the file system's clients and also performing block creation, deletion, and replication on the command from the NameNode.

On the HDFS runs a key-value database called DDB. This database stores pairs of documents as values and their hashes as keys. All data is crawled via internet with the use of a special program called Spider. All documents are indexed and preprocessed to obtain their words lemmas.

8 Algorithms

Similarity search algorithms can be divided into two main steps – candidate generation and candidate verification. In the step of candidate generation we select pairs of objects that are good candidates for having similarity above the given threshold. During candidate verification phase, the similarity of pairs is verified against the threshold by exact computation of the similarity or other method [1].

The classic approach to this problem such as kd-trees and R-trees works well only in low dimensions data sets. Invention of Locality Sensitive Hashing (see section 4) made a big impact on computing very large scale data sets [3,12,1].

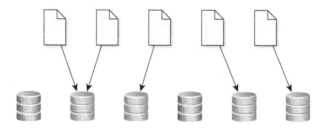

Fig. 1. Candidate generation phase

8.1 Candidate Generation Phase

In this step we used LSH method MinHash (min-wise independent permutations) described in section 5 adapted to Google MapReduce paradigm from section 6.1.

What was really handy was the use of the basic implementation of MinHash on Hadoop, that is the use of library Likelike [13]. The library was adapted to our specialised data input format and also it was adjusted to cooperate with DDB database working on Hadoop.

For all words in a document (exactly its lemma) hash value is counted by function h. Depending on MinHash variant with single hash function (see section 5.2), we calculate MinHash function value $m_k(S)$ defined as k smallest values of integers from vector v produced by hash function h. From that subset of v we calculating signature represented by single integer value. This signature lets us to assign this document to proper bucket or in the other words to proper cluster. This step was presented on figure 1.

8.2 Candidate Verification Phase

In this phase we must verify the similarity of all pairs of objects received from a single bucket. For that purpose we use the computation of the similarity of two documents based on Jaccard similarity coefficient shown in section 3. This step was presented on figure 2.

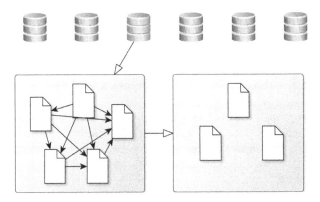

Fig. 2. Candidate verification phase

9 Summary of Results

In this article, we have presented Locality Sensitive Hashing scheme approach for similarity search problem using MapReduce paradigm on large scale data set. In candidate generation phase we used MinHash (min-wise independent permutations) scheme implemented in Likelike library. We adjust this approach and library to our needs and technical requirements. The results of similarity search were used to eliminate duplicated web pages from search results in search engine from Natively Enhanced Knowledge Sharing Technologies project.

As we predicted, locality sensitive hashing allows us to compute this task in finite and short time in comparison to traditional methods like kd-trees or R-trees. For example computing candidate generation phase on our cluster takes 15 mins, 07 sec for 8 167 022 documents and produced 6 348 635 baskets. Computational complexity of this task was linear, what is presented on figure 3.

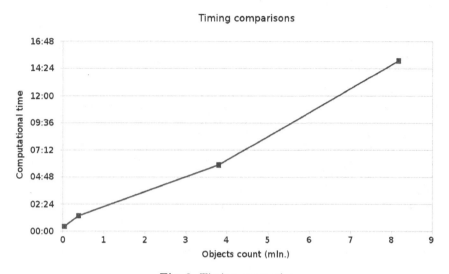

Fig. 3. Timing comparisons

10   Future Work

In the next step of research on similarity search problem we recommend to use the idea described in [14], namely to hash only sentences instead of whole documents. In this approach we are able to measure similarity also between some pairs of documents, for example citation, inclusion, partial copy. We can also hash lemmas instead of words omitting meaningless words, giving in this way a method for semantic and partial similarity comparison which is a very interesting topic for future research.

Acknowledgments. The author would like to acknowledge the contributions of NEKST team, especially his coordinator Dariusz Czerski. This research project was supported by funds from the science budget of the Republic of Poland and is cofounded by the European Union from resources of the European Regional Development Fund, Project Innovative Economy [15].

References

1. Venu Satuluri, S.P.: Bayesian locality sensitive hashing for fast similarity search. In: Proceedings of the VLDB Endowment (2012)
2. Yuan, P., Sha, C., Wang, X., Yang, B., Zhou, A., Yang, S.: XML structural similarity search using mapreduce. In: Chen, L., Tang, C., Yang, J., Gao, Y. (eds.) WAIM 2010. LNCS, vol. 6184, pp. 169–181. Springer, Heidelberg (2010)

3. Piotr Indyk, R.M.: Approximate nearest neighbors: towards removing the curse of dimensionality. In: Proceedings of the Thirtieth Annual ACM Symposium on Theory of Computing (1998)
4. Broder, A.: On the resemblance and containment of documents. In: Proceedings of Compression and Complexity of Sequences 1997, pp. 21–29 (1997)
5. Broder, A.Z., Charikar, M., Frieze, A.M., Mitzenmacher, M.: Min-wise independent permutations. JCSS 60(3), 630–659 (2000)
6. Broder, A.Z., Charikar, M., Frieze, A.M., Mitzenmacher, M.: Min-wise independent permutations. In: Proc. 30th ACM Symposium on Theory of Computing, STOC 1998 (1998)
7. Das, A., Datar, M., Garg, A.: Google news personalization: Scalable online collaborative filtering. In: Industrial Practice and Experience, Banff, Alberta, Canada, May 8-12 (2007)
8. Foundation, A.S.: Apache^{TM} hadoop®, http://hadoop.apache.org/
9. Cloudera: Hadoop and big data, http://www.cloudera.com/content/cloudera/en/why-cloudera/hadoop-and-big-data.html
10. Dean, J., Ghemawat, S.: Mapreduce: Simplified data processing on large clusters. In: OSDI 2004: Sixth Symposium on Operating System Design and Implementation, pp. 1–13 (2004)
11. Chansler, R., Kuang, H., Radia, S., Shvachko, K., Srinivas, S.: The hadoop distributed file system, http://www.aosabook.org/en/hdfs.html
12. Gionis, A., Motwani, P.I.R.: Similarity search in high dimensions via hashing. In: VLDB (1999)
13. Ito, T.: Likelike - an implementation of locality sensitive hashing with mapreduce., http://code.google.com/p/likelike/
14. Ceglarek, D., Haniewicz, K.: Fast plagiarism detection by sentence hashing. In: Rutkowski, L., Korytkowski, M., Scherer, R., Tadeusiewicz, R., Zadeh, L.A., Zurada, J.M. (eds.) ICAISC 2012, Part II. LNCS, vol. 7268, pp. 30–37. Springer, Heidelberg (2012)
15. NEKST: Natively enhanced knowledge sharing technologies (2009), http://www.ipipan.waw.pl/nekst/

Stabilization of Users Profiling Processed by Metaclustering of Web Pages

Michał Dramiński[1], Błażej Owczarczyk[2], Krzysztof Trojanowski[1,2],
Dariusz Czerski[1], Krzysztof Ciesielski[1], and Mieczysław A. Kłopotek[1]

[1] Institute of Computer Science of the Polish Academy of Sciences
[2] Cardinal Stefan Wyszyński University in Warsaw

Abstract. In this paper we report on an ongoing research project aiming at evaluation of the hypothesis of stabilization of Web user segmentation via cross site information exchange. We check stability of user membership in segments derived at various points of time from the content of sites they visit. If it is true that users of the same service share segments over time that pulling together clustering information over various services may be profitable. If not then the way how users are profiled or clustered needs to be revised.

1 Introduction

Profiling of users is nowadays viewed as an important way to improve quality of various services, especially of information services. The idea is to support the user in finding the piece of information he needs by exploiting the background knowledge about the group of users the user probably belongs to.

So one seeks to split the set of users into homogenous segments such that they can be described by features useful for the purposes of the service to be delivered. This may be done using some clustering methods or by other techniques.

One of the problems encountered is the instability of segments that are susceptible to noisy behaviour due to the sparseness of the set of users in particular if the number of potential interesting segments is large. In this paper we want to pose the question if we can be helped by pulling together clustering information from various services, potentially with disjoint sets of users, but with a similar type of service, in creating more robust or stable clusters than it is the case for a single service.

Imagine we have applied a clustering procedure to a set of session data and obtained a clustering of user profiles (splitting of data into clusters) and a clustering rule. Then new data come. We can both apply the clustering rule to assign the profiles in new data to the existing clusters or (re)cluster the old and new data from scratch. We will say that the clustering is stable if:

- the optimal number of clusters did not change or new clusters (after reclustering) are subclusters of existing ones
- new session data of old users (the users that were present in old data) fall into the same clusters as the old ones if we apply the clustering rule

M.A. Kłopotek et al. (Eds.): IIS 2013, LNCS 7912, pp. 179–186, 2013.

– after reclustering old users from the same old cluster fall into the same new cluster.

Within this paper we try to address the question whether or not there exist user behaviours that allow us to assume that such a stabilizing of clustering / segmentation is possible.

We report on an experiment concerning stability of user membership in segments derived at various points of time from the content of sites they visit. If it is true that users of the same service share segments over time that pulling together clustering information over various services may be profitable. If not then the way how users are profiled or clustered needs to be revised.

1.1 Metaclustering / Consensus Clustering

It has been long noticed that different algorithms may result in different clusterings of the same set of objects. In our case we look at profiles of the same users perceivable at different points in time. In each case there is a business need to find the most appropriate clustering. Two approaches to this issue can be distinguished in the literature:

– the meta-clustering where it is proposed to cluster the clusterings to find out which clusterings are similar to one another (see [5], also compare [12,4,7,6])
– the consensus clustering (called also in various brands ensemble clustering or cluster aggregation) where a similarity measure between clusterings is introduced and data is re-clustered to get a clustering close to the original ones or groups of clusters are formed (a kind of meta-clustering) where the meta-clusters compete for objects performing just a re-clustering (see [13] and also [9,10,8]).

In this paper we are interested in a middle way between these two approaches: Though our goal would be to construct a consensus clustering, we want ask first if we can cluster together pairs of clusters from different clusterings.

1.2 User Profiling

User profiling means usually inferring unobservable information about users from observable information about them. The inferred unobservable information is usually one of business value while the observable not.

The goal of profiling is usually to achieve some degree of adaptation meaning different (more appropriate) behaviour for different users. In particular in e-commerce applications the user or customer profile is used to make personalized offers and to suggest or recommend products the user is supposed to like.

In the context of internet systems, in the past various features of observed user behaviour have been used to obtain user profiles. In [14] a limited number of features generated from an IP address were used, like generated package similarity. Profiles were grouped together by a hierarchical clustering algorithm. In [1] click streams in short time intervals formed a basis to group people.

The short term group memberships were put together into longer vectors which were again subject of various clustering analyses.

In this paper we cluster the users based on textual content of documents they clicked as a result of queries they submit.

1.3   Clustering Stability

An excellent overview of the topic of clustering stability is given in [11]. They understand clustering algorithm instability for splitting into K clusters for sample sizes n $Instab(K, n)$ as the expected value of the distance between two clusterings $C_K(S_1), C_K(S_2)$ obtained for samples S_1, S_2. Samples can be collected in various ways (e.g. in [3] by sampling without replacement from the original set).

It is worth noting that clustering instability may have various roots [2]. The first one can be the structure of clusterings where multiple minima of the cluster optimization function may exist. The second source may be the sampling process itself resulting in cluster variance. The third one may the lack of computing resources preventing from achieving the global optimum.

It is claimed that for an ideal K-means algorithm (the one that is able to find global optimum) clusters will be unstable if K is too large, but for the proper K or lower they will be stable. For realistic K-means the noise level and uniform convergence are of significant impact.

1.4   Our Contribution

In this paper we investigate a very specific brand of cluster stability related first of all to the search behaviour of users over time, measured in terms of content of documents they visit. We explain the way how data for such investigation can be obtained, what kind of preprocessing work is needed and what difficulties are encountered in such investigations due to the sparseness of users common to various clustering points in time. We present the results and attempt to find an explanation why the clusters of user profiles seem to be apparently unstable over time.

2   Data

2.1   AOL Data

Our metaclustering experiment has been carried out on the so-called AOL data set. The collection includes 20 million keywords typed in the search engine by 650,000 users over three months (from March 1 to May 31, 2006). User queries are together with the information about clicked link for a given search results. User names in the data were replaced by numbers (user index).

The data is stored in the form of undirected bigraph with labeled nodes and edges. There are 2 types of nodes: *query* and *URL*. The nodes of the first type are described by the label containing the keywords typed into a search engine, the other nodes represent web pages with URL label. The existence of the edge between *URL* and *query* means that at least one user looking for *query* clicked in the result of the *URL* address. Edges are described by four following attributes:

- *click* - the number of clicks on the *URL* address on the search results page for keywords *query*
- *session* - IDs of users who have chosen the result *URL* for the *query*
- *time* - click date/time UNIX timestamp format
- *rank* - outcome position in search results

The graph contains 6 444 438 nodes (4 811 650 *query* and 1 632 788 *URL*) and 10 741 956 undirected edges.

3   The Experiment

The experiment is based on building of profiles of AOL users. These profiles are created separately for two different time periods (before and after some chosen date). We assume that each user is represented by a profile built on the web pages visited in a given period. For each of the two periods separated clustering is processed and finally groups from both periods are compared in a sense of users belonging.

Downloading the Web Pages. The first step was to download the contents of sites located at addresses described by *URL*. For this purpose Apache Nutch (crawler) in combination with Apache Solr (search engine - in this case used as a fast NoSQL database) has been used. Downloading using 10 threads took 74 days and the result has been correctly recorded for about 1.1 million pages.

Some web pages are currently unavailable because of:

- status http 403 - Forbidden
- status http 404 - Not Found
- status http 500 - Internal server error
- did not answer within 30 seconds

The content of properly downloaded pages has been filtered to remove html tags using Apache Tika and then uploaded to Solr.

Separation of Periods. Investigation of the users stability behavior over time requires two disjoint sets of profiles. The division can be set on the basis of cut-off date and collections resulting from the split will be called *before* and *after*.

Users who were active in only one of the periods do not affect on the results of the experiment and can be removed. On the other hand, we need the maximum number of profiles and it is important that the number of removed users is minimal. This number depends on the choice of cut-off date.AOL collection contains information about the sites visited between March 1st and May 31th (2006). In the middle of this range is the date of April 15th and it seemed to be the best candidate for cut-off date. In the next step we launched a program to select the best cut-off date. Date that allows to build the largest number of profiles of users who have been active in *before* and *after*. The number of active users was calculated for each day (time 00:00) in the range. As expected, the maximum value of active users corresponded to April 15th and it was 321 307.

Building of Users Profiles. The next step was to combine together the content of the pages visited by the user in one period. The following schema describes the method to obtain one document as the user's profile:

```
 1: function MERGEUSERSDOCUMENTS(Users)
 2:     for all range in (before, after) do
 3:         for all user in Users do
 4:             document ← CREATEEMPTYDOCUMENT
 5:             Pages ← GETPAGESVISITEDBYUSER(user)
 6:             for all page in Pages do
 7:                 document.content += page.content
 8:             end for
 9:             SAVEDOCUMENT(document)
10:         end for
11:     end for
12: end function
```

As a result of this operation we abtained 2 * 321 307 documents. Two for each user (*before* and *after*).

3.1 Text Analysis

The first step in the analysis of documents (in fact profiles) is tokenization. The result of tokenization are words (tokens) substracted from the document. Next these tokens are lower case normalized and filtered. Filtering removes *stop words* and tokens that contain characters other than the Latin alphabet. *Stop words* are selected based on total frequency. If token exists in more than 60% of documents we assume it is a *stop word*.To represent text documents we used VSM (Vector Space Model) model and to determine the importance of word we selected popular TFxIDF measure.

These steps have been performed on both sets of profiles generated previously (*before* and *after*) using the Apache Mahout. As a result we received two binary files containing objects org.apache.mahout.math.VectorWritable class. Result files before and after the cut-off date occupied respectively 5.7 and 5.9 GB of disk space.

Profiles have been used for clustering by k-means algorithm. This algorithm divides tokens vectors into k groups, trying to minimize the quantization error. To determine the measure of similarity between the two documents we used cosine measure. It defines the similarity between two vectors based on cosine of the angle between the directions of the n-dimensional space.

3.2 Quality Measures

As a result of metaclustering we obtained two separated sets of clusters with assigned users respectively for both periods. To investigate the stability of users there was needed to define a measure of similarity of two clusterings. It was decided to treat the data as a classification task and describe similarity by typical classification quality indicators. The result of the *before* period was considered as a reference point for the *after* one.

Accuracy is very good indicator of the overall quality of classification. For calculation of accuracy it is necessary to connect all clusters from two periods into pairs i (*before*) and j (*after*) to maximize TP_i^j (True Positive) factor. In other words we connect clusters where maximal number of same users appeared.

$$accuracy = \frac{\sum_{i,j=1}^{k} Max(TP_i^j)}{M}$$

$Max(TP_i^j)$ maximum TP for pair of clusters i and j
k number of clusters
M number of profiles

4   Results

The experiment was repeated 9 times with different number of groups. Table 1 presents accuracy for a defined number of groups. Second column contains experiment's result, the third column contains the value of accuracy that would result from randomly assigning profiles to groups. The last column shows the ratio of the real accuracy and that one related to random mapping. Values greater than 1 indicate a better result than a random assigning.

Table 1. Accuracy - number of clusters

clusters (k)	$Accuracy$ (%)	$Accuracy_{random}$ (%)	$\frac{Accuracy}{Accuracy_{random}}$
5	9.24	20	0.46
10	11.07	10	1.11
20	2.65	5	0.53
40	2.39	2.5	0.96
50	4.88	2	2.44
55	1.96	1.81	1.08
60	2.48	1.66	1.49
80	2.43	1.25	1.94
100	1.67	1	1.67

5 Summary

In this paper We investigated stability of user membership in segments derived at various points of time from the content of sites they visit. It turned out that users of the same service change segments over time for AOL data. This means on the one hand that pulling together clustering information over various services is of questionable value at least for the approach to clustering as pursued in this paper. Therefore it is necessary to look for different ways of user profiling or to apply different clustering procedures than those presented in this paper to achieve the goal of clustering stability.

As an implication of this apparently negative result, one shall consider the following issues:

- the possibility that users are in fact strongly different in their behavior over time so that no "flock of sheeps" behavior can be observed, at least in terms of their interests spread over a day
- the level of noise / instability induced by the K-means algorithm and the possibility to use a different clustering algorithm or an "incremental" K means in which second clustering starts with the results of the first and while clustering the data points of the first clustering are stepwise removed and replaced by the new data points
- the quality of search engine underlying the available data - whether or not it returns data really relevant to the information needs of the user
- the possibility of clustering either alone on the basis of queries or on text fragments "close enough" to the content of the query.

References

1. Antonellis, P., Makris, C., Tsirakis, N.: Algorithms for clustering clickstream data. Preprint Submitted to Information Processing Letters, IPL October 29 (2007), http://students.ceid.upatras.gr/~tsirakis/publications/Algorithms-for-Clustering-ClickStream-Data-TSIRAKIS.pdf
2. Ben-David, S., von Luxburg, U., P'all, D.: A sober look at clustering stability (2006), http://www.kyb.mpg.de/fileadmin/user_upload/files/publications/attachments/BenLuxPal06_%5B0%5D.pdf
3. Ben-Hur, A., Elisseeff, A., Guyon, I.: A stability based method for discovering structure in clustered data. In: Pacific Symposium on Biocomputing (2002)
4. Bifulco, I., Iorio, F., Napolitano, F., Raiconi, G., Tagliaferri, R.: Interactive visualization tools for meta-clustering. In: Proceedings of the 2009 conference on New Directions in Neural Networks: 18th Italian Workshop on Neural Networks: WIRN 2008, pp. 223–231. IOS Press, Amsterdam (2009), http://dl.acm.org/citation.cfm?id=1564064.1564092
5. Caruana, R., Elhawary, M., Nguyen, N., Smith, C.: Meta clustering. In: Proceedings of the Sixth International Conference on Data Mining, ICDM 2006, pp. 107–118. IEEE Computer Society, Washington, DC (2006), http://dx.doi.org/10.1109/ICDM.2006.103

6. Cui, Y., Fern, X.Z., Dy, J.G.: Learning multiple nonredundant clusterings. ACM Transactions on Knowledge Discovery from Data (TKDD) 4, 15:1–15:32 (2010), http://doi.acm.org/10.1145/1839490.1839496

7. Dasgupta, S., Ng, V.: Which clustering do you want? inducing your ideal clustering with minimal feedback. J. Artif. Int. Res. 39, 581–632 (2010), http://dl.acm.org/citation.cfm?id=1946417.1946430

8. Ghosh, J., Acharya, A.: Cluster ensembles. Wiley Interdisc. Rew.: Data Mining and Knowledge Discovery 1(4), 305–315 (2011)

9. Goder, A., Filkov, V.: Consensus clustering algorithms: Comparison and refinement. In: Munro, J.I., Wagner, D. (eds.) Proceedings of the Workshop on Algorithm Engineering and Experiments, ALENEX 2008, San Francisco, California, USA, January 19, pp. 109–117 (2008), http://www.siam.org/proceedings/alenex/2008/alx08_011godera.pdf

10. Hore, P., Hall, L.O., Goldgof, D.B.: A scalable framework for cluster ensembles. Pattern Recogn. 42(5), 676–688 (2009), http://dx.doi.org/10.1016/j.patcog.2008.09.027

11. von Luxburg, U.: Clustering stability: An overview. Foundations and Trends in Machine Learning 2(3), 235–274 (2009)

12. Niu, D., Dy, J.G., Jordan, M.: Multiple non-redundant spectral clustering views. Proc. ICML 2010 (2010), http://citeseerx.ist.psu.edu/viewdoc/download?doi=10.1.1.170.1490&rep=rep1&type=pdf

13. Strehl, A., Ghosh, J.: Cluster ensembles — a knowledge reuse framework for combining multiple partitions. J. Mach. Learn. Res. 3, 583–617 (2003), http://dx.doi.org/10.1162/153244303321897735

14. Wei, S., Mirkovic, J., Kissel, E.: Profiling and clustering internet hosts. In: Proc. WorldComp2006 (2006), http://www.isi.edu/~mirkovic/publications/DMI8155.pdf

Towards a Keyword-Focused Web Crawler

Tomasz Kuśmierczyk[1] and Marcin Sydow[2,1]

[1] Institute of Computer Science, Polish Academy of Sciences, Warsaw, Poland
[2] Polish-Japanese Institute of Information Technology, Warsaw, Poland
t.kusmierczyk@phd.ipipan.waw.pl, msyd@poljap.edu.pl

Abstract. This paper concerns predicting the content of textual web documents based on features extracted from web pages that link to them. It may be applied in an intelligent, keyword-focused web crawler. The experiments made on publicly available real data obtained from Open Directory Project[1] with the use of several classification models are promising and indicate potential usefulness of the studied approach in automatically obtaining keyword-rich web document collections.

1 Introduction and Motivation

Web crawler is a network application that automatically fetches large collections of web documents via http protocol according to some clearly defined crawling strategy. It is an essential module in various applications including search engines, for example. For some applications it is important to limit the fetching process only to documents that satisfy some criteria concerning their content, for example presence of specific keywords, specific topic of document, etc. Such task is known as *focused crawling*.

A crawler generally works in iterations that, in short, are as follows. Picking a bulk of URL addresses to be fetched, out of an internal priority queue, fetching them via http protocol, parsing and recording the fetched documents, pushing the parsed links that lead to new web documents into the priority queue. In real systems, the process is much more complicated, but the idea is generally as presented.

One of the key technical problems in focused crawling is that the fact whether a document to be fetched is worth fetching (i.e. satisfies the specified criteria) may be verified only *after* it is fetched. In practice, the ratio of web documents satisfying the focused-crawling criteria to all documents that are available in standard, BFS-like crawling scheme may be arbitrarily low. Thus, to save crawler's resources such as network bandwidth, hard disk, CPU, etc. and to efficiently fetch large collection that is rich of documents that satisfy the crawling criteria it is necessary to *predict* the contents of documents to be fetched *without fetching them*.

This can be stated as a binary classification problem: given some specific criterion and the set of already-crawled documents that contain links to an unknown web document x, predict whether x satisfies the criterion without fetching it. More precisely, a supervised learning approach can be used, i.e. the model is learnt on a portion of linked web documents and it is subsequently applied to unknown portion of the web.

---

[1] http://www.dmoz.org/

M.A. Kłopotek et al. (Eds.): IIS 2013, LNCS 7912, pp. 187–197, 2013.
© Springer-Verlag Berlin Heidelberg 2013

In this paper, we study a specific problem of predicting the presence of pre-specified keyword phrase on a web page rather than its topicality that makes it subtly different from most of approaches previously studied in the literature.

Such a specified task has many important applications that usually involve preparing a corpus of documents rich in specific keywords to be further processed by other tools. It may be then used for various tasks ranging from information extraction to statistical analysis of keyword presence to be subsequently used for tuning keyword-based web ad campaigns, for example.

1.1 Related Work

The idea of biasing the crawled collections towards a pre-specified criteria has been intensively studied since early times of web mining. Below we list a selection of representative early works on the topic.

Focused crawling based on a classifier was proposed in [4] where a naive Bayes approach was applied to predict categories of web pages to be fetched.

The phenomenon of "topical locality", i.e. a topical correlation of web documents in a link neighbourhood in WWW was studied in [5].

The idea of taking into account, during web content prediction, the pages that are a few links away, with the concept of context graphs was studied in [6].

Most works concerning the topic use naive Bayesian classifier, though [8] studies many other models and observes that other models may perform better, e.g. SVM (Support Vector Machine). In this paper we apply SVM and CART-Trees, besides Bayesian classifier to evaluate our approach. At this level of work our goal is not to select the best possible classifier and configuration but to gain some knowledge and intuition about their properties in context of the task. Therefore, we decided to use three popular approaches that are also known to be successful in solving similar problems. In further research one can carry additional experiments leading to slight increase in quality.

The concept of intelligent crawler that learns during the crawling was introduced in [1]. The same work proposes to measure the quality of intelligent or focused crawling with *harvest rate* – the proportion of documents "relevant" to the crawl criteria to all harvested documents. The same measure is used in our paper.

As an example of a recent survey, [2] studies various algorithms for prioritising the pages to be crawled with a PageRank-based importance measure.

In contrast to the cited works, and many others, our work focuses on a specific task of crawling web pages that are rich in pre-specified *keywords* rather than of a specific topic. In addition, while we adapt a combination of the machine-learning approaches studied in other works before, including context-graphs, for example, the techniques presented in this paper are very simple, efficient and topic-independent.

2   Problem Statement

In the work described in this paper we focus on a specific issue of short crawls based on usage of a small list of keywords with well chosen seed pages. This keywords might be user's queries or names of entities therefore their length is limited to just several words. By short crawls we understand crawls going no farther than ten or twenty jumps from layer of seed pages (in experiments we used 25 layers). By well chosen seed we understand the set of pages' URLs with high initial Harvest Ratio:

$$HR = \frac{|valuable\ pages|}{|fetched\ pages|}$$

where we define $valuable\ pages =\{$pages from set $fetched\ pages$ that contain each of keywords at least once$\}$ and by $fetched\ pages$ we understand all pages downloaded by crawler in specific set of crawl layers (layer = set of pages fetched by crawler in single work cycle).

3   General Ideas and Design

In our approach to focused crawling we utilized two main concepts in this area. Our design of a classifier can be understood as a combination of simplified content and link (graph context) analysis approaches. In contrast to the first type of crawlers we decided to use simple keyword-based features that can be computed in a very fast way. Also context is analysed in a simplified way: possible partial overlapping of different link paths is not investigated.

General design of a classification scheme is shown on Figure 1. The scheme presents a process of deciding whether to fetch or not considered page. The process is composed of several steps that produces different outcomes. Outcomes are denoted with consecutive letters of alphabet. The result of last step is a final decision that can be then applied by fetching module. This decision can be interpreted as mentioned in introduction "prediction of content" e.g. system predicts whether considered page contains keywords or not.

The first step of a decision making process is to extract features (denoted with letter A on the Figure 1) of all link paths that lead to the considered URL. It is obvious that only paths included in known part of the web-graph are considered. To avoid loops and filter out irrelevant paths we consider only these links that lead from lower to higher layer. In our implementation we limited paths' length to tree hops.

For every link in the path simple features are extracted:

- whether it points out at valuable (in the sense of the criteria) page or not (of course this feature is not known for the last link in path)
- how many hops backward is needed to get to valuable page
- what is minimum/average distance (measured in number of words) between link position on the page and criteria keywords
- what is the number of keywords occurrences in the link source page
- what would be the fraction of valuable pages considering layers up to the one where the source page is placed if we have not applied cutting-off

As one can see at this point we exploit textual content of previously fetched pages. Nevertheless the content is used in a very simplified and therefore low-cost way e.g. single occurrences and relative positions of keywords are considered. Such an approach

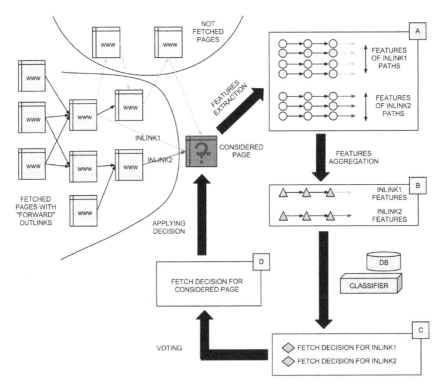

Fig. 1. General schema of features extraction and classification process

uses only small part of available information but as further experiments showed final result, after incorporating these features into graph context structures, is very promising.

During the evaluation process we tested three different subsets of features. First, denoted as Rich, consist of all possible features. In the second, denoted as Poor, we include only 5 features: number of keywords for all pages in considered path (3 features), whether previous page was valuable or not (1 feature) and what is the minimum distance between link and keywords in the current page (1 feature). Third set of features, denoted as Medial, includes a number of features in between Rich and Poor sets.

In the second step, lists of features for paths are grouped according to the last link in the path and then aggregated. For example, having two in-links for the considered URL we obtain two vectors of features (one per each URL). These vectors (denoted with letter B on the Figure 1) are used in classification process: either for training or for test/final classifying.

Classifiers need to define positive and negative class for them. The simplest approach (denoted Simple) is to select links that directly point to a valuable page. Fetching or not of some page may influence reachabilitiy of other pages. Therefore we also considered strategies based on harvest ratio estimation: link is added to positive class if fraction of valuable pages reachable (in farther layers) from link destination page fulfils condition:

$$C \cdot fraction > harvestRatioEstimation$$

General idea is to teach classifier whether link leads to some valuable (e.g. richer in valuable pages than the average) sub-graph or not. Right side of the inequality has the meaning of what is current believe on what is average harvest ratio. It is calculated basing on pages fetched up to the current moment. Left side consist of real (known during learning, but not known after deployment) fraction of future-reachable, valuable pages and constant C that controls what level of harvest ratio is satisfying. It is important to remember that some of the pages in the reachable sub-graph are also reachable from other links that also will be considered, therefore C has not obvious meaning. It can be interpreted as a measure of how much we want to risk fetching unsuitable pages. For $C = 1.0$ we denote this fetch criteria as Harvest0, for $C = 0.3$ as Harvest1 and for $C = 0.001$ as Harvest2.

The last step in URL classification process is to decide whether page should be fetched or not basing on decisions for all in-links (denoted with letter C on the Figure 1). This decision (denoted with letter D on the Figure 1) is made by voting. If there is $\geq F$ votes then page is fetched; otherwise not. Empirically we chose $F = 0.95$ what in practise means that all votes must say 'yes' for fetching.

At current level of advance of our project we set up experimental environment using *python* scripts. The scripts process already downloaded results of crawls and simulate behaviour of focused crawler on off-line data. The data was gathered with Apache Nutch 1.6 crawler and logical consequence of current works would be to reimplement system using Java language as a plug-in to this crawler.

4   Experiments

4.1   Data Characterisation

In experiments we used results of crawls gathered by Apache Nutch 1.6. For seed URLs we used three publicly available Open Directory Project directories:

1. business/e-commerce (655 URLs)
2. recreation/theme parks (485 URLs)
3. computers/mobile computing (510 URLs)

For each of these sets we crawled the web with depth parameter set to 25 layers and maximum breadth set to 1000. It led to fetching more than 20 thousand of pages with hundreds of thousands of links. We analysed the resulting crawls with different sets of keywords. On Figure 2 we show dependence of harvest ratio in different layers for different keywords in considered crawls. Brief review of this figure leads to the conclusion that typical assumption that the ratio of the pages satisfying the crawling criteria decreases with the distance from the seed set, is not necessarily true when taken verbatim. However, after smoothing (not shown) the charts, although quite flat, they generally indicate weak signals of such phenomenon.

4.2   Links Classifier Parameters Selection

Classification process that is shown on Figure 1 depends on many parameters. To choose them we performed several experiments using first crawl results (for business/e-commerce seed). We split links basing on layers into two sets: training set out of layers

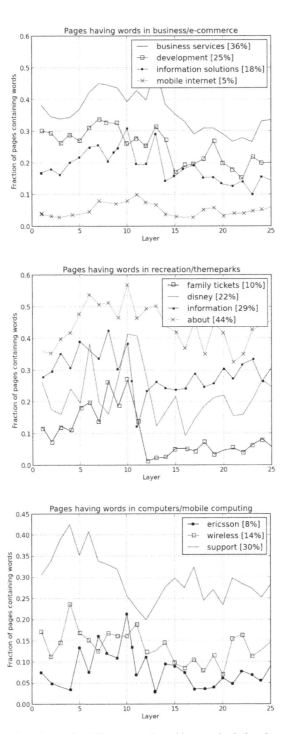

Fig. 2. Harvest ratio in layers for different crawls and keywords (in brackets means are given)

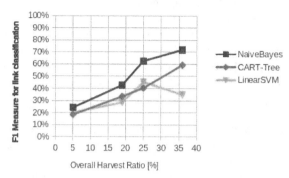

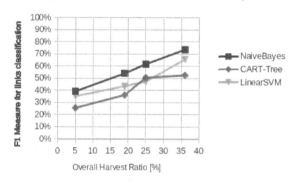

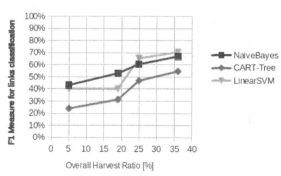

Fig. 3. Link classification quality (F_1) for different classifiers

3-10 and test set out of layers 11-25. For various keyword sets (shown on Figure 2) we tested different classifiers (Gaussian Naive Bayes [7], CART-Tree [3], Linear-SVM [9]), sets of features (Poor, Medial, Rich) and fetch criteria (Simple, Harvest0/1/2).

To select the best classifier we compared plots of F_1 measures for test set. We fixed other parameters and measured quality for different keywords with different overall harvest ratio (harvest ratio calculated for whole crawl results). All of the plots look similarly to each other. Three sample plots are shown on Figure 3. In general Gaussian Naive Bayes classifier performed the best. The worst results were obtained for CART-Trees. What can also be observed is that results of link classification increase with number of valuable pages. It can be an effect of better representation of positive class in training set.

To select the best subset of features and fetch criteria we performed similar procedures. Table 1 shows averaged values of F_1 for different features subsets and Table 2 for different fetch criteria. Final conclusion is that the best results are obtained for the features denoted as Poor with either Simple or Harvest0 fetch criteria.

Table 1. Average (over different keyword sets) F_1 of links classification for different sets of features [Fetch Criteria = Simple]

Set of Features	NaiveBayes	CART-Tree	LinearSVM
Poor	61%	41%	59%
Medial	52%	40%	44%
Rich	52%	39%	35%

Table 2. Average (over different keyword sets) F_1 of links classification for different Fetch Criteria [Features = Poor]

Fetch Criteria	NaiveBayes	CART-Tree	LinearSVM
Simple	61%	41%	59%
Harvest0	61%	42%	49%
Harvest1	59%	43%	44%
Harvest2	57%	42%	49%

4.3   Pages Classification

To evaluate classification system's ability to select properly pages to be fetched we performed further simulation. We used layers 3-10 as a training set and 11-25 as a test set. At first we calculated harvest ratio without cutting-off any branches (Original Harvest Ratio). Then we calculated harvest ratio using classification system to cut-off some URLs (and eventually branches). It is important to mention that this behaviour would be quite different in real, on-line focused crawler whereas skipped (cut-off) pages would be replaced with another ones. Anyway, assuming that in this new set of pages we can also successfully perform classification, final ratio would be even better.

Figure 4 presents plots of harvest ratio before and after cutting-off for different fetch criteria. Change of these criteria should strongly influence behaviour of the whole system. Intuitively, when changing this parameter we change what classifier is learned to achieve: either to predict that a single page satisfies the criteria or it contains links that can lead to such. Short analysis of this figure shows that the best results are obtained for strategy Simple and Harvest0.

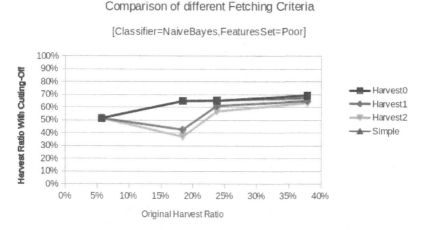

Fig. 4. Harvest ratio for different fetch criteria

Figure 5 presents changes of harvest ratio in test set in crawl results for business/e-commerce seed. For all of considered keyword sets quality increased visibly. Ratio improved in the best case of 50%.

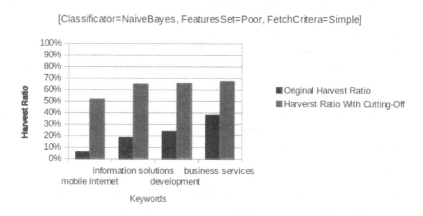

Fig. 5. Harvest ratio increase in crawl for business/e-commerce seed

4.4 Final Evaluation

To confirm that our results apply to different crawl results and keyword sets we repeated simulation for the rest of configurations from Figure 2. In each case we split pages

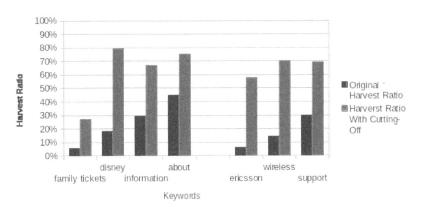

Fig. 6. Harvest ratio increase in crawls for computers/mobile-computations and recreation/theme-parks seed sets

into training and test sets similarly as before. Then, we performed classification and measured harvest ratio change. Charts are shown on Figure 6. These results indicate that the approach is quite successful as the harvest ratio clearly increases. The improvement factor varies from about 1.5 (e.g. business/e-commerce:"business services") to about 10 times (e.g. computers/mobile computations:"ericsson").

5   Conclusions and Future Work

We proposed a machine-learning approach to efficiently predict the presence of pre-specified keywords on unknown textual web pages, based on features extracted from web pages in a close link neighbourhood. The features are based both on link structure and textual content. The studied issue has applications in designing an efficient crawler that effectively collects web documents that are rich in pre-specified keywords.

In the reported experimental evaluation we tested numerous combinations of several parameter settings, including various feature sets, classification algorithms and keyword sets. Preliminary experimental results, that are done in a repeatable manner on a publicly available set of web documents from the dmoz.org web site are promising and indicate that the applied approach seems to be successful in obtaining keyword-rich web document collections, despite the simplicity of the applied model.

A continuation of this work would involve more systematic and extensive experimentation, including statistical significance analysis, larger data sets and more sophisticated prediction models, including multi-phrase criterion, for example.

An important improvement of the presented approach would involve incorporating the prediction module into an intelligent crawler that incrementally learns on-line, during the crawling process instead of the off-line learning model presented in this paper. This would also make it possible to apply even more practical evaluation measures that take into account also the consumption of important resources such as crawling time, used bandwidth, etc.

Acknowledgements. The first author was supported by research fellowship within "Information technologies: research and their interdisciplinary applications" agreement between IPS PAS and Polish Ministry of Science and Higher Education POKL.04.01.01-00-051/10-00, the second author was supported by PJIIT grant ST/SI/02/2011.

References

1. Aggarwal, C.C., Al-Garawi, F., Yu, P.S.: Intelligent crawling on the world wide web with arbitrary predicates. In: Proceedings of the 10th International Conference on World Wide Web, WWW 2001, pp. 96–105. ACM, New York (2001),
   http://doi.acm.org/10.1145/371920.371955
2. Alam, M., Ha, J., Lee, S.: Novel approaches to crawling important pages early. Knowledge and Information Systems 33, 707–734 (2012),
   http://dx.doi.org/10.1007/s10115-012-0535-4
3. Breiman, L., Friedman, J., Olshen, R., Stone, C.: Classification and Regression Trees. Wadsworth and Brooks, Monterey (1984)
4. Chakrabarti, S., van den Berg, M., Dom, B.: Focused crawling: a new approach to topic-specific web resource discovery. Computer Networks 31(11-16), 1623–1640 (1999),
   http://www.sciencedirect.com/science/article/pii/S1389128699000523
5. Davison, B.D.: Topical locality in the web. In: Proceedings of the 23rd Annual International ACM SIGIR Conference on Research and Development in Information Retrieval, SIGIR 2000, pp. 272–279. ACM, New York (2000),
   http://doi.acm.org/10.1145/345508.345597
6. Diligenti, M., Coetzee, F., Lawrence, S., Giles, C.L., Gori, M.: Focused crawling using context graphs. In: Proceedings of the 26th International Conference on Very Large Data Bases, VLDB 2000, pp. 527–534. Morgan Kaufmann Publishers Inc., San Francisco (2000),
   http://dl.acm.org/citation.cfm?id=645926.671854
7. John, G.H., Langley, P.: Estimating continuous distributions in bayesian classifiers. In: Proceedings of the Eleventh Conference on Uncertainty in Artificial Intelligence, UAI 1995, pp. 338–345. Morgan Kaufmann Publishers Inc., San Francisco (1995),
   http://dl.acm.org/citation.cfm?id=2074158.2074196
8. Pant, G., Srinivasan, P.: Learning to crawl: Comparing classification schemes. ACM Trans. Inf. Syst. 23(4), 430–462 (2005), http://doi.acm.org/10.1145/1095872.1095875
9. Steinwart, I., Christmann, A.: Support Vector Machines, 1st edn. Springer Publishing Company, Incorporated (2008)

Threshold ML-KNN: Statistical Evaluation on Multiple Benchmarks

Michał Łukasik[1] and Marcin Sydow[2,1]

[1] Institute of Computer Science, Polish Academy of Sciences, Warsaw, Poland
[2] Polish-Japanese Institute of Information Technology, Warsaw, Poland
m.lukasik@phd.ipipan.waw.pl, msyd@poljap.edu.pl

Abstract. This paper concerns the performance of a recently proposed multi-label classification algorithm called Threshold ML-KNN. It is a modification of the established ML-KNN algorithm. The performance of both algorithms is compared on several publicly available benchmarks. Based on the results, the conclusion is drawn that Threshold ML-KNN is statistically significantly better in terms of accuracy, f-measure and hamming loss.

1 Introduction

Multi-label classification is a problem, in which objects can be assigned more then one label. Document classification might be considered as an example of multi-label classification [3]. Threshold ML-KNN is a multi-label classification algorithm, which has been recently proposed in [3]. It is a modification of an established algorithm: ML-KNN [6][5].

In [3], the algorithm was evaluated on a single dataset without deeper statistical analysis. It is therefore unknown, whether it is usually better to use ML-KNN or Threshold ML-KNN. Purpose of this work is to perform experimental comparison of the 2 algorithms, using multiple established benchmarks and statistical methods. This would allow to make some conclusions about the relative performance of the 2 classifiers.

The rest of this work is organised as follows: in section 2 we introduce the 2 studied classifiers: ML-KNN and Threshold ML-KNN. In section 3 we explain, how to compare 2 classification algorithms across multiple domains. Section 4 contains short overview of datasets on which algorithms have been evaluated. In section 5 we describe the experiments and interpret the results. We end the paper with section 6, in which we summarize our work.

2 Classifiers

In a multi-label classification problem we are given a dataset X and a set of labels L. Each element $x \in X$ may be described by a set $L_x \subset L$.

2.1 ML-KNN

ML-KNN (Multi-Label KNN) is an algorithm proposed by Zhang in [6]. It is basically a Naive Bayes classifier, which uses features induced from the neighbourhood of an object, therefore it uses the concept of KNN.

M.A. Kłopotek et al. (Eds.): IIS 2013, LNCS 7912, pp. 198–205, 2013.

Let us denote by $l(x)$ an event that label l describes object x. Furthermore, let $E_{x(l)}$ be an event, that amongst k nearest neighbours of x there are $x(l)$ objects described by label l. In such case, we shall assign label l to an object x if the following holds: $P(l(x)|E_{x(l)}) > P(\neg l(x)|E_{x(l)})$. According to the Bayes rule, this can be rewritten to the inequality shown in (1).

$$P(E_{x(l)}|l(x))P(l(x)) > P(E_{x(l)}|\neg l(x))P(\neg l(x)) \tag{1}$$

Variables that appear in inequality (1) can be estimated using the training set. Prior probabilities of occurrence of a label can be estimated by frequencies in the set. Posterior probabilities are approximated by counting neighbourhoods of all objects. Complete algorithm with pseudocode can be found in [6].

2.2   Threshold ML-KNN

In [3] it has been shown that ML-KNN may perform poorly on a real dataset because of noise in the data. A solution to the problem has been proposed: instead of estimating the Bayes probabilities, a single threshold t can be assigned to each label l. After selecting a threshold value, label l is assigned to object x when at least t objects of class l are found in the neighbourhood of x.

For a given label l, let us denote by c_l^i number of objects in the training set described by label l, that have exactly i objects with label l assigned in their neighbourhood. We will denote by d_l^i number of objects in the training set, that have exactly i objects with label l assigned in their neighbourhood and which are not described by label l.

In order to choose value for a threshold, one can traverse through all $t \in \{0, \ldots, k\}$ and check, for which t some utility function is the highest. We will consider utility functions, which for a fixed t and the set of values c_l^i, d_l^i can be measured using the following variables:

- FN (false negatives), number of objects incorrectly classified as not belonging to class l. It can be calculated as $\sum_{i<t} c_l^i$,
- TP - (true positives), number of objects correctly classified as belonging to class l. It can be calculated as $\sum_{i \geq t} c_l^i$,
- TN - (true negatives), number of objects correctly classified as not belonging to class l. It can be calculated as $\sum_{i<t} d_l^i$,
- FP - (false positives), number of objects incorrectly classified as belonging to class l. It can be calculated as $\sum_{i \geq t} d_l^i$.

Example of utility function for choosing threshold value t is f-measure, as was the case in [3], which can be expressed by the formula: $f1 = H(\frac{TP}{TP+FP}, \frac{TP}{TP+FN})$, where $H(x, y) = \frac{2xy}{x+y}$. One can use any other criterion, for example accuracy. In such case, one would seek for maximizing the following expression: $acc = \frac{TP+TN}{TP+FN+TN+FP}$.

The modification presented is a way of shrinking the parameter space, which makes the algorithm less prone to noise in the training data. Also, the time complexity of modification is the same as of ML-KNN. The complete description of Threshold ML-KNN with pseudocode and deeper analysis can be found in [3].

2.3   Criterion for Choosing Threshold in Threshold ML-KNN

In general, it is good to choose the criterion according to the data that one has to work on. For example, in [3] the criterion chosen was F-measure and allowed obtaining good classification results. However, when there are some classes with very few members, f-measure tends to maximize recall at the cost of precision, which in the end gives low accuracy and f-measure for the whole classifier. It can be easily seen why this is the case when we consider a dataset where some label l has only a few members. Then, for high threshold value, recall becomes very low (around zero). In order to compensate this, classifier chooses lower thresholds, which elevates recall, making precision drop to lower numbers. Accuracy does not have the drawback of not dealing with the small categories count.

As for the problem what criterion to choose in order to obtain as general solution as possible, we have decided to choose accuracy maximization criterion, since it seems more resistant to the problem with small number of labels.

Furthermore, we shall examine an algorithm which uses a simple sum of acc and $f1$ as a criterion for choosing thresholds. Any combination can be chosen and the choice should answer to a problem one poses to himself, that is what type of data he or she is dealing with or what measure he or she is mostly interested in maximizing. However, in this work we are interested in as universal methods as possible, therefore in the second approach we do not emphasize any of the 2 classification measures more.

To sum up, we are going to use 2 types of Threshold ML-KNN:

- Threshold ML-KNN with the criterion for choosing threshold being accuracy,
- Threshold ML-KNN with the criterion for choosing threshold being sum of accuracy and F-measure.

3   Problem Statement

We are given 2 algorithms: A and B. We also have several datasets. Based on the results received for each data set by the 2 classifiers, we are interested in determining, which algorithm is better. The procedure of determining this consists of the following steps:

- calculating some classification measure $f_{c,d}$ for each classifier c on each dataset d
- using a statistical test on the measures calculated to determine, whether one classifier is generally better than the other

As for the first step, different measures exist for multi-label classification. Below we describe some of them that we are going to use. Afterwards, we shortly describe a statistical test for comparison of 2 classifiers on multiple datasets.

3.1   Classification Measures for Multi-label Classification

Each object x has a set of labels L_x assigned to it. On the other hand, algorithm A assigns to it set of labels L_x^A. Now, for all $x \in X$, using sets L_x and L_x^A we want to measure how well the classifier A performs. We use the following measures.

We use the following definition of multi-label accuracy: $\frac{1}{|X|} \sum_{x \in X} \frac{|L_x \cap L_x^A|}{|L_x \cup L_x^A|}$. It does not distinguish error of choosing too many labels from not choosing labels needed.

Precision measures what part of labels from L_x have been chosen. Its formula is as follows: $\frac{1}{|X|} \sum_{x \in X} \frac{|L_x \cap L_x^A|}{|L_x|}$.

Recall allows to see, how many labels from L_x^A have been really needed. Recall is calculated as: $\frac{1}{|X|} \sum_{x \in X} \frac{|L_x \cap L_x^A|}{|L_x^A|}$.

The measure that balances between recall and precision is F-measure. For each classified item, the harmonic mean of precision and recall is calculated. Then, the result is averaged over all items: $\frac{1}{|X|} \sum_{x \in X} H(\frac{|L_x \cap L_x^A|}{|L_x|}, \frac{|L_x \cap L_x^A|}{|L_x^A|})$, where $H(x, y) = \frac{2xy}{x+y}$.

Hamming Loss counts, how many labels are on average misclassified to be or not to be assigned to an object. The formula is as follows: $\frac{1}{|X|} \sum_{x \in X} L_x \Delta L_x^A$, where Δ stands for symmetric difference.

3.2 Statistical Test

When a classification measure is fixed, based on values $f_{c,d}^i$, we want to check for statistical difference between 2 classifiers. According to [2], a good test for this is Wilcoxon signed ranks test. In this test, difference between performances on each dataset d is calculated: $s_d = f_{c_A,d} - f_{c_B,d}$. The differences are sorted according to their absolute value. Then, values R^A and R^B can be calculated, which denote: the sum of ranks where algorithm A was better and the sum of ranks where algorithm B was better, respectively. The test statistic is the minimum of the 2 sums.

There are a few arguments why Wilcoxon signed ranks test should be used instead of other popular tests like t-test. One of them is that it does not assume commensurability: results for different datasets can be very different. Furthermore, normal distributions of results are not assumed. Such assumption is rarely met when dealing with classification results[2].

4 Datasets

We evaluated classifiers on multi-label datasets: scene, emotions, genbase, yeast, medical, CAL500. All of them are available on-line on: http://mulan.sourceforge.net/datasets. html. The criterion for choosing datasets was only their size - datasets with too many samples and features have been excluded for computational reasons.

Scene dataset contains features of natural scene images, together with a few labellings stating, what the picture shows. Each scene image is divided into 49 blocks of pixels. Blocks are described by their first and second moments.

Emotions data consists of songs described by emotions that they cause. The features were calculated based on the signal, such as amplitude spectrogram characteristics or parameters of signal in frequency domain acquired after FFT.

Genbase dataset contains motifs associated to protein families. Feature vectors point, which proteins are present in the family.

Yeast dataset poses a problem of predicting gene functional classes of Yeast Saccharomyces cerevisiae. Genes are described by micro-array expression data and phylogenetic profile, preprocessed accordingly. The set of functional classes is structured into hierarchies and only functional classes in the top hierarchy are considered.

Medical dataset contains ICD-9-CM codes assigned to clinical free text. It is about assigning surgical, diagnostic and therapeutic procedures that should be applied, based on information about patients.

CAL500 contains annotated musical tracks. The features describing songs are based on the FFT.

In Table 1 we show basic statistics of the used datasets. In particular, the following statistics concern multi-label datasets: cardinality (how many labels on average are assigned to an object) and density (what percentage of labels is on average assigned to an object).

Table 1. Basic statistics of datasets used for comparison of classifiers

name	domain	instances	labels	features	cardinality	density
scene	image	2407	6	294	1.074	0.179
yeast	biology	2417	14	103	4.237	0.303
medical	text	978	45	1449	1.245	0.028
genbase	biology	662	27	1186	1.252	0.046
emotions	music	593	6	72	1.869	0.311
CAL500	music	502	174	68	26.044	0.150

5   Experiments

We extended Orange framework [1] in order to implement Threshold ML-KNN. We also used tools from the framework to perform analysis of multi-label measures. Statistical analysis was performed using R programming language [4].

As in [6] we have also not noticed big change in obtained results when changing parameter k for the classifiers, therefore we decided to use value 10 for all datasets.

In this section we evaluate 3 classifiers introduced in section 2. We list them below, giving their shorter names which we are going to use in the rest of this section:

- ML-KNN
- Threshold ML-KNN with the criterion for choosing threshold being accuracy, denoted as T-ML-KNN Acc for short,
- Threshold ML-KNN with the criterion for choosing threshold being a sum of accuracy and F-measure, denoted as T-ML-KNN F1 Acc for short.

5.1   Experiment 1

First we compared all of the 3 classifiers on each dataset separately. In Tables 2, 3, 4 we show how means and standard deviations vary in results given by each classifier, according to Hamming loss, accuracy, F-measure. The simple statistics are calculated on results of 10-fold cross validation. The best results have been emphasized.

As for T-ML-KNN Acc it can be noticed, that for dataset CAL500 there is a drop in quality according to all measures used. However, for other datasets, this type of Threshold ML-KNN outperforms ML-KNN. For example in terms of accuracy, for all datasets except for CAL500, Threshold ML-KNN performs much better. Similarly when F-measure is considered. It can also be noticed, that the performance drop for CAL500 is much smaller compared to how Threshold ML-KNN improves upon other datasets.

Table 2. Hamming Loss (mean±std) for ML-KNN, T-ML-KNN Acc and T-ML-KNN F1 Acc

Dataset	ML-KNN	T-ML-KNN Acc	T-ML-KNN F1 Acc
emotions	0.1981 ± 0.02247205	**0.1950 ± 0.02035522**	0.200 ± 0.02133588
genbase	0.004534 ± 0.001490837	0.001958 ± 0.001217603	**0.001789 ± 0.0009050165**
medical	0.01592 ± 0.0009839629	**0.01544 ± 0.001136067**	0.02160 ± 0.001906117
scene	0.08634 ± 0.004665552	**0.0857 ± 0.004970515**	0.08863 ± 0.007205567
yeast	0.1912 ± 0.007809137	**0.1909 ± 0.00768696**	0.2148 ± 0.01478159
CAL500	**0.1384 ± 0.004184808**	0.1389 ± 0.003986446	0.1830 ± 0.005210248

Table 3. Accuracy (mean±std) for ML-KNN, T-ML-KNN Acc and T-ML-KNN F1 Acc

Dataset	ML-KNN	T-ML-KNN Acc	T-ML-KNN F1 Acc
emotions	0.5291 ± 0.05421192	0.5451 ± 0.04333727	**0.5677 ± 0.05035647**
genbase	0.9488 ± 0.01075993	0.9823 ± 0.007310215	**0.9831 ± 0.006521904**
medical	0.5656 ± 0.03622595	**0.6027 ± 0.02660085**	0.5767 ± 0.01889509
scene	0.6643 ± 0.0194494	0.6691 ± 0.01711195	**0.7194 ± 0.02449533**
yeast	0.5188 ± 0.02101427	0.5212 ± 0.02024027	**0.5405 ± 0.02609525**
CAL500	0.1964 ± 0.0110821	0.1934 ± 0.01100551	**0.2878 ± 0.01146733**

Table 4. F-measure (mean±std) for ML-KNN, T-ML-KNN Acc and T-ML-KNN F1 Acc

Dataset	ML-KNN	T-ML-KNN Acc	T-ML-KNN F1 Acc
emotions	0.6049 ± 0.04901216	0.623 ± 0.03599063	**0.6551 ± 0.04584066**
genbase	0.9575 ± 0.01037667	0.9881 ± 0.005401398	**0.9887 ± 0.005131296**
medical	0.592 ± 0.04060414	**0.630 ± 0.02828658**	0.6297 ± 0.02032625
scene	0.6776 ± 0.01807858	0.6827 ± 0.01611694	**0.7444 ± 0.02582574**
yeast	0.6230 ± 0.02219235	0.6252 ± 0.02113644	**0.647 ± 0.02493529**
CAL500	**0.323 ± 0.01513205**	0.3194 ± 0.0154195	0.2878 ± 0.01146733

On the other hand, T-ML-KNN F1 Acc yields even better results as far as F-measure and accuracy are concerned. In terms of F-measure, T-ML-KNN Acc performs better then T-ML-KNN F1 Acc only on medical and CAL500 datasets. However, in case of Hamming Loss, T-ML-KNN F1 Acc almost always yields worse results then T-ML-KNN Acc.

5.2   Experiment 2

Second experiment is performing Wilcoxon signed rank test for detecting difference in performances of ML-KNN and T-ML-KNN Acc on all datasets considered at once. The null hypothesis is that both classifiers behave the same whereas the alternative hypothesis is that Threshold ML-KNN behaves better. The results for this statistical test are shown in table 5.

Table 5. Wilcoxon test for differences in performances of ML-KNN and T-ML-KNN Acc

	H-Loss	Accuracy	F-measure
p-value	0.07813	0.04688	0.04688

Results show, that in terms of all measures used, except for Hamming loss, T-ML-KNN Acc is statistically significantly better under significance level 5%. This proves, that T-ML-KNN F1 Acc is universally better, unless one is interested mainly in Hamming Loss quality. However, as far as Hamming Loss is concerned, it can also not be stated, that T-ML-KNN F1 Acc is not worse then ML-KNN, since the p-value is not high. Under 10% significance it can be stated, that in terms of Hamming Loss T-ML-KNN F1 Acc behaves better then ML-KNN.

5.3   Experiment 3

Third experiment is performing Wilcoxon signed rank test for detecting difference in performances of ML-KNN and T-ML-KNN F1 Acc. The results for this statistical test are shown in table 6.

Table 6. Wilcoxon test for differences in performances of ML-KNN and T-ML-KNN F1 Acc

	H-Loss	Accuracy	F-measure
p-value	0.9531	0.01563	0.01563

The dominance over ML-KNN in terms of accuracy and F-measure is bigger in case of T-ML-KNN F1 Acc then T-ML-KNN Acc. When one is interested in maximizing overall accuracy or F-measure, this version of Threshold ML-KNN helps gain a more sure advantage over ML-KNN. However, according to Hamming Loss, T-ML-KNN F1 Acc does not perform well. We also conducted Wilcoxon signed ranks test for H-Loss difference where null hypothesis was that algorithms behave the same whereas alternative hypothesis was that algorithms do not behave the same (note that this time alternative hypothesis is different then in calculations for tables 5 and 6). We got p-value equal 0.1563, which is also not very big. Still, we can presume that Threshold ML-KNN does have some drawbacks as far as this criterion is concerned.

6 Conclusions

In our work we have evaluated ML-KNN and 2 types of Threshold ML-KNN classifiers on multiple datasets, using various classification measures. We have shown, using Wilcoxon signed ranks test, how Threshold ML-KNN with criterion of accuracy measure for choosing threshold performs statistically significantly better then ML-KNN, as far as accuracy or f-measure are concerned. We have also shown, that in case of Hamming Loss, Threshold ML-KNN does not behave worse.

On the other hand, Threshold ML-KNN with the criterion for choosing threshold being a sum of accuracy and F-measure performs much better then ML-KNN in terms of accuracy and F-measure. However, it is probably behaving worse then ML-KNN in terms of Hamming Loss.

The conclusion is that the more universal improvement over ML-KNN is Threshold ML-KNN with accuracy criterion. However, when one is interested mainly in maximizing either accuracy or F-measure, he or she should rather choose the second approach.

Acknowledgements. Study was supported by research fellowship within "Information technologies: research and their interdisciplinary applications" agreement between IPS PAS and Polish Ministry of Science and Higher Education POKL.04.01.01-00-051/10-00.

References

1. Curk, T., Demšar, J., Xu, Q., Leban, G., Petrovič, U., Bratko, I., Shaulsky, G., Zupan, B.: Microarray data mining with visual programming. Bioinformatics 21, 396–398 (2005), http://bioinformatics.oxfordjournals.org/content/21/3/396.full.pdf

2. Demšar, J.: Statistical comparisons of classifiers over multiple data sets. J. Mach. Learn. Res. 7, 1–30 (2006), http://dl.acm.org/citation.cfm?id=1248547.1248548

3. Łukasik, M., Kuśmierczyk, T., Bolikowski, Ł., Nguyen, H.S.: Hierarchical, multi-label classification of scholarly publications: Modifications of ML-KNN algorithm. In: Bembenik, R., Skonieczny, Ł., Rybiński, H., Kryszkiewicz, M., Niezgódka, M. (eds.) Intell. Tools for Building a Scientific Information. SCI, vol. 467, pp. 343–364. Springer, Heidelberg (2013)

4. R Core Team: R: A Language and Environment for Statistical Computing. R Foundation for Statistical Computing, Vienna, Austria (2012), http://www.R-project.org ISBN 3-900051-07-0

5. Tsoumakas, G., Katakis, I.: Multi-label classification: An overview. IJDWM 3(3), 1–13 (2007)

6. Zhang, M.L., Zhou, Z.H.: Ml-knn: A lazy learning approach to multi-label learning. Pattern Recognition 40(7), 2038–2048 (2007)

Supervised Content Visualization of Scientific Publications: A Case Study on the ArXiv Dataset

Theodoros Giannakopoulos, Harry Dimitropoulos, Omiros Metaxas,
Natalia Manola, and Yannis Ioannidis

Management of Data, Information, and Knowledge Group of the Department of
Informatics & Telecommunications of the University of Athens 15784, Greece
{tyiannak,harryd,omiros,natalia,yannis}@di.uoa.gr

Abstract. A supervised approach to visualization of collections of scientific documents is presented. We have implemented a text classification module, which leads to class probability estimations, along with a dimensionality reduction technique which represents each class in the 2-D space. Integrating those two procedures, any collection of unlabelled documents can be visualized. The arXiv dataset has been adopted for training the classification and visualization modules. We demonstrate the system's functionality on a corpus of automatically detected publications of particular EU FP7 funding categories.

1 Introduction

The task of visualizing text content is crucial since it provides a representation of what particular collections of documents refer to and it can lead to reinforcement of human cognition, with regards to abstract text. In particular, scientific documents define a subject of major interest in the field of text analytics, while their content richness and diversity are remarkably high. In this work we present a method for supervised classification and visualization of scientific content, trained on the arXiv data [1]. We present intermediate results of this procedure, applied on a particular use case, according to which we are interested in visualizing the content of collections of publications which *share a common funding scheme* (e.g. FP7-ICT). The adopted methodology is implemented under the OpenAIRE+ EU project ("2nd-Generation Open Access Infrastructure for Research in Europe" - 283595), which is an information infrastructure of publication and data repositories and implements ECs open access policies, effectively connecting publications to research data and funding. Therefore, in such context, content classification and visualization, when aggregated to funding schemes is a powerful tool that can be used by research administrators to assist them in strategy or policy making processes.

2 Overall Architecture

In Figure 1 the proposed architecture is presented. The following sub-modules can be distinguished: (1) **Content-based classification and class representation**

M.A. Kłopotek et al. (Eds.): IIS 2013, LNCS 7912, pp. 206–211, 2013.

module. The purpose of this module is two-fold: (a) to classify a document to a set of predefined classes. (b) To represent content classes. Towards this end, we have selected a dictionary extraction technique: each class is represented by a dictionary of terms and a list of respective weights. The same dictionaries are used in the classification process. **(2) 2D Class representation module** Each class is represented in a high - dimensional feature space, based on the dictionaries extracted by the first module. Then a dimensionality reduction approach is adopted, in order to represent the classes in the 2-D feature space.

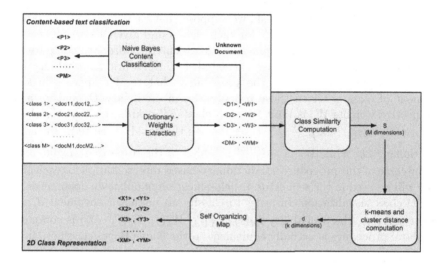

Fig. 1. Overall architecture of the proposed method

3   Content-Based Classification and Class Representation

3.1   Adopted Taxonomy: arXiv

In order to train the content classifier and the visualization model, supervised knowledge is needed, i.e., mappings of documents to classes. Towards this end, we have adopted the taxonomy provided by `arXiv` [1], which is an electronic archive of scientific documents, covering a wide range of content. The `arXiv` categorization uses a two-level hierarchy: each "super-class" (e.g. Computer Science) is divided into a set of sub-classes. We have not made use of this hierarchical labeling structure. Instead, *we have used those sub-classes as classes* in all involved supervised tasks. In order to retrieve documents for training / testing, we have made use of the `arXiv.org` API [2]. Finally, a maximum number of documents per class was set equal to 5000, when retrieving documents through the API. A list of the adopted `arXiv` categories can be found in `http://arxiv.org/help/api/user-manual`.

3.2   Class Representation and Classifier Training

In order to proceed with the classification and visualization modules, each class needs to be represented. First, each text document d is represented as vector according to the following text analysis steps:

1. Tokenization: the initial stream text is broken into individual words
2. Stop word removal: NLTK's stop words list has been adopted ([5])
3. Stemming: the Wordnet lemmatizer of NLTK has been adopted ([5])
4. For each unique term t its frequency $df_d(t)$ is extracted

In the context of a supervised task, we suppose that each document is mapped to one or more classes. Therefore, for each class c and given a set of respective documents, the aforementioned procedure is executed, in order to compute df_d. In the sequel, $P(t)$ and $P(t|c)$ are extracted, i.e., the a-priori probability that term t can appear, along with the probability that term t appears in some document of class c. Given those probabilities, a dictionary D_c and an array of respective weights W_c is built for each class c. Towards this end, for class c and for each term t, if $\frac{P(t|c)}{P(t)} > T$ (user-defined threshold), then term t is added to dictionary D_c, while $W_c(t) = \frac{P(t|c)}{P(t)}$ is added to the respective weights array. The outcome of this procedure is a dictionary-based representation for each class, which will be used in the sequel for: (a) classification of unknown documents and (b) 2-D class visualization. In order to classify an unknown document d, with terms $t_1, \ldots, t_N$, the probability $P_d(c) = \prod_{i=1}^{N} W_c(j : D_c(j) = t_i)$ is computed. The above procedure is actually equivalent to the Naive Bayes classifier [4].

4   Visualization of Text Content

4.1   Class Representation in the 2-D Space

The purpose of this module is to map each class to a point in the 2-D space, so that classes of similar content are close. This can be seen as a dimensionality reduction task, though in that case we need to reduce *class* representations, instead of sample representations. At first, a class similarity matrix is extracted, based on the computed class dictionaries and respective weight arrays (Section 3.2). In particular, for any pair of classes c_1 and c_2, with respective dictionaries D_{c_1} and D_{c_2}, weights W_{c_1} and W_{c_2} and number of terms per dictionary N_1 and N_2, the following similarity measure is computed:

$$S(c_1, c_2) = \frac{\sum_{i=1}^{N_1} W_{c_2}(k : D_{c_1}(i) = D_{c_2}(k))}{\sum_{i=1}^{N_2} W_{c_2}(i)} + \frac{\sum_{i=1}^{N_2} W_{c_1}(k : D_{c_2}(i) = D_{c_1}(k))}{\sum_{i=1}^{N_1} W_{c_1}(i)}$$

In that way, we directly use the extracted dictionaries, in order to calculate the similarity between the respective classes. Other measures could also be used, based on sample-to-sample similarities, though the extraction of that class-based similarity measure is of very low computational cost and it makes direct use of the information extracted in the training phase of the content classifier.

The class similarity matrix S is a way of representing the class distributions in the $\mathbb{R}^M$ space (M: total number of classes). Our purpose is to reduce the dimensionality of this space to 2 using discretized class representations. Experiments we conducted showed that this cannot be achieved directly, due to the fact that the initial feature space is rather high. Therefore, before proceeding with the core dimensionality reduction procedure, we reduce the feature space via a clustering technique. In particular, we first apply k-means [6] on S, assuming raws are samples. k was selected to be equal to 20. The outcome of the k-means algorithm is a set of k cluster centers, say $Cl_i, i = 1, \cdots, k$. This leads to clusters of similar classes, based to the dictionary-based similarity criterion. Then we compute the Eucledian distance between each row i of the S matrix and each cluster j: $d(i,j)$. d can be assumed as a set of M samples in the k feature space. Each class is now represented by its distances from the extracted k-means clusters. This lower dimensional space (k) is used by a self organizing map (SOM), in order to extract a 2-D discretized representation of the classes [7]. The reason why we selected to express the original feature space as a linear combination of distances from cluster centers, before proceeding with the main SOM algorithm is to avoid numerical and computational issues that stem from the high initial dimensionality and the large number of classes involved in the SOM training procedure. Reducing the class dimensionality to $k = 20$ makes the training of the SOM faster and more accurate.

4.2   Content Representation of Unlabelled Document Collections

The aforementioned modules form a system that can (a) classify an unknown document to a set of classes, providing soft outputs (probability estimations) and (b) represent each of the classes in the 2-D space. Applying those two modules for a collection of unlabeled documents, we can provide a visual interpretation of the collection's content. In particular, we apply the content classification module for every document $i, i = 1, \ldots, N_d$ (N_d: total number of documents in the collection), leading to a set of output probabilities $P_i(c)$ for each class $c = 1, \ldots, M$. When this document-level classification procedure is completed, we can represent the collection's content using a 3-D vector for each class c: $[X_c, Y_c, \frac{\sum_{i=1}^{N_d} P_i(c)}{N_d}]$, where, X_c, and Y_c are the estimated 2-D class coordinates described in Section 4.1. In other words, each collection of documents is represented for each class of the adopted taxonomy, using the 2-D estimated coordinates, along with the accumulated (average) estimated content class probability. We have selected to adopt the "balloon" representation for the visualization of this type of 3-D data, provided by Google.

5   Results

In Figure 2(a) we present the estimated 2-D content distribution of the arXiv dataset. The size of the balloons is not used here, since we are only interested in presenting the distribution of the classes in the 2-D space. The "super-classes"

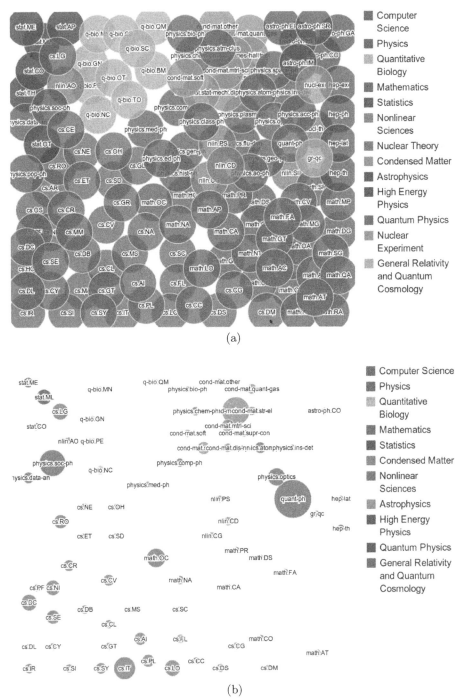

Fig. 2. (a) Overall content distribution of the `arXiv` dataset (b) Content distribution of almost 1000 publications of the `arXiv` dataset that where part of FP7-ICT funded research projects

(e.g., Computer Science) are just groups of classes used in the `arXiv` hierarchy and *are not used* in our supervised models: we just present them in the visualization results. Figure 2(b) presents the content distribution for a collection of `arXiv` documents that share a common funding scheme. Funding information is a very important type of metadata that can be useful in scientific document analytics, e.g. to discover and present trends in a temporal way. In this example we present content representation from FP7-ICT funded publications. In order to extract funding information a "funding metadata extractor module" has been developed in the context of `OpenAIRE+` which scans each publication and finds matches against the current known lists of project grant agreement numbers and/or acronyms for various funding bodies. As explained in Section 4.2, balloon sizes represent the average (estimated) probability that a publication from the input collection belongs to the respective content class. *More visualizations of various types of publication collections can be found at* `http://www.di.uoa.gr/~tyiannak/contentAnalysis.html`.

6 Conclusions and Ongoing Work

We have presented a method towards automatic visualization of collections of scientific publications using supervised knowledge. We have trained both the content classifier and the visualization module based on the data and the taxonomy of the `arXiv` dataset. A visualization example of scientific publications funded by FP7-ICT EU projects has been presented. We currently conduct ongoing research towards the following directions:

1. Detailed *Evaluation* of both the document collection visualization.
2. Visualization enhancement by adding other types of content descriptors, e.g., a tag cloud for each estimated class probability.
3. Adopt semi-supervised techniques (e.g., probabilistic topic modeling [8]).

References

1. arXiv.org: Cornel University Library article archive
2. `http://arxiv.org/help/api/index`: The arXiv.org API
3. Manning, C.D., Prabhakar, R., Hinrich, S.: Introduction to Information Retrieval. Cambridge University Press (2008)
4. Rish I.: An empirical study of the naive bayes classifier. In IJCAI 2001 Workshop on Empirical Methods in AI (2001)
5. Bird, S.: NLTK: the natural language toolkit. In: Proceedings of the COLING/ACL on Interactive Presentation Sessions, pp. 69–72. Association for Computational Linguistics, Stroudsburg (2006)
6. Theodoridis, S., Koutroumbas, K.: Pattern Recognition, 4th edn. Academic Press (2008)
7. Kohonen, T.: Self-Organizing Maps. In: Schroeder, M.R., Huang, T.S. (eds.), 3rd edn., Springer-Verlag New York, Inc., Secaucus (2001)
8. Ramage, D., Hall, D., Nallapati, R., Manning, C.D.: Labeled LDA: A supervised topic model for credit attribution in multi-labeled corpora. In: Conference on Empirical Methods in Natural Language Processing (2009)

A Calculus for Personalized PageRank

Mieczysław A. Kłopotek, Sławomir T. Wierzchoń, Dariusz Czerski,
Krzysztof Ciesielski, and Michał Dramiński

Institute of Computer Science of the Polish Academy of Sciences
ul. Jana Kazimierza 5, 01-248 Warszawa Poland

Abstract. This paper proposes a calculus for computing personalized
PageRank for complex categories given a precomputed set of primitive
categories. This is a work in progress aiming at reduction of the necessary number of precomputed PageRanks for a set of (next to disjoint)
categories.

Keywords: PageRank, composite personalization, combining PageR-
anks.

1 Introduction

Ranking of returned documents has been a headache for search engines since
the time when vast majority of queries started returning large numbers of documents containing user keywords. Among various proposals HITS algorithm [5,1]
attracted attention due to its ability to exploit link information when ranking
documents. But it suffered from the serious drawback that the computation had
to be done on-line among the retrieved documents and the iterative computation process was time- and resource consuming. So a great advantage was the
proposal of the PageRank ranking method [8] where the static ranking could
be pre-computed and easily accessed to rank the retrieved documents, hence it
earned much popularity and became component of many in formation retrieval
systems. However, a drawback here was that documents, being highly ranked
for some reason, could be ranked highly also for queries for which they are irrelevant just because containing by chance some keywords [2,11]. Therefore idea
was born to compute PageRank in various variants specific for the conceptual
category of the query so that a chosen ranking would really be representative
for the domain of the query (Personalized PageRank [3], Topical PageRank [4],
Query-Dependent PageRank [10] etc., see [6] for an exhaustive bibliography).
This meant of course precomputation of multiple PageRanks so that only a
limited number of categories can be taken into account at the stage of precomputation. In this paper we would like to focus on some possibilities of composing
personalized PageRanks from precomputed personalized PageRanks hoping to
contribute towards bridging the gap between pre-computation and flexible responding to user queries.

M.A. Kłopotek et al. (Eds.): IIS 2013, LNCS 7912, pp. 212–219, 2013.

2   Ideas behind PageRank

One of many interpretations of PageRank states that it is the probability that a knowledgeable (i.e. knowing addresses of all Web pages) but mindless (for randomly choosing next link to go) walker will visit a Web page. More precisely, it is a stationary distribution of a special random walk on Web graph. That is: upon entering a particular Web page, if it has no outgoing links, the walker jumps to any Web page with uniform probability. If there are outgoing links, he chooses with uniform probability one of the outgoing links and goes to the selected Web page, unless he gets bored. If he gets bored (which may happen with a fixed probability ζ on any page), he jumps to any Web page with uniform probability.

This model refers to the original, "objective" PageRank. At the other extreme we can consider a mindless page-u-fan random walker who is doing exactly the same, but in case of a jump out of boredom he does not jump to any page, but to the page u. A page ranking obtained in this way belongs to the category of "subjective" or personalized PageRank. Note that if there exists one page-fan for each web page then the PageRank vector of the knowledgeable walker is the average of PageRank vectors of all these page-fan walkers. Also there are plenty possibilities of other mindless walkers between these two extremes. E.g. a bored walker can jump to a page from a set U with a uniform probability or with probability proportional to the out-degree of the pages from this set.

Let us formalize these concepts. Let r denote a (column) vector of ranks: r_j will mean the PageRank of page j of the oriented Web graph W (edges corresponding to links). Let $\sum_{j \in W} r_j = 1$, and $r_j \geq 0$ for all $j \in W$. Let A be a matrix (called balanced connection matrix) such that if there is a link from page j to page i, then $A_{i,j} = \frac{1}{outdeg(j)}$, where $outdeg(j)$ is the out-degree of node j. If a node had an out-degree equal 0, then prior to construction of A the node is replaced by one with edges outgoing to all the other nodes of the network. Under these circumstances PageRank r is defined as

$$r = (1 - \zeta) \cdot A \cdot r + \zeta \cdot s \tag{1}$$

where s is the so-called "initial" probability distribution (again a column vector such that $\sum_{j \in W} s_j = 1$, and $s_j \geq 0$ for all $j \in W$). s is interpreted as a vector of Web page preferences. It has been proven that for $\zeta \in (0,1)$ the vector r exists and is unique, [7]. Hence we can define a function $r(A, s)$ as $r(A, s) = r$, where r is the vector being the solution to eq. (1). For a knowledgeable walker for each node j of the network W $s_j = \frac{1}{|W|}$, ($|W|$ is the cardinality of the set of nodes of W). For a page-u-fan we have $s_u = 1$, and for any other page $j \neq u$ $s_j = 0$. For a uniform-set-U-fan we get $s_j = \frac{1}{|U|}$ for all $j \in U$, and $s_j = 0$ for all $j \notin U$. The following property is easy to show: If A is a balanced connection matrix as defined above and s_1, s_2 be two vectors of Web page preferences, and $r_1 = r(A, s_1), r_2 = r(A, s_2)$ and $\beta \in (0, 1)$, then

$$(\beta r_1 + (1 - \beta)r_2) = (1 - \zeta) \cdot A \cdot (\beta r_1 + (1 - \beta)r_2) + \zeta \cdot (\beta s_1 + (1 - \beta)s_2)$$

or expressing it differently

$$r(A, \beta s_1 + (1 - \beta)s_2) = \beta r(A, s_1) + (1 - \beta)r(A, s_2) \tag{2}$$

which will be exploited subsequently.

3   Personalized PageRank for Exclusive Categories

Let us consider subsequently the concept of personalized PageRank which shall be identical with a page visit probability for a uniform-set-U-fan walker.

It is frequently claimed that Web page ranking would be better if for a query the category of its topic would be identified and then the personalized PageRank for this category would be applied when answering the query. For example we would define categories like "sports", "music" etc. and for a query like "skies" we would use the ranking of "sports". However, as each personalized PageRank requires time for precomputing and space for storage, we face the problem how many categories we shall distinguish. Whatever decision we make, we will always encounter queries that do not fit one single category and then there is a problem which one to choose.

Subsequently we want to know if having personalized PageRanks for several disjoint categories which may be considered as disjoint sets of Web pages sets $U_1, U_2, ..., U_n$ we can compute personalized PageRanks for other sets, obtained from these ones by set-theoretic operators of of union, difference or complement or their combination. Such considerations are of particular interest within ontology-like frameworks (e.g. a simple lattice or TBox of concepts [9]).

These computations should be of course trivial compared to the direct time-consuming operation of finding the eigen-vector so that they can be executed on the fly while answering a query.

Let $I^{(U)}$ be an indicator vector such that $I_j^{(U)} = 1$ if $j \in U$ and $I_j^{(U)} = 0$ otherwise. So for the balanced connection matrix A the Personalized PageRank for the (non-empty) set of pages U equals $r(A, I^{(U)}/|U|)$.

In this section we focus on a family of disjoint sets $U_1, U_2, ..., U_n$ which may be thought of as categories assigned to Web pages such that the search engine may easily infer the categories of interest from user query. In such a setting the operation of intersection or difference is pointless so we will restrict ourselves to the set-theoretic union postponing consideration of complementary sets to the next section.

Consider first two disjoint sets U_1, U_2 with PageRank vectors r_1, r_2. Can we compute PageRank for $U_1 \cup U_2$ for them? The clue is of course in easy construction of $s_{12} = I^{(U_1 \cup U_2)}/|U_1 \cup U_2|$ from $s_1 = I^{(U_1)}/|U_1|$, $s_2 = I^{(U_2)}/|U_2|$. In fact this is trivial: as the sets are disjoint, $I^{(U_1 \cup U_2)} = I^{(U_1)} + I^{(U_2)}$ therefore

$$I^{(U_1 \cup U_2)}/|U_1 \cup U_2| = \frac{|U_1|}{|U_1 \cup U_2|}I^{(U_1)}/|U_1| + \frac{|U_2|}{|U_1 \cup U_2|}I^{(U_2)}/|U_2|$$

which via eq.(2) implies

$$r\left(A, \frac{I^{(U_1 \cup U_2)}}{|U_1 \cup U_2|}\right) = \frac{|U_1| r(A, I^{(U_1)}/|U_1|) + |U_2| r(A, I^{(U_2)}/|U_2|)}{|U_1 \cup U_2|} \tag{3}$$

In general

$$r\left(A, \frac{I^{(\cup_{i=1}^{n} U_i)}}{|\cup_{i=1}^{n} U_i|}\right) = \sum_{i=1}^{n} \frac{|U_i|}{|\cup_{i=1}^{n} U_i|} r\left(A, \frac{I^{U_i}}{|U_i|}\right) \tag{4}$$

4   Personalized PageRank with Negation

Let us turn now to the issue of PageRank for a complementary set, a kind of "negation" of category membership. Obviously, if for our disjoint categories $W = U_1 \cup U_2 \cup ... \cup U_n$ would hold, then the complement of U_1 (denoted here $\neg U_1$) would be equal to $W - U_1 = U_2 \cup ... \cup U_n$ and its personalized PageRank can be computed from the above formula (4). But it would be easier if the "objective" PageRank vector would be available that is $r(A, I^{(W)}/|W|$. Then, using again the equation (4) we would derive

$$r(A, I^{(\neg U)}/|\neg U|) = \frac{|W|}{|W| - |U|} \cdot r(A, I^{(W)}/|W|) - \frac{|U|}{|W| - |U|} \cdot r(A, I^{(U)}/|U|) \tag{5}$$

In case of the above formula there is of course a risk getting negative rank values (due e.g. to rounding errors) so that corrections may be necessary (e.g. changing negative values to 0).

5   Personalized PageRank for Concept Hierarchies

We can distinguish two basic brands of context hierarchies: simple ones (tree-like) and directed-acyclic graphs.

In both cases we could imagine that hierarchy leaves have precomputed personalized PageRanks and the PageRanks of higher level concepts are obtained by transforming them into unions of leaf concepts and then one applies equation (4). However, if queries touching higher level concepts are more frequent then this may be inefficient.

Therefore it may be reasonable for simple hierarchies to pre-compute PageRank at each level of hierarchy for all the child nodes of a given node except for the least frequent one (in whatever sense) and then to use a mixture of equation (4) and equation (5) at appropriate levels of the hierarchy.

Note that a similar approach is possible for general acyclic directed graphs of concepts. Note that under such a setting the idea of concept intersection may make sense because concepts may have common children.

6   Personalized PageRank for Non-exclusive Categories

The beauty of the formulas derived in sections 3 and 4 relies on the fact that both r's and cardinalities of categories can be precomputed and stored with easy access so that the formulas are directly applied. Non-disjoint categories of Web pages may entail two types of relationship:

- the categories form a hierarchy in which at the leaves subcategories are exclusive, or
- the above case does not apply

The first case was treated in the preceding section 5.

The second case does not have a direct solution because there exists no arithmetic operation applying to indicator vectors allowing to compute intersection indicator vector other than direct eigenvalue computation. Therefore a workaround is necessary.

Suppose that $\mathbf{U} = \{U_1, .., U_n\}$ is a set of (overlaping) categories, and let $\mathcal{U} = U_1 \cup \cdots \cup U_n$ denotes the set of Web pages covering all these categories. To compute the Personalized PageRank for this set, $r(A, I^{(\mathcal{U})}/|\mathcal{U}|)$, we introduce generalized membership functions defined as follows

$$I_j^{(U_i)} = \begin{cases} \dfrac{1}{|\{U : U \in \mathbf{U} \wedge j \in U\}|} & \text{if } j \in U_i \\ 0 & \text{otherwise} \end{cases} \quad , \quad i = 1, \ldots n \qquad (6)$$

In other words, $I_j^{(U_i)}$ represents the probability with which a node j can be assigned to the set U_i. Denote further

$$|I^{U_i}| = \sum_{j \in W} I_j^{(U_i)}$$

The intuition behind this formula is to favor the pages that belong to a single category so that the representation of a category is as sharp as possible.

Having a representation like this, we would further treat the categories as if they were disjoint and whenever a query is issued we would transform the expression for the set being base for personalized PageRank computation to a union of these formally "disjoint" categories, and then compute

$$r\left(A, \frac{I^{(U_1 \cup U_2)}}{|I^{(U_1 \cup U_2)}|}\right) = \frac{|I^{U_1}|}{|I^{(U_1 \cup U_2)}|} r\left(A, \frac{I^{(U_1)}}{|I^{(U_1)}|}\right) + \frac{|I^{U_2}|}{|I^{(U_1 \cup U_2)}|} r\left(A, \frac{I^{(U_2)}}{|I^{(U_2)}|}\right)$$

where we apply the formal principle:

$$I^{(U_1 \cup U_2)} = I^{(U_1)} + I^{(U_2)}$$

In general

$$r(A, I^{(\cup_{i=1}^n U_i)}/|I|^{(\cup_{i=1}^n U_i)}|) = \sum_{i=1}^n \frac{|I^{(U_i)}|}{|I^{(\cup_{i=1}^n U_i)}|} r(A, I^{(U_i)}/|I^{(U_i)}|) \qquad (7)$$

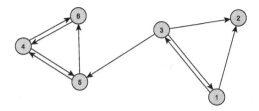

Fig. 1. A simple Web graph

Table 1. Details of computing $r(A, I^{(U_1 \cup U_2)}/|I^{(U_1 \cup U_2)}|)$ with $\alpha = 0.9$

$I^{(U_1)}$	1	0	1	0	1/2	0
$I^{(U_2)}$	0	1	0	0	1/2	0
$r(A, I^{(U_1)}/|I^{(U_1)}|)$	0.0759	0.0701	0.0847	0.3224	0.2010	0.2460
$r(A, I^{(U_2)}/|I^{(U_2)}|)$	0.0223	0.0990	0.0249	0.3606	0.2179	0.2752
$r(A, I^{(U_1 \cup U_2)}/|)I^{(U_1 \cup U_2)}|$	0.0558	0.0809	0.0623	0.3367	0.2073	0.2570

To be more concrete, consider a small example. Assume that the Web graph has the form as depicted in figure 1. Assume that $U_1 = \{1, 3, 5\}$ and $U_2 = \{2, 5\}$. According to the equation (7) we should compute the generalized indicators $I^{(U_1)}, I^{(U_2)}$. They are shown in first and second row of Table 1. On the other hand, if we know the vectors r_1 and r_2, we should only compute the vector $r(A, I^{(U_1 \cap U_2)}/|U_1 \cap U_2|)$ and we can combine already possessed information with this new one by means of the equation (8).

Unfortunately, the formula (7) requires a re-computation of Personalized PageRank with starting vectors $I^{(U_i)}/|I^{(U_i)}|$ instead of $U_u/|U_i|$. However we can make use of the formula (5). Let U_1, U_2 be two overlapping categories, and let $U_{12} = U_1 \cap U_2$. Denote $r_i = r(A, I^{(U_i)}/|U_i|)$ for $i = 1, 2$). As these values are already known, we can compute the Personalized PageRank vector $r(A, I^{(U_1 \cup U_2)}/|U_1 \cup U_2|)$ as follows

$$r\left(A, \frac{I^{(U_1 \cup U_2)}}{|U_1 \cup U_2|}\right) = \frac{r_1|U_1| + r_2|U_2| - |U_1 \cap U_2| r\left(A, \frac{I^{(U_1 \cap U_2)}}{|U_1 \cap U_2|}\right)}{|U_1 \cup U_2|} \qquad (8)$$

That is the only effort is concerned with the computation of the vector $r(A, I^{(U_1 \cap U_2)}/|U_1 \cap U_2|)$.

Finally, let us return to the problem of finding rankings for a "negation" of a given category. Suppose that we have two rankings: $r(A, I^{(U_1)}/|U_1|)$, $r(A, I^{(U_2)}/|U_2|)$ for two categories $U_1 \subset U_2$. Let V be a category such that $U_1 \cap V \neq \emptyset$ and $U_1 \cup V = U_2$. Then, applying the equation (8) we obtain

$$r\left(A, \frac{I^{(V)}}{|V|}\right) = \frac{|U_2| r\left(A, \frac{I^{(U_2)}}{|U_2|}\right) - |U_1| r\left(A, \frac{I^{(U_1)}}{|U_1|}\right) + |U_1 \cap V| r\left(A, \frac{I^{(U_1 \cap V)}}{|U_1 \cap V|}\right)}{|V|}$$

$$(9)$$

Again, in this case we should only find the vector $r(A, I^{(U_1 \cap V)}/|U_1 \cap V|)$, and combine it with the two already defined rankings.

7   Contextual Personalized PageRank

Let us consider briefly the issue of growing interest of seeking for documents in the context of larger groups (usually domains) where first we ask a query for the domain and then for a particular document content. We would suggest using our proposal separately for determining personalized PageRanks for the domains and for the documents and then to apply the eq. (2) to combine both PageRanks treating the domain PageRank as the PageRank of each of the documents within it.

8   Personalized PageRank and User Preferences

The advantage of the proposed framework lies in the fact one can smoothly integrate user preferences in case that these are defined in terms of weights of the categories. Assume that the user gives weight w_1 to the category U_1 and w_2 to the (disjoint) category U_2 and that both of them constitute a background of a query.

Then the equation (3) can be re-interpreted as follows. The indicator vector would now be weighted

$$I^{(U_1 \cup U_2)} = w_1 \cdot I^{(U_1)} + w_2 \cdot I^{(U_2)} \text{ therefore}$$

$$I^{(U_1 \cup U_2)}/|I^{(U_1 \cup U_2)}| = \frac{w_1 \cdot |U_1|}{|I^{(U_1 \cup U_2)}|} I^{(U_1)}/|U_1| + \frac{w_2 \cdot |U_2|}{|I^{(U_1 \cup U_2)}|} I^{(U_2)}/|U_2|$$

which via eq. (2) implies

$$r(A, I^{(U_1 \cup U_2)}/|I^{(U_1 \cup U_2)}|) = \frac{w_1 \cdot |U_1|}{|I^{(U_1 \cup U_2)}|} r(A, I^{(U_1)}/|U_1|) + \frac{w_2 \cdot |U_2|}{|I^{(U_1 \cup U_2)}|} r(A, I^{(U_2)}/|U_2|)$$

9   Final Remarks

Currently, a set of experiments is planned on to what extent the ideas expressed in this paper may prove helpful in improving responses to user queries in a large scale search engine. We expect being able to serve thousands of different category contexts while having to store up to 40 precomputed PageRanks.

Acknowledgements. The research is supported by POIG.01.01.02-14-013/09 grant at the Institute of Computer Sciences, Polish Academy of Sciences, aiming at building NEKST, an experimental, semantically enhanced web search engine particularly adapted for Polish language.

References

1. Deng, H., Lyu, M.R., King, I.: A generalized Co-HITS algorithm and its application to bipartite graphs. In: Proc. of the 15th ACM SIGKDD International Conf. on Knowledge Discovery and Data Mining, KDD 2009, June 28-July 1, pp. 239–248. ACM, New York (2009)

2. Geng, X., Liu, T.Y., Qin, T., Arnold, A., Li, H., Shum, H.Y.: Query dependent ranking using k-nearest neighbor. In: Proceedings of the 31st Annual International ACM SIGIR Conference on Research and Development in Information Retrieval, SIGIR 2008, pp. 115–122. ACM, New York (2008)

3. Haveliwala, T., Kamvar, S., Jeh, G.: An analytical comparison of approaches to personalizing PageRank. Technical Report 2003-35, Stanford InfoLab (June 2003), http://ilpubs.stanford.edu:8090/596/

4. Haveliwala, T.H.: Topic-sensitive PageRank: A context-sensitive ranking algorithm for web search. IEEE Trans. Knowl. Data Eng. 15(4), 784–796 (2003)

5. Kleinberg, J.M.: Authoritative sources in a hyperlinked environment. J. ACM 46(5), 604–632 (1999)

6. Langville, A.N.: An annotated bibliography of papers about Markov chains and information retrieval (2005), http://www.cofc.edu/~langvillea/bibtexpractice.pdf

7. Langville, A.N., Meyer, C.D.: Google's PageRank and Beyond: The Science of Search Engine Rankings. Princeton University Press (2006)

8. Page, L., Brin, S., Motwani, R., Winograd, T.: The PageRank citation ranking: Bringing order to the web. Technical Report 1999-66, Stanford InfoLab (November 1999), http://ilpubs.stanford.edu:8090/422/

9. Ren, Y., Pan, J.Z., Zhao, Y.: Soundness preserving approximation for tbox reasoning in r. In: Grau, B.C., Horrocks, I., Motik, B., Sattler, U. (eds.) Description Logics. Proceedings of the 22nd International Workshop DL 2009, Oxford, UK, July 27-30. CEUR Workshop Proceedings, vol. 477, CEUR-WS.org (2009)

10. Richardson, M., Domingos, P.: The Intelligent Surfer: Probabilistic Combination of Link and Content Information in PageRank. In: Advances in Neural Information Processing Systems 14. MIT Press (2002), http://citeseer.ist.psu.edu/460350.html

11. Zhang, L., Zhang, X., Shum, H.Y.: Qsrank: Query-sensitive hash code ranking for efficient ϵ-neighbor search. In: 2012 IEEE Conference on Computer Vision and Pattern Recognition, pp. 2058–2065 (2012)

Finding the Number of Clusters
on the Basis of Eigenvectors

Małgorzata Lucińska[1] and Sławomir T. Wierzchoń[2,3]

[1] Kielce University of Technology, Kielce, Poland
[2] Institute of Computer Science Polish Academy of Sciences, Warsaw, Poland
[3] University of Gdańsk, Gdańsk, Poland

Abstract. Finding the number of clusters is a challenging task. We suggest a new method for an assessment of a group number. Our solution uses only simple properties of signless Laplacian eigenvectors. The novel method has been incorporated to our previous spectral algorithm. The performance of the modified version is competitive to existing solutions. We empirically evaluate the proposed approach using standard test sets and show that it is able to find correct partitioning even for weakly separated groups of varying densities.

Keywords: spectral clustering, nearest neighbor graph, signless Laplacian.

1 Introduction

Clustering refers to a process of classifying data points into disjoint groups such that elements belonging to same cluster are similar while elements belonging to different clusters are dissimilar. Being a powerful tool it has been successfully applied in many research areas, which include data mining [4], document clustering [3], and large scale search engines [11], to name a few.

One of the main challenges clustering algorithms cope with, is an automatic estimation of the number of groups data should be divided in. Many approaches come down to finding the number of clusters with a help of some functions that measure the quality of grouping. Unfortunately, it results in additional computation costs.

One of the techniques that offer promising tools for solving the problem is spectral clustering. Eigenvalues and eigenvectors of a suitably chosen matrix are used in spectral algorithms in order to partition a dataset. The matrix is an affinity matrix (or a matrix derived from it) built on the basis of pairwise similarity of objects to be grouped. Gaps between eigenvalues and structures of eigenvectors are used as indicators of the cluster number.

The recently proposed Data Spectroscopic (`DaSpec`) clustering algorithm [21] constitutes an example of the second approach. The algorithm estimates the group number by finding eigenvectors with no sign change (up to a small threshold) in the top spectrum of an affinity matrix and assigns labels to each point

M.A. Kłopotek et al. (Eds.): IIS 2013, LNCS 7912, pp. 220–233, 2013.

based on these eigenvectors. The method fails, however, in case of close or over-lapping subsets with different densities. Shi *et al* notice that smaller, or less compact groups may not be identified using just the very top part of the spectrum. More eigenvectors need to be investigated to see these clusters. On the other hand, information in the top few eigenvectors may also be redundant for clustering, as some of these eigenvectors may represent the same group.

In order to overcome the problem, we have employed a hybrid method in our Speclus algorithm [13]. It enables to establish the number of groups automatically and employs both a structure of eigenvectors and a modularity function [18] which measures the quality of partitioning. To limit the influence of not well separated clusters or cluster varying densities on affinity matrix structure, we have introduced the new similarity measure. In the Speclus algorithm the similarity between pairs of points is deduced from their neighborhoods. The resulting affinity matrix reflects true relationships between data points.

The main contribution of this paper is to propose the modification of the Speclus algorithm, called Speclum. The novelty of the last algorithm lies in the new way of establishment of the cluster number. It is assessed only on the basis of eigenvector structures, without the use of an additional quality function. Our method results from observations of spectral algorithms using eigenvectors related to the biggest eigenvalues. Only some of the eigenvectors – these with relatively large absolute mean value of their coordinates – play a significant role in grouping. In other words, the mean values seem to be better indicators of the eigenvector usefulness in partitioning than their related eigenvalues. Apparently, the similarity measure and the resulting affinity matrix, introduced in the Speclus algorithm, play also an important role in the automatic establishment of the cluster number.

In section 2 the notation and related terms are presented. The next section describes some ways of establishing the number of clusters. The main concepts used in the Speclus algorithm are explained in section 4. Then, in section 5, we present the policy of selecting eigenvectors that reflect the structure of dataset. Section 6 includes the description of experiments and results obtained with the use of the Speclum algorithm. Finally, in section 7, the main conclusions are drawn.

2   Notation and Related Terms

Let $\mathbf{X} = (\mathbf{x}_1, \mathbf{x}_2, \ldots, \mathbf{x}_n)$ be the set of data points to be clustered. For each pair of points i, j an adjacency $a_{ij} \in \{0, 1\}$ is attached. The value $a_{ij} = 1$ implies the existence of an undirected edge $i \sim j$ in the graph G spanned over the set of vertices $\mathbf{X}$. Let $A = [a_{ij}]$ be the adjacency matrix. Let $d_i = \sum_j a_{ij}$ denote the degree of node i and let D be the diagonal matrix with d_i's on its diagonal. A clustering $\mathcal{C} = (C_1, C_2, \ldots, C_l)$ is a partition of $\mathbf{X}$ into l nonempty and mutually disjoint subsets. In the graph-theoretic language the clustering represents a multiway cut in G [6]. In many spectral algorithms instead of the affinity matrix the graph Laplacian matrix is used. The unnormalized Laplacian matrix associated with G is the $n \times n$ matrix $L = (l_{ij})$, defined as $L = D - A$ with entries given by:

$$l_{ij} = \begin{cases} d_i \text{ if } i = j \\ -1 \text{ if } i \neq j \text{ and there is an edge } \{i,j\} \in E \\ 0 \text{ otherwise} \end{cases}$$

The normalized Laplacian is defined as $L_{sym} = D^{-1/2}LD^{-1/2}$.

In the `Speclum` algorithm a signless Laplacian $M = D + A$, introduced by Cvetković [5], is used.

A non-zero vector x is an eigenvector of a matrix M with a corresponding eigenvalue λ if x and λ satisfy the following equation:

$$Mx = \lambda x$$

3   Establishing the Number of Connected Components in a Graph

The multiplicity of one as an eigenvalue of L_{sym} (or of zero for unnormalized Laplacian L) is equal to the number of connected components of the graph. An eigenvector with one eigenvalue is a function on the vertices whose value at i is the weighted average of its values on the neighbors of i, each neighbor weighted by the number of edges joining it to i. Considering a vertex where the maximum absolute value is achieved, we see that the same value occurs on all neighbors, so the function is constant on connected components. In particular, if the graph is connected, the one eigenvalue (called trivial) has multiplicity 1; the other eigenvalues are nontrivial. The eigenvectors for the trivial eigenvalue are the constant vectors.

The above theorem explains why most of the spectral algorithms use for clustering one or a few eigenvectors of an appropriate matrix. The eigenvectors are related to the l closest to one (in case of normalized and signless Laplacians) or closest to zero (for unnormalized Laplacian) eigenvalues. However, for real, noisy, not very well separated datasets it is usually very difficult to distinguish which eigenvalues are related to connected components.

In Figure 1 we show a few largest eigenvalues of the normalized Laplacian for two different datasets. The first one consists of two very well separated homocentric circles. The other set of two noisy rings (2R3D.2) constitutes much more difficult task for clustering and is presented in section 6 (Figure 3). The way of the Laplacian calculation is exactly the same as in the NJW algorithm [20] that is described later in section 6 together with details concerning its affinity measure. One can indicate easily the number of clusters in the first case, as there are two eigenvalues equal to one. As far as the other set is concerned it is impossible to distinguish the right number of clusters on the basis of the eigenvalues. In other words the Laplacian eigenvalues do not suffice when it comes to finding the number of clusters.

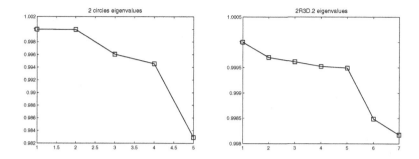

Fig. 1. Normalized Laplacian eigenvalues for two sets: 2 circles (left) and 2R3D.2 (right)

4   Main Contributions of the Speclus Algorithm

In order to estimate the number of groups and divide data into clusters the
`Speclum` algorithm utilizes structure of eigenvectors of the signless Laplacian,
similarly to its predecessor the `Speclus` algorithm. According to works [7] and
[21], the top eigenvectors of sparse matrices, related to points creating disjoint
subsets, reflect the structure of the data set. Figure 2 shows an ideal example,
when three clusters are completely separated and each of them can be presented
in the form of the regular graph of the same degree. The top three eigenvectors
of the signless Laplacian show clearly its structure. Each cluster is represented
by an eigenvector, which assumes relatively large values (of one sign) for points
belonging to the cluster and zero values for points from other clusters. The
additional regularity can also be seen – if a point is close to a cluster center
its value in the corresponding eigenvector is large. The points that lay on the
border of a cluster have relatively small values of the appropriate eigenvector.

In real situations, when subsets are close to each other, overlap or have different densities, the picture of data structure given by the top eigenvectors can
be a little confusing. First of all a graph representing such a dataset is no longer
regular and eigenvectors of an affinity matrix, or matrices derived from it, fail to
represent each cluster clearly. A few eigenvectors may represent the same group,
whereas two different groups can be reflected in one eigenvector. In the `Speclus`
algorithm the problems are solved with the help of a novel similarity measure
based on nearest neighbor approach.

The new similarity measure is described in [13] , and here we will present
only its general concept. Specifically the k mutual nearest neighbor graph is
constructed with points as the vertices and edges as similarities. First, for each
of the points k symmetric nearest neighbors are found with Euclidean distance
as the distance metric. Then for each two vertices $\mathbf{x}_i$ and $\mathbf{x}_j$ the connecting edge
v_{ij} is created if the vertex $\mathbf{x}_i$ belongs to the k-nearest neighbors of vertex $\mathbf{x}_j$
and vice versa. Afterwards additional edges are created between vertices with

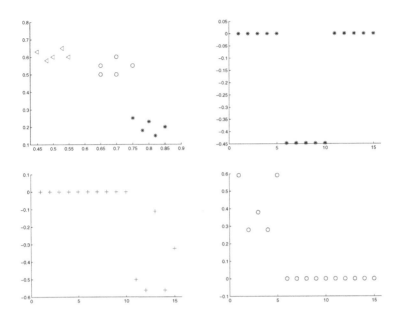

Fig. 2. Perfectly separated clusters (top right) and their eigenvectors (top left and bottom)

low degrees (smaller than a half of the average degree in the set). For each pair of nodes $\mathbf{x}_i$ and $\mathbf{x}_j$ in such a graph the value a_{ij} is set to one if and only if there is an edge joining the two vertices. Otherwise a_{ij} equals 0. Also all diagonal elements of the affinity matrix A are zero. Because the number of edges k going out from one point is usually small, we achieve sparse matrix, however weakly connected nodes are not separated from one another.

The policy is meant to improve regularity of a graph, so that the resulting affinity matrix is close to block-diagonal. As it is usually not perfectly block-diagonal, another tool should be used in order to chose the right eigenvectors. In the Speclus algorithm for this purpose we apply the modularity function. If two eigenvectors indicate two different divisions of the set, the modularity is calculated in order to choose a better cut in terms of modularity maximization. The modularity function being a well known, recognized cut quality measure has, however, some drawbacks. It prefers, for example, divisions to larger numbers of groups. The use of the modularity also involves execution and evaluation of preliminary cuts, thus increasing complexity of the process of clustering.

Here we select the most suitable eigenvectors on the basis of their simple statistic properties: mean value, maximum, and minimum values, without any additional quality functions.

5   Properties of Signless Laplacian Eigenvectors

In the `Speclum` algorithm we utilize special features of eigenvectors related to the signless Laplacian of a regular graph. Each top eigenvector (i.e. related to the eigenvalue equal 1) represents one connected component of the graph and its coordinates indicate the degree of point affiliation to the component. All coordinates have the same sign and they are large if the related points belong to the group and equal zero if they do not. The coordinate values of other eigenvectors (related to smaller eigenvalues) change sign within the same connected component. This means that the absolute mean value of the eigenvector carrying information about the data structure is relatively large. The rest of eigenvectors, whose mean values are relatively small and they do not differ a lot from one another, usually repeat structures of the previous ones or include misleading patterns.

For irregular graphs, some eigenvectors representing particular groups may not belong to the top spectrum. If their coordinates differ in sign, their mean values will be smaller than in the case of top eigenvectors. In other cases, they may correspond not only to one cluster, but also to parts of other groups. Such situation causes misleading increase in the eigenvector mean value. In order to execute the correct division, we have to find not only eigenvectors with reasonably large absolute mean value but also establish which of them constitute a true and single representation of clusters.

For the above reasons we will examine both eigenvector mean values and their minimum and maximum values. As our task is to indicate all the eigenvectors reflecting a dataset structure, we have to take into consideration two features of each vector – its mean value and the change of sign of its coordinates. Our policy is the following:

1. Calculate a few eigenvectors (about 20) of the signless Laplacian
2. Put them in descending order in terms of their absolute mean values
3. Find the first eigenvector with a large sign change
4. Select eigenvectors with absolute mean values bigger than the one of the first eigenvector with the sign change
5. Execute division on the basis of the selected eigenvectors

According to our assumption an eigenvector changes the sign of its coordinates if its minimum value is smaller than minus a half of its maximum for vectors with positive coordinates, and appropriately for negative coordinates the maximum value should be larger than minus a half of the minimum. The following formula shows the above mentioned policy:

$$min > -0.5 * max \text{ if } mean > 0$$
$$max < -0.5 * min \text{ if } mean < 0$$

where $mean$ is a mean value of eigenvector coordinates, max and min stand for the vector coordinate maximum and minimum respectively.

Our policy can be clarified in the following way. If a graph is regular, the top eigenvectors of the signless Laplacian, related to the largest eigenvalues, have the largest absolute mean values. Other eigenvectors corresponding to smaller eigenvalues change the sign of their coordinates. When a graph is not regular, the structure is disturbed and the eigenvectors reflecting single components may not be related to the largest eigenvalues. Their absolute mean value, however, remains still relatively large. At least larger than that of eigenvectors that change the sign of their coordinates. One should notice that in case of strongly irregular graphs such rules cannot be applied, because eigenvector structures are deeply disturbed.

6   The Speclum Algorithm and Experiments

The main steps of the Speclum algorithm are very similar to these of the Speclus algorithm (presented in details in [13]) and they look in the following way:

The Speclum algorithm

```
Input: Data X, number of nearest neighbors k
Output: C clustering of X
Algorithm:
1. Compute, in the following order
     k-nearest neighbors for each x
     mutual nearest neighbors for each x
     additional neighbors in case degree of x < half of the
     average degree in X
2. Create the affinity matrix S and the signless Laplacian M=D+S
3. Find the set of eigenvectors A, each representing one cluster
4. Assign each point x to one eigenvector from the set A,
     having the biggest entry for x
```

The main difference between the two solutions lies in the way the third step is executed. The change concerns the method of establishing the number of clusters and choosing the eigenvectors that carry most information about graph structure. In the Speclum algorithm the third step is realized as described in section 5. The new version establishes the number of clusters in a very natural way and does not require any preliminary cuts and calculation of a quality function, contrary to the previous solution.

We have compared the performance of the Speclum algorithm (implemented in MATLAB) to two other methods: the NJW algorithm [20] and the PIC algorithm introduced by Lin *et al* [12]. The first one is a standard spectral algorithm, which uses normalized Laplacian. The other one applies power iteration to the row-normalized affinity matrix. Both of them utilize k-means for final clustering and need the number of clusters as an input parameter.

The NJW algorithm uses the similarity measure based on the Gaussian kernel function defined as:

$$A(i,j) = \exp(-\|\mathbf{x}_i - \mathbf{x}_j\|^2/(2\sigma^2)) \tag{1}$$

where $\|\mathbf{x}_i - \mathbf{x}_j\|$ denotes the Euclidean distance between points $\mathbf{x}_i$ and $\mathbf{x}_j$. The kernel parameter σ influences the structure of an affinity matrix and generally it is difficult to find its optimal value. For the sake of algorithm comparison, the values of the σ parameter were chosen manually, as described by Fischer *et al* [8].

The PIC algorithm uses the affinity matrix based on the cosine similarity:

$$A(i,j) = \frac{\mathbf{x}_i \cdot \mathbf{x}_j}{\|\mathbf{x}_i\|^2 \|\mathbf{x}_j\|^2} \tag{2}$$

where $\mathbf{x}_i$ is a point. Such a metric avoids tuning the σ parameter.

In our experiments we use both artificial and real data sets of different structures, sizes, dimensions, densities, and noise levels. First, we test the algorithms with the help of the same benchmark data sets as for the Speclus algorithm: 2R3D.2, RG, 2S, 4 Gaussian, 5 Gaussian, Iris, Wine, and Breast cancer, the sets are described in details in [8]. Another group consists of three handwritten digit sets Pen17, Opt17, and Opt1000. The first one derives from the Pen-based recognition of handwritten digits dataset [2] with digits "1" and "7". The second and third one are subsets of Optical recognition of handwritten digits dataset [10] consisting of digits "1" and "7", and all the digits respectively. Some network datasets have also been applied: Polbooks (a co-purchase network of 105 political books [19]), UBMGBlog (a network of 404 liberal and conservative political blogs [9]), and AGBlog (another network of 1222 liberal and conservative political blogs [1]). The sets 20ng* derive from the 20 newsgroups text dataset [17] and are selected by Lin *et al* [12]. 20ngA contains 100 documents from 2 newsgroups: misc.forsale and soc.religion.christian. 20ngB adds 100 documents to each group of 20ngA. 20ngC adds 200 from talk.politics.guns to 20ngB. 20ngD adds 200 from rec.sport.baseball to 20ngC.

All the datasets are labeled, which enables evaluation of the clustering results against the labels using cluster purity and normalized mutual information (NMI), as measures of division quality. For both measures higher number means better partitioning. We refer an interested reader to [14] for details regarding the measures.

In case of datasets 2R3D.2, RG, 2S, 4 Gaussian, 5 Gaussian, Iris, Wine, Breast cancer, Pen17, Opt17, and Opt1000 an appropriate metric for each algorithm has been applied, i.e.: Gaussian kernel for NJW, cosine for PIC, and original similarity measure of the Speclum algorithm. As far as networks are concerned, all the algorithms use the same affinity matrix that is simply $a_{ij} = 1$ if an edge exists between vertices i and j, and $a_{ij} = 0$ otherwise. Similarly for the text datasets in all the cases, feature vectors are created on the basis of word counts, with only stop words and singleton words removed.

In the first part of experiments, our intention has been to check whether our new algorithm allows to find the most suitable eigenvectors and to establish the right number of groups. If it succeeds, the results will be of course the same as for the `Speclus` algorithm. We start with three datasets: the first (2R3D.2) is a very noisy one, the second (RG) consists of two rather high density rings and the Gaussian cluster with very low density, and the third (2S) is created by two S-shaped clusters with varying densities within each group. In Figure 3 we present the dataset partitioning obtained with the use of the `Speclum` algorithm, eigenvalues (squares), and absolute mean values of eigenvectors of the signless Laplacian (circles). The absolute mean values of eigenvectors and the eigenvalues are sorted in descending order. The filled marks indicate the related eigenvectors that are used for partitioning. The figure shows that despite varying densities and noisy, weakly separated groups, the numbers of clusters are established correctly and the dataset divisions are correct. One can notice that in many cases the chosen eigenvectors are not the ones related with the largest eigenvalues. For example, in case of the set of two Gaussian rings (2R3D.2) the selected vectors correspond with the second and third highest eigenvalue and for the set with three clusters to the first, fourth, and tenth eigenvalue. Moreover, there is usually a visible gap between the absolute mean values of the chosen eigenvectors and the rest of them.

We have also tested the presented algorithm on the rest of the benchmark sets (used for the `Speclus` algorithm) which include both artificial and real data: Iris, Wine, Breast cancer and 4 Gaussian sets. In all these cases one is able to detect the right number of clusters and choose proper eigenvectors revealing data structure. Figure 4 illustrates absolute mean values of eigenvectors (sorted in descending order) for the sets.

The most interesting is the four-dimensional set 5G, consisting of five Gaussian clusters of different densities. As can be seen in Figure 5 the four groups can be detected easily both on the basis of absolute mean values of eigenvectors as well as eigenvalues. The fifth one is found by the `Speclum` algorithm with the help of the eigenvector related to the 30-st eigenvalue. So it is practically inseparable for methods relying on the handful of top eigenvectors.

Table 1 and Table 2 summarize the partitioning results obtained by the `Speclus`, `NJW`, and `PIC` algorithms. In cases where the original similarity measure of the `Speclum` algorithm is used (the first 11 sets) its results are slightly better than that of the `NJW` algorithm and far better than these for the `PIC` algorithm. The last solution failed to find the partitioning in reasonable time (1 hour on 4 GHz processor). For the other sets, when the affinity matrices are the same for all the algorithms, our solution is the runner-up, performs slightly worse than the `PIC` algorithm, but better than the `NJW` algorithm. One should remember, however, that the `Speclum` algorithm does not require the number of clusters to be given manually, but finds it in an automatic way. Even in cases when another metric is used, our method is able to find the right number of clusters for all the sets except for the Polbooks set.

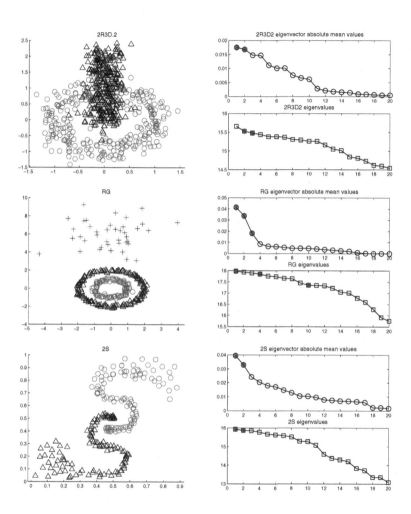

Fig. 3. Data sets, their eigenvalues (squares) and absolute mean values of their eigenvectors (circles). The filled marks indicate related eigenvectors that are used for partitioning.

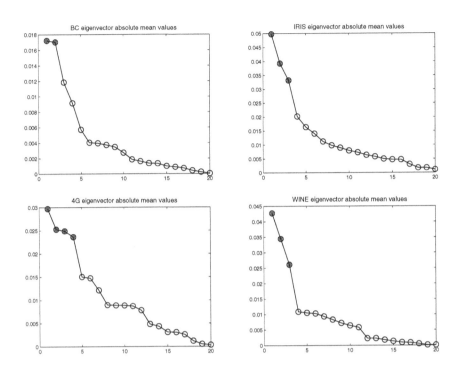

Fig. 4. Absolute mean values of eigenvectors for different datasets. The filled marks indicate eigenvectors that are used for partitioning.

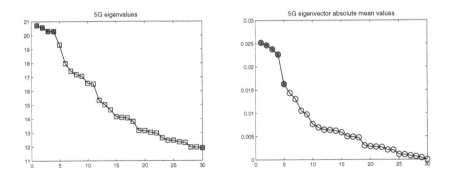

Fig. 5. Eigenvalues (left) and absolute mean values of eigenvectors (right) for the set of 5G, sorted in descending order.

Table 1. Comparison of NJW, PIC, and Speclum algorithms in terms of purity and NMI. For each algorithm its original similarity measure has been used. n denotes number of points, l – number of clusters, D – data dimension, and ls – number of clusters obtained by the Speclum algorithm.

Data	n	D	l	ls	NJW		PIC		Speclum	
					purity	NMI	purity	NMI	purity	NMI
2R3D.2	600	2	3	3	0.9867	0.9038	0.5083	0.00004	0.9800	0.8585
RG	290	2	3	3	1.0000	1.0000	0.5172	0.0138	1.0000	1.0000
2S	220	2	2	2	1.0000	1.0000	0.7227	0.3112	1.0000	1.0000
4G	200	3	4	4	0.9100	0.8012	0.8500	0.7210	0.9850	0.9469
5G	250	4	5	5	0.8640	0.7394	0.6160	0.5232	0.9560	0.9041
Iris	150	4	3	3	0.9067	0.8058	0.9800	0.9306	0.9067	0.7649
Wine	178	13	3	3	0.9663	0.8781	0.7360	0.5019	0.9494	0.8666
BC	683	9	2	2	0.9722	0.8144	0.6501	0.0502	0.9707	0.8048
Pen17	200	16	2	2	0.7900	0.2587	0.7900	0.2587	0.8250	0.3342
Opt17	200	64	2	2	0.8900	0.5953	0.8850	0.5838	0.8850	0.5838
Opt100	1000	64	10	10	0.7890	0.8248	na	na	0.9400	0.894
average					0.9159	0.7838	0.7255	0.3894	0.9453	0.8144

Table 2. Comparison of NJW, PIC, and Speclum algorithms in terms of purity and NMI. For each algorithm the same affinity matrix has been used. n denotes number of points, l – number of clusters, and ls – number of clusters obtained by the Speclum algorithm.

Data	n	l	ls	NJW		PIC		Speclum	
				purity	NMI	purity	NMI	purity	NMI
Polbooks	105	3	2	0.8286	0.5422	0.8667	0.6234	0.8572	0.6244
UBMCBlog	404	2	2	0.9530	0.7375	0.9480	0.7193	0.7871	0.2884
AGBlog	1222	2	2	0.5205	0.0006	0.9574	0.7465	0.8568	0.4779
20ngA	100	2	2	0.9600	0.7594	0.9600	0.7594	0.9200	0.6050
20ngB	200	2	2	0.5525	0.0842	0.8700	0.5230	0.8450	0.3997
20ngC	400	3	3	0.6317	0.3488	0.6933	0.4450	0.7233	0.3070
20ngD	600	4	4	0.5150	0.2959	0.5825	0.3133	0.4963	0.1778
average				0.7088	0.3955	0.8397	0.5900	0.7844	0.4114

7 Conclusions

We have presented a new spectral clustering algorithm that is a modification of our previous work. Similarly to its predecessor it uses signless Laplacian eigenvectors and a novel affinity matrix. It is simpler than the previous one, because it does not require executing preliminary cuts and calculating a cut-quality function. Its novelty lies in making a good use of simple statistics properties of eigenvectors. Our experiments show superiority of clustering on the basis of eigenvector absolute mean values over eigenvalues. The presented way of establishing the number of groups can have applications in many other clustering problems.

References

1. Adamic, L., Glance, N.: The political blogosphere and the 2004 U.S. election. In: WWW Workshop on the Weblogging Ecosystem, pp. 36–43 (2005)
2. Alimoglu, F., Alpaydin, E.: Combining multiple representations and classifiers for handwrittendigit recognition. In: Proc. of ICDAR, pp. 637–640 (1997)
3. Andrews, N.O., Fox, E.A.: Recent Developments in Document Clustering. Technical Report TR-07-35, Computer Science, Virginia Tech (2007)
4. Berkhin, P.: Survey of Clustering Data Mining Techniques (2002), http://citeseer.nj.nec.com/berkhin02survey.html
5. Cvetkovic, D.: Signless Laplacians and line graphs. Bull. Acad. Serbe Sci. Arts, Cl. Sci. Math. Natur., Sci. Math. 131(30), 85–92 (2005)
6. Deepak, V., Meila, M.: Comparison of Spectral Clustering Methods. UW TR CSE-03-05-01 (2003)
7. Elon, Y.: Eigenvectors of the discrete Laplacian on regular graphs a statistical approach. J. Phys. A: Math. Theor. 41, 1–17 (2008)
8. Fischer, I., Poland, J.: Amplifying the Block Matrix Structure for Spectral Clustering. Technical Report No. IDSIA-03-05, Telecommunications Lab, pp. 21–28 (2005)
9. Kale, A., Karandikar, A., Kolari, P., Java, A., Finin, T., Joshi, A.: Modeling trust and influence in the blogosphere using link polarity. In: Proc. of ICWSM 2007 (2007)
10. Kaynak, C.: Methods of combining multiple classifiers and their applications to handwritten digit recognition. Master's thesis, Institute of Graduate Studies in Science and Engineering, Bogazici University (1995)
11. Langville, A.N., Meyer, C.D.: Google's PageRank and Beyond: The Science of Search Engine Rankings. Princeton University Press, Princeton (2006)
12. Lin, F., Cohen, W.W.: Power iteration clustering. In: Proc. of ICML–2010, pp. 655–662 (2010)
13. Lucińska, M., Wierzchoń, S.T.: Spectral clustering based on k-nearest neighbor graph. In: Cortesi, A., Chaki, N., Saeed, K., Wierzchoń, S. (eds.) CISIM 2012. LNCS, vol. 7564, pp. 254–265. Springer, Heidelberg (2012)
14. Manning, C.D., Raghavan, P., Schütze, H.: Introduction to Information Retrieval. Cambridge University Press (2008)
15. Meila, M., Shi, J.: A random walks view of spectral segmentation. In: Proc. of 10th International Workshop on Artificial Intelligence and Statistics (AISTATS), pp. 8–11 (2001)

16. Meila, M., Verma, D.: A comparison of spectral clustering methods. Technical Report UW TR CSE-03-05-01 (2003)
17. Mitchell, T.: Machine Learning. McGraw Hill (1997)
18. Newman, M.E.J.: Detecting community structure in networks. European Physics. J. B 38, 321–330 (2004)
19. Newman, M.E.J.: Finding community structure in networks using the eigenvectors of matrices. Physical Review E 74, 036104 (2006)
20. Ng, A., Jordan, M., Weiss, Y.: On spectral clustering: Analysis and an algorithm. In: Advances in Neural Information Processing Systems 14 (2001)
21. Shi, T., Belkin, M., Yu, B.: Data spectroscopy: eigenspace of convolution operators and clustering. The Annals of Statistics 37(6B), 3960–3984 (2009)

Study on the Estimation of the Bipartite Graph Generator Parameters

Robert A. Kłopotek

Institute of Computer Science, Polish Academy of Sciences,
ul. Jana Kazimierza 5, 01-237 Warsaw, Poland
`robert@klopotek.com.pl`

Abstract. One of possible ways of studying dynamics of real life networks is to identify models of network growth that fit a given network.

In this paper, we consider the evolution of bipartite graphs generated from graph generator proposed in [1]. We propose a method of capturing generator parameters from the network and evaluate it on artificial networks generated from the very same generator.

It seems possible to discover these parameters from the network to an extent allowing for generation of similar graphs in terms of several graph metrics.

Keywords: bipartite graph, graph model, graph generator, parameter identification, social network analysis.

1 Introduction

Graphs are used nowadays to model various interesting real world phenomena. Much interest of researchers is attracted e.g. by social networks which can be modeled in many cases via bipartite graphs.

Vertices of bipartite graph can be divided into two disjoint sets U and V such that every edge connects a vertex in U to one in V; that is, U and V are independent sets. These sets can be for example customers and products. If a customer u_i buys a product v_j there is an edge between vertex u_i and v_j and there are no edges between customers and between items. In case of an Internet forum one could have also two modalities: one for users and the other for threads they participate in. Many other kinds of bipartite networks occur in real life [2].

These kinds of networks are characterized by one important dimension - their evolution in time. There are many questions concerning graph growth over time. One of main questions concerns real graph evolution over time and extraction of growth patterns in real life networks. Many studies have discovered patterns in static graphs, identifying properties in a single snapshot of a large network, or in a very small number of snapshots. This data is sometimes not enough for extracting interesting features, behavior of network or predicting trend in the future which is useful in i.e recommending systems. The graph properties between existent snapshots may be of interest e.g. when evaluating link analysis algorithms.

M.A. Kłopotek et al. (Eds.): IIS 2013, LNCS 7912, pp. 234–244, 2013.

One of possible ways to study network dynamics is to construct growth models of the network. If we fit a growth model to a real graph growth phenomenon by e.g. getting good estimates on network parameters, we can model graph growth in future and hence make for example better business decisions.

The quality of a model is usually evaluated by investigating if the model can generate graphs "similar" to real world graphs. This similarity is evaluated in terms of similarity of various graph metrics computed for the original graph and for the one generated from the model. If they are close then we assume that the growth model is useful.

Many real graphs exhibit properties like power law of degree distribution, densifying over time, shrinking of average distance between nodes, in contrast to the conventional wisdom that such distance parameters should increase slowly as a function of the number of nodes (see [3, 4]). Prediction of structure is much more complicated when we have more than one component (see [5]). In real world data it is very common that we have one giant component and many small ones. Kumar et al. [5] pointed out a possible examination. Structure outside the giant component is largely characterized by stars. The creation of stars is largely a result of the dynamics of invitation, in which many people are invited to the social network, but only a small fraction choose to engage more deeply than simply responding to an invitation from a friend. Thus in this paper we will consider only connected graphs or giant component (biggest connected subgraph) when we have more.

The frequently used graph metric, estimating graph density, is called local clustering coefficient (LCC) and for a vertex i it is defined as:

$$LCC(i) = \frac{|(a, b) \in E : (a, i) \in E \wedge (b, i) \in E|}{k_i(k_i - 1)/2} \tag{1}$$

where E is set of all edges, V is set of all vertices, $a, b \in V$ are vertices and k_i is degree of vertex i. For the whole graph G clustering coefficient is just $LCC(G) = \sum_{i \in V} \frac{LCC(i)}{|V|}$.

In bipartite graph for all vertices a, b in the same set we don't have any edges between them, so we always get 0. This means a serious problem when studying bipartite graphs and is an obstacle in adopting traditional graph generators to the case of bipartite ones. Therefore in [1] another suitable metric was proposed - bipartite clustering coefficient (BLCC).

$$BLCC(u) = 1 - \frac{|N_2(u)|}{\sum_{v \in N_1(u)}(k_v - 1)} \tag{2}$$

W is set of all vertices, $N_s(n)$ — set of neighbors of vertex $n \in W$, which are $s \geq 1$ steps away. In other words $N_s(n) = \{a \in V : K(n, a) = s\}$, where $K(i, j)$ is minimal distance (number of edges) between vertices i and j. In [1] it is shown that graph metric LCC and $BLCC$ are similar in classical graphs.

Over the last decade a number of growth models for bipartite graphs have been proposed [6–8]. Unfortunately their bipartite graph generators have some drawbacks. They create bipartite graphs with limited reproduction of real-life graph properties and they create two graph structures which complicates the models a lot.

In this paper we consider the graph generator of Chojnacki [1] that can be viewed as a graph growth model with five parameters. In [1] it has been demonstrated that the model qualitatively reflects quite well properties of real life bipartite graphs. Our long term goal is to investigate whether or not it can be used also for a quantitative analysis.

In this paper we concentrate at the first stage of this research that is on methods of reconstructing generator models from the graph at some stage of development. We propose a method to capture the parameters from the actual graph and verify the similarity of metrics between the original graph and the one obtained from the model.

But in this study we want to go one step further, trying to estimate to what extent the model parameters can be properly recovered from the graph. Therefore we study artificial graphs generated from Chojnacki model and apply our model recovery method to them.

The paper is structured as follows: In section 2 we briefly recall the Chojnacki generator. In section 3 we propose a method of parameter identification from a graph. In section 4 we present experimental results on parameter recovery and model quality. Section 5 contains some concluding remarks.

2   Bipartite Graph Generator

Generator presented in [1] is more flexible than graph generators mentioned in [9] (Erdös-Réni model), [10] (Bárabasi-Albert model), [11] (Vázquez model), [12] (White model) and [13] (Liu model). In this paper we will examine model without "bouncing parameter". Bouncing parameter is adaptation of surfing mechanism in classical graphs (see [11]). Bouncing mechanism is used only to the edges which were created according to preferential attachment.

For simplification we will consider graph with set of vertices $W = U \cup I$, $U \cap I = \emptyset$, where set U we will call "users" and set I we will call "items". We consider both uniform attachment, where incoming nodes form links to existing nodes selected uniformly at random, and preferential attachment, when probabilities are assigned proportional to the degrees of the existing nodes (see [14]). The generator has 6 parameters:

1. m - initial number of edges
2. δ - probability that new vertex v added to graph in iteration t is a user $v \in U$, so $1 - \delta$ means probability that new vertex v is an item $v \in I$
3. d_u - number of edges added from vertex of type user in one iteration
4. d_v - number of edges added from vertex of type item in one iteration
5. α - probability of *item* preferential attachment, $1 - \alpha$ - probability of *item* uniform attachment
6. β - probability of *user* preferential attachment, $1 - \alpha$ - probability of *user* uniform attachment

The Chojnacki's procedure for generating synthetic bipartite graphs consists of steps given below:

1. Initialize graph with m edges (we have $2m$ vertices)
2. Add new vertex to the graph of type *user* with probability δ otherwise it is of type *item*
3. The choice of how to join neighbors to the new vertex:
   (a) if node is *item* add d_v edges from this node to type *user* vertices, but with probability α by preferential attachment mechanism and otherwise with uniform attachment
   (b) if node is *user* add d_u edges from this node to type *item* vertices, but with probability β by preferential attachment mechanism and otherwise with uniform attachment
4. Repeat steps 2 and 3 T times

It is easy to see that after t iteration we have $|U(t)| = m + \delta t$ vertices of type *user* and $|I(t)| = m + (1-\delta)t$ vertices of type *item*. Average number of edges attached in one iteration is $\eta = d_u \delta + (1 - \delta)d_v$. After very big number of iterations we can skip m initial edges in further calculations. Thus we can show that average numbers of vertex of type *user* and of type *item* depend only on tine given by iteration t and does not depend on m, d_v, d_u. This is not a good news, because we cannot use them to estimate all parameters of the generator, especially δ, β and α.

So let us exploit another relationship. After many calculation (see [1]) involving relaxation of degree to real positive number, defining probability density function over degrees, we get following equation:

$$\Phi\{k_u(t) < k\} = 1 - \left(\frac{\beta\eta + \delta(1 - \beta)k}{\beta\eta + \delta(1 - \beta)d_u} \right)^{\frac{-\eta}{(1-\delta)(1-\beta)d_v}} \tag{3}$$

where $\Phi\{k_u(t) < k\}$ is probability that user vertex u has degree k_u, which is less than threshold value k and other parameters are given from model. Analogously we can construct following equation:

$$\Phi\{k_v(t) < k\} = 1 - \left(\frac{\alpha\eta + (1 - \delta)(1 - \alpha)k}{\alpha\eta + (1 - \delta)(1 - \alpha)d_v} \right)^{\frac{-\eta}{\delta(1-\alpha)d_u}} \tag{4}$$

where $\Phi\{k_v(t) < k\}$ is probability that item vertex v has degree k_v, which is less than threshold value k.

3   Parameter Estimation

Theoretical equations from previous section after some modification are useful to estimate parameters of bipartite graph generator. The simplest one is δ.

$$\delta = \frac{|U|}{|U \cup I|} \tag{5}$$

For computation of β we have to modify equation (3) to obtain an expression depending solely on the variable β, (leaving only δ, as it is easily obtained from the former formula). Let $\Phi\{k_u(t) < k\} = \Phi_k$ We rewrite this equation into:

$$\Phi_k = 1 - \left(\frac{\beta\eta + \delta(1-\beta)k}{\beta\eta + \delta(1-\beta)d_u}\right)^{\frac{-\eta}{(1-\delta)(1-\beta)d_v}} \tag{6}$$

Consider following fraction:

$$\frac{1 - \Phi_{k+1}}{1 - \Phi_k} = \frac{\left(\frac{\beta\eta+\delta(1-\beta)(k+1)}{\beta\eta+\delta(1-\beta)d_u}\right)^{\frac{-\eta}{(1-\delta)(1-\beta)d_v}}}{\left(\frac{\beta\eta+\delta(1-\beta)k}{\beta\eta+\delta(1-\beta)d_u}\right)^{\frac{-\eta}{(1-\delta)(1-\beta)d_v}}} = \left(\frac{\frac{\beta\eta+\delta(1-\beta)(k+1)}{\beta\eta+\delta(1-\beta)d_u}}{\frac{\beta\eta+\delta(1-\beta)k}{\beta\eta+\delta(1-\beta)d_u}}\right)^{\frac{-\eta}{(1-\delta)(1-\beta)d_v}} \tag{7}$$

Hence

$$\frac{1 - \Phi_{k+1}}{1 - \Phi_k} = \left(1 + \frac{\delta(1-\beta)}{\beta\eta + \delta(1-\beta)k}\right)^{\frac{-\eta}{(1-\delta)(1-\beta)d_v}} \tag{8}$$

Thus

$$\log\left(\frac{1 - \Phi_{k+1}}{1 - \Phi_k}\right) = \frac{-\eta}{(1-\delta)(1-\beta)d_v} \log\left(1 + \frac{\delta(1-\beta)}{\beta\eta + \delta(1-\beta)k}\right) \tag{9}$$

To calculate somehow β from equations above, we construct a function $F(\beta)$ such that $F(\beta) = 0$ for optimal β. Consider

$$\frac{\log\left(\frac{1-\Phi_{k+2}}{1-\Phi_{k+1}}\right)}{\log\left(\frac{1-\Phi_{k+1}}{1-\Phi_k}\right)} = \frac{\log\left(1 + \frac{\delta(1-\beta)}{\beta\eta+\delta(1-\beta)(k+1)}\right)}{\log\left(1 + \frac{\delta(1-\beta)}{\beta\eta+\delta(1-\beta)k}\right)} \tag{10}$$

From equation 10 we get our desired function $F(\beta)$

$$F(\beta) = \frac{\log\left(1 + \frac{\delta(1-\beta)}{\beta\eta+\delta(1-\beta)(k+1)}\right)}{\log\left(1 + \frac{\delta(1-\beta)}{\beta\eta+\delta(1-\beta)k}\right)} - \frac{\log\left(\frac{1-\Phi_{k+2}}{1-\Phi_{k+1}}\right)}{\log\left(\frac{1-\Phi_{k+1}}{1-\Phi_k}\right)} \tag{11}$$

From equation (10) we can easily see that $F(\beta) = 0$ for optimal β. For given bipartite graph from iteration t we can calculate $\eta = \frac{|E(t)|}{|U(t)|+|I(t)|}$ and $\delta = \frac{|U(t)|}{|U(t)|+|I(t)|}$. To compute β it is enough to use some root finding method on function $F(\beta)$. Estimates for $\Phi_k = \Phi\{k_u(t) < k\}$ can be computed as a cumulative sum of vertex degrees from

$$\Phi_k = \frac{\sum_{i=1}^{k-1} |\{u \in U : |N(u)| = i\}|}{|U|} \tag{12}$$

To estimate α parameter we can construct $F(\alpha)$ in full analogy to $F(\beta)$.

4   Experimental Results

Equation (11) is computably complicated and moreover it's theoretical, when number of vertices grows to infinity and we relaxed property of degrees to any real number. Also this equation gives us no insight what k should we choose. For proper estimation we made several experiments to find out, how good this estimation of parameters is.

4.1   Choosing Threshold k

Intuitively we should choose such k that best represents our graph. Experiments for estimation β from equation (3) and α from (4) are shown in figures 1 and 2. We can see that when size of our graph grows, we get less accuracy on smaller k. For other value of parameter δ relations are similar, but relative error of β is little smaller with decreasing δ and little higher with increasing δ, and relative error of α otherwise. It can lead to some false conclusion that it is better to choose bigger k, because from power law distribution of vertices degrees there is very little number of vertices with high degrees and therefore this does not represent well graph properties. So in our experiment we took such k, that sum $k, k+1, k+2$ of vertices degrees was maximal. For $d_u = d_v = 2$ we chose threshold $k = 3$.

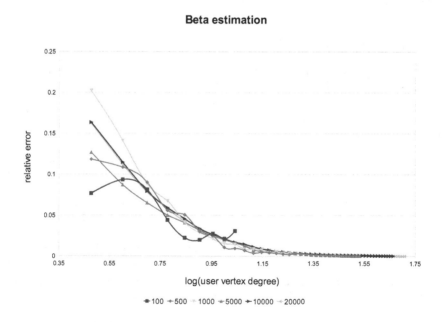

Fig. 1. Relative error for estimation β for different graph sizes (eq. 3), $d_v = d_u = 2$, $\delta = 0.5$, $\alpha = 0.5$. On horizontal axis is logarithm of user vertex degree.

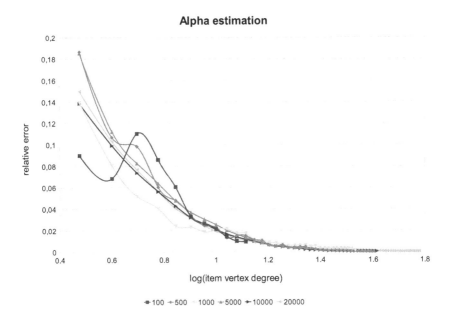

Fig. 2. Relative error for estimation α for different graph sizes (eq. 4), $d_v = d_u = 2$, $\delta = 0.5$, $\beta = 0.5$. On horizontal axis is logarithm of item vertex degree.

4.2 Estimation of α and β Parameters

Tables 2, 4, 6 present relative error of 3 estimated parameters of our generator. Estimation of parameter δ is very good, because it is simple to compute. The best estimation of α and β is when sets of items and users have equal sizes($\delta = 0.5$),

As one might expect, with the growth of the network (see Iter column meaning the number of iterations) the predictions improve.

4.3 Evaluation of α and β Estimation Using Graph Properties

The quality of model identification (hence in particular of the quality of parameter estimation) should be in general evaluated based on reconstruction of various graph metrics.

For $d_v = d_u = 2$ there was no important difference between selected properties of the original graph from which parameters were extracted and graph generated from estimated parameters. As one would expect the following graph properties were recovered correctly (as they are easy): number of vertices, number of edges, average degree, density.

In tables 1, 3, 5 experimental results (relative errors) for the following important graph properties are presented:

- Modularity - measures how well a network decomposes into modular communities, a high modularity score indicates sophisticated internal structure. This structure, often called a community structure, describes how the network is compartmentalized into sub-networks (communities)
- Comm num - number of communities (sub-structures)
- User Count - number of vertices of type "user"
- Item Count - number of vertices of type "item"
- Avg Item BLLC - average bipartite clustering coefficient (see equation (2)) for items
- Avg User BLLC - average bipartite clustering coefficient (see equation (2)) for users

We present balanced experiment where $\alpha = \beta = 0.5$ and we vary δ. For not extreme values of $\alpha \in (0.1, 0.9)$ and $\beta \in (0.1, 0.9)$, relative errors are more or less the same.

From tables 1, 3, 5 we can see that all properties are estimated well except Avg Item BLLC and Avg User BLLC. These two graph properties are in strong relations with quality of graph generator parameters, thus they can contain important information of how two graphs differ. Graph properties Avg Item BLLC and Avg User BLLC are estimated better for middle range generator parameters that is when these parameters are recovered in a more reliable way.

Table 1. Graph relative error of properties for original parameters $\alpha = 0.5$, $\beta = 0.5$, $\delta = 0.7$

Iter	Comm Num	Modularity	User Count	Item Count	Avg Item BLCC	Avg User BLCC
100	0	0.0127	0.0357	0.0887	1.27E-04	0.3169
500	0.0690	0.0125	0.0087	0.0183	2.50E-05	0.0745
1000	0.0130	0.0035	0.0125	0.0283	3.53E-06	0.0066
5000	0.0429	0.0013	0.0036	0.0083	2.55E-07	0.0698
10000	0.0278	0.0021	0.0043	0.0101	2.13E-07	0.0111
20000	0.0085	0.0005	0.0014	0.0034	2.29E-08	0.0447

Table 2. Graph relative error of estimation model parameters for original parameters $\alpha = 0.5$, $\beta = 0.5$, $\delta = 0.7$

Iter	Alpha	Beta	Delta
100	0.5000	0.3709	0.0185
500	0.4310	0.9857	0.0333
1000	0.5000	0.3303	0.0094
5000	0.2372	0.2435	0.0010
10000	0.3027	0.1750	0.0034
20000	0.6273	0.1891	0.0026

Table 3. Graph relative error of properties for original parameters $\alpha = 0.5$, $\beta = 0.5$, $\delta = 0.7$

Iter	Comm Num	Modularity	User Count	Item Count	Avg Item BLCC	Avg User BLCC
100	0.0833	0.0035	0.0365	0.0238	0.1370	0.0262
500	0.0172	0.0039	0.0087	0.0097	0.0705	0.0309
1000	0.0130	0.0027	0.0158	0.0102	0.0264	0.0718
5000	0.0274	0.0036	0.0034	0.0035	0.0294	0.0107
10000	0.0213	0.0005	0.0021	0.0022	0.0666	0.2295
20000	0.0117	0.0003	0.0057	0.0056	0.0370	0.0697

Table 4. Graph relative error of estimation model parameters for original parameters $\alpha = 0.5$, $\beta = 0.5$, $\delta = 0.5$

Iter	Alpha	Beta	Delta
100	0.5000	1.49E-08	0.0139
500	0.5000	0.0002	0.0167
1000	0.2183	0.4417	0.0030
5000	0.1853	0.0296	0.0155
10000	0.0309	0.3327	0.0046
20000	0.0222	0.2853	0.0005

Table 5. Graph relative error of properties for original parameters $\alpha = 0.5$, $\beta = 0.5$, $\delta = 0.3$

Iter	Comm Num	Modularity	User Count	Item Count	Avg Item BLCC	Avg User BLCC
100	0	0.0144	0.0133	0.0071	0.1118	0.0050
500	0.0164	0.0023	0.0622	0.0278	0.1214	0.0580
1000	0	0.0079	0.0166	0.0071	0.4686	0.7184
5000	0.0071	0.0004	0.0032	0.0014	0.1472	0.1564
10000	0.0899	0.0012	0.0022	0.0010	0.1294	0.3452
20000	0.0167	0.0018	0.0019	0.0008	0.0169	0.1733

Table 6. Graph relative error of estimation model parameters for original parameters $\alpha = 0.5$, $\beta = 0.5$, $\delta = 0.3$

Iter	Alpha	Beta	Delta
100	0.2709	4.47E-08	0.1574
500	0.7279	0.1925	0.0285
1000	0.3076	0.5000	0.0030
5000	0.1116	0.1694	0.0038
10000	0.2808	0.2995	0.0166
20000	0.0542	0.3730	0.0047

5   Remarks and Conclusions

Estimation of parameters of considered bipartite graph generator is a hard task. Exact values are difficult to obtain from theoretical properties. But if we compare parameter estimation by properties of obtained graphs [3] then this estimation can be sufficient. We found that those 3 parameters (out of 6) have big influence on network growth and Chojnacki's model of bipartite graphs is able to capture patterns observed in real life networks.

One can say that the investigated problem of estimation of model parameters can be viewed as a multidimensional optimization or machine learning problem in 6 variables out of which only 3 are continuous. In a separate research, not reported here, linear regression, SVN and logistic regression methods were used to train a predictive model based on graph properties, but the models performed poorly. Only δ parameter was estimated quite well with 10% relative error. This failure led to trying out the approach described in this paper.

As a side effect of the performed experiments, we have noticed that the generated graphs tend to pull together the nodes into a large, dominating connected component. However, as stated in [3], social network contain often more than half of their mass outside the giant component and this type of network appears to travel through distinct stages of growth. Therefore Chojnackis model needs some improvements to simulate correctly such a type of behaviors. The multistage growth of network problem is a good research area for further investigations.

There are many other questions one may ask about a real bipartite dynamic network. One of them is to what extent does the theoretical model fit real SN graphs and how realistic parameter recovery would be in that case. Although Chojnacki's model is very flexible, Kumar et al. [5] pointed out that real network appears to travel through distinct stages of growth, characterized by specific behavior in terms of density, diameter, and regularity of component structure. This observation leads us to new open problems in which point of time we have to change parameters.

Acknowledgments. The author would like to acknowledge Szymon Chojnacki of ICS PAS for help with understanding the bipartite graph generator. This research project is co founded by the European Union from resources of the European Social Fund. Project PO KL "Information technologies: Research and their interdisciplinary applications".

References

1. Chojnacki, S.: Analiza technicznych własności systemów rekomendujących za pomocą algorytmów losowych. PhD thesis, Institute of Computer Science, Polish Academy of Sciences, Warsaw, English title: Analysis of Technical Properties of Recommender Systems with Random Graphs (2012)
2. Krebs, V.E.: Uncloaking terrorist networks. First Monday 7(4) (2002)

3. Leskovec, J., Kleinberg, J., Faloutsos, C.: Graphs over time: densification laws, shrinking diameters and possible explanations. In: Proceedings of the Eleventh ACM SIGKDD International Conference on Knowledge Discovery in Data Mining, KDD 2005, pp. 177–187. ACM, New York (2005)
4. Berger-Wolf, T.Y., Saia, J.: A framework for analysis of dynamic social networks. In: Proceedings of the 12th ACM SIGKDD International Conference on Knowledge Discovery and Data Mining, KDD 2006, pp. 523–528. ACM, New York (2006)
5. Kumar, R., Novak, J., Tomkins, A.: Structure and evolution of online social networks. In: Proceedings of the 12th ACM SIGKDD International Conference on Knowledge Discovery and Data Mining, KDD 2006, pp. 611–617. ACM, New York (2006)
6. Birmelé, E.: A scale-free graph model based on bipartite graphs. Discrete Appl. Math. 157(10), 2267–2284 (2009)
7. Zheleva, E., Sharara, H., Getoor, L.: Co-evolution of social and affiliation networks. In: Proceedings of the 15th ACM SIGKDD International Conference on Knowledge Discovery and Data Mining, KDD 2009, pp. 1007–1016. ACM, New York (2009)
8. Guillaume, J.L., Latapy, M.: Bipartite structure of all complex networks. Inf. Process. Lett. 90(5), 215–221 (2004)
9. Erdös, P., Rényi, A.: On the evolution of random graphs. In: Publication of The Mathematical Institute of the Hungarian Academy of Sciences, pp. 17–61 (1960)
10. Barabasi, A.: Linked - how everything is connected to everything else and what it means for business, science, and everyday life. Plume (2003)
11. Vázquez, A.: Growing network with local rules: Preferential attachment, clustering hierarchy, and degree correlations. Phys. Rev. E 67, 056104 (2003)
12. White, D.R., Kejzar, N., Tsallis, C., Farmer, D., White, S.: Generative model for feedback networks. Phys. Rev. E 73(1) (January 2006)
13. Liu, Z., Lai, Y.C., Ye, N., Dasgupta, P.: Connectivity distribution and attack tolerance of general networks with both preferential and random attachments. Physics Letters A 303(5-6), 337–344 (2002)
14. Fotouhi, B., Rabbat, M.G.: Network growth with arbitrary initial conditions: Analytical results for uniform and preferential attachment. CoRR abs/1212.0435 (December 2012)

Expected Value
of the Optimization Algorithm Outcome

Krzysztof Trojanowski[1,2] and Marcin Janiszewski[3]

[1] Institute of Computer Science, Polish Academy of Sciences
Ordona 21, 01-237 Warsaw, Poland
[2] Cardinal Stefan Wyszyński University
Faculty of Mathematics and Natural Sciences
Wóycickiego 1/3, 01-938 Warsaw, Poland
[3] University of Zielona Góra
Faculty of Electrical Engineering, Computer Science and Telecommunications
Podgórna 50, 65-246 Zielona Góra, Poland

Abstract. In this paper, we study the influence of the constrained computational resources on the expected value of the algorithm outcome. In our case, time is the limited resource, that is, the search process can be interrupted in any moment by the user who requests the current best solution. Different characteristics of the user behavior are discussed and a method for evaluation of the expected value is proposed. One of the characteristics is selected for experimental analysis of the algorithm outcome. The expected values of a given search process outcome for different user characteristics are evaluated and compared.

Keywords: Heuristic optimization, dynamic optimization, expected value of the algorithm outcome.

1   Introduction

In this paper, we are interested in a single-objective dynamic optimization in multimodal fitness landscapes. Particularly, the aim is evaluation of expected value of the optimization algorithm outcome. Heuristic optimization approaches are usually based on the iterative process of continuous improvement of the current solution or set of solutions. Due to the iterative nature of the search process, the raw outcome of the algorithm activity is always a series of values obtained for each of the executions of the algorithm main loop. Regardless of whether the measured value is the quality of the current best-found solution, the error level or the Euclidean distance to the optimum, the outcome is represented as a series of values. The length of this series is controlled by the stopping criterion of the algorithm.

The outcome is reported in publications in one of the two following ways: (1) graphs with series of values or (2) single statistic values like, for example, the averaged best values obtained for each of the time intervals between subsequent changes in the fitness landscape, or averages of a series of values measured in

M.A. Kłopotek et al. (Eds.): IIS 2013, LNCS 7912, pp. 245–253, 2013.
© Springer-Verlag Berlin Heidelberg 2013

subsequent time steps. The first type of the answer representation was applied mostly in the early publications devoted to dynamic optimization. Very quickly it was replaced by the second type, which is much more useful for comparisons. The second type of the answer representation has many versions which differ in the type of measured value and the frequency of measurements. For the evaluation of a single statistic value, it is always taken for granted, that the user is ready to wait for the result for the full time interval between one change in the landscape and the next one. It can be seen in the way of the outcome evaluation. Clearly, either all the values in the series participate in evaluation of the final result with the same weight, that is, they are equally significant, or the maximum value for the series is returned as the final result.

However, this does not have to be the case in the real world situations. The fact is, that in the real world there are usually two unknown parameters we have to cope with: the time, we have to the next change in the environment, and the time, which the user is going to wait for the recovery of the result after the last change. We assume, that the former one is always greater than the latter one.

In spite of the full access to the entire series of values measured during simulations for each of the time intervals between subsequent changes, we need to take into account stochastic nature of both time interval length and the user impatience. Particularly, we have to assume that after each time step the user can break the search process and request the solution. The user decision, concerning selection of a time step for the break, may be related with a number of circumstances, for example, with quality of the algorithm current outcome. However, here we assume that the user motivation to stop the search process comes solely from outside and the quality of the algorithm current outcome does not influence the user decision. For example, in the case of an airport, where flights are disrupted due to thick fog, we can use the optimization algorithm to find the optimal sequence for departures of delayed planes when the fog lifts. In this case, the optimization can be performed as long as possible because the more computation is performed, the better solution can be obtained. The only stopping criterion is the fog lifting which is the moment when the current best found solution has to be provided to the airport control center.

Therefore, a new method of the algorithm performance evaluation is proposed in this paper. The expected value of the algorithm outcome is evaluated respectively to the user tendency to request the result before the end of the given time. The evaluation is based on the previously obtained dataset containing the algorithm outcome for a selected fitness landscape. We assume, that the dataset represents the algorithm performance for the class of problems being a subject of simulations and thus being also the source of the dataset. In the case of dynamic optimization, the method evaluates expected values for each of the time interval between subsequent changes in the landscape.

The paper consists of three sections. Section 2 presents a new idea of evaluation of the expected value of the algorithm outcome. Section 3 contains sample evaluation of the algorithm outcome according to the method presented in Sect. 2. Section 4 concludes the paper.

2   Evaluation of the Algorithm Outcome Respectively to the User Preferences

The solution request in the m-th time step, that is, a stopping time can be represented as a random variable $\tau(m) = m$. The variable $\tau(m)$ takes values being numbers from the interval $[1, \ldots, M]$, where M represents the maximum number of time steps between subsequent changes in the fitness landscape.

   The physical implementation of the random number generator for τ can be represented as an array of M independent continuous random number generators. The generators produce uniformly distributed real numbers from the interval $[0, 1]$. The user single decision to request the solution at m-th time step depends on the generator in the m-th cell of the array and a threshold assigned to this generator. The m-th threshold represents probability of the user request at m-th time step. The value generated by the generator is compared with the threshold. When the value is above the threshold, the user is ready to wait and the optimization process continues. Otherwise, the user requests for the solution. Clearly, the higher threshold the stronger impatience of the user.

   Chances, that the user requests the solution precisely just in m-th time step from the last change, can be calculated as follows. Let p_{true}^m represents probability that the generator in the m-cell of the array returned a value below the threshold, that is, the user requests the solution. Then, for example, the case where the user requested the solution just after the third time step represents the following situation: the generator in the first cell returned a value above the threshold, the generator in the second cell also returned a value above the threshold but the generator in the third cell returned a value below the threshold. Thus, the expected value of the algorithm outcome in the m-th time step equals:

$$E[\Delta | \tau = m] = E\Delta(m). \tag{1}$$

In our analysis, it is assumed that the algorithm outcome for the given optimization problem is already known, that is, it is deterministic. For example, this is the case when experiments have already been done and a dataset, which contains the algorithm entire outcome, is saved. Lets have a series of outcome values for subsequent time steps averaged over the number of runs for the same optimization problem, the same algorithm configuration and the same starting conditions. Now, we want to evaluate an expected value of the outcome for the case where there exist randomness originating from the user as described above. Thus, the expected value Δ of the outcome in the m-th time step equals:

$$E[\Delta | \tau = m] = \Delta(m). \tag{2}$$

In practice, the probabilities p_{true}^m for the subsequent generators in the array can differ to each other. Clearly, the user is ready to wait for the solution for some time, however, the probability of his request changes in subsequent time steps. The impatience can grow or decline. Example graphs of the thresholds varying in subsequent time steps are depicted in Fig. 1. In the graphs, it is assumed that there are 50 steps between subsequent changes. The graphs can be divided into two subgroups which represent: decreasing impatience of a user (Fig. 1 – the top row) and increasing impatience ((Fig. 1 – the bottom row). Both types of impatience are expressed by the threshold which changes linearly (the first column), with acceleration (the second column), or with delay (the third column).

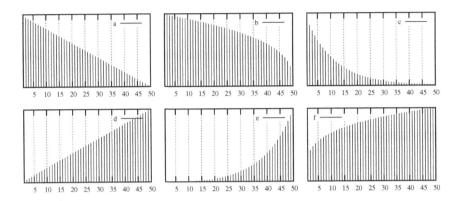

Fig. 1. Example threshold functions which represent chances that the user requests the solution precisely just after m-th time step from the last change; $N = 50$

In this case, the expected value Δ of the algorithm outcome for the time steps from $[1, \ldots, N]$ equals:

$$E[\Delta] = \sum_{m=1}^{N} \Delta(m) \cdot p_m \qquad (3)$$

where $\Delta(m)$ is the algorithm outcome for the m-th time step and p_m represents the chances for selection any of the time steps from $[1, \ldots, N]$. The total of chances have to be equal 1, that is, the formula for evaluation of p_m is as follows:

$$p_m = \begin{cases} \left[\prod_{k=1}^{m-1}(1 - p_{true}^k)\right] \cdot p_{true}^m & \text{if } m < N \\ 1 - \sum_{m=1}^{N-1}\left[\prod_{k=1}^{m-1}(1 - p_{true}^k)\right] \cdot p_{true}^m & \text{if } m = N \end{cases} \qquad (4)$$

For each of the user characteristics depicted in Fig. 1, respective graphs with the subsequent values of p_m for $m \in [1, 50]$ are shown in Fig. 2. The graphs in Fig. 2 were generated for p_{true}^m varying within the range $[0, 1]$. As can be seen, in every case there are a few highest values of p_m which are at least several orders of magnitude higher than the remaining values of p_m present in the sequence. Unfortunately, this makes the characteristic rather useless. The problem is, that the expected value of the algorithm outcome $E[\Delta]$, evaluated according to Eq. (3), shall be dominated by a few of the outcome values in the series, that is, the ones which are multiplied by the few highest values of p_m. The graph of p_m generated for characteristic "e" is the exception. In this case, quite a large

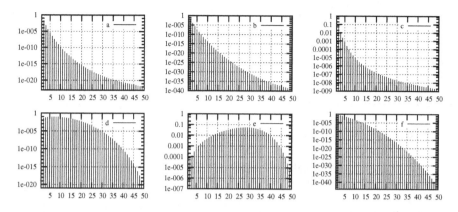

Fig. 2. Graphs with the subsequent values of p_m for $N = 50$ evaluated for respective characteristics given in Fig. 1

fraction of values in the series (for $n = 50$ this is about a half) belonging to the group of the largest differ to each other by no more than one order of magnitude.

The formula of the threshold evaluation for subsequent generators according to the characteristic "e" is:

$$f_e(m) = \frac{\exp((m/N)^q) - \exp(0)}{\exp(1) - \exp(0)} \qquad (5)$$

where q is the parameter which controls the strength of acceleration. The probabilities p_m for the function $f_e(m)$ where $q \in [1, 15]$ and $m \in [1, 5000]$ are depicted in Fig. 3.

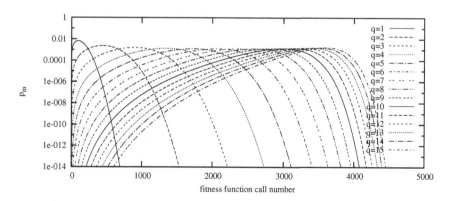

Fig. 3. Graphs with the probabilities p_m of the solution request by the user in the m-th step for the function $f_e(m)$ where $q \in [1, 15]$

Therefore, the characteristic "e" was selected for experimental part of the research. In this part, we evaluated the expected value of the offline error returned by a heuristic optimization algorithm during an experiment with a single dynamic fitness landscape.

3   Experimental Research

Among a number of existing metaheuristics, we selected a differential evolution (DE) for the research. This approach is recently a subject of growing interests and has already been studied from many points of view (for detailed discussion see, for example, monographs [3] or [4]). Our attention has been paid to the self-adaptive version of the DE algorithm [1]. This version differs form the basic approach in that a self-adaptive control mechanism is used to change the control parameters F and CR during the run. Eventually, for our research we reimplemented the version of jDE presented in [2]. Our experiments were conducted with the version extended by a new mutation operator inspired by a mechanism originating from the particle swarm optimization approach [5].

A test-case for optimization was generated by Syringa dynamic landscape generator [5]. The properties of the fitness landscape dynamics can be described as four types of changes modifying the components: horizontal and vertical translation, scaling and rotation. These modifications occur at regular time intervals in the environment. The components of landscape are various functions defined by the same base formula but different parameters. In Syringa, there are several types of functions describing the components and several types of changes for the parameters of these functions. In our case, each of the components is generated by spherical function: $f(\mathbf{x}) = \sum_{i=1}^{N_{\dim}} x_i^2$ where $x \in [-100, 100]$ and $N_{\dim}$ is the number of search space dimensions. For spherical function, the following type of the parameters change was chosen which is called "a small change":

$$\Delta = \alpha \cdot r \cdot (max - min) \cdot \phi_{severity} \qquad (6)$$

where: $\alpha = 0.04$; $r = U(-1, 1)$; and $\phi_{severity} = 5$. The parameters max and min represent lower and upper boundary of the parameter range of values. $U(-1, 1)$ is a random number generated from uniform distribution. Evaluation of the solution $\mathbf{x}$ for the time step t is performed according to the formula:

$$F(\mathbf{x}, \phi, t) = \sum_{i=1}^{N} (w_i \cdot (f_i'((x - O_i(t) + O_{iold})/\lambda_i \cdot M_i) + H_i(t))) \qquad (7)$$

where:
    N – the number of component functions,
    t – the discrete time,
    ϕ – the landscape parameters for $\phi = (O, M, H)$, where
    H – the vector of height coefficients,
    M – the rotation matrix for each i-th component (the matrices remain unchanged during the entire run of the algorithm),

$O_i(t)$ – optimum point coordinates for $f_i(\mathbf{x})$,

O_{iold} – initial optimum point coordinates for $f_i(\mathbf{x})$ (which is zero for each component function).

Furthermore, function components should be normalized:

$$f_i(\mathbf{x})^{'} = C \cdot f_i(\mathbf{x})/|f_i^{max}| \tag{8}$$

where $C = 2000$ and f_i^{max} is the value of the current optimum.

Table 1 contains values of some of the parameters from the eq. (6) and (7).

Table 1. Values of parameters used for GDBP

param	value
m	10
t	$\in [1, 5000]$
H	$\in [10, 100]$
max	100
min	10

The landscape was generated in 5-dimensional search space where there exist 10 moving components. 60 changes occur in the landscape during a single call of algorithm.

The offline error (oe) represents the average deviation from the optimum of the best solution value since the last change in the landscape. The values of oe were averaged over 30 experiments repeated for the same parameters of the algorithm and the same landscape.

The graph of subsequent values of oe obtained for the time of the first six changes in the fitness landscape is depicted in Fig. 4 (the top graph).

There were performed evaluations for five versions of the user impatience characteristic: $f_e(m)$ where $q \in \{1, 3, 6, 9, 12\}$. Graphs with subsequent results of multiplication p_m by average values of oe are presented in Fig. 4 (the bottom graph).

Values of expected value of oe for the six subsequent shapes of the fitness landscape are presented in Table 2. As can be seen in Fig. 4, the expected value of oe decreases as q grows which is easy to explain. Simply, the range of values of m occupied by the fraction of values of p_m belonging to the group of the largest moves to the right as q increases (see Fig. 3). At the same time, in the given six data subseries the oe values decrease during the algorithm run. The differences between expected values of oe for subsequent values of q are significant. This confirms our hypothesis that even little changes in the shape of user impatience characteristic should not be regarded as negligible.

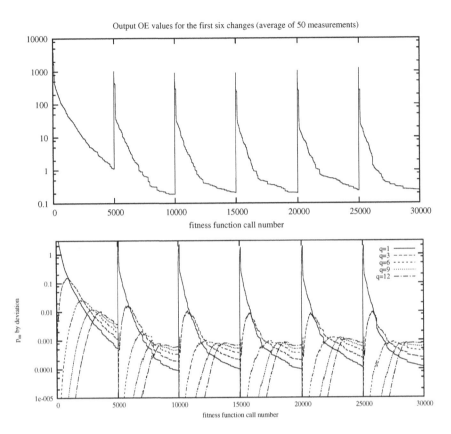

Fig. 4. Graph with subsequent average values of *oe* for the first six changes in the fitness landscape (the top figure) and graphs with subsequent results of multiplication average values of *oe* by respective values of p_m (the bottom figure)

Table 2. Expected value of *oe* for 6 subsequent shapes of the fitness landscape evaluated for $q \in \{1, 3, 6, 9, 12\}$

shape nr	1	3	6	9	12
0	0.422553	0.037594	0.008986	0.004455	0.003070
1	0.060331	0.003576	0.000693	0.000360	0.000274
2	0.045394	0.002228	0.000491	0.000340	0.000294
3	0.035660	0.001710	0.000446	0.000334	0.000288
4	0.035365	0.001848	0.000610	0.000464	0.000394
5	0.037326	0.001753	0.000445	0.000342	0.000306

4   Conclusions

In this paper, we present a new approach to the optimization algorithm evaluation considering the user preferences and, particularly, the user constraints. One of these constrains is a maximum time interval given the algorithm for computation. This interval represented as a maximum available number of evaluation can be non deterministic due to some external conditions. Therefore, we have to evaluate an expected value of the algorithm outcome rather than just the value of the outcome. In the first part of the paper, we have proposed a method of evaluation of such an expected value based on the characteristic of the user behavior, that is, probability of interruption of the search process before it ends. The characteristics describing random stopping time has significant influence on the expected value of the outcome. The proposed model allows for application of different characteristics of the user request and one of them was particularly discussed above.

In the experimental part of the research, we applied the proposed model to the sample algorithm output. This way we showed how the expected value changes respectively to different user preferences. This confirmed significance of the model and showed dependency between the user impatience characteristic and the expected values of the outcome.

Acknowledgments. The authors would like to thank prof. Mieczysław A. Kłopotek, prof. Lesław Socha, and prof. Jan Mielniczuk for their valuable comments and feedback. This research has been partially supported by the European Regional Development Fund with the grant no. POIG.01.01.02-14-013/09: *Adaptive system supporting problem solution based on analysis of textual contents of available electronic resources.*

References

1. Brest, J., Greiner, S., Boskovic, B., Mernik, M., Zumer, V.: Self-adapting control parameters in differential evolution: A comparative study on numerical benchmark problems. IEEE Trans. Evol. Comput. 10(6), 646–657 (2006)
2. Brest, J., Zamuda, A., Boskovic, B., Maucec, M.S., Zumer, V.: Dynamic optimization using self-adaptive differential evolution. In: IEEE Congr. on Evolutionary Computation, pp. 415–422. IEEE (2009)
3. Feokistov, V.: Differential Evolution, In Search of Solutions. Optimization and Its Applications, vol. 5. Springer (2006)
4. Price, K.V., Storn, R.M., Lampinen, J.A.: Differential Evolution, A Practical Approach to Global Optimization. Natural Computing Series. Springer (2005)
5. Trojanowski, K., Raciborski, M., Kaczyński, P.: Self-adaptive differential evolution with hybrid rules of perturbation for dynamic optimization. Journal of Telecommunications and Information Technology, 18–28 (April 2011)

Solving Travelling Salesman Problem Using Egyptian Vulture Optimization Algorithm – A New Approach

Chiranjib Sur, Sanjeev Sharma, and Anupam Shukla

Soft Computing and Expert System Laboratory,
ABV - Indian Institute of Information Technology & Management
Gwalior, Madhya Pradesh, India - 474010
{chiranjibsur,sanjeev.sharma1868,dranupamshukla}@gmail.com

Abstract. Travelling Salesman Problem (TSP) is a NP-Hard combinatorial optimization problem and many real life problems are constrained replica of it which possesses exponential time complexity and requires heavy combination capability. In this work a new nature inspired meta-heuristics called Egyptian Vulture Optimization Algorithm (EVOA) is being introduced and presented for the first time and illustrated with examples how it can be utilized for the constrained graph based problems and is utilized to solve the various dimensional datasets of the traditional travelling salesman problem. There are not many discrete optimization bio-inspired algorithms available in the literature and in that respect it is a novel one which can readily utilized for the graph based and assignment based problems. This EVOA is inspired by the natural and skilled phenomenal habits, unique perceptions and intelligence of the Egyptian Vulture bird for carry out the livelihood and acquisition of food which is inevitable for any kind of organisms. The Egyptian Vulture bird is one of the few birds who are known for showing dexterous capability when it comes to its confrontation with tough challenges and usage of tools with combinations of force and weakness finding ability. The results show that the Egyptian Vulture Optimization meta-heuristics has potential for deriving solutions for the TSP combinatorial problem and it is found that the quality and perfection of the solutions for the datasets depend mainly on the number of dimensions when considerable for the same number of iterations.

Keywords: egyptian vulture optimization algorithm, discrete domain problems, combinatorial optimization, graph based constrained problems, nature inspired heuristics, travelling salesman problem.

1   Introduction

Mathematical operation modeling or rather what we call algorithms for constrained discrete domain problems and graph based NP hard problems which represent many real life scenarios are very difficult to achieve. The same goes for

M.A. Kłopotek et al. (Eds.): IIS 2013, LNCS 7912, pp. 254–267, 2013.

both mathematically significant problems (like sequential ordering problems) and path planning like combinational optimization problems. These kinds of problems require algorithms which are randomized, converging and capable of synthesizing combinations efficiently and thus after considerable iterations the near optimized solution may be hit upon. With so many nature inspired heuristics for optimization like Particle Swarm Optimization [4], Honey Bee Swarm [5], League Championship Algorithm [6], Cuckoo search via Levy flights [7], Bat-Inspired Algorithm [8], Simulated Annealing [9], Harmony Search [12], Honey-bees mating optimization (HBMO) algorithm [14], Krill Herd Algorithm[21], Virus Optimization Algorithm[24] etc most of them are suitable and naturally favorable for continuous domain problem optimization and are more suitable for exploration of variation of parameters based search problems than the sequential search problems which have discrete states for acceptance. Only Ant Colony Optimization [3], Intelligent Water Drops Algorithm [16] etc are among the few which are randomized graph search algorithms or coordinated cum cooperative graph traversing based search algorithms involved with both exploration and exploitation for achievement of global optimization. The bio-inspired algorithms described in [3-24] are mostly the continuous domain combination capable and if ever they are forced to be applied on the discrete domain problems one drawback persists that once a series or sequence is formed either the whole is modified or a restricted part (if possible) of it but lack the operator of deriving the change of sequence in between. So in this work we have introduced for the first time another biologically inspired meta-heuristics called Egyptian Vulture Optimization Algorithm which readily applicable for the graphical problems and node based continuity search and optimization capability and there is no requirement of local search in the continuous space. The main advantage of the EVOA is its capability for different combination formation and at the same time prevents loop formation and also in many problem cases (like TSP, Knapsack etc) insertion and depletion of node sequence at will for development of the solution and at the same time generation of new solution sequence. As illustration and performance analysis of the Egyptian Vulture Optimization Algorithm we have optimized the traditional travelling salesman problem with its varied range of dimension with the new algorithm and capability of the Egyptian Vulture Optimization Algorithm is reflected through the results. However the improvement of the results for long dimensional datasets can be achieved with the increase in the number of iterations. Literature has revealed many procedures for optimization of the TSP problems both for deterministic approaches like [28-31] and non-deterministic approaches like [26-27].

The remaining portion of this documentation is organized with Section 2 for life-style of the Egyptian Vulture bird, Section 3 for EVOA algorithm and its scope and details, Section 4 for the implementation details of the algorithm for the TSP, Section 5 for results and 6 for conclusion and future works.

2   History and Life Style of Egyptian Vulture

The Egyptian Vulture, also known as White Scavenger Vulture (Scientific Name: *Neophron percnopterus*) [1], is one of the most ancient kinds of vulture that existed on this earth and shares it features with the dinosaurs family with respect to its food habit, strength, endurance and has surpassed them in intelligence as well, but unfortunately a few species of its kind has become extinct. Like any other vulture species, the primary food habitat of the Egyptian Vulture is meat, but the opportunistic feature for food habit which makes the species unique and thus lead to the meta-heuristic is that they eat the eggs of the other birds available.

Fig. 1. Egyptian Vulture at Work

However for larger and strong (in terms of breakability) eggs they toss pebble hard on them, using the pebbles as hammer, and thus break them. Also the Egyptian Vultures have the knack of rolling things with twigs, which is another distinguish feature of the Egyptian Vulture. Relatively the Egyptian Vulture possess a sedentary life apart from hunting for food, but their level of performance and technique have been unique among all the member of the class Aves and this makes them the best lot. However due to some unavoidable reasons of the unscrupulous activity of the human beings like poaching, cutting down of forests, global warming, etc there has been a decrease in their numbers in population. The breed has been famous among the Pharaohs of Egypt and was considered as a symbol of royalty and was known as "Pharaoh's Chicken". In India, there are a lot of superstitious believes are associated with the bird. The sight of this bird is considered as unlucky and their shrilling calls believed to signify downfall, hardship or even death. However there are tribal groups who can actually tame them and read the activity of the vultures to detect natural calamity or incidents. Another superstitious belief is considered in [1]. A temple situated at Thirukalukundram in Chengalpattu (India) was reputed for a pair of Egyptian Vulture that used to visit the place for centuries. These Egyptian Vultures were fed ceremonially by the priests of the temple and used to arrive just before noon to feed on offerings made from traditional Indian foods like rice, ghee, sugar and even wheat. Although Egyptian Vultures are normally punctual in their arrival, but in case there is failure of the Egyptian Vultures to turn up, it is attributed to the presence of any "sinners" among the onlookers. Also according to mythology legend has it the vultures (or "eagles") represented eight sages who were punished by Lord Shiva (Hindu God), and in each of a series of epochs two of them leave. The Egyptian Vultures possess the reputation of practicing the habit of coprophagy that is being fed on faeces of other animals.

3 Egyptian Vulture Optimization Algorithm

The Egyptian Vulture Optimization Meta-Heuristics Algorithm has been described here as steps, illustration through examples and explanations. The two main activities of the Egyptian Vulture, which are considered here or rather transferred into algorithm, are the tossing of pebbles and the ability of rolling things with twigs. Before describing the algorithmic steps, brief description of the data structure used for solution set is provided in the corresponding Section 4, its limitations and imposed constraints are also discussed and what are we looking for at the end of the algorithm.

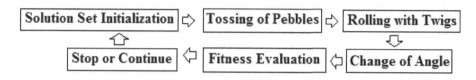

Fig. 2. Steps for Egyptian Vulture Optimization Algorithm

The overall generalized algorithm can be framed into the following steps unless some steps are deformed or restricted to cope up with the constraints of the problem.

Step 1: Initialization of the solution set or string which contain the representation of parameters in form of variables. The String represents a set of parameters which as a whole represents a single state of permissible solution.
Step 2: Refinement of the variable representatives, checking of the superimposed conditions and constraints.
Step 3: Tossing of Pebbles at selected or random points.
Step 4: Rolling of Twigs on selected or the whole string.
Step 5: Change of angle through selective part reversal of solution set.
Step 6: Fitness Evaluation.
Step 7: Check Condition for stopping.

So at the end of the simulation the main objective of the algorithm is derivation of a solution whose sequence respects some constraints and thus establishes a sequence of serially connected events or states which is optimized with some parameter(s) individually or as a whole. The solution can approached in two ways, one is starting from an arbitrary sequence of all the nodes when it should contain all and then performing the operator on them or starting with small number of nodes and try creating a path between the source and the destination when the solution dont contain all the nodes.

3.1 Pebble Tossing

The Egyptian Vulture uses the pebbles for breakage of the eggs of the other birds with relatively harder eggs and only after breakage they can have the food inside. Two or three Egyptian Vulture continuously toss the pebbles on the egg with force until they break and they try to find the weak points or the crack points for success. This approach is used in this meta-heuristics for introduction of new solution in the solution set randomly at certain positions and hypothetically the solution breaks into the set and may bring about four possibilities depending upon probability and the two generated parameters for execution of the operations and selection of extension of the performance. Figure 3 provides the pictorial view of the pebble tossing step of the Egyptian Vulture. Here the numerical values are representation of nodes or discrete events for a solution string or array where each element of the string is represented as a parameter. This is applicable for all the figures 3-5. The three cases generated are the probables and in actuality only one takes place. However all the three probables are shown for clarification.

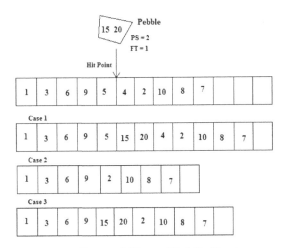

Fig. 3. Pictorial View of Pebble Tossing

The two variables for the determination of the extent of the operation are:

PS = Pebble Size (level of occupy) where $PS \geq 0$
FT = Force of Tossing (level of removal) where $FT \geq 0$.
Hence, If $PS > 0$ Then "Get In" Else "No Get In"
Also If $FT > 0$ Then "Removal" Else "No Removal"

where "Get In" denotes occupancy and "Removal" is for removing. Now the Level of occupy denotes how many solutions should the pebble carry and must intrude forcefully into the solution set. Level of removal implies how many solutions are removed from the solution set. Both are generated randomly within a certain limit and the pebbles carrying PS number of nodes are also generated randomly considering that the combination can produce new solution set. Now FT denotes the number of nodes that are removed from either side of the point of hitting. Overall there are four combinations of operations are possible and are:

- Case 1: Get In & No Removal
- Case 2: No Get In & No Removal
- Case 3: Get In & Removal
- Case 4: No Get In & No Removal

The last combination is of no operation and is another way refusal of operation on the solution. Another criterion is the point of application of the step.

It is to be pointed out that the application is sole decider of up to what extent the operation combination will take place and whether it is permissible to allow combinations where PS FT which means that the removal and occupy or both will be of unequal length and thus introduces the concept of variable string length which is perhaps very necessary for route finding problems. However for problems like TSP the required combination is always PS = FT to justify the constraint of constant number of cities and without duplicity.

Point of hitting is another criterion which requires attention and strategy must be determined for quickening the solution convergence process. Like for TSP problem any point can be chosen for application of Tossing of Pebble step but for path finding problem the best strategy is considered if the discontinuous positions are targeted for application. In a similar way for continuous domain problems any point and relevant and mapped positions can be the hit point and way for removal and occupy for experimentation and combination trials.

3.2   Rolling with Twigs

The rolling with twigs is another astonishing skill of the Egyptian Vulture with which they can roll an object for the purpose of movement or may be to perform other activity like finding the position or weak points or just giving a look over the other part which is facing the floor. Rolling of the objects requires not only power but also the art of holding tight the stick with their beak and also finding the proper stick. This is perhaps the inherited skill of any bird for finding the right stick for any object they are trying to create or execute. Several birds have given testimony of making high quality nests during laying eggs. Such selection of sticks is mainly made for making the nest or positioning the right bend of the stick at the right place. Even some birds have given evidence of sewing the soft twigs with their beak. This activity of the Egyptian Vulture is considered as rolling of the solution set for changing of the positions of the variables to change the meaning and thus may create new solutions which may produce better fitness value and also better path when it comes for multi-objective optimization. Also when the hit point is less and the numbers of options are more, it may take a long time for the finishing event to take place or in other words the appropriate matching of the random event to occur. In such case this kind of operations can be helpful. Figure 4 illustrates the effect of the "Rolling with Twigs" event for graph based problems for a particular state and for certain parameter value of the probabilistic approach which is discussed in the subsequent paragraphs. Here the whole string is considered for shifting (with two possibilities of either left or right and is determined probabilistically), but in the TSP we have considered only partial shifting and the partial string is generated randomly. The main criteria of determination of what should be adopted is the application itself and what far it can tolerate so that the validity of solution string is not hampered. For the "Rolling with Twigs" to occur there is required another two more parametric variables which will direct the mathematical formulation of the event and also guide the implementation of the step. These two criteria for the determination of the extent of the operation are:

DS = Degree of Roll where $DS \geq 0$ denoting number of rolls. DR as Direction of Rolling where probabilistically we have:
$DR = 0$ for Right Rolling/Shift
     $= 1$ for Left Rolling/Shift

where 0 and 1 is generated randomly and deterministically the equation can be framed as:

DR = Left Rolling/Shift for RightHalf > LeftHalf
     = Right Rolling/Shift for RightHalf < LeftHalf

where RightHalf is the secondary fitness for the right half of the solution string and LeftHalf is for left half. The reason behind this is if the RightHalf is better, then this will be a provision to extent the source with the connected node portion and same is for LeftHalf, which can be connected with the destination.

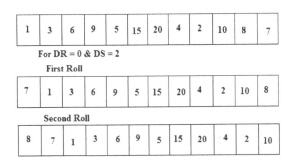

Fig. 4. Pictorial View of Rolling with Twigs for DS = 2

Another scheme that can be implemented in constraint environment without hampering the partial derived solution occurs for mainly problems like path finding etc. Here only the unstructured solution string is modified and not the partial path already found. Link and in orderness are important factors of these kind of constraint problems, but for problems like the datasets of the TSP, where a path exist between every node and distance is the Euclidean distance between them, shifting of the partial string holds the same information as that of the whole string as each can give rise to new solution and hence the search procedure is more versatile and global solution can be attended easily.

3.3 Change of Angle

This is another operation that the Egyptian Vulture can perform which derives its analogy from the change of angle of the tossing of pebbles so as to experiment with procedure and increase the chance of breakage of the hard eggs. Now the change of the angle is represented as a mutation step where the unconnected linked node sequence are reversed for the expectation of being connected and thus complete the sequence of nodes. Figure 5 gives a demonstration of such a step. This step is not permanent and is incorporated if only the path is improved.

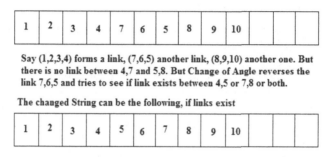

Say (1,2,3,4) forms a link, (7,6,5) another link, (8,9,10) another one. But there is no link between 4,7 and 5,8. But Change of Angle reverses the link 7,6,5 and tries to see if link exists between 4,5 or 7,8 or both.

The changed String can be the following, if links exist

Fig. 5. Pictorial View of Change of Angle

   This Change of Angle step can be multi-point step and the local search decides the points, number of nodes to be considered and depends on the number of nodes the string is holding. If the string is holding too many nodes and Pebble Tossing step cannot be performed then this step is a good option for local search and trying to figure the full path out of it.

3.4 Brief Description of Fitness Function

The fitness function is of utmost importance when it comes for the decision making of the system and optimization selection, but it is noticed that in majority graph based problems, obsessed with multi-objective optimization, that the complete path is reached after a huge number of iterations and by the mean time it is very difficult to clearly demarcate the better incomplete result from the others and it is in this case the act of probabilistic steps can worsen the solution. Also the acts of the operations need to be operated in proper places mainly on the node gaps where there is yet to make any linkage. Hence a brief description of the secondary fitness function needs to be addressed. This secondary fitness value can be of several types:

1) The technique used in the simulation finds the linked consecutive nodes and is numbered with a number which denotes how many nodes are linked together at that portion. Then the secondary fitness is calculated as (summation of the fitness)/(number of nodes). High secondary fitness denotes that more numbers of nodes are linked together as a unit than the other solution string. But for the TSP as there occurs a link between every node, the secondary fitness will always be constant and will be of no use.

2) Another partial solution fitness evaluation can be through the use of the number of partial solution that is linked portion are present in that string which can have high probability of being processed into a complete path than the isolated ones. Here on the count of the linked sections present in the solution string are kept as secondary fitness value. But contrary to the previous method, this method provides minimum as best result.

3.5   Adaptiveness of the EVOA

The Egyptian Vulture Optimization Algorithm provides the option of adaptive experimentation for the problem which can be multi-variable during the initial positions and gradually decreases with iterations and with the length of the path. Also for constant length combinatorial optimization, it can be modified accordingly and can be regarded as a special case of the algorithm. There can be situations when the linkage between two path segments can be done through single or multiple numbers of nodes and this requires the need of adaptive flexibility in the operators. Also the operators like "rolling of twig" and "change of angle" can be operated on selected part of the solution string and hence can generate partly good solution which later can be united to create the complete one.

4   EVOA for Travelling Salesman Problem

The following are the details of the steps of the Egyptian Vulture Optimization Algorithm used for Travelling Salesman Problem Application.

Step 1: Initialize N (taken as 20) solution strings with random generation of all the nodes present for a dataset without repetition. The String represents a set of parameters which as a whole represents a single state of permissible solution. Here the strings have the unrepeated nodes. However generation of the solution strings involved Tossing of Pebbles step where the sequence of cities is generated through the random arrival of nodes and duplicate prevention step. So at this point the strings with no node will rise to its maximum length and is equal to the dimension of dataset. Later the Tossing of Pebbles step in Step 3 will create changes in the string through the same procedure but the length of string will remain intact following the criteria of valid TSP solutions.

Step 2: Initialize the primary fitness matrix (array) only, as secondary fitness is unnecessary as all the nodes are connected. Evaluate the initial fitness of the strings.

Step 3: Perform Tossing of Pebbles operation at selected or random points depending upon implementation on deterministic approach or probability. The best combination can be achieved if the selected node(s) are optimized with respect to distance and is placed with the node with which it has the least distance by performing a local search in a bounded area (as always searching through the whole string is not possible, the search space is restricted to some portion between position S_{max} and S_{min} where S_{max} < (dimension of TSP) and $S_{min} > 0$ and $S_{max} - S_{min}$ < threshold and threshold determines how many maximum nodes are to be searched and is held for the computational complexity of the algorithm.) Placement and replacement of nodes is compensated by shifting of the nodes or the vacancies whichever required. Accept the new sequence if it surpass the old sequence in fitness. This step will help in gradual reducing the distance between two nodes.

Step 4: Perform Rolling of Twigs operation on selected portion only as the operation on the whole string will not make any sense so far as the solution quality is concerned. It can also be done by choosing a certain length with node positions as L_{start} and L_{end} where $L_{start} < L_{end}$ and L_{end} - L_{start} < (Dimemsion of TSP) as if the whole string is shifted (right or left) the fitness value of the string remains unchanged, however only the starting and ending cities gets changed.

Step 5: Perform Change of Angle operation through selective reversal of solution subset. This is some kind of extra effort introduced by the bird for efficient result. It is mutation operator for combination. Accept the new sequence if it surpass the old sequence in fitness. Same procedure of L_{start} and L_{end} is followed.

Step 6: Evaluate the fitness of each string that is the minimum distance connecting them.

Step 7: If New solution (derived out of combination of operation(s)) is better, then replace the old else dont.

Step 8: Select the best result and compare with global best. If better then set it as global best.

Step 9: After each iteration replace X% worst solutions with random initialization. (X depends on N and according to the exploration requirement)

Step 10: If number of iteration is complete then stop else continue from Step 3.

Note: It is to be mentioned here that "Tossing of Pebbles" operation occurs under influence of some swarm of vulture bird agents each generating different elements at different positions and this accelerates the solution generation much quickly. The number of birds in a swarm depends on the dimension of the dataset and how much quickly the combination is required to be varied. However the other two operations ("Rolling of Twigs" and "Change of Angle") are also performed under influence of a swarm but the number of agents in swarms are relative lower.

5   Computational Results

In this section we have provided the results consisting of mean, standard deviation (SD), best, worst and mean error in a tabulated form while it is compared with the optimum value with dim denoting the dimension of the datasets. The simulation of the EVOA on Travelling Salesman Problem datasets [25] ranging from the 16 to 280 dimensions provides that the range of 4.7 and 28.7 percent when all the datasets are run for 25000 iterations.

Table 1. Table for result

DATASETS			EVOA				
Name	**Dim**	**Optimum**	**Mean**	**SD**	**Best**	**Worst**	**Error**
Ulysses16.tsp	16	74.11	77.56	1.16	75.16	79.53	4.6552
att48.tsp	48	3.3524e+004	3.7119e+004	23.89	3.3781e+004	4.1136e+004	10.7237
st70.tsp	70	678.5975	730.676	105.6	694	802	7.6744
pr76.tsp	76	1.0816e+005	1.2941e+005	219.1	1.1295e+005	1.5898e+005	19.6468
gr96.tsp	96	512.3094	659.11	46.7	599.2	1002	28.6547
gr120.tsp	120	1.6665e+003	1.8223e+003	106	1.7552e+003	2.1825e+003	9.3489
gr202.tsp	202	549.9981	886.92	92.2	650.2	1202	61.2587
tsp225.tsp	225	3919	4597	196	4216	6112	17.3003
a280.tsp	280	2.5868e+003	2.9943e+003	1213	2.7976e+003	3.8236e+003	15.7531

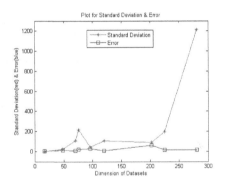

Fig. 6. Plot for Standard Deviation & Error

The figure 6-8 also reveals the graphical view of the table with reference to the dimension of the datasets provided in table 1. The result clearly reveal the ability of the EVOA as a successful algorithm for TSP and experimentation has revealed that with the increase in the number of dimensions the iteration number must increase to get a better result.

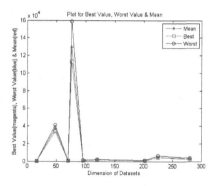

Fig. 7. Plot for Best Value, Worst Value & Mean

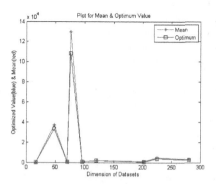

Fig. 8. Plot for Mean & Optimum Value

6   Conclusion and Future Works

So in this work we have contributed by introducing for the first time yet another member for the nature inspired computing family, now for the discrete
combinatorial optimization problems and graph based search and path planning
problems mainly due to the availability of large number of continuous domain
problems. This Egyptian Vulture Optimization Algorithm is capable of combining well the options but is as usual depends on probability. It is applied well
on the TSP and the results are converging towards the best with the number
of iterations increasing with the increased number of dimensions. The EVOA
can easily be used for all kinds of node based search problems and the fitness
evaluation strategy and validation checking strategy differs in each case. Local
searches like placing the node with the nearest node without random placements
can however be good strategy when facing constraint-less problems and can help
in quick convergence but the continuous addition of such local search based may
destroy the previously placed nearest one. However it needs to be experimented

with many other real life problems and other combinatorial optimization problems before coming to any conclusion and there can be other aspects related to its performance in its future works.

Acknowledgement. The first author gratefully acknowledges the motivation, guidance and support of Prof. Anupam Shukla, Professor, ABV-Indian Institute of Information Technology and Management, Gwalior, India. His time to time critics and reviews has been very helpful for the work's improvement. The work is motivated by a slide of Prof Ajith Abraham.

References

1. Egyptian Vulture details, http://en.wikipedia.org/wiki/Egyptian_Vulture
2. Vulture Photo, http://www.flickr.com/photos/spangles44/5600556141
3. Blum, C., Roli, A.: Metaheuristics in Combinatorial Optimization: Overview and Conceptual Comparison. ACM Comput. Survey 35, 268–308 (2003)
4. Kennedy, J., Eberhart, R.: Particle Swarm Optimization. In: IEEE International Conference on Neural Networks, vol. 4, pp. 1942–1948 (1995)
5. Karaboga, D.: An Idea Based on Honey Bee Swarm for Numerical Optimization. Technical Report TR06, Erciyes University (2005)
6. Kashan, A.H.: League Championship Algorithm: A New Algorithm for Numerical Function Optimization. In: International Conference of Soft Computing and Pattern Recognition, pp. 43–48. IEEE Computer Society, Washington, DC (2009)
7. Yang, X.S., Deb, S.: Cuckoo search via Levy flights, In: World Congress on Nature & Biologically Inspired Computing, pp. 210-214. IEEE Publication, USA (2009)
8. Yang, X.-S.: A New Metaheuristic Bat-Inspired Algorithm. In: González, J.R., Pelta, D.A., Cruz, C., Terrazas, G., Krasnogor, N. (eds.) NICSO 2010. SCI, vol. 284, pp. 65–74. Springer, Heidelberg (2010)
9. Kirkpatrick, S., Gelatt Jr., C.D., Vecchi, M.P.: Optimization by Simulated Annealing. Science 220(4598), 671–680 (1983)
10. Storn, R., Price, K.: Differential Evolution - A Simple and Efficient Heuristic for Global Optimization Over Continuous Spaces. Journal of Global Optimization 11(4), 341–359 (1997)
11. Farmer, J.D., Packard, N., Perelson, A.: The Immune System, Adaptation and Machine Learning. Physica D 22, 187–204 (1986)
12. Geem, Z.W., Kim, J.H., Loganathan, G.V.: A new heuristic optimization algorithm: harmo-ny search. Simulation 76, 60–68 (2001)
13. Krishnanand, K., Ghose, D.: Glowworm swarm optimization for simultaneous capture of multiple local optima of multimodal functions. Swarm Intelligence 3(2), 87–124 (2009)
14. Haddad, O.B., et al.: Honey-bees mating optimization (HBMO) algorithm: a new heuristic approach for water resources optimization. Water Resources Management 20(5), 661–680 (2006)
15. Tamura, K., Yasuda, K.: Primary Study of Spiral Dynamics Inspired Optimization. IEEE Transactions on Electrical and Electronic Engineering 6, S98–S100 (2011)
16. Hamed, S.H.: The intelligent water drops algorithm: a nature-inspired swarm-based optimization algorithm. International Journal of Bio-Inspired Computation 1, 71–79 (2009)

17. Civicioglu, P.: Transforming geocentric cartesian coordinates to geodetic coordinates by using differential search algorithm. Computers & Geosciences 46, 229–247 (2012)
18. Tayarani-N, M.H., Akbarzadeh-T, M.R.: Magnetic Optimization Algorithms a new synthesis. In: IEEE Congress on Evolutionary Computation, pp. 2659–2664 (2008)
19. Reynolds, C.W.: Flocks, herds and schools: A distributed behavioral model. Computer Graphics 21, 25–34 (1987)
20. Kaveh, A., Talatahari, S.: A Novel Heuristic Optimization Method: Charged System Search. Acta Mechanica 213, 267–289 (2010)
21. Gandomi, A.H., Alavi, A.H.: Krill Herd Algorithm: A New Bio-Inspired Optimization Algorithm. Communications in Nonlinear Science and Numerical Simulation (2012)
22. Tamura, K., Yasuda, K.: Spiral Dynamics Inspired Optimization. Journal of Advanced Computational Intelligence and Intelligent Informatics 15, 1116–1122 (2011)
23. Wolpert, D.H., Macready, W.G.: No free lunch theorems for Optimization. IEEE Transactions on Evolutionary Computation 1, 67–82 (1997)
24. Liang, Y.C., et al.: Virus Optimization Algorithm for Curve Fitting Problems. In: IIE Asian Conference (2011)
25. Dataset Library, http://elib.zib.de/pub/mp-testdata/tsp/tsplib/tsplib.html
26. Lin, S., Kernighan, B.W.: An effective heuristic algorithm for the travelling salesman problem. Operations Research 21, 498–516 (1973)
27. Helsgaun, K.: An effective implementation of the linkernighan travelling salesman heuristic. European Journal of Operational Research 126(1), 106–130 (2000)
28. Applegate, D., Bixby, R.E., Chvátal, V., Cook, W.: TSP Cuts Which Do Not Conform to the Template Paradigm. In: Jünger, M., Naddef, D. (eds.) Computational Combinatorial Optimization. LNCS, vol. 2241, pp. 261–304. Springer, Heidelberg (2001)
29. Hahsler, M., Hornik, K.: TSP Infrastructure for the Travelling Salesperson Problem (2007)
30. Dantzig, G.B., Fulkerson, D.R., Johnson, S.M.: Solution of a Large-scale Traveling Salesman Problem. Operations Research 2, 393–410 (1954)
31. Miller, P.J.: Exact Solution of Large Asymmetric Traveling Salesman Problems. Science 251, 754–761 (1991)

Author Index